Rituals of Islamic Spirituality

A Study of Majlis Dhikr Groups in East Java

Rituals of Islamic Spirituality

A Study of Majlis Dhikr Groups in East Java

Arif Zamhari

THE AUSTRALIAN NATIONAL UNIVERSITY

E PRESS

E PRESS

Published by ANU E Press
The Australian National University
Canberra ACT 0200, Australia
Email: anuepress@anu.edu.au
This title is also available online at: http://epress.anu.edu.au/islamic_citation.html

National Library of Australia
Cataloguing-in-Publication entry

Author:	Zamhari, Arif.
Title:	Rituals of Islamic spirituality: a study of Majlis Dhikr groups in East Java / Arif Zamhari.
ISBN:	9781921666247 (pbk) 9781921666254 (pdf)
Series:	Islam in Southeast Asia.
Notes:	Includes bibliographical references.
Subjects:	Islam--Rituals. Islam Doctrines. Islamic sects--Indonesia--Jawa Timur. Sufism--Indonesia--Jawa Timur.
Dewey Number:	297.359598

Cover design and layout by ANU E Press

Islam in Southeast Asia Series

Theses at The Australian National University are assessed by external examiners and students are expected to take into account the advice of their examiners before they submit to the University Library the final versions of their theses. For this series, this final version of the thesis has been used as the basis for publication, taking into account other changesthat the author may have decided to undertake. In some cases, a few minor editorial revisions have made to the work. The acknowledgements in each of these publications provide information on the supervisors of the thesis and those who contributed to its development. For many of the authors in this series, English is a second language and their texts reflect an appropriate fluency.

Contents

Foreword xiii

Dedications xv

Acknowledgement xvii

Abstract xxi

Abbreviations and glossary xxiii

Transliteration xxxi

Chapter I 1

1.1. The Significance of the Study 1

1.2. The Understanding of *Tasawuf, Tarekat* and *Majlis Dhikr* Group in Indonesian Islam 10

1.3. The Variety of *Majlis Dhikr* Groups in Java 14

1.4. Meaning and Implications of the Classification: *Mu'tabarah* 17

1.5. Sufism in the *Pesantren* Tradition 21

Chapter II: Innovation or Aberration: *Majlis Dhikr* in Contemporary Indonesian Islamic Discourse **25**

2.1. Source of Disputes: Understanding the Concept of *Bid'ah* (innovation within Islam) within Indonesian Islam 26

2.2. Theological Debates on *Dhikr* Ritual 35

2.3. Conclusion 46

Chapter III: The Intellectual Response of Indonesian *Majlis Dhikr* Groups to Some Aspects of Their Ritual Practices 49

3.1. *Ṣalawāt* As a Means to Approach God 49

3.1.1. *Majlis Dhikr* Groups' Understanding of *Ṣalawāt* 54

3.2. The Concepts of Sainthood (*Wali*) and Miracle (*Karamah*) 58

3.2.1. The Concepts of Sainthood (*Wali*) and Miracle (*Karamah*) as Understood by *Majlis Dhikr* Groups 64

3.3. The Concept of *Tawassul* 69

3.3.1. Understanding the Concept of *Tawassul* Among *Majlis Dhikr* Groups 76

3.4. Sending the Merit of Pious Deeds to Deceased Persons 80

3.4.1. The *Majlis Dhikr* Groups' Understanding of Sending the Merit of Pious Deeds to Deceased Persons 84

3.5. Seeking Blessing (*barakah, tabarruk*) 86

3.5.1. The Concept of *Tabarruk* As Understood by *Majlis Dhikr* Groups . . 90

3.6. Conclusion 93

Chapter IV: 'Turn to God and His Prophet': The Spiritual Path of the *Ṣalawāt Wāḥidiyat* Group 95

4.1. The Foundation of *Ṣalawāt Wāḥidiyat* 95

4.2. External Conflict in *Wāḥidiyat* 107

4.3. Internal Conflict in *Wāḥidiyat* 115

4.4. The Teaching of *Wāḥidiyat* 125

4.5. The Ritual of *Mujāhada in Wāḥidiyat*: Spiritual Pilgrimage 133

4.6. The Strategy to Preaching *Ṣalawāt Wāḥidiyat* (*Da'wah Wāḥidiyat*) in Implementing Sufi Tolerance: The Role of *Pesantren* 145

4.7. Spiritual Experience and Spiritual Authority in *Wāḥidiyat* 157

Chapter V: The Veneration of *Wali* and Holy Persons: The Case of *Istighāthat Iḥsāniyyat* **165**

5.1. The Foundation of *Istighāthat Iḥsāniyyat* *165*

5.2. Local Rivalry and Challenges 176

5.3. The Ritual of *Iḥsāniyyat* 180

5.4. The Structure of the Group 188

5.5. From Tombs to Mosques: Implementing Sufi *Dakwah* and Religious Tolerance 192

Chapter VI: The Awakening of the Negligent: The *Dhikr al- Ghāfilīn Group* **207**

6.1. The Foundation of the group 207

6.2. The Ritual Practice of the Group 212

6.3. *Gus* Mik: a Living Saint and Controversial *Kyai* 219

6.4. *Gus* Mik: His *Karamah* 227

6.5. *Gus* Mik: His Teachings 231

6.6. The Group after *Gus* Mik 235

6.7. Conclusion 244

Conclusion **245**

Appendix **251**

Bibliography **253**

List of Plates

Plate 4.1: The text of *Ṣalawāt Wāḥidiyat* and its instruction how to recite it 104

Plate 4.2: Sticker of Wāḥidiyat displaying the logo of the group and Nidā' Yā Sayyidī yā Rasūl Allah (the exclamation). 105

Plate 4.3: The Logo of Ṣalawāt Wāḥidiyat group and Pesantren Kedunglo (Yayasan Perjuangan Wahidiyah dan Pondok Pesantren Kedunglo) in Kediri. . . 124

Plate 4.4: The Logo of Ṣalawāt Wāḥidiyat group (Penyiar Sholawat Wahidiyah, PSW) in Ngoro, Jombang. 124

Plate 4.5: Female participants waiting for a pisowanan session. 137

Plate 4.6: Female participants during a pisowanan session 137

Plate 4.7: Male participants at a Mujāhada Kubrā waiting for a pisowanan session. 138

Plate 4.8: Male participants kissing their leader's hand during pisowanan session. 138

Plate 4.9: The participants at a Mujāhada Kubrā praying at the tomb of Kyai Abdul Madjid Ma'ruf (the founder of the Wāḥidiyat group) 139

Plate 4.10: Children crying during Mujāhada Kubrā ritual in Pesantren Kedunglo, Kediri. 139

Plate 4.11: Female participants, including young girls, listening to fatwa during Mujāhada Kubrā ritual in Pesantren Kedunglo, Kediri. 140

Plate 4.12: Female students crying during a prayer session in Mujāhada Kubrā ritual in Pesantren Kedunglo, Kediri 141

Plate 4.13: The leader of Wāḥidiyat, Kyai Abdul Latif Madjid giving edicts (fatwa) in Mujāhada Kubrā. 144

Plate 5.1: Gus Abdul Latif (Gus Latif), the founder and the leader of the Istighāthat Iḥsāniyyat group. 169

Plate 5.2: People using trucks to get to the Istighāthat Iḥsāniyyat ritual Banyuwangi 183

Plate 5.3: Female participants at a Istighāthat Iḥsāniyyat group ritual in Kediri. 183

Plate 5.4: Gus Abdul Latif (wearing a white hat) and the researcher left) after conducting istighāthat ritual at the shrine of a Muslim saint 203

Plate 5.5: The Yamisda group holding istighāthat at Kyai Ihsan Dahlan's tomb. 203

Plate 5.6: The participants of istighāthat at a Muslim saint's tomb. 204

Plate 5.7: The Book of Istighāthat Iḥsāniyyat. 206

Plate 6.1: Gus Mik meeting with Ir. Akbar Tanjung, the former minister in Suharto era 223

Plate 6.2: Gus Mik with his followers in a pub in Surabaya. 225

Plate 6.3: Gus Mik chatting with Sultan Hameng Kubuwono X (The Ruler of Yogyakarta) 226

Plate 6.4: The front cover of the Dhikr al-Ghafīlīn book published by Gus Sabut Panoto Projo 240

Plate 6.5: The back cover of the Dhikr al-Ghafīlīn book published by Gus Sabut Panoto Projo 241

Plate 6.6: The front cover of the Dhikr al-Ghafīlīn book published by Gus Farih Fauz 242

Plate 6.7: The back cover of the Dhikr al-Ghafīlīn book published by Gus Farih Fauzi 243

List of Figures

Figure 4.1: The Organizational Structure of Ṣalawāt Wāḥidiyat 150

Figure 5.1: Orgnizational Structure of Iḥsāniyyat Group................. 189

Figure 6.1: Kyai Hamim Jazuli's (Gus Mik's) Family.................... 238

Figure 6.2: Kyai Ahmad Siddīq's Family............................ 239

List of Maps

Map 1: Indonesia xxxiii

Map 2: East Java xxxiii

Map 3: Residency of Kediri xxxiv

Map 4: Pesandren Kedunglo, Kediri 148

Foreword

This beautiful study by Arif Zamhari offers a rare glimpse into the practices of Islamic spirituality in contemporary Java. Dr Zamhari focuses on three distinct groups in East Java who gather under the inspired religious leadership of a notable *kyai* to invoke the Divine Names in the remembrance of God *(Dhikr Allah*). Each of the groups is remarkably different yet they adhere to a common tradition that has deep historical roots. At present, these groups are the popular manifestation of a resurgent devotional Islam – an open, active, and engaging form of Sufi worship.

Dr Zamhari's study also provides remarkable insights into the working of *Nahdlatul Ulama* (NU) at a grass-roots level. Each of the groups, which Dr Zamhari designates as *Majlis Dhikr*, has established itself under the broad umbrella of NU orthodoxy. Yet none of *Majlis Dhikr* has been given the formal recognition of *mu'tabarah* that NU has accorded *tarekat* such as Naqshabandiyah, Qadiriyah, Shattiriyah or Tijaniyah. Indeed the issue of recognition has arisen primarily in relation to just one of these groups, the *Ṣalawāt Wāḥidiyat*; the other two groups, the *Istighāthat Iḥsāniyyat* and the *Dhikr al-Ghāfilīn*, are even less formally constituted.

Thus in studying Sufi devotional practice that occurs outside the bounds of organized *tarekat*, Dr Zamhari has had to develop an appropriate terminology to locate such diverse groups within a pertinent frame of reference. His efforts are as innovative as they are revealing. Although these groups and others like them can not be considered as *tarekat*, they share much in common with *tarekat* and are part of a spiritual continuum that is closely linked to the *tarekat* tradition on Java. As Dr Zamhari makes clear, to understand Islam on Java, it is essential to perceive the full spectrum of its religiosity.

This book leads into the world of *tasawuf* – the mystic teachings of Islam. Dr Zamhari devotes considerable attention to an exegesis of critical concepts underlying the spiritual practices of the *Majlis Dhikr* and the interpretative basis for these practices within orthodox teaching. At the same time, he is able to tie his exegesis to a living tradition. He is also able to show how *kyai* act as charismatic religious leaders and to provide a portrait of some of these remarkable *ulama*.

Dr Zamhari's portrayal of the *kyai* who founded the three *Majlis Dhikr* that he examines – *Kyai* Abdul Madjid Ma'ruf, the founder of *Ṣalawāt Wāḥidiyat*, *Kyai* Abdul Latif Muhammad, known as *Gus* Latif, founder of *Istighāthat Iḥsāniyyat* and *Kyai* Hamin Jazuli known as *Gus* Mik, founder of the *Dhikr al-Ghāfilīn* – is a study in contrasts. The deep spirituality and learning of each of these *kyai* is evident; their genealogical ties within the NU community are made clear, and yet their individuality and their differences in religious approaches are particularly notable. The *kyai* of NU are a diverse group.

The person of the *kyai* is central to the development of these Ṣufi groups and each has its base in a particular *pesantren*. Dr Zamhari is able to weave all of these elements together – personal, sociological and theological – in a clear, coherent and sympathetic exposition.

Dr Zamhari's ability to create this work is based on his intimate knowledge of East Java and of its *pesantren* community. Dr Zamhari was born in Lamongan and educated there at Madrasah Bustanul Ulum before taking up further study in Malang at Pesantren Miftahul Huda, then at Pesantren Sabilurrasyad and, thereafter, at IAIN Sunan Ampel Malang. He did his PhD in the Department of Anthropology in the Research School of Pacific and Asian Studies at the ANU from 2003 to 2007 and has since returned to Indonesia where he lectures at different institutions: at UIN Malang, Ma'had Aly Al-Hikam, UIN Syarif Hidayatullah and Paramadina University in Jakarta, and at IAIN Sunan Ampel in Surabaya

Dedications

To my parents who always encouraged me to seek knowledge

And to those who always fill my life:

My beloved wife, Yuni Arovah,

My son, Balya Muhammad Izzat,

My daughter, Taliah Aqilah Farnaz,

My baby, Muhammad Haikal Makarim

Acknowledgments

Alhamdulillah, all praises due to Allah, I can finally complete this study and my study. I would like to acknowledge several people in Australia and Indonesia for the contribution they made to this study. I would also like to apologise to anyone whom I forget to mention here.

First of all, my thanks go to the Australian government who offered me sponsorship through Australian Development Scholarship (ADS) for conducting my study. I am grateful to Australian government for this funding. Without this funding, it would not have been financially possible for me to come to study at The Australian National University. I am also grateful for the kind assistance I received from the AusAid liaison officers at ANU: Carol Laslett, Louise Jackson, Debra Reed, Anthony Bowden, and Stephanie Black, thank you all very much.

I owe great debt to Professor James J. Fox who has been my principal supervisor since I began my studies in the Department of Anthropology, Research School of Pacific and Asian Studies, The Australian National University. I would like to thank him for his considerable assistance at important moments of my study. Before studying in Australia, I met him first time at the Anthropology Conference at the University of Udayana, Bali. I remember that at that time, even though I never met him before, he seemed to me like a *guru* who is always interested in his *murid*'s study. I cannot forget that he was the first professor in Australia who gave me a strong recommendation before formally applying for an ADS Scholarship and studying at the Australian National University. As my principal supervisor he even visited me during my fieldwork in Kediri. His guidance has continued even while he was on leave at Harvard University. He is like a father who always cares for his children.

My Co-Supervisor on this work, Prof. Kathryn Robinson, has also been very helpful to me in many respects. She initiated several informal meeting and discussion before I presented my paper at the International Conference at The National University of Singapore (NUS). During this informal discussion, I received invaluable feed back from her and from other participants. The discussion with her before and after midterm seminar has shaped my idea about *Majlis Dhikr* groups in Indonesia. She also helped me with information regarding literature and seminars which are closely related to my field. I would like to express my thanks to *Ibu* Kathy.

In addition to Professor Fox and Professor Robinson, my advisor on this work, Prof. Virginia Hooker (*Mbak* Nia), has been very helpful to me. I would like to express my thanks for her patience and attention. Her deep understanding of Indonesian Islam and Indonesian Islamic texts has enriched my perspective of the subject. She not only provided me with references which are related to my subject but also sent them to my mail box. I also thank my advisor Dr Greg Fealy for his assistance especially in dealing with Indonesian terms and providing me with literature on Islam.

There are too many people in Kediri to whom I am indebted. Without their willingness to spare their time and to share their perceptions with me, it would not have been possible for me to complete my study. I express my thanks to the family of *Pak* Mahmud and *Ibu* Mahmud, especially *Mbak* Ati and *Mas* Mughni, who have introduced me to *Pesantren* Jampes, Kediri. My deep thanks go to friendly people such as *Gus* Latif Muhammad (the leader of *Ihsāniyyat* group), *Kyai* Misbah (the senior *kyai* in Jampes), *Kyai* Zainuddin (the vice leader of the *Wāḥidiyat* group), *Kyai* Saiful (from the *Dhikr al-Ghāfilīn* group), and *Gus* Fahri Fauzi (the leader of the *Dhikr al-Ghāfilīn* group) for their deep understanding of Islamic ritual. These persons are busy persons with their students, family and *ummat;* however they generously shared their time and ideas with me and enthusiastically answered my questions .

My thanks also go to those who have always been kind and willing to help me in the department of Anthropology: Prof. Mark Mosko, as the head of department; Ben Cauchi, the late Leon Nolan and Chris Thomson who were always willing to help with IT problems; Fritha Jones, Penelope Judd and Ann Buller who were really kind and helpful and shared their warm friendship; and the administrator of the department, Fay Castles who was always been lovely and kind.

I also thank to Drs. Syu'aib Mallombasi, the Director of the State of Islamic Studies (STAIN) Kendari, Southeast Sulawesi who has given permission me to leave my duties as a lecturer. He and his family gave me a warm place when I firstly came to Kendari and supported me to study abroad.

To my friends in the Anthropology department, Lintje Pelu, Joice, Murni Mahmud, Jayne Curnow, Angie Baxley, Shu Ling, Joy Bai, Traci Smith, Gilly, Monika Doxey, Ann Thararat, Ana Dragojlovic, Adelyn Lim, Jayne Munro, Nanlai Cao, Warren Mayes, Yasir Alimi and many others, thanks for your warm friendship. I specially thank to Garry Kildea for his patience in teaching me how to make a good film shot.

To my friends in Nahdlatul Ulama (NU) in Canberra, *Mbak* Wahidah, *Pak* Kacung Marijan, *Mas* Zahrul and *Mbak* Mellani, *Mas* Taufik and *Mbak* Rosa, *Mas* Eko and Ida, *Kang* Lili and Ana, Nia and Hilmi, *Pak* Umar and Ijah, Farid and Eva, *Pak* and *Bu* Marfuddin, Sita and Mega, Ulfa and Rahman, *Pak* Imam Rafi'i, thanks for being together in *khataman* and *ratiban*. Also for my friends in NU in Melbourne, Tony Indranada, Su'aidi, Masdar Hilmi, Aliformen, in Brisbane, *Pak* Suseno Hadi, in Perth *Mas* Gaffar Abdulkarim, in Wollonggong, *Shaikh* Nadirsyah Hosen thanks for being together in introducing moderate Islam of Nahdlatul Ulama in Australia.

Thanks also to my brothers and sisters: Abid, Enik Amiroh, Qibtiyah thanks for all your support. My deepest gratitude goes to Bapak Hasyim Muzadi and Ibu Mutammimah for their prayers during my difficult times.

My beloved wife, Yuni Arovah, has supported me during my studies in Canberra. She has given me enormous power to complete my studies. I realise how difficult her life in Australia has been with two kids and a new baby born in Canberra during my final period of study. My three little sweeties: Balya Muhammad Izzat, Taliah Aqilah Farnaz, and Muhammad Haikal Makarim have been a great inspiration for me during my study in Canberra. I dedicated my work to them.

Finally, my parents, *Abah* and *Umi,* and *Mbah* have given their love and support to me when I have faced difficulties in my study. I dedicate this work to them. Thank you all for praying for me.

Abstract

This study attempts to elucidate the emergence of forms of Islamic spirituality in Indonesian Islam identified as *Majlis Dhikr* groups. Despite the increasing popularity of Sufi groups (*tarekat*) among Indonesian Muslims, these *Majlis Dhikr* groups have proliferated on Java in the last two decades both in urban and rural areas. These groups have attracted followers from a wide social base to their practices, hence contributing significantly to the improvement of religious performance among Indonesian Muslims. The diverse aspects of these *Majlis Dhikr* groups are examined in this study: their rituals and teachings, their understanding of their rituals, their contestation with critics and opponents, their strategies to disseminate their teachings and expand their membership, their role in the preaching Islam among Indonesian Muslims and the role of the *pesantren* in developing these groups.

Detailed analyses of specific *Majlis Dhikr* illustrate how these groups consider themselves as an alternative way for Indonesian Muslims to experience Islamic spirituality. Careful examination of their rituals, teachings and their theological debates with other Muslim groups reveals how *Majlis Dhikr* groups regard their activities as legitimate ritual practices that are in accordance with the legacy of Islamic Sufism based on the interpretation of the Qur'anic and the Prophetic tradition.

This study examines how *Majlis Dhikr* are used by Indonesian Muslims as another institution to maintain Islamic tradition in Indonesia in general and among Javanese Muslims in particular.

Abbreviations and glossary

'Ālim	a learned person
'Ain al-yaqīn	vision of certitude
Amal jariah	contributions of wealth to facilitate the carrying out of God's purposes, for which the reward continues after the contributor's death
'Ujb	self proud
'Ulamā'	Muslim scholars
'Uzla	seclusion, lesser retreat
'Ilm al-yaqīn	knowledge of certitude
Āmil	employees of zakat
Abangan	nominal Javanese Muslims; the term is used in some areas of Central and East Java and sometimes has negative connotations
Adab	courtesy
Ahlussunnah wal Jama'ah	Sunni distinguished from the Shī'ah; in Java this refers to traditional Islam which basically follows Ash'arite theology. Shāfi'ite fiqh, and al-Ghazālī's Sufism
Akhlāq	Islamic morality, ethics
Akhlakul karimah	good behaviour based on Muslim values
Al-Fātiḥat	The first chapter of the Qur'an
Alun-alun (Jav.)	town square
Amar ma'rufnahi munkar	enjoining what is right and forbidding what is wrong
Asmaul Ḥusnā	the beautiful names of God
Athar	report of the Prophet's Companions
Auliyaullah	the saints of God, friends of God
Barakah	blessing
Bay'at	vow of allegiance to a Sufi leader
Berjamaah	in unison
Bid'ah	innovation within Islam
Bid'a sayyiat, ḍalālat	innovation within Islam categorized as illicit

Bisikan gaib	unseen whisper believed to come from God and Angels
Bupati	the Chief of Executive of the District
Dā'ī	male preacher
Dā'iyyat	female preacher
Dakwah	Islamic propagation
DDII	Dewan Dakwah Islam Indonesia (The Indonesian Council for Islamic Preaching)
Dhikr	repetitive prayers
Dosa besar	cardinal offence
Du'ā	Islamic prayers
Dukun santet	sorcerer
Fana'	annihilation
Faqīr	the needy
Fatwā	legal opinion, edict
Fīsabilillah	persons who struggle in the cause of Allah
Fiqh	Islamic jurisprudence
Fuqahā	Muslim jurists, singular form of Faqīh
Gemblengan	a form of invulnerability
Ghārim	a debtor
Ghairu mu'tabarah	non-recognised; it is used to refer to Sufi groups which do not have a chain of transmission back to the Prophet
Gus or Agus	a title used to address sons of kyai in most Javanese pesantren
Hadas besar	impurity that requires a Muslim to carry out a full ritual ablution (A., ghusl) as for example after having a wet dream or sexual intercourse with one's spouse
Hadas kecil	impurity that requires a Muslim to carry out a minor ablution (A., wuḍū') as for example after passing wind, urinating, and defecating
Hadith	a documented tradition purporting to preserve the decisions, actions, and utterances of the Prophet Muhammad
Hadith qudsī	a documented tradition containing revelation from God phrased in the Prophet's own words
Haji	the pilgrimage to Mecca
Halal	lawful
Ḥaqīqat	ultimate goal and final stage of the mystical path of God

Ḥaqq al-yaqīn	real certitude
Ḥasad	jealous
Ḥaul	anniversary of the birth of the founder of a Sufi order or of a kyai
Ḥisāb	reckoning stage in the hereafter
Himmat 'āliyat	a high-aiming endeavour
Ḥusn al-ẓann	to think well
Ḥusn al-khātimat	good death
Ibadah	worship
Ibn sabīl	wayfarers
Iḥlāṣ	sincerity
Iḥsān	goodness
Ijāza	a license or an authorization
Ijtihad	independent judgment based on recognized sources of Islam on legal or theological question
Ilmu	knowledge
Ilmu kekebalan	invulnerability power
Imām	leader of communal prayers or dhikr ritual
Imān	faith, belief
Insān al-Kāmil	The Perfect Man; Sufis regard Muhammad as The Perfect Man
Islam kaffah	a comprehensive Islamic practice
Isnād	chain of transmitter
Istighāthat	dhikr ritual that mentions some of the Ninety Nine Attributes of God and other prayers; it is commonly conducted among Nahdlatul Ulama members
Istighfār	requesting God's forgiveness
Istighrāq	the state of immersion in God
Istijrāj	miracles given by God to non-Muslims just to spoil
Istikhāra	A particular prayers conducted to seed guidance from God when one is faced with a problem to which no solution is apparent
Istiqāmat	Steadfastness
Jaranan (Jav.)	hobby-horse dance
Jawara	expert in martial arts
Jodoh	soul mate
Juru kunci	custodian of tombs

Karamah	miracles performed by Muslim saints
Kesakten (Jav.)	potency; supernatural power
Kesembuan	healing
Ketua	chairperson
Khāriq al-'āda	extraordinary deeds performed by Muslim saints
Khadam	assistant
Khalīfat	vice-regent; the successor of the Shaikh of a Sufi order
Khamr	alcohol
Khataman	graduation in a pesantren
Khilāfiyyat	disputed matters in Islamic teachings
Khurafat	myth; superstition
Khusū'	feeling of intimacy with and remembrance of God
Kiblat	the particular direction toward Mecca that Muslims face when they perform prayers
Kitab kuning	'yellow books' that signify the classical Arabic texts used in Salaf pesantren (traditional pesantren)
Kurban	sacrifice
Kyai	Javanese name for 'ulamā'
Leang-leong	Chinese dragon dance
Ma'rifahbillah	Gnosis of God, the highest spiritual experience obtained by those who practise Sufism
Ma'rifat	divine gnosis; intuitive of knowledge of God
Madhhab	Islamic legal schools
Madrasah 'Āliyat	Islamic high school
Madrasah Ibtidāiyat	Islamic elementary school
Madrasah Thanāwiyyat	Islamic secondary school
Maḥabba	Love
Mahr	dowry
Majlis Dhikr	Dhikr group
Maksiat	immoral acts
Manāqiban	reciting a particular Sufi saint's biography
Maqāmāt	stations on the Sufi path to gnosis
Masyumi	Majelis Syuro Muslim Indonesia (Consultative Council of Indonesian Muslims)

Mau'iẓat al-hasanat	religious lecture
Miskīn	the poor
MTQ	Musabaqah Tilawatil al-Qur'an, competition in reciting the Qur'an
Mu'allaf	people who convert to Islam
Mu'tabarah	recognized; this term is used to refer to Sufi group which have a chain of transmission back to the Prophet
Mubādhir	useless
Mubāḥ	permitted deeds
Muballigh	Islamic preacher
Mubdi'	Innovator; someone who carries out bid'ah
Mufassir	exegete
Mujaddid	a Muslim reformer; it is believed that he or she comes at the end of every century to revitalize Islam and save society from moral and spiritual decadency
Mujāhada	striving, an intense spiritual effort that leads to levels of spiritual ecstasy
Muqaddam	deputy of a renowned Sufi master, leader of a regional branch of Sufi order
Murabbi	spiritual teacher
Murid	a disciple of a Sufi master
Murshid	a leader of tarekat group (Sufi group)
Mustaḥiq	people who are eligible to receive zakat (tax)
Musyāhadat	spiritual vision
Naḥw	Arabic grammar
Narkoba	narcotics
Ninja	popular term used in Indonesia to refer to dangerous shadowy figures with martial arts ability who are believed to carry out executions
NU	Nahdlatul Ulama (Revival of the Religious Scholars, Indonesia's largest Islamic organization)
Nuzūl al-Qur'an	Revelation of the Qur'an
Nyadran	visiting tombs to fulfil a vow after having made request
Nyai	wife of a Kyai
ONH	Ongkos Naik Haji (the cost of pilgrimage to Mecca)

Orang nakal	bad individuals
Orang pangkat	Nobles: persons with positions, titles
Orang pinggiran	marginalized people
Orang ruwet	difficult people
PAN	Partai Amanat Nasional (The National Mandate Party)
Pancasila	The Five Basic Principles; the ideological and political foundation of the Republic of Indonesia
PDIP	Partai Demokrasi Indonesia Perjuangan (The Indonesian Democratic Party of Struggle)
Pejabat	government officials
Pendopo Kabupaten	the office of the Chief of Executive of the district
Pengajian umum	general religious lecture
PERSIS	Persatuan Islam (Islamic Union)
Pesantren	Islamic boarding schools
Pesantren salaf	Pesantren which still use classical Arabic texts in their curriculum
PKB	Partai Kebangkitan Bangsa (The National Awakening Party)
Preman	local hoodlums
Qutb	literally means 'the Axis, Pole'; in Sufi traditions this term refers to the spiritual pole of the age, the supreme saint of a given epoch
Rābiṭa al'Ālam al-Islāmiy	The Islamic World League; the name of an Islamic organization established in Saudi Arabia
Rabīṭa	one's heart's connection with a Sufi master; this should be conducted in the ritual of Sufi groups
Ramaḍān	name of the month in the Islamic calendar during which Muslims are obliged to fast
Reog	tiger-masked dance
Riḍā	contentment
Riqāb	freed slaves
Riyā'	vainglory, showing off
Ruh	spirit
Ru'ya al- ṣadiqa	true vision
Ruwatan	a sacred ceremony in the Javanese tradition to ward off misfortune

Ṣāliḥin	virtuous Muslims
Ṣabr	patience
Ṣaḥabāt	The Prophet Companions
Ṣalawāt	invoking the blessing on the Prophet
Ṣaraf	Arabic morphology
Sāmi'īn	listeners
Sabu-sabu	opium
Salaf al-ṣāliḥīn	pious forebears, early generation of Muslims
Salafi	Muslim groups that follow the Prophet and the next three generations
Sampah masyarakat	the dregs of society
Santri	students of pesantren, pious Muslims in Java
Selapanan	thirty five days; term used to denote a cycle in the Javanese calendar
Semaan	listening carefully to the recitation of the Qur'an
Shadaqat	charity
Shafā'at	intercession
Shahāda	witness of faith
Shahādatain	the two sentences of the declaration of faith
Sharī'at	Islamic Law, the formal aspects of Islam
Shirk	polytheism
Shuhadā'	martyrs
Shukr (gratitude)	gratitude
Silsilah	a chain; spiritual genealogy of a Sufi master or of a Sufi community
Sū' al-khātimat	bad death
Sunnah	The Prophetic Tradition
sunnat	recommended deeds
Sunnatullah	The Custom of God
Syuriah	supreme religious council in an Indonesian Muslim organisation such as NU
Ta'awwudl	Islamic phrase to seek refuge from Satan
Tābi'īn	Successors of the Companions of the Prophet
Tābi'it al-tābi'īn	Successors of the Successors of the Companions of the Prophet
Tārikh	Islamic history

Tabib	*Muslim healer*
Taḥmīd	*reciting the phrase of praise to God*
Tahajjud	*optional night prayers*
Tahayyul	*superstition*
Tahlīl	*recitation of lā ilāha illa Allah; a ritual commonly practised to ask forgiveness for deceased Muslims.*
Takabbur	*pride, arrogant*
Takhalluq bi akhlāq al-rasūl	*to imitate the Prophet's ethics*
Tarekat	*a Sufi group*
Taṣawwur al-shaikh	*to visualize the master, a ritual that is carried out by the followers of some Sufi groups (tarekat)*
Tasawwuf	*Sufism, mystic knowledge*
Ṭarīqat pl. ṭurūq	*method of spiritual education practiced by a Sufi master or Sufi order*
Tasbīḥ	*a phrase to glorify God*
Taubat	*repentance*
Taushiyah	*religious advice*
Tawḥīd	*Islamic theology; knowledge of the Oneness of God*
TPA	*Taman Pendidikan Al-Qur'an, Qur'anic Kindergarten*
Umarā' (sing. Amīr)	*Arabic term forgovernment officials*
Ummat	*Islamic community*
Wājib	*obligatory deeds*
Wali	*saint of God*
Wasīlat	*intermediary*
Wirid	*routine program of dhikr*
Wuṣūl	*attainment of union with God*
Yaqdhah	*wakening state, in active mind*
Yaum al-ḥisāb	*The Day of Judgment*
Zakat fitrah	*poll tax*
Zakat profesi	*wealth tax*
Zuhud	*asceticism*

Transliteration

This work contains many Arabic words and names. For writing these Arabic names and words, I use the system of Arabic words and names used by Institute of Islamic Studies, McGill University.

gh	=	غ	z	=	ز	b	=	ب
f	=	ف	s	=	س	t	=	ت
q	=	ق	sh	=	ش	th	=	ث
k	=	ك	ṣ	=	ص	j	=	ج
l	=	ل	ḍ	=	ض	ḥ	=	ح
m	=	م	ṭ	=	ط	kh	=	خ
n	=	ن	ẓ	=	ظ	d	=	د
h	=	ه	ʿ	=	ع	dh	=	ذ
w	=	و	y	=	ي	r	=	ر

Short: a = ◌َ ; i = ◌ِ ; u = ◌ُ

Long: ā = ا ; ī = ي ; ū = و

Diphthong: ay = اي ; aw = او

Maps

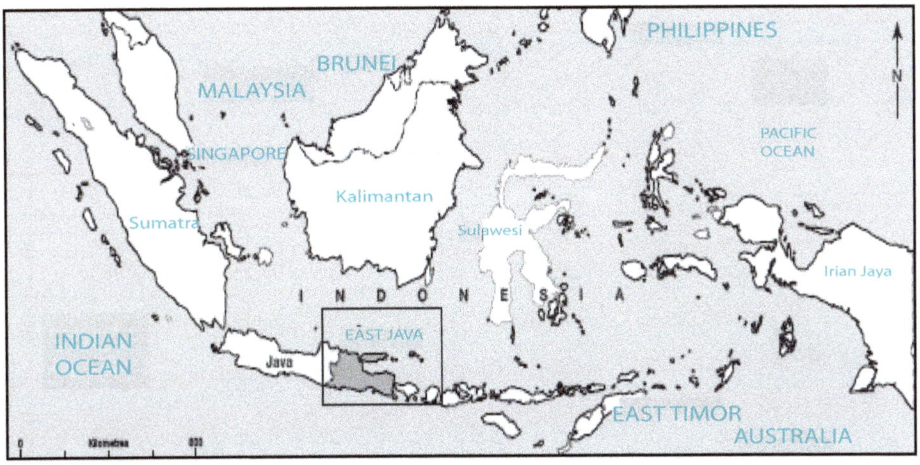

Map.1. Indonesia

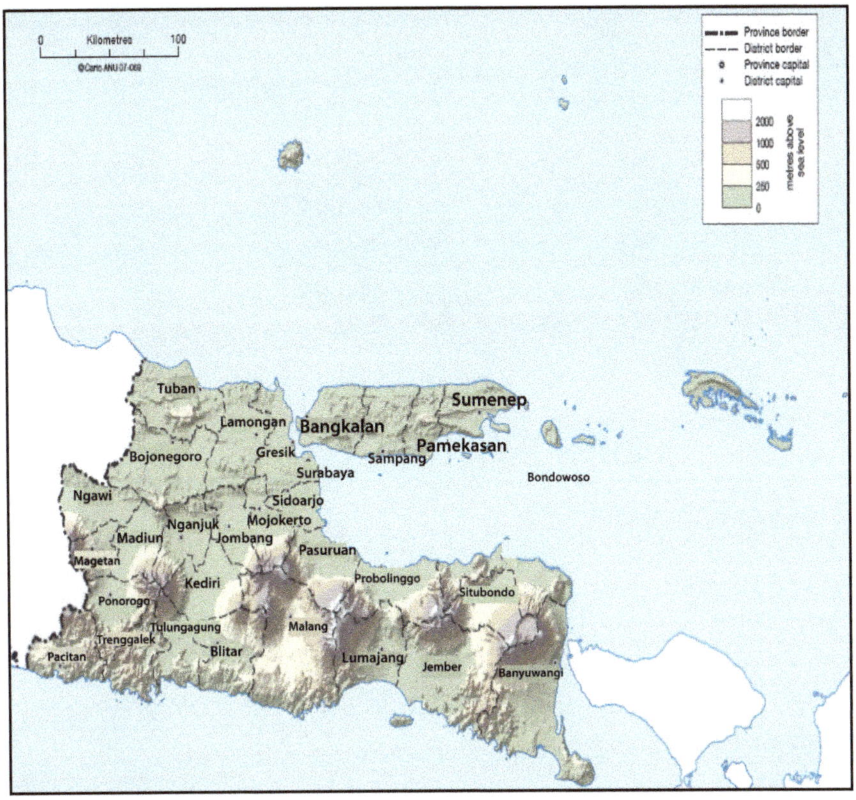

Map.2. East Java

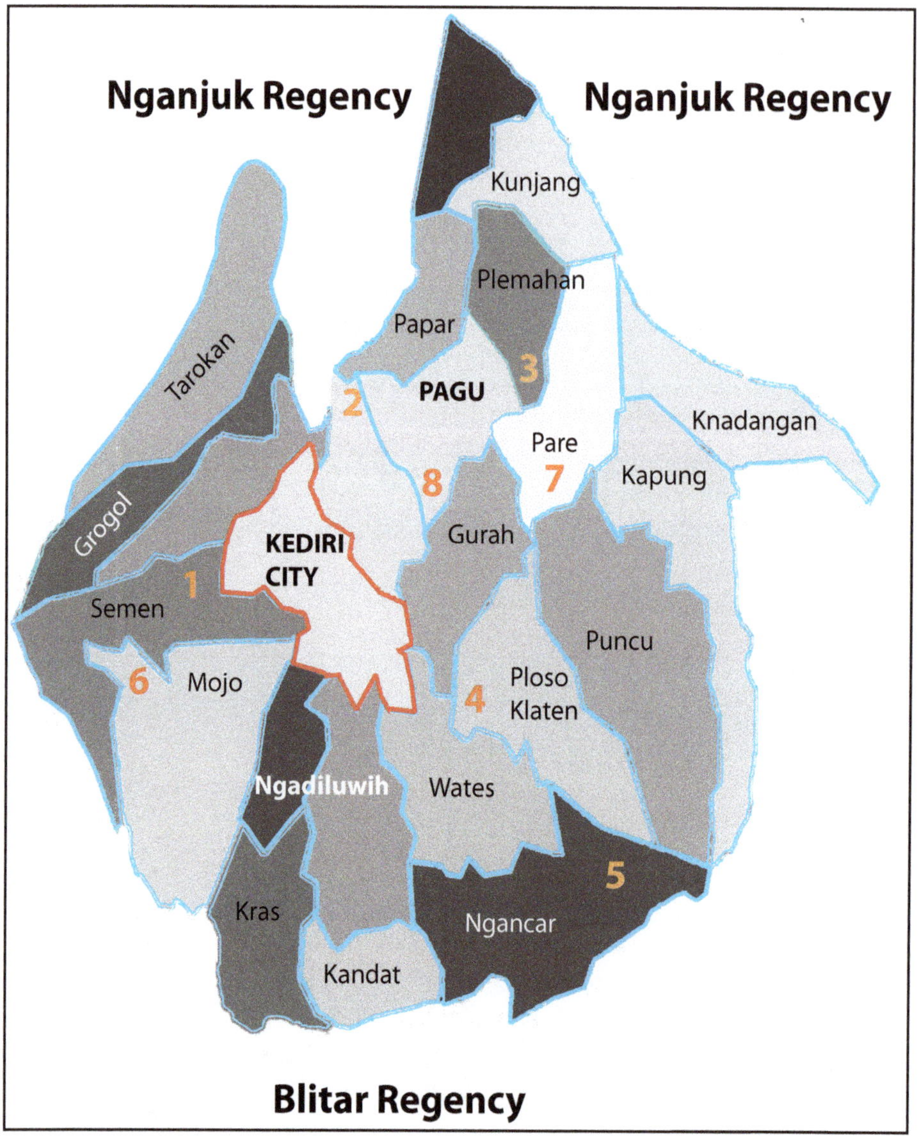

Map.3. Residency of Kediri

Chapter I

1.1. The Significance of the Study

This is a study of developments in Islamic spiritual practice in East Java. It focuses on groups organized with the specific purpose of chanting of various Islamic litanies. The study of these groups, designated by the name, *Majlis Dhikr*, is a neglected area of research within the study of Islamic ritual groups in Indonesia. In contrast to the abundance of studies of Sufi groups (I., *tarekat*), such as Tijaniyah, Qadiriyah, Naqshabandiyah, Qadiriyah wa Naqshabandiyah, and Shatariah, there has not yet been any comprehensive study devoted to examining the development of *Majlis Dhikr* in the Indonesian Islamic context. This lack of research is, unfortunately, accompanied by negative images of these groups. Nahdlatul Ulama, as an organization, does not accord these groups official recognition as *mu'tabarah*. Many Indonesian scholars and other Muslim groups consider these *Majlis Dhikr* to be local *tarekat* that lack *silsilah* (proper genealogy of transmission, *isnād*) or to represent unorthodox or pseudo-Sufi organizations. Often these groups have been considered syncretic because they incorporate strong local elements, both in their ritual and in their teachings. For the Indonesian Salafi group, the ritual practices of *Majlis Dhikr* are considered as *bid'ah* (innovation within Islam) because they claim that they have no sanction in the Prophetic tradition.

One reason that *Majlis Dhikr* groups are not considered to be *mu'tabarah* (recognised) is that they do not meet the criteria laid down by the *Jam'iyyah Ahl al-Thariqah al-Mu'tabarah,* which was established in 1957 under the Nahdlatul Ulama (NU) organization as the forum for recognized Sufi orders in Indonesia. One of these criteria is that a group can only be regarded as *mu'tabarah* if its *wirid* or ritual practices can be traced through an unbroken line of links between its *murshid* and the Prophet, and its teachings and doctrines should be relevant to the Islamic law (A., *sharī'at*) (Turmudi 2003:65). Any Islamic group, which does not meet these criteria, cannot be regarded as *mu'tabarah.*

Although the teachings of *Majlis Dhikr* groups conform to *sharī'at,* nevertheless, according the *Jam'iyyah,* they do not have an unbroken line of links between their founders and the Prophet. In other words, the Prophet never practised the *wirid* used by these groups and never passed it to the founders through a genealogy of spiritual leaders. As a result, for the *Jam'iyyah,* no *Majlis Dhikr* group can be regarded as an acknowledged Sufi order (I., *tarekat yang mu'tabarah*) because they do not have such links.

A similar response to *Majlis Dhikr* groups, especially for the *Ṣalawāt Wāḥidiyat* group, was given by *Kyai* Machrus Ali, a prominent '*ulamā'* with a Nahdlatul Ulama background, who regarded the *Ṣalawāt Wāḥidiyat* group as a non-*mu'tabarah* group because of its lack of direct connection between the founder of the group and the Prophet. According to him, the founder of *Wāḥidiyat*established and practised his ritual based on his encounter with the Prophet in a dream. According to *Kyai* Machrus, dreams cannot be used as a theological basis for establishing a *tarekat.*

The Dutch scholar Martin van Bruinessen has categorised *Majlis Dhikr* groups such as *Wāḥidiyat*as local *tarekat* whose practices and rituals are inseparable from those in some other mystical groups (I., *golongan kebatinan*). As a result of this notion, seemingly influenced by a Geertzian idea of Javanese Islam, Bruinessen considers *Wāḥidiyat*and the like as spiritualist and syncretic movements (*gerakan-gerakan kebatinan yang sinkretis*) which has eventually prompted several *tarekat,* such as Qadiriyah, Naqshabandiyah and other mainstream *tarekat* to establish the NU-affiliated *Jam'iyyah Ahl al-Thariqah al-Mu'tabarah* as an institution to disassociate themself from such syncretic groups (Bruinessen 1992:171).

Likewise, Lukman Hakim, one of the members of a prominent *tarekat* group in Indonesia, has maintained that Sufism or *tasawuf* cannot be practised without joining an acknowledged *tarekat* (*tarekat yang mu'tabarah*).[1] He argues that the practice of *tasawuf* without being member of an acknowledged *tarekat* (I., *bertasawuf tanpa tarekat*) and without the supervision of a spiritual master (A., *murshid*) can only lead to a superficial level of spiritual experience (A., *'ilm al-yaqīn*) and can never reach *'ain al-yaqīn* and *ḥaqq al-yaqīn.* In other words, in order to attain the deepest level of spiritual experience (A., *ḥaqq al-yaqīn*), Muslims should affiliate with an acknowledged *tarekat* whose ritual is clearly derived through an unbroken line of links connected to the Prophet. The implication of this notion is that any Islamic spiritual group including any *Majlis Dhikr* group, which does not have a spiritual genealogy going back to the Prophet, cannot be used as a means to practise *tasawuf.* Lukman Hakim has argued that

> Those who practise Sufism without tarekat only attain the experience of *'ilm al-yaqīn.* They never reach *'ain al-yaqīn* and *ḥaqq al-yaqīn*. This is because they only believe (I., *yakin*) based on their theoretical philosophy. They do not believe practically (I., *secara amaliah*), even though they claim that they believe *secara amaliah.* In fact, this belief happens only in their imagination, as if they believe *secara amaliah.*

1 Interviewed with Lukman Hakim, Jakarta, 24 July 2005.

A stronger rejection of the rituals and practices of the *Majlis Dhikr* groups which has emerged over the last two decades comes from the supporters of Indonesian Salafi groups which are strongly influenced by Wahabbism, a reform movement aimed at purifying Islam of local accretions. For instance, Abu Amsaka and Jawas, who champion the Islamic puritan movement in Indonesia, have argued that the ritual practice of Indonesian *Majlis Dhikr* groups mostly falls into the practise of *bid'ah.* They criticise these groups mainly because of the way they recite *dhikr* vocally in a group. In their view, such a practice is not sanctioned by the teachings of Qur'an, which urges Muslims to recite *dhikr* quietly (Amsaka 2003:85; Jawas 1423:150-51).

In contrast to these various critics, I will argue in this study that although *Majlis Dhikr* groups have been strongly criticised by other Muslims groups as not *mu'tabarah,* or as pseudo-Sufism or as *bid'ah,* nevertheless the existence of these groups is significant. The fact that these groups have attracted many followers demonstrates that the interest of Indonesian Muslims in joining these groups is strong and is increasing. Despite the increasing popularity of Sufi orders (*tarekat*) among Indonesian Muslims, these *Majlis Dhikr* groups have not only expanded and introduced their ritual and teachings widely but have also continued to gain new followers in both rural and urban areas.

Understanding these *Majlis Dhikr* groups becomes particularly important in the context of the Islamic preaching (I., *dakwah Islam*) in Indonesia. These groups have attracted followers from a wide social base to their practices, hence contributing significantly to the improvement of religious practice among Indonesian Muslims who were not strict in their daily observance of Islamic practice. Based on their understanding of the teachings of *tasawuf,* instead of rejecting nominal Muslims, these *Majlis Dhikr* groups have shown respect for and accommodation to all kinds of cultural symbols used by these Muslims groups. In doing so, the presence of these *Majlis Dhikr* groups in the landscape of Indonesian Islam has contributed to narrowing the gap between *santri* Muslims and nominal Muslims, who have long been ideologically opposed to one another. This study of *Majlis Dhikr* groups thus sheds light on increasing Islamic spiritual life and practice in Indonesia.

My research also explores the role that *Majlis Dhikr* groups are playing in improving the quality of interfaith dialogue and searching for a harmonious religious life in Indonesia. This important role can be seen from the fact that these groups allow the followers of other religions to share in and experience their rituals without asking them to convert. This respectful attitude toward followers of other religions can be attributed to a deep understanding of Islamic Sufi teachings, which strongly emphasise respect for people as human beings and God's creatures, irrespective of their religion. Without doubt, this tolerant attitude and emphasis on the spiritual aspects of religiosity are needed to create a peaceful religious life in Indonesia.

Contrary to accusations by other Muslim groups that *Majlis Dhikr* groups are practising *bid'ah*, are syncretic and represent pseudo-Sufism, these groups have, in fact, been strongly influenced by orthodox *tasawuf* teachings, and the members of these groups operate in the framework of mainstream Sufi practices. For example, many of the terms and symbols used within the teachings of *Majlis Dhikr* groups are adopted from similar Islamic terms and symbols commonly used by acknowledged Sufi groups. Moreover, most of the teachings of *Majlis Dhikr* groups result from their response to, and interpretation based on the two sources of Islamic law, that is, the Qur'an and hadith, as well as the views of other prominent Muslim Sufi scholars. Therefore, instead of practising *bid'ah* and carrying out syncretic rituals, I argue in this study that these groups have creatively interpreted and adapted the Qur'anic and hadith teachings in order to make themselves relevant in a mainstream Indonesian Islamic context. These groups also claim that the aim of their rituals is to attain closeness to God, which is also similar to the aim of the ritual practice conducted by *tarekat* groups. These *Majlis Dhikr* groups can thus be utilized as another means for Indonesian Muslims to seek spiritual closeness to God.

Another significance of this study is that it challenges Geertz's research on the development of Sufism in Muslim-majority countries. In his view, economic development and the expansion of modern sectors in many Muslim countries will result not only in the demise of Sufi orders in those countries but also lead to the triumph of Muslim scripturalist groups. Research conducted by Julia Howell has proved the inaccuracy of Geertz's prediction. According to Howell, despite their challenge and rejection by Indonesian Muslim revivalist or reformist groups, Sufi groups in Indonesia have not only shown signs of vigorous growth but also have attracted an increasing diversity of participants (Howell 2001:722). Not only has there been a proliferation of Sufi orders in current Indonesian Islam, but also a proliferation of other Islamic spiritual groups, such as *Majlis Dhikr* groups, in both rural and urban areas.

As far as I am aware, no comprehensive or specific studies have been conducted on *Majlis Dhikr* groups in Indonesia. Since scholars have erroneously regarded these groups as Sufi groups (*tarekat*), these groups have usually been discussed in studies either on general topics such as urban Sufism or Sufi groups in Indonesia, or on the religious revival in Java. In fact, *Majlis Dhikr* groups are not the same as Sufi groups (*tarekat*). As a result, little attempt has been made to provide a critical analysis of the teachings and rituals of these groups in the context of Islamic Sufism, how they disseminate their teachings or how they respond to various aspects of practical Sufism, as well as how these groups regard their rituals as legitimate practice within Islam.

In comparison, as M. Bruinessen has observed, the quantity and the quality of studies of *tarekat* (Sufi group) has proliferated during the last decade of the twentieth century, following the increasing popularity of *tarekat* in many parts of the Islamic world including Indonesia. Since the 1990s, people have witnessed an abundance of the works about Sufism in different regions, such as the Middle East, South Asian, Southeast Asia, West Africa, East Africa, and even, Europe. In addition, several international scholarly conferences on Sufism have been held to discuss different Sufi groups, as for example conferences on Naqshabandiyah (Paris 1985), Bektashiyah (Strasburg, 1986), Malamatiyah (Istanbul, 1987) and Mawlawiyah (Bamberg, 1991), and a debate between proponents and opponents of Sufism held in Utrecht in 1996. In response to this increasing interest in Sufism, several big publishers such as Hurst & Co., Curzon Press, and E.J. Brill have published books on Sufism. E. J. Brill, the renowned publisher of 'The Encyclopaedia of Islam', is preparing to publish *TheEncyclopaedia of Sufism*(Sujuti 2001a:xv). All this indicates an increasing scholarly interest in Sufism.

Likewise, studies of *tarekat* in Indonesian Islam gained popularity among Indonesian and Western researchers during 1990s and the early part of the current century. Publications include those by as AG. Muhaimin (1995; 2006), Endang Turmudi (1996; 2006), Howell (2001), Martin van Bruinessen (1992), Sukamto (1999), Sujuti (2001), Zamkhasari Dhofier (1982; 1999), and Zulkifli (2000). Among these studies, Zamakhsari Dhofier's study of *pesantren* traditions is regarded as a pioneering and important examination of Islamic traditional practices including the history and practice of the Qadiriyah Naqshabandiyah in Rejoso Jombang, East Java. This group is presently one of the orders with the largest following in Indonesia. In his study, Dhofier argues that *tarekat* have been an important means of spreading Islam since the early period of Islamization in the Indonesian archipelago. Through the leadership of the *kyai* in *pesantren,tarekat* have spread Islamic teachings among Javanese in particular. Furthermore, *pesantren* have become places for providing the leadership of *tarekat*. This can be seen in the case of *Pesantren* Tebuireng in Jombang, which has played an important role in providing most of the influential leaders of Qadiriyah Naqshabandiyah in East and Central Java. All of these figures were graduates from this *pesantren*, even though *Pesantren* Tebuireng is not a *pesantren tarekat* (Dhofier 1999: 151).

Another important study on *tarekat* was conducted by a Dutch scholar, Martin Van Bruinessen. His work might be considered as the most complete work that has ever been written on the Naqshabaniyah order and its networks, particularly in Indonesia. According to Bruinessen, Naqshabandiyah is significant because it is the most internationalised of orders compared to other *tarekat*, having branches in many countries including Yugoslavia, Egypt, Indonesia and China. In Indonesia, moreover, this *tarekat* has three important branches with different names: Naqshabandiyah Khalidiyah, Naqshabandiyah Mazhariyah and Qadiriyah wa Naqshabandiyah. Qadiriyah wa Naqshabandiyah is a combination of two *tarekat* set up by the Indonesian Sufi, Ahmad Khatib Sambas, who taught in Mecca in the mid-nineteenth century. In Java in particular, the Naqshabandiyah *tarekat* has attracted many followers in Central Java (Semarang, Girikusumo, Rembang, Blora, Banyumas, Purwokerto and Cirebon), the southern areas of East Java (Kediri, Blitar, Madiun, Magetan) and in Madura. It is important to note here that most of the leaders or *murshid* of Naqshabandiyah *tarekat* in Java belong to *pesantren*. They use their *pesantren* as a basis to spread the teachings of the *tarekat*. In other words, *pesantren* still play an important role in spreading the Sufi teachings and recruiting new members to the *tarekat*.

Muhaimin's study of the Islamic traditions of Cirebon has also greatly contributed to the understanding of the origin and the spread of Shattariyah and Tijaniyah *tarekat*. Tijaniyah is considered the fastest growing *tarekat* in Java. Like Dhofier, Muhaimin argues that Islamic traditions in Cirebon and probably elsewhere in Java has been maintained within Javanese Muslim society through the combination of *pesantren* and *tarekat* (Muhaimin 1995:355). It is not an exaggeration to say that those institutions are the hallmark of traditional Islam in Java. In line with this, looking at *Pesantren* Buntet in Cirebon, Muhaimin observes that the *pesantren* has become the base for both Shattariyah and Tijaniyah. As argued by Muhaimin, not only has Buntet become an important door-way for spreading Tijaniyah in Java, particularly West Java, but it has also become the model of a *pesantren* able to accept the practice of two different *tarekat* groups, something that is not found in other *pesantren* in Java. The *kyai* responsible for making *Pesantren* Buntet the centre of two *tarekat* were two brothers, *Kyai* Anas and *Kyai* Abbas. *Kyai* Anas was the leader of the Tijaniyah long before his brother *Kyai* Abbas was initiated into this group. *Kyai* Abbas was able to break the Tijaniyah rule which requires individuals to abandon their previous order before joining Tijaniyah. *Kyai* Abbas joined Tijaniyah while still affiliated with Shatariyah. Later, he became a *muqaddam* (leader) of Tijaniyah (Muhaimin 1995:353).

Turmudi's study of the changing leadership roles of *kyai* in Jombang has also added to the scholarly literature on the political dynamics of *tarekat* in Java.

Even though this study focuses on local *pesantren* leadership, it also considers the significant role of *tarekat* in several *pesantren* in Jombang. Turmudi examines how *kyai* who lead *tarekat* are involved in politics. Like Dhofier, Turmudi focused his attention on the influential Sufi group, Qadiriyah wa Naqshabadiyah in Jombang which was the first *tarekat* in Java to initiate a new tradition of establishing a political relationship with a ruling political party. *Kyai* Musta'in Ramli, the leader of the Qadiriyah wa Naqshabandiyah group in Jombang, supported the ruling party, *Golongan Karya* (GOLKAR) prior to the 1977 general election. His involvement in politics was seen in various ways by his followers. Some *kyai* who were members of the *tarekat* considered *Kyai* Ramli's political affiliation with GOLKAR as a violation of NU's commitment to support PPP (*Partai Persatuan Pembangunan,* The United Development Party), which was seen as the representative of Indonesian Muslims. As a result, these *kyai* withdrew their support for *Kyai* Mustain's group by establishing new *tarekat* groupings in *Pesantren* Cukir in Jombang and *Pesantren* Kedinding Lor in Surabaya. In contrast, *Kyai* Mustain's obedient followers regarded his involvement with GOLKAR as a new strategy to engage in the wider political context. This view was supported by *Kyai* Musta'in's wife who argued that the defection of her husband occurred because he had seen another way to achieve the political ends of 'the Islamic struggle'. While *Kyai* Mustain wanted to avoid further division in the Islamic community, his defection to GOLKAR nevertheless resulted in the splitting of Qadiriyah wa Naqshabandiyah into three different groups, namely, a Rejoso group, a Cukir group and a Kedinding Lor group (Sujuti 2001a:71). Turmudi's study of the leadership of *kyai* in *tarekat* shows how the involvement of *kyai* in politics can lead to changing loyalty among followers. Although the authority of a *kyai* to influence his followers' political affiliation is not absolute, nonetheless many followers do indeed follow their *kyai*'s example.

Adding to his predecessors' attempts to understand Java's *pesantren* traditions, Zulkifli's work, *The Role of the Pesantren in the Maintenance of Sufism in Java* (2002) addresses the issue of the transmission of *tasawuf* teachings through prominent scholars such as *Shaikh*Nawāwī Banten, *Shaikh*Maḥfūdh Termas and *Kyai* Kholil Bangkalan. *Kyai*Nawāwī was a student of *Shaikh* Ahmad Khāṭib in Mecca, and both are regarded as important figures in teaching and practising rituals associated with *tasawuf,* even though they reportedly did not join a *tarekat*. *Kyai* Kholil Bangkalan was also an important figure whose influence is evident among a generation of distinguished Javanese *kyai.*

The importance of Zulkifli's study lies in his comparison of two of the most important *pesantren* in Java, *Pesantren* Tebuireng in East Java and *Pesantren* Suryalaya in West Java. He looks at the role and strategies of the leaders in both *pesantren* in the development of the Qadiriyah wa Naqshabandiyah. Zulkifli argues that the two *pesantren* have different roles in the maintenance of Sufism in Java. *Pesantren* Tebuireng, established by *Kyai* Hashim Ash'ari, is known as a *pesantren sharī'at,* yet it maintains the teachings of Sufism including sincerity, asceticism, modesty, patience and the Sufi rituals such as prayers, *dhikr,* and *wirid.* Through the figure of *Kyai* Hashim Ash'ari, this *pesantren* has played an indirect role in the spread of the Qadiriyah wa Naqshabandiyah in East Java, controlling the practices of the leaders and the followers of the group and preventing them from deviation from orthodox Sufi teachings. Not only that, this *pesantren* has also produced the leaders of Qadiriyah wa Naqshabandiyah, since most of the *murshid* of the group in Java are graduates from *pesantren* Tebuireng. In contrast, *Pesantren* Suryalaya, represented by the figure of Shaikh Abdullah Mubarak, known as Abah Sepuh ('The Old Abah'), and his successor, Ahmad Shohibulwafa Tadjul Arifin, known as Abah Anom ('The Young Abah') have maintained Sufi traditions by establishing their *pesantren* as the centre of Qadiriyah wa Naqshabandiyah. Under the leadership of Abah Anom, Qadiriyah wa Naqshabandiyah has attracted many followers, not only from other regions in Indonesia but also from other countries, such as Malaysia and Singapore.

Important information about the diversity of the followers of *tarekat* in Java derives from research conducted by Howell, Subandi, and Nelson (2001) in several branches of Suralaya's Qadiriyah wa Naqshabandiyah. Comparing the results of a previous survey of members of the *tarekat* in 1990 with a survey carried out in 1997, their study makes clear that this group has experienced dramatic growth in membership during Suharto's New Order regime and the range of its membership has been extended from villagers to educated urban professionals and managers. This study also reveals an increase in women members of the *tarekat* compared to the previous period.[2] Therefore, Howell et al. suggest conducting further research on different groups of *tarekat,* focusing on analysing the membership in terms of age, education and gender.

All of these studies show that *tarekat* and *pesantren* are not separable institutions in maintaining Islamic traditions in Java. Most *pesantren* in Java function as places to mould students with Islamic knowledge, while some also function as an instrument for the recruitment of members of a *tarekat,* each of which is organized around the figure of a particular scholar and teacher (*kyai).*[3] None of these studies, however, analyse specifically the rise of *Majlis Dhikr* groups,

2 These findings are unlikely to be true of other *tarekat* groups.

3 See James J. Fox's foreword in Zulkifli's work of 'The Role of the *Pesantren* in the Maintenance of Sufism in Java' (2001)

which also use *pesantren* to spread and maintain their rituals and teachings. These groups should be taken into account in the analysis of the maintenance of traditional Islam within the Javanese Muslim community.

Julia Howell's study on Sufism and the Indonesian Islamic revival is pioneering research which helps particularly to understand the new trends in Sufism developing in urban areas (Howell 2001). Howell argues that in the latter part of twentieth century, numerous *tarekat* experienced new growth with new kinds of participants. She suggests that traditional Sufism in Indonesian during this period has undergone institutional innovation and modification to accommodate social needs. Since her study focuses on the development of Sufism in urban areas, particularly in Jakarta, Howell does not specifically examine the increasing development of *Majlis Dhikr* groups in other parts of Indonesia.

Inspired by Julia Howell's work, Ace Hasan Syadzily's work (2005) on the figure of Arifin Ilham, an urban preacher, and his *Majlis Dhikr* group has also added to an understanding the development of Islamic ritual groups, especially in urban areas. Similar to Howell, Syadzily finds that the participants in the *dhikr* ritual held by Arifin's group are mostly middle class urban residents who are relatively well-established economically and educationally. Since the focus of this work is to show that modernization and secularisation do not necessarily lead urban people to set aside religion, his study does not specifically look at how this *dhikr* group or its members consider their ritual as a theologically legitimate practice within Islam. In addition, this book did not critically analyse the response of members of this group to important issues concerning its specific practices.

Ahmad Syafi'i Mufid, a researcher in the Agency for Religious Research and Development at the Indonesian Ministry of Religious Affairs, recently conducted another important study on Sufism in Indonesian Islam. His work is about the role of *tarekat* Qadiriyah Naqshabandiyah in the north coastal area of Java in improving the religiosity of Javanese people in that area. He concluded in his work that Javanese people in the area have readily accepted the teaching of Sufism because it is relevant to their worldview. As a result, he claims that this process of Islamization mirrors the process of Islamization in the Malay Archipelago many centuries ago, which also involved Sufi inspiration. Although Mufid included the study of Islamic spiritual groups other than *tarekat* in his research such as *Ṣalawāt Wāḥidiyat* group, he did not analyse critically the teaching of these groups nor how they creatively establish their teaching by interpreting the Qur'an and hadith (Mufid 2006).

This work is designed to contribute to the body of work of those scholars who have discussed the proliferation of Islamic spiritual groups in contemporary Indonesian Islam. It aims to fill a gap in the literature by examining how Indonesian *Majlis Dhikr* groups regard themselves as legitimate groups within Islam. A more specific question related to the rituals and teachings of these groups is to what extent these rituals and teachings are related to the teachings of the Qur'an and hadith and the general teachings of Islam and orthodox Sufism. As regards the preaching of Islam, the question is what strategies these groups use to disseminate their teachings to other Muslims. As these *Dhikr* groups derive from the context of the *pesantren,* another question is what role *pesantren* play in facilitating the development of these *Majlis Dhikr* groups.

1.2. The Understanding of *Tasawuf, Tarekat* and *Majlis Dhikr* Group in Indonesian Islam

For the purpose of this study, it is important to explain important terms such as *tasawuf, tarekat,* and *Majlis Dhikr* (or *Jama'ah Dhikr*), which have been used interchangeably by researchers on Indonesian Islam. This explanation is necessary to understand the phenomenon of the proliferation of various Islamic spiritual groups within the Indonesian Islamic context and the development of studies about Islamic spiritual groups in Indonesia.

As far as the definition of *tasawuf* is concerned in classic Arabic understanding, this term was defined variously by Sufi scholars. Al-Qushairy (d. 475/1074) (2002:337-41) in his book *al-Risālat* and Al-Hujwiri (d.1082)(1997:43-55), in his book *Kashf al-Maḥjūb,* enumerate the various definitions of *tasawuf* put forward by different Muslim Sufi. These diverse definitions of Sufism demonstrate how difficult is to provide an exact definition of *tasawuf*. Perhaps, because of this difficulty, Chittick argues that it is difficult to distinguish which Muslims have been Sufi and which have not (Chittick 1995). Closer examination of these definitions shows that they are concerned with the practical aspects of the inner life which have eventually formed a body of knowledge. When *tasawuf* became a particular form of knowledge, like other categories of Islamic knowledge such as *fiqh, hadith,* and Islamic theology (*kalam*), it comprised theoretical teachings that needed to be put into practice. Therefore, as a form of knowledge, *tasawuf* was named as *'īlm al-bātin* (the knowledge of the inner self), a term used in opposition to other traditional sciences, such as the study of hadith or Islamic jurisprudence (*fiqh*), which were known as perceptible knowledge (A., *'ilm al-ẓāhir*)

The word *tasawuf* is frequently defined in broad terms in Indonesian Islam. For instance, citing Trimingham, Syafi'i Mufid defines *tasawuf* as the spiritual teaching, knowledge and practices of Muslim individuals or groups for the purpose of purifying the spirit in order to approach God. Another definition is given by Julia Howell who has defined *tasawuf* as personal intensification and interiorization of Islamic faith and practice. These broad definitions thus encompass not only the spiritual practices of *tarekat* (Sufi groups) but also the practices of others, including *Majlis Dhikr* groups, as well as study groups and intensive courses on practical *tasawuf* which all aim at the purification of soul in approaching of God.

So, the term *tasawuf* is able to accommodate a range of meanings which are put forward by different groups. Expanded terms such as modern *tasawuf* (I., *tasawuf modern*), and positive *tasawuf* (I., *tasawuf positif*), have recently been introduced in the literature of *tasawuf* study in Indonesia. Thus *tasawuf* is no longer restricted to the description of practices by *tarekat* (Sufi groups).

The term *tasawuf modern* was first introduced by Hamka in the study and practice of *tasawuf* in Indonesia. Using this term, Hamka tried to disengage the concept of *tasawuf* from the concept of *tarekat*. Moreover, by introducing this term, Hamka criticised Muslims who practise *tasawuf* as a way of avoiding worldly matters and regarding them as unimportant (Hamka 1990:5-6). For Hamka, *tasawuf* should be understood in its original meaning, that is,

as a method to 'leave off offensive behaviour and to take on praiseworthy manners by purifying the self, improving and training the stature of human personality, renouncing greed and caprice and controlling the sexual desire from exceeding what is normal for a sound individual'(Hooker 2006:103-4).

Inspired by the idea of *tasawuf* put forward by al-Ghazālī (d.1111) in his book *Ihyā'Ulūm al-din,* Hamka urged Muslims to cultivate the inner spiritual life within the outer forms of religiosity. Hamka considered this as an urgent need, particularly to achieve a deeper emotional richness of devotion. Based on his interpretation of *tasawuf*, Hamka is regarded as the person responsible for popularising *tasawuf* to the educated urban middle class in Indonesia.

Another term introduced by Indonesian scholars is *tasawuf positif* (positive *tasawuf*). This term has become popular within the study of Indonesian Islam following the increasing interest in *tasawuf* among urban Muslims and well-to-do cosmopolitan Muslims. Similar to the idea of *tasawuf modern,* the concept of *tasawuf positif* aims to make the practice of *tasawuf* more an individual responsibility rather than heavily relying on the guidance of *murshid* (masters) of particular *tarekat.* This kind of *tasawuf* stresses individual effort to mould praiseworthy manners without joining a particular *tarekat.* Those who champion the idea of *tasawuf positif* actively promote what they regard as practising *tasawuf* without *tarekat* (Sufi groups) (I., *tasawuf tanpa tarekat*). Instead, they can independently practise and actively learn *tasawuf* teachings through intensive courses or workshops, and religious study clubs as is evident in urban organisations such as Yayasan Paramadina, Yayasan Tazkiyah, ICNIS (Intensive Course and Networking for Islamic Science), *Pusat Pengembangan Tasawuf Positif dan Klinik Spiritualitas Islami* (Centre for the Development of Positive Tasawuf and Clinic for Muslim Spirituality), and IiMAN (the Indonesian Islamic Media Network). According to the initiators of *tasawuf positif,* Muslims can practise *tasawuf positif* since many Muslims *tasawuf* scholars have actively practised and deeply understood the teaching of *tasawuf* even though they never joined any *tarekat*(Anwar 2002:13-16).

Another term that is important to elaborate further in this study is *tarekat.* This term is widely used in Indonesian Islam to refer to the practice of *tasawuf* in particular communal ritual through 'an organised Sufi order'. According to the *pesantren* tradition, *tarekat* can be divided into two kinds: *tarekat 'ammah* (the general way), pious acts which are continually practised with good intention, and *tarekat khassah* (the specific way) relying on certain ritual *dhikr* which are performed with the guidance of a *murshid* who is linked in his knowledge through a spiritual genealogy going back to the Prophet Muhammad. This form of *tarekat* has formal requirements. For example, in order to become a member of such a *tarekat,* disciples should make a vow of allegiance (I., *baiat* or *talqin*) to the master of the *tarekat* concerned. Through this *baiat,* disciples (*murid*) put themselves under the guidance of the *murshid* to purify themselves in their to approach God (Aqib 1999:98). The *baiat* is an important condition for the validity of the spiritual journey of *murid.* It is commonly believed in the *tarekat* world that following the *tasawuf* path without the guidance of a *murshid* is like following this path under the guidance of Satan.

The proponents of *tarekat* are convinced that a *murshid* has an important role in the spiritual development of his *murid.* Without the guidance of a *murshid,* a *murid* cannot obtain authentic spirituality. The proponents of *tarekat* claim that if there are Muslims who claim that they have achieved *wusul* or *ma'rifat* (gnosis), in the absence of a *murshid* to guide them, what they have achieved consists of the whispers and tricks (I., *tipu daya*) of Satan. It is believed in the *tarekat* world that without the guidance of a *murshid,* Muslims cannot distinguish between the whispers of God and his Angels and the whisper of Satan.

In this study, I use the term *Majlis Dhikr* to refer to groups who practise reciting *dhikr* and *Ṣalawāt*in unison (I., *berjamaah*) in order to achieve perfection and closeness to God with no structural connection to any *tarekat* order. Comprehending the term *Majlis Dhikr* as used in this study is important, particularly to approach and analyse the current proliferation of Islamic spiritual groups in Indonesia.

In this argument, I differ with scholars such as Bruinessen (1992), Dhofier (1999), Turmudi (2003), Mufid (2006), and Abdurrahman (1978). For example, *Majlis Dhikr* groups do not require followers to take an oath (*baiat*) to the leader of these groups. In other words, exclusive membership is not recognised. People are able to join *Majlis Dhikr* groups and practise their *dhikr* without taking an oath of allegiance to the leader of any particular group. As a result, people can voluntary join one group while also being members of other *Majlis Dhikr* groups, something which is not, generally, possible for members of *tarekat* in Java.[4]

Another obvious difference from *tarekat* is in the *dhikr* recited by *Majlis Dhikr*. The *dhikr* text recited by these *Majlis Dhikr* are generally created by their leaders or taken from *dhikr* formulas taught by the Prophet or widely practised by previous prominent *'ulamā'*. In contrast, *dhikr* formulas recited by *tarekat* orders are claimed to have been transmitted by a series of unbroken links between the *mursyid* and the Prophet. Unlike *tarekat,* the members of *Majlis Dhikr* groups are also able to practise the group's ritual intermittently without any sanction, even though the leaders of these groups recommend members to practise the ritual continuously.

Distinguishing clearly between the *Majlis Dhikr* groups and other Islamic spiritual groups in Indonesia is critical to an analysis of the position of these *Majlis Dhikr* groups in the context of current Indonesian Muslim life. The proliferation of *Majlis Dhikr* indicates that such *Majlis Dhikr* have been accepted by Indonesian Muslims as an alternative vehicle to practise the teachings of *tasawuf*.

---

4 In the past, there were no clear cut boundaries between numerous different *tarekat* either in their doctrines and ritual or their memberships. Disciples did not necessarily adhere to one *tarekat*; they could become a member of different *tarekat* and take allegiance to different *murshid* of those *tarekat*. The best exemplar of this was Muḥammad Yūsuf al-Maqassārī (1037-1111/1627-99) the seventeenth century Malay Sufi, who affiliated himself with several *tarekat* such as Qadiriyah, Kkhalwatiyah and Naqshabandiyah (Azra 1992:420-27). *Kyai* Abbas form *Pesantren* Buntet, Cirebon, can also be added in this category as a *Kyai* who joined two different *tarekat,* Shattariyah and Tijaniyah.

1.3. The Variety of *Majlis Dhikr* Groups in Java

Despite the increasing popularity of *tarekat* among the Javanese, *Majlis Dhikr* groups have also gained popularity in many rural and urban areas in Java over the last two decades. Like *tarekat,* these groups offering a new mode of Islamic ritual practice have captured the interest of people of various ages and genders from villagers to well educated persons, and even a number of national elites. In contrast to the *tarekat,* which necessarily require members to aged forty or more to be able to practise its ritual, *Majlis Dhikr* groups do not have this requirement. As a result, in several *Majlis Dhikr* groups, one might easily find persons categorised as teenagers and even children following and practising the rituals of the group.

The presence of *Majlis Dhikr* is evident in the landscape of Indonesian Islam. Several such groups have been set up in Java during the last two decades. Most of these have been established by Islamic leaders (I., *kyai*) who have strong connection with *pesantren.* As a result, the activities of these groups cannot be separated from those of *pesantren.* However, some groups have been set up by independent Islamic leaders who do not have a strong affiliation with a particular *pesantren.* As far as the organization of these groups is concerned, most have organizational structures with branches in many regions, while others do not have an organizational structure. To give an overview of the range of these groups, this subsection will briefly introduce the *Majlis Dhikr* groups in Java that have attracted large numbers of followers and participants in their rituals in recent years.

One of these groups is the *Majlis Dhikr al-Maghfira* which was established in 1984 by Ustadz Haryono (b. 1970) from Pasuruan, East Java. This group has a home base in *Pesantren* Al-Madinah, Pasuruan, East Java (Haryono 2006:xxxii). Before establishing his group, Ustadz Haryono was known as a *tabib* (an Islamic healer) who was able to heal sickness using alternative methods which are unknown to the medical world. For instance, before healing his patients, he asked them to provide a goat. Using his spiritual power, he transferred the patients' disease to the goat, and then slaughtered the goat. He still uses this method and many other healing methods to cure his patients. Perhaps because of his profession as a healer, his group is known by his followers as *Majlis Dhikr Penyembuhan* (The Healing *Dhikr* Group). Before becoming widely known nationally, this group initially conducted its ritual from house to house (*dari rumah ke rumah*) and in several small village mosques, attended by only a few people. Since 2000, the ritual of this group has attracted thousands of people, and can now only be held in mosques with a large park or in a sport stadium. This group now conducts *dhikr* ritual in forty eight towns throughout

Indonesia (Damarhuda and Mashuri 2005:74) and in Malaysia, Brunei and Singapore. During my research, the ritual of this group was widely broadcast by national and local television. In Surabaya, East Java, this group is sponsored by JTV, a local TV station owned by the *Jawa Pos* Media Group, which always broadcasts Ustadz Haryono's *dhikr* ritual when it is held in cities in East Java. This *Majlis Dhikr* group conducts its ritual by reciting the *Ratib al-al-Ḥaddād,* a prayer composed by a famous Hadrami Muslim saint, 'Abd 'Allah Ibn 'Alawī al-Ḥaddād (d.1720) consisting of a collection of Qur'anic verses, a declaration of belief, praise and exaltation of God, and particular invocations.

Another group is *Majlis Dhikr al-Dhikra,* which was established by a young Muslim preacher Arifin Ilham (b. 1969). During his youth, Arifin Ilham was a proponent of the religious ideas of Muhammadiyah, who strongly criticized reciting vocal *dhikr,* especially after the five daily prayers, as is popularly done among Nahdlatul Ulama's members. However, after suffering severe sickness because of a snake bite, he began to realize the importance of reciting *dhikr,* and he popularised the vocal recitation of *dhikr* in unison (I., *berjamaah*). This group was initially established in 1999 from a small group of seven people who recited *dhikr* weekly in the *Al-Amr bi al-Taqwa* mosque in Mampang Indah, Jakarta. This group has now attracted the attention of thousands of Muslims, mostly in urban areas, who attend its ritual. In order to organise this group, Arifin Ilham established an organization consisting of an executive board (I., *Dewan Tanfidhiah*) and a consultative board (I., *Dewan Syuriah*). With this organization, this group serves not only as an institution for conducting *dhikr* ritual but also as an institution to provide social services for the community. For example, one of the units in this group, *Titian Keluarga Sakinah,* gives advice to teenagers and adults on family and marriage matters. Other units established in this group include a *Panti Asuhan Yatama Az-Zikra* (orphanage), the *Tasbih* magazine and a *Tim Khadimatul Ummah* (Team for Social Service) (Syadzily 2005:50-54).

Like other *Majlis Dhikr* groups, Arifin Ilham's group recites several *dhikr* formulae taken from the Qur'an and hadith such as *ta'awwudl, tasbīḥ, taḥmīd, tahlīl,* several short chapters of the Qur'an, *Asmaul Husna* (the beautiful names of God), and the exaltation of the Prophet (I., *salawat nabi*). This ritual is conducted after a short lecture (I., *taushiyah singkat*) by Arifin Ilham. It is interesting to note that participants are strongly encouraged to wear white clothes and white caps (I., *peci haji*) during this ritual (Syadzily 2005:67). In 2003, this group successfully held the *dhikr* ritual entitled *Indonesia Berdzikir* in the *Istiqlal* mosque, the biggest mosque in Southeast Asia. This ceremony was attended by senior Indonesian politicians, several Indonesian Muslim leaders, and thousands of people from the Jakarta area. The increasing popularity of

Arifin Ilham and his group among Indonesian Muslims nationally has been strengthened by wide publicity in the media. For example, the activities of Arifin Ilham and his group are widely reported on by Indonesian electronic and print media. Like Abdullah Gymnastiar (known as AA Gym), a famous young Muslim preacher, Arifin Ilham's face and his *dhikr* activities regularly appeared on national television programs during the period of my research. Furthermore, cassettes and CDs of his *tausiyah* (I., *ceramah*, religious lecture) and *dhikr* ritual are readily found in many music shops. His face is also visible on the covers of many books in big bookshops in Indonesia such as Gramedia and Gunung Agung bookshop.

The *Ṣalawāt Wāḥidiyat* group is another important *Majlis Dhikr* group in Java, with members in many cities throughout Indonesia and also overseas. This group was set up in 1963 by *Kyai* Abdul Madjid Ma'ruf, believed by his followers to have experienced a dream of the Prophet. Focusing its ritual on the recitation of *Ṣalāwa* (the exaltation of the Prophet), the group has set up branches in many cities in Indonesia, with its central board in Kediri, East Java. In order to spread its teachings, beside using Kedunglo *pesantren* as a home base, this group has established an organizational structure which consists of a central board office with representatives in provinces, regencies, sub-districts, and villages, something which has not been done by other *Majlis Dhikr*. The highest authority and decision-making body in the *Wāḥidiyat* is in the hands of *Kyai* Abdul Latif Madjid, the son of the founder, who acts as the guardian of the *Wāḥidiyat* and as the head of its foundation and organization. Among *tarekat* groups, *Wāḥidiyat* is considered by some to be an unacknowledged *tarekat* (*ghairu mu'tabarah*) since it does not have an unbroken a chain of transmission that can be traced back to the Prophet. Despite its popularity, this group keeps no official record of the number of its members.

Another significant *Majlis Dhikr* group is called *Istighāthat Iḥsāniyyat*. Compared to the two previous groups, the*Istighāthat Iḥsāniyyat* is a relatively group, established in Kediri in 1999 by *Kyai* Abdul Latif, a *kyai* from *Pesantren* Jampes, Kediri. The ritual of this group focuses on the recitation of *dhikr* formulae written by *Kyai* Abdul Latif. This ritual is not only held regularly at several Muslim saints' graves, but also in other places in East Java, Central Java and Bali. Unlike *Ṣalawāt Wāḥidiyat* group, *Iḥsāniyyat* does not have an organizational structure to spread its teachings. Nevertheless, it has several coordinators in various regions who facilitate events held by the group in those regions. This group was established initially to cater for those categorised as *orang ruwet,* nominal Muslims, and those negatively categorised as the dregs of society (*sampah masyarakat*), such as those who were previously addicted to narcotics (I., *narkoba*), alcohol, ecstasy tablets, and opium (*sabu-sabu*).

Iḥsāniyyat thus accommodates cultural modes prevalent among such people in its *dakwah* strategy. For instance, this group allows Javanese popular arts such as the horse dance (J., *jaranan*), tiger-masked dance (I., *reog*), music of Malay Orchestras (I., *Orkes Melayu*), Chinese dragon dance (*leang-leong*), and *ruwatan* to be performed on its annual anniversary.

Another important *Majlis Dhikr* group in Java is *Dhikr al-Ghāfilīn* which was established in 1973 by the late *Kyai* Hamim Jazuli (*Gus* Mik) who was seen as a controversial *kyai*. The ritual of this group is held at several Muslim tombs in Kediri, East Java and many other places throughout Indonesia. This ritual is often combined with *Semaan al-Qur'an*, a recitation of all the chapters of the Qur'an by memorizers, followed by other participants called *sāmi'īn* (literally, listeners). This group has now established many branches in many cities in Java and other islands, attracting numerous members from different social levels. The group even holds its annual ritual in the Yogyakarta palace (*Alun-alun Utara*), where a member of the palace's family acts as its coordinator. Since the death of *Kyai* Hamim Jazuli, this group has been independently run by different leaders, each with their own followers. The exact number of its followers is unknown since no official record is kept of its membership.

1.4. Meaning and Implications of the Classification: *Mu'tabarah*

In the study of Islamic practices, the concept of *mu'tabarah* might be known only in the context of Indonesian Islam, particularly within the Nahdlatul Ulama (NU) tradition. This term literally means 'recognised' and 'legitimate'. However, it is used by NU not only to refer to particular books that can be appropriately used as literature in the NU's *pesantren* and as references on which to base religious legal opinions, but it is also used to refer to particular Sufi groups which can be joined by NU members.

According to this concept, books that can be categorised as *mu'tabarah* are those which are compatible with the doctrine of *Ahlussunnah wal Jama'ah*(Muhammad 2004:77), a doctrine which is strongly held by the NU members as the basis of their religious practices. According to this doctrine, those books should conform to one of four *madhhab* (Islamic legal schools) in matters of Islamic jurisprudence; in matters of Islamic theology they should follow the teachings of Abū Ḥasan al-Ash'ārī and Abū Manṣūr al-Māturidī, and in matters of *tasawuf* they should comply with the teaching of al-Ghazālī and Junaid al-Baghdādī. In addition, another criterion used to identify books as *mu'tabarah* in the NU tradition is the credibility of their authors. According to *Kyai* Misbah, a senior leader of *pesantren* Jampes in Kediri, particular books (I., *kitab kuning*) can be considered *mu'tabarah* as long as their authors meet four criteria. Firstly, they must be learned persons (A., *'ālim*). Secondly they must have displayed good behaviour (I., *akhlakul karimah*). Thirdly, they must express a high-aiming endeavour (A., *himmat 'āliyat*) to follow the practice of the Prophet. Fourthly, they should display refined speech when discussing others' opinions.[5] Based on these criteria, books written by Ibn Taymiyyah and his student, Ibn al-Qayyim al-Jauziyah, for example, are rarely found in NU's *pesantren* literature and curriculum because these authors do not use refined speech. Instead, they usually use provocative and abusive language in expressing their disagreement with other Muslim scholars' views. Books such as *Bidāyat al-Mujtahid*written by Ibn al-Rushd, and *Subul al-Salām*written by al-Shan'ānī are not used in *pesantren* curricula or as references because these authors are Shiites, a group which is different from *Ahlussunnah wal Jama'ah.*

The concept of *mu'tabarah* is also applied to the practice of *tarekat* (Sufi groups) under the umbrella of NU. It is used by an association founded in 1957 under the NU umbrella and known as *Pucuk Pimpinan Jam'iyyat Ahli Thoriqoh Mu'tabarah* (Central Executive Committee of the Association of Members of Respected *Tarekat* Orders) to identify Sufi groups that can be joined by a member of NU based on the criteria laid down by this association (*Jam'iyyat*). These criteria make clear that the teachings of the *tarekat* must conform to the Islamic Law (A., *sharī'at*) and the *wirid* practised by the *tarekat* must have a spiritual genealogy (I., *silsilah*) going back to the Prophet. Turmudi argues that these criteria were established by the *Jam'iyah* to ensure that the *wirid* were not invented by the founders of *tarekat,* but were practised by the Prophet himself. Any *tarekat* that does not meet these criteria is not recognized or not given the 'respect' accorded to other *tarekat* (A., *ghairu mu'tabarah*), and as a result should not be joined by NU members (Turmudi 2003:65).

It is clear that the concept of *mu'tabarah* is significant in regard to the ritual practices among *tarekat* members because it cannot only give strong legitimacy for *tarekat* groups involved in the *Jam'iyyah* but can also enhance the members' faith in their rituals and teaching. Furthermore, by using the concept of *mu'tabarah,* those groups involved in the *Jam'iyyah* can make a clear-cut distinction between their rituals and various other ritual practices considered incompatible with Islamic law (Dhofier 1999:144). In other words, the concept of *mu'tabarah* is internally effective to protect these groups from other unorthodox spiritual groups.

5 Interview with *Kyai* Misbah, Kediri, June 2005.

Nevertheless, the concept of *mu'tabarah* used by the *Jam'iyyat* has not prevented the proliferation of ritual groups which are incompatible with the criteria laid down by the association. For instance, at one of its official meetings held in 1957 in Magelang, Central Java, the association declared that *Tarekat* Shiddiqiyah,[6] headed by an NU *kyai,* could not be regarded as *mu'tabarah* because it does not have an acceptable *silsilah* and *murshidship.* Despite this decision, *Tarekat* Shiddiqiyah keeps growing and recruits many members from different regions, particularly in East Java and Central Java (Qawa'id 1992:89). It also continues to operate like other recognized *tarekat.*

In fact, the concept of mu'tabarah was debated within NU before the Jam'iyyat was formally founded. For example, in its 6th Congress on August 1931 held in Cirebon, NU faced a difficulty in determining whether or not Tijaniyah could be regarded as being mu'tabarah so that its teachings could be practised by NU members. This problem arose due to the fact that some of the participants of the Congress considered that the Tijaniyah did not have an acceptable silsilah because the founder of this group Aḥmad al-Tijānī (1737-1815), who lived in North Africa and founded his group in 1781-2,[7] claimed that he received the wird for his tarekat from the Prophet when he was fully conscious and in active mind (A., yaqdhat), not dreaming. Another objection to the Tijaniyah is related to its teaching that the Tijaniyah followers will be given a place in paradise without passing the reckoning stage (hisab), and that they should give up their membership in their former orders (Pijper 1987:89). Despite strong objections from some of its members, after a long and exhausting debate, the Congress chaired by Kyai Hasyim Asy'ari eventually declared that the Tijaniyah can be considered mu'tabarah (Muhaimin 1995:345). Instead of referring to the criteria of *silsilah,* this decision was based on the notion that the litanies including *dhikr, Ṣalawāt* and *istighfār,* practised in Tijaniyah ritual are compatible with Islamic teaching (Bruinessen 1995:108). In other words, even though the Tijaniyah does not have an acceptable *silsilah* that can be traced back to the Prophet, its litanies are legitimate and can be practised by Nahdlatul Ulama members; the Congress was silent about the *tarekat*'s more extreme claims (Pijper 1987:97).

It is interesting to analyse why NU, in its 6th Congress, agreed to consider the Tijaniyah as being *mu'tabarah* based only on the content of its litanies, despite strong objections from within the NU circle. The decision was made by NU to put an end a conflict which threatened to divide the organisation. As mentioned by Bruinessen, both apologists and proponents of Tijaniyah were members of NU and had close relations with NU leaders. *Kyai* Anas, the *Muqaddam* (leader)

6 This *tarekat* was established by *Kyai* Muchtar Mu'thi in early 1950s in Ploso, Jombang, East Java.

7 During this period, al-Tijani claimed that he received a waking vision of the Prophet who taught him the litanies for his new order.

of Tijaniyah was a leading member of NU as well as being the student of *Kyai* Hasyim Asy'ari, the founder of NU. To maintain the unity of the organisation, NU accommodated both sides and allowed them to coexist peacefully. Moreover, this decision was taken because NU did not want to offend *Kyai* Abbas (1879-1946) who was the host of the Congress and the elder brother of the *Muqaddam* of Tijaniyah, *Kyai* Anas (Bruinessen 1999:721-22).

Kyai Abbas was also an important figure who bridged the gap between the followers of Tijaniyah and other *tarekat*. Several years after the congress, despite being the *murshid* (leader) of Shatariyah, following his brother, *Kyai* Abbas took an initiation in Tijaniyah and then became the *muqaddam* (leader) of Tijaniyah. (Muhaimin 1995:350). According to the teaching of Tijaniyah, once Muslims become members of the Tijaniyah, they should abandon their previous *tarekat*. However, *Kyai* Abbas did not abandon his former *tarekat* and even became the leader of two *tarekat*. Without doubt, this unique position of *Kyai* Abbas broke the strict Tijaniyah rule which necessitates its members abandon previous *tarekat*. *Kyai* Abbas might have deliberately taken this position to put an end to the dispute over the exclusiveness of Tijaniyah and, as result, this might have helped to put an end to greater conflicts which threatened the unity of NU organisationally. Until now the *mu'tabarah* status of Tijaniyah has remained unshaken and it was one of forty six *tarekat mu'tabarah* considered as *mu'tabarah* in the Congress held by the association on 26th-28th February 2000 in Pekalongan, Central Java (Anonymous 2000:222).[8]

It is clear that in an emergency situation, the concept of *mu'tabarah* can be negotiated and interpreted by the important figures in the NU. These key figures are significant in deciding whether particular *tarekat* can be regarded as being *mu'tabarah* or not, based on their understanding of the general concept of *Ahlussunnah wal jamaah* embraced by NU members. Part of this understanding is that preventing evil takes precedence over any consideration of gaining benefit from something (A., *dar'ul mafāsid muqaddam alā jalb al-maṣālih*). This notion, which is taken from Islamic legal theory, might have inspired the NU leaders to decide on the status of Tijaniyah. Therefore, instead of considering Tijaniyah to be non-*mu'tabarah* on the basis of the criteria prevalent in the organisation, the leaders of NU found a compromise formula which not only allowed the followers and opponents of Tijaniyah to coexist peacefully, but also avoided a possible conflict threatening the unity of NU organisationally.

8 See Appendix

1.5. Sufism in the *Pesantren* Tradition

The forms of Islam that first came to Malay Archipelago were probably colored by Sufi doctrine and practice. It is no historical coincidence that the first century of the Islamization of South Asia (the thirteenth century) was the golden period of medieval Sufism that saw a proliferation of Sufi orders (*tarekat).* Thus, for example, al-Ghazālī, the proponent of orthodox Sufism, died in 1111; Abd al-Qādir al-Jaylānī to whom the teachings of the *tarekat* Qadiriyah are attributed, died in 1166; a year later saw the death of Abd al-Qāhir al-Suhrawardī with whom *tarekat* Suhrawardiyah is associated; Najm al-Dīn al-Kubrā, the founder of *tarekat* Kubrawiyyah and the key influential figure of the Naqsabandiyah order died in 1221; Ibn al-'Arabī whose thoughts and teachings greatly influenced Malay Sufi thinking died in 1240; Abu al-Ḥasan al- Shādhilī who originated from North Africa and established the Shadhiliyah order died in 1258 (Bruinessen 1994a:2).

In Anthony Johns's view, individual Sufi and Sufi orders played an important role in the Islamization of Malay Archipelago beginning in the thirteenth century. After the fall of Baghdad in 1258, there began a wave of active Sufi wanderings that did much to unify the Islamic world (Johns 1961:14). The teachings of Sufism founded fertile ground within indigenous religions and belief. The indigenous population could easily accept mystical thoughts of Ibn 'Arabī because they were closely related to the previous Indic mystical ideas prevalent in the region. In addition, the Sufi ideas of the Perfect Man (A., *Insān al-Kāmil)* and of sainthood (A., *wilāyat*) gave a mystical legitimation to local rulers enabling them to use these notions for political or economical reasons. Instead of radically changing traditional beliefs and practices, Sufism emphasized the continuity of indigenous tradition and belief, coloring them with Islam. Al-Attas argues that it is the characteristic of Sufism to allow non Islamic elements within Islamic Sufism providing that they do not contradict Qur'an revelation (Al-Attas 1985: 171).

The second wave of Islamic intellectualism that influenced Sufism in the *pesantren* tradition was brought by 'traditional' Muslim scholars who studied in Mecca and Medina during the early nineteenth century. It was in this century that intellectual links between the heart of Islam in Middle East and the Malay world experienced greater consolidation. Due to the easing of restrictions on the *hajj* and the improved of availability in transport, more students from Southeast Asia, particularly from Indonesia, were able to study in Mecca and Medina. Many prominent Indonesian '*ulamā*' studied there during this period: Shaikh Akhmad Khāṭib Sambas (d.1875), *Shaikh* al-Nawāwī al-Bantānī al-Tanari (d. 1897), Mahfūdz al-Tirmīsī (d.1919), Ahmad Rifā'ī Kalisalak (d.1875), *Kyai*

Saleh Darat (1903), *Kyai* Khalil Bangkalan (d.1925), *Kyai* Hasyim Asy'ari (d.1947) and *Kyai* Asnawi Kudus (d.1959) Rahman (1997:94). Three prominent Indonesian *'ulamā'*, Shaikh al-Nawāwī al-Bantānī, *Shaikh* Akhmad Khāṭib Sambas and *Kyai*Mahfūdz al-Tirmīsī, who taught at the Ḥaram mosque in Mecca shaped the intellectual traditions of the *pesantren* because almost all *kyai* from prominent *pesantren* in Java studied with these *'ulamā'*(Bruinessen 1994b:137).

This wave of intellectualism placed great emphasis on the reconciliation between Sufism and *sharī'at*. This can be seen clearly from texts taught in the two holy cities –Mecca and Medina – during the period. As observed by Snouck Hurgronje, the primary texts on Sufism taught at the Ḥaram mosque in Mecca were the works of al-Ghazali (Zulkifli 2002:24). During this period, there was a change in the theological orientation of Sufism and other Islamic knowledge in the *pesantren*. For example, mystical texts containing the theosophical or philosophical mystic ideas of *Waḥdat al-Wujūd* and *Martabat Tujuh* were no longer taught in many *pesantren*. L.W.C. van den Berg who conducted research in a number of *pesantren* in Java and Madura in 1880 and compiled a list of Arabic texts used in these *pesantren* indicates that books containing *Wujudiyah* doctrine or *Insān al-Kāmil* (the 'perfect man') teaching were absent from the curriculum. Instead in those *pesantren* with direct contact with the center of orthodoxy, most texts on Sufism were dominated by Ghazāli's works or commentaries on them (Bruinessen 1994b).[9]

Another salient feature of the second wave of intellectualism coming to Indonesia was the growth of Sufi orders in Indonesia. The growth of Sufi orders during the period was made possible because of the increase number of pilgrims performing the *hajj*. Several Sufi orders played an important role in anti-colonial rebellions during the late 19th and early 20th centuries.

The nature of the second wave of intellectualism contributed significantly to the development of Sufism in *pesantren*. Key pesantren affiliated with Sufi orders were: *Pesantren* Darul-'Ulum in Rejoso, Jombang; *Pesantren* Sawapulo, *Pesantren* al-Fitrah both in Surabaya (Sujuti 2001b: 59); *Pesantren* Suralaya in Tasikmalaya, West Java (Zulkifli 2002: 71); *Pesantren* Al-Falah, Pegantongan in Bogor, *Pesantren* Mranggen in Central Java, *Pesantren* Ploso in Jombang (Dhofier 1978:141) and *Pesantren* Buntet in Cirebon (Muhaimin 1995). On the other hand, other *pesantren* that chose not to affiliate themselves with Sufi orders nevertheless focused on the study of Sufism: *Pesantren* Langitan in Tuban, East Java; *Pesantren* Lirboyo in Kediri, *Pesantren* Blok Agung in

9 Bruinessen speculates that in some *pesantren* works on *Waḥdat al-Wujūd* or the seven grades of being may have been given to select students.

Banyuwangi, *Pesantren* Kajen in Pati and many other *pesantren.* As a result of these different responses, the community of *pesantren* generally distinguish between Sufi and the followers of Sufi orders (*ahli tarekat*). They base this argument on the fact that al-Ghazali was a Sufi but he never belonged to a particular Sufi order (Zulkifli 2002: 30).

Regardless of their strategy, Sufism is an important subject in pesantren. The inclination towards Sufism shown by most pesantren is closely related to the fact that pesantren are institutions that aim not only to transfer Islamic knowledge but also to transfer values (akhlāq). Sufism provides a set of moral and religious values which are needed by pesantren to mould the character of their students and develop their spiritual life. As a result, aspects of tasawuf are often taught under the heading of akhlāq (Islamic ethics) and sometimes it is hard to distinguish the teachings on akhlāq from those of Sufism. Pesantren traditions require not only the understanding of the teachings of Sufism through the Sufi texts but also require the implementation of those teachings into practice under the guidance of a teacher. This understanding of Sufism in the pesantren tradition is relevant to the definition of tasawuf as put forward by some kyai such as Kyai Shohibulwafa Tajul Arifin, known as Abah Anom who stated that 'tasawuf cleanses the heart's passion and its heinous inclinations by teaching exercises to control passion, to develop a noble character and to follow the teachings of the Prophet Muhammad as persistently as possible.' Similarly, *Kyai* Shamsuri Badawi defined *tasawuf* as the purification of the soul from disgraceful characteristics (Zulkifli 2002:27).

Among the Sufi texts taught in *pesantren,* al-Ghazālī's works are most prominent. Bruinessen who carried out research on the Arabic classical books (I., *kitab kuning)* used in *pesantren* concludes that Sufism texts taught in *pesantren* are dominated by Ghazali's works such as *Ihyā' 'Ulūm al-Dīn, Minhāj al-'Ābidīn* and *Bidāyat al-Hidāyat* (excerpted from his *Ihyā'*) (Bruinessen 1994b). Some *pesantren* such as *Pesantren* Darunnajah, Bendo, Pare, Kediri; *Pesantren* Bustanul Ulum, Batoan, Mojo, Kediri and Fathul Ulum, Wagean, Kepung, Pare, Kediri specialize in the teaching of *Ihyā'*. In most *pesantren, Ihyā' 'Ulūm al-Dīn* holds high rank. It is seen as the final stage of an intellectual journey that involves the the study law and theology. This book is taught to those students who have finished their study in formal classes in *pesantren.*

The reason why Ghazali's works on Sufism have dominated the teaching of Sufism has to do with to the doctrine of *Ahlussunnah wa al-Jama'ah* prevalent in *pesantren,* particularly those affiliated with NU, that strongly emphasize the balance between Islamic Law and Sufism. These *pesantren* adhere to the teaching of Imam al-Junaid al-Baghdādī and al-Ghazālī. Al-Ghazālī is regarded as the Muslim scholar who succeeded in harmonizing and reconciling orthodox Islam (the exoteric dimension of Islam) with the mystical ideas of Sufism (the esoteric dimension of Islam). This can be seen clearly in his magnum opus *Ihyā' 'Ulūm al-Dīn, Minhāj al-'Ābidīn* and *Bidāyat al-Hidāyat.*

Chapter II: Innovation or Aberration: *Majlis Dhikr* in Contemporary Indonesian Islamic Discourse

Some Indonesianists have predicted that the practice of *tarekat* prevalent in the rural areas would disappear following the proliferation of Islamic modernist movements in Indonesia. This prediction, however, proved to be unfounded. Surprisingly, not only has there been an increase and expansion of Sufi orders in Indonesia, there is also currently a rise of other Islamic spiritual groups, such as *Majlis Dhikr* groups together with various Islamic spiritual courses. These groups have also undergone an increase in membership. Besides those categorized as peasants who have increased their interest in these groups, the urban middle class, together with many educated Muslims, have been attracted to join these groups.

The proliferation of these new Islamic spiritual groups has raised strong criticism and has prompted polemical debates regarding the validity of their ritual practices. This criticism can be conceived as a continuation of previous religious debates on the teaching of Sufism which were first put forward by the supporters of puritanical Islamic groups in the late nineteenth and the early twentieth centuries.[1] In a broader context, these debates constitute an integral part of the internal debates which has taken place in the Islamic tradition for several centuries. Therefore, in this chapter, I will examine the main factors have led to these polemical debates on the ritual practices of *Majlis Dhikr*. I intend to discuss the views of both the proponents and opponents of *Majlis Dhikr* in contemporary Indonesia.

---

1 As Bruinessen observed, Ahmad Khatib (1852-1915), a West Sumatra Muslim scholar who spent his life in Mecca, was an outspoken critic of Naqshabandiyah. He and other West Sumatran reformers vigorously charged the teachings of *tarekat* and its practices with misleading *bid'ah* and heresy. From 1906 to 1908 he wrote three polemical treatises about Naqshabandiyah which have been used as the main references for subsequent debates and criticism toward the group. Those three writings include '*Iẓhāru Zaghl al-Kādhibīn fī Tashabbuhihim bi al-Shādiqīn* ('Revealing the falseness of the deceivers who wear the mask of truth'), *Al-Āyāt al-Bayyināt li al-Munsifīn fī Izāla Khurafāt ba'dh al-Muta'assibin*' ('The true evidence of virtuous persons for eradicating the superstition of the fanatics'), and '*Al-Asāif al-Battār fī Maḥqi Kalimāti Ba'ḍl Ahl-al-Ightrār*' ('The cutting sword that fights the words of the arrogant) (Bruinessen 1994: 110-13).'

2.1. Source of Disputes: Understanding the Concept of *Bid'ah* (innovation within Islam) within Indonesian Islam

Polemical debates on theological matters have become a general phenomenon among Muslims around the world, including in Indonesia. For those who are familiar with the history of Islamic thought in Indonesia, polemical debates on religious matters have characterized Indonesian Islamic thought from the formative centuries of the coming of Islam to the present.[2] The root of these polemical debates is mainly on the question of orthodoxy and authenticity in Islam. This includes the question of whether particular religious practices can be categorized as a part of Islamic orthodoxy or whether they can be considered as new practices in Islam, which have no sanction either in the Qur'an or hadith, leading their performers to be labeled with misguidance.

The rise of Islamic purification and reformism movements in the early twentieth century in Egypt strongly influenced similar movements among Indonesian Muslims (Fealy et al. 2006:43-44). For instance, the ideas of reformism initiated by Al-Azhar's scholars such as Jamāl al-Dīn al-Afghānī (1839-97), Muḥammad 'Abduh (1849-1905) and his successor, RashīdRiḍā (1865-1935) attracted new generations of Indonesian Muslims to come to Cairo as an alternative to Mecca (Fox 2004:2-3). Inspired by these ideas, Muhammadiyah (1912) and Persatuan Islam (Islamic Union, PERSIS) (1923) were the first modern Indonesian Muslims organizations that championed the call for a return to pristine teachings of the Qur'an and the Prophet, the abandonment of various traditional practices deemed to be tainted with *bid'ah* (innovation), *tahayyul* (superstition) and *khurafat* (myth), and the call to conduct *ijtihad* (independent judgment based on recognized sources of Islam on legal or theological question) by reference to the Qur'an and hadith. Without doubt, these themes, in turn, have not only been directed toward 'nominal Muslims' who remained practising their traditional ritual practices but also toward 'traditionalist' Muslim groups and Sufi groups (*kelompok tarekat*) who were alleged by reformist groups to be practising innovation in their rituals (Fox 2004:4; Howell 2001:705).

The struggle to purify traditional, local custom and alleged *bid'ah* in belief and practice, threatened the rituals of Sufi groups which had been practised

2 The 16th and the 17th centuries were seen as periods when disputes in Sufism among Malay Muslim scholars occurred in the Islamic Malay world. The ideas of philosophical Sufism of Ibn 'Arabī introduced by Hamzah Fansuri (d. 1590) and his student Shams al-Dīn al-Sumatrānī (1575-1630)which had been prevalent in Aceh for a century were challenged by the orthodox notions of Nur al-Dīn al-Ranirī. The views of Hamzah and Sumatrāni were subject to accusations of heresy by al- Ranirī (Azra 1992:379).

by Indonesian Muslims for centuries. Throughout the twentieth century, the vehement rejection of Sufi practices among reformist groups represented by Muhammadiyah spread widely. In line with their idea of purification, Muslim reformist groups saw in Sufism a toleration of local idolatry, the excessive veneration of a spiritual master, and a hierarchical structure which led to deviation from devotion to the Oneness of God (I., *tauhid*). According to them, all of these practices had no sanction either in the Qur'an and hadith. These reformist groups regarded Sufism as 'the Islam that is not Islam' (I., *Islam yang bukan Islam*) (Howell 2001:706).

However, during the last decade of twentieth century, Muhammadiyah seems no longer to stress its puritanical *dakwah*. Instead, Muhammadiyah has given more emphasis to social and cultural *dakwah* than puritanical *dakwah*. As a result, Muhammadiyah no longer fiercely challenges alleged *bid'ah* rituals that they had previously accused the Nahdlatul 'Ulama community, nominal Muslims and followers of Sufi groups of carrying out. Instead, Muhammadiyah has begun to consider 'Sufism' in its *dakwah*. For example Munir Mulkhan, a Muhammadiyah activist, as quoted by Howell, argues that in its National Congress held in Aceh 4-5 July 1995, in Banda Aceh,[3] Muhammadiyah began to consider the importance of the inner aspect of Islamic teachings that used to be the subject of its criticism. Inspired by Hamka, to implement this notion, Muhammadiyah has revitalized and accommodated the spiritual teachings of Sufism without asking its members to join particular Sufi groups and without lessening its character as a modern and rational organization. The Congress, for instance, encouraged Muhammadiyah members to develop community ritual life by performing prayer and *dhikr* according to the Prophetic tradition (I., *sunnah*) and by promoting *tahajjud* prayer (night prayers), especially for strategic groups in the middle class, such as managers and executives in large cities. According to Mulkhan, this strategy was taken due to the fact that the Muhammadiyah's previous *dakwah* strategy had failed to convince nominal Muslims to set aside rituals seen by reformist groups as *bid'ah*, such as the Sufi practices of *dhikr* and *wird* (Howell 2001:712). Furthermore, Martin Van Bruinessen, in his foreword of Mahmud Sujuti's book, even observed that there are members of Muhammadiyah who have joined *tarekat*, even though they are not numerous (Sujuti 2001:xiv).

3 Along with the idea of accommodation of spiritual Islam, it was in this Congress that Muhammadiyah realized the importance of implementing the strategy of *Dakwah Kultural* (cultural Islamic preaching). This strategy was officially enforced in the subsequent Congress in 2000 in Jakarta and in the *SidangTanwir* Muhammadiyah in Denpasar January, the 24th- 25th 2002 . This strategy was taken by Muhammadiyah because the puritanical *dakwah* strategy that has been applied by Muhammadiyah preachers since its inception did not accommodate the Indonesian traditional culture and its positive values (Tanthowi 2003:131-32).

In contrast, PERSIS seems to have retained its trademark as the Islamic organization which has consistently stressed the importance of puritanical Islamic *dakwah*. PERSIS, which has been known as the most radical of Islamic organizations in its rejection of spirit beliefs, *adat* rituals and traditional Muslim practices with no sound basis in the Qur'an and hadith, propagated its views under the theme of purifying belief, worship, and ethics (I., *Islahul Akidah, Ibadah,* and *Akhlak*). Moreover, as argued by Shiddiq Amien, the chairman of PERSIS, currently, the biggest challenge of its *dakwah* project is concerned with the spread of superstition (*tahayyul*), illicit innovation within Islam (I., *bid'ah*) and myths (*khurafat*), often shortened to TBC (which stands for 'tuberculosis') but also concerned with SIPILIS (Indonesian term for 'syphilis') which stands for secularism (I., *sekularisme*), pluralism (I., *pluralisme*) and liberalism (I., *liberalisme*). The SIPILIS is regarded by PERSIS as an ideology that has degraded the truth of Islam as a divine religion since PERSIS claims that its proponents regard all religions as equal (Amien 2005).

Along with the current worldwide growth of the Salafi movement in the latter part of twentieth century, puritanical themes of *dakwah* have regained currency in Islamic activism in Indonesia. Like Muhammadiyah and PERSIS, as Noorhaidi has argued, the main concern of Indonesian Salafi is to purify *tauḥīd*(the doctrine of the unity of God), by calling for a return to strict religious practices and by putting emphasis on individual integrity. With this concern, the Indonesian Salafi movement stresses the need to call Indonesian Muslims to return the pristine Qur'anic and hadith teachings and to avoid any practices deemed to be tainted with *bid'ah,* superstition, and myths (Noorhaidi 2005:24-25). With these campaigns, the Indonesian Salafi movement not only rejects Sufi devotional practices but also other ritual practices such as those of the *Majlis Dhikr.*

There is no doubt that the spread of the world wide Salafi movement has been inspired ideologically by the most puritanical Islamic sect, Wahabbism, developed by Muḥammad Ibn 'Abd al-Wahhāb (1703-1792). The aim of the Wahabi movement has been to fight the superstitions and Sufi devotional practices prevalent in Arab society, which are considered as misleading *bid'ah,* as well as to attack un-Islamic behaviour by Muslims. Although Wahabbism was distinguished from Salafism in older academic discourse, contemporary Salafism can be seen as reorganised Wahabbism since its opponents invariably refer to the thoughts formulated by Aḥmad Ibn Taymiyyah, Ibn Qayyim al-Jauzī (1292-1350) and Muḥammad Ibn 'Abd al-Wahhāb and rely on contemporary Wahabbist '*ulamā*'such as 'Abd al-'Aziz 'Abd Allah bin Baz (d.1999) and Muḥammad Nāṣir al-Dīn al-Albani (Fadl 2005:74; Noorhaidi 2005:24-25). According to Fadl the word Salafi, however, did not become associated with the

Wahabbism creed until the 1970s. The word Salaf initially means predecessors, but in this context, Salaf usually refers to the period of the Prophet, his Companions, and their successors. The word Salafi means people who follow the Salaf. This word can also connote authenticity and legitimacy. Therefore, any religious movement that claims authenticity in Islam may easily exploit the term for its purposes (Fadl 2005:75).

The Indonesian Council for Islamic Preaching (*Dewan Dakwah Islamiah Indonesia*, DDII) is one of the Islamic organizations in Indonesia whose characteristic is Salafi. The DDII, which was established in 1967 by ex-Masyumi party[4] (*Partai Majlis Syuro Muslim Indonesia*) members, has a strong connection not only with the Saudi Arabian government but also with the Islamic World League (*Rābiṭa al'Ālam al-Islāmiy*), an organization which is regularly funded by the Saudi Kingdom and often seen as part of a campaign to spread the strict ideology of Wahhabism across the world (Noorhaidi 2005:30-32). With this strong connection, it is not surprising that DDII is mainly concerned with the propagation of Islam and the purification of Islamic belief, attacking practices deemed as *bid'ah*. Initially, this organization attacked Indonesian Shi'ite groups but in recent years it has regularly criticized the idea of Islamic modernism, liberalism, and neo-modernism (Jaiz 2004:214-35).

Hartono Ahmad Jaiz is one of the most outspoken proponents of DDII who actively calls for the implementation of pristine Islamic teachings as sanctioned by the Qur'an and hadith. He is also a prolific writer on several issues including political Islam. Most of his works, however, are polemical, and to some extent apologetic. He, for example, wrote a book which specifically attacks Sufi practices and rituals which have been widely conducted by Indonesian *tarekat* groups. According to Hartono, these practices and rituals are tantamount to the practices conducted by polytheists (I., *orang musyrik*) because none of them was practised by the Prophet and His Companions. In his view, reciting vocal *dhikr*, and silent *dhikr*, a ritual which has become the main ritual within *tarekat* groups is deemed as a novelty which can be categorized as illicit innovation (I., *bid'ahyang sesat*) because all such practices have no sanction in the Qur'an and hadith. He has lamented that despite these polytheistic rituals, Muslims scholars who have deep understanding of Islamic knowledge keep practising these rituals. He specifically considers that all technical terms as used in Sufi teachings such as *sharī'at, ḥaqīqat,* and *ma'rifat* have no precedent either in the Qur'an and hadith. Not only that, the method used in the practices of *tarekat*

4 The Masyumi party was the biggest Islamic party in Indonesia. In 1960, Soekarno banned the party because some of its activists were involved in the PRRI (regional rebellion) against him.

including *zuhud* (asceticism), *wasīlat* (reliance on an intermediary), *rabīṭa* (one's heart's connection with a Sufi master), and *'uzla* (withdrawing from society) are not found in the Islamic teachings (Jaiz 1999:132).

Meanwhile, along with the proliferation of *Majlis Dhikr* groups in urban areas, other proponents of the contemporary Indonesian Salafi thinking strongly criticize the reciting of vocal *dhikr* in unison (I., *zikir berjamaah*) practised by those groups. Like previous criticism addressed to Sufi practices, the objection of the Salafi toward the reciting of vocal *dhikr* in unison is partly related to the fact that this kind of ritual is claimed never to have been practised by the Prophet and the first generation of Muslims (A., *salaf al-ṣāliḥīn*). Since this ritual was supposedly never been conducted by the Prophet, it can be considered as *bid'ah* (innovation). Based on certain hadith, the Salafi believe that since every innovation is misguidance, it cannot be practised. Likewise, since the reciting of *dhikr* in unison is considered as *bid'ah,* it cannot be practised as part of worship (I., *ritual ibadah*).

The roots of the Indonesian polemical debates on religious matters particularly concerning the validity of reciting vocal *dhikr* in unison can be traced back to different views and understanding of the concept of *bid'ah* in Islam. These debates on the definition of *bid'ah* among Indonesian Muslims are inseparable from the same debates in the history of Islamic theology involving Muslim theologians several centuries ago. Differences in defining the concept of *bid'ah,* in turn, lead to the differences in defining whether a ritual practice can be justified in the light of the Qur'anic and Prophetic teachings or whether it is considered to be un-Islamic ritual and not supported by Islamic law; they also relate to whether or not practices, which were never carried out by the Prophet during his life, are able to be practised by His followers.

The differences in understanding the term *bid'ah* can be attributed to the Prophetic hadith which reportedly stated that every innovation is misguidance and all misguidance leads into hellfire. Citing the book *Fatawa Azhariyah* (1997) Muhammad Niam has argued that Muslims can be divided into two broad groups as far as their approaches in defining the concept of *bid'ah.* The first group approaches the term *bid'ah* from an etymological perspective and the second approaches it from a terminological perspective (Ni'am 2007).

The first group defines *bid'ah* as innovation or creation of something which has no precedent. Based on this definition, every innovation or creation in religious matters that has no precedent during the lifetime of the Prophet can be regarded as *bid'ah,* regardless of whether it is good or bad. This definition is justified by the fact that the derivatives of root *b-d-'* are often used to signify either good or bad things. Therefore, with this definition, Imam Shāfi'ī, the founder of Shāfi'ite school of Islamic law, argued that there are two kinds of innovation in religious matters. The first one is the innovation which contradicts the teaching of the Qur'an, the example of the Prophet, His Companions and Successors, or the consensus of Muslims scholars; this is illicit and objectionable *bid'ah*. The second one is the innovation in religious matters which is not evil in itself and does not contradict those authorities and may be good or praiseworthy (Fierro 1992:205-06). 'Iz al-Dīn Ibn 'Abd al-Salām (d.660/1262), a prominent scholar of Shafi'ite school, came to distinguish *bid'ah* according to five legal norms depending on whether or not it violated a revealed text, a judiciary consensus or a Companion's report (A., *athar*) (Hallaq 2001:536-537). These categories include 1) mandatory innovation (A., *bid'ah wājiba*), 2) prohibited innovation (A.,*bid'ah muḥarrama*), 3) recommended innovation (A., *bid'ah mandūba*), 4) reprehensible innovation (A.,*bid'ah makrūha*), and 5) permissible innovation (A., *bid'ah mubāḥa*) (Rispler 1991:324)

In contrast, the second group defines *bid'ah* as all newly invented activities in religious matters which are believed to be part of religion but in fact not part of religion. Some of the proponents of this group argue that *bid'ah* can be applied only in the matters of worship. Therefore, following this definition, they argue that every innovation in matters of worship can be labeled as misguidance and therefore cannot be categorized as recommended or permissible innovation as argued by the first group. In other words, this group implements the term *bid'ah* as indicated by the Prophetic hadith cited in regard to any kind of innovation; all such innovation is misguidance. This group bases its argument on the prominent view of Mālik Ibn Anas (710-795), the founder of Malikite school of Islamic law, who stated that Muslims who innovate something in Islam while deeming it to be a good innovation thus allege that Muhammad (peace and blessings be upon him) has concealed part of God's message.

The Indonesian Salafi group follows this second group in defining their concept of *bid'ah*. Therefore, for this group, every new practice in religious matters which is not sanctioned by the Qur'an, hadith and juridical consensus among Muslim scholars can be categorized as illicit innovation. Following Ibn Taymiyyah's view, they argue that every good innovation in worship which does not have clear evidence (A., *adillat*) is unlawful (Jahar 1999:46). Their definition of *bid'ah* is based on the belief that Islam is a perfect religion. For them, the perfection of Islam as religion can be conceived from the fact that Islam regulates not only major matters but also small matters such as the ethics of entering a toilet or a house. Because of this perfection, they believe that Islam has already explained everything in all matters of worship including its ways, forms and conditions (Amsaka 2003:36). In order to prove the perfection of Islam, like previous Muslim reformist groups, the Indonesian Salafi cite the Qur'anic verse (5:3), 'This day I have perfected your religion for you, completed My favor upon you, and have chosen for you Islam as your religion.' For the Salafi, this verse is evidence of the perfection of Islam. Therefore, based on this verse, Islam does not need any accretions in the matters of worship because it has been completely prescribed in the Qur'an and hadith and at the same time there is no need for reduction in the matters of worship. Further, the Salafi argue that those who add new ritual practices in the matters of worship are like those who do not only believe that God has completed Islam as a religion but also believed that the Prophet has not completely delivered the message of God to his people (Amsaka 2003:32).

According to the Salafi, in matters of worship people are not able to create new rituals of worship except ones that have been prescribed by God and His Prophet. The types, forms and ways of worship cannot be derived by human reasoning, even though they are being used to obtain closeness to God, such as reciting vocal *dhikr* in unison (I., *zikir dengan suara dan berjamaah*) and other ritual practices as in Sufi groups. These types, forms and ways of worship have to be conducted in accordance with the revelation from God. In other words, one should do precisely what the Prophet did based on revelation. In this regard, the Indonesian Salafi hold the view that in the matters of worship everything is prohibited except that which is commanded (Amsaka 2003:53). In contrast, in worldly matters, everything is permitted except that which is prohibited. Therefore, in line with their definition of the concept of *bid'ah*, the Salafi believe that innovation in matters of worship is misguidance and illicit and its innovators (A., *mubdi'*) belong in hellfire (Jaiz 1999:18).

For the Indonesian Salafi, conducting any ritual worship to obtain closeness to God has to be based on a precise order as prescribed by the Qur'an and hadith. In their view, if such ritual practice as reciting vocal *dhikr* in unison can be used to approach God, then God would have ordered the Prophet to conduct that ritual because there was no obstacle during his lifetime to conduct it. As a result, conducting some practices which were never practised by the Prophet, even though for the purpose of obtaining closeness to God, can be seen as changing and thus violating the teaching of God (Shiddieqy 1983:41).

The view of the Salafi group on the matter of worship becomes, however, problematic when it is used to explain the case of *zakat* from personal income (I., *zakat profesi,* wealth tax), which is currently widely practised among Muslims worldwide. The practice of *zakat* from personal income (I., *zakat profesi*) is categorized as a matter of worship (I., *ibadah*) but was never practised as such during the lifetime of the Prophet and His Companions. Since there can be no addition or reduction in the matter of *ibadah, zakat profesi* can be categorized as *bid'ah* according to the definition held by the Salafi. Yet despite its innovation, almost all Muslims agree to practise *zakat profesi.* No one will argue that those who practise *zakat profesi* should be cast into hellfire because they have conducted *bid'ah* in worship.

As a consequence of their definition of *bid'ah,* the Indonesian Salafi strongly stress that those who practise innovation will be charged with fierce punishment in the hereafter as stated by the Prophet through his many hadith. For example, one hadith states that the perpetrators of innovation will not obtain any reward from their own good virtues such as their prayers, fasting, pilgrimage and their charity (Shiddieqy 1983:24-28).

In contrast to Salafi group, the proponents of *Majlis Dhikr* define *bid'ah* as religious ritual which was not known during the Prophet's lifetime. Moreover, for them, *bid'ah* can also be defined as accretion to or reduction of religious matters that has occurred after the period of the Prophet with no permission from God and His Prophet (A., *shāri'*). In other words, every single practice that has no sanction explicitly and implicitly during the period of the Prophet can be considered as *bid'ah* (Badruzzaman 2003:30-31; Satori 2003:107). With this definition of *bid'ah,* the proponents of *Majlis Dhikr* believe that every Muslim who conducts the practices of *bid'ah* will be punished with painful torment in the hereafter as described by several hadith. However, in their view, not all *bid'ah* will be accorded this punishment and only those practices categorized as illicit (A., *bid'ah sayyia, ḍalāla*) will be charged of the punishment. In contrast, those who conduct practices categorized as praiseworthy innovation will not be charged with severe punishment. Thus according to Badruzzaman, the *Sharī'at*board member of *Majelis Zikir al-Dhikra,* if Muslims perform the praiseworthy innovation sincerely, they will gain good rewards. (Badruzzaman 2003:54). In other words, the proponent of *Majlis Dhikr* argue that in regard to the new practices, one should not judge them as negative *bid'ah* without carefully looking at whether or not these new practices contradict Islamic Law (*Sharī'at*). If these new practices contradict the Sunnah of the Prophet, this is an innovation which is an error (A., *bid'ah ḍalāla*), while if these novelties are not evil in itself and do not contradict the authority of Islam, this is unobjectionable novelty (A., *fahādhihī bid'ah ghairu maẓmūma*) (Badruzzaman 2003:38).

The category of *bid'ah* used by the proponents of *Majlis Dhikr* follows the ideas proposed by the great legal scholars, Imām Shāfi'ī (d.204/819), Abū Zakaria Yaḥyā ibn Sharaf al-Nawāwī (d.676/1277), Abd al-Haqq al-Dahlawī. In the view of Badruzzaman, one of proponents of *Majlis Dhikr,* the categorization of *bid'ah* proposed by Imam. Shāfi'ī stems from his deep understanding of one of the authoritative hadith. The hadith attributed to Prophet's Companion, 'Umar ibn al-Khaṭṭāb, reported that when he asked Muslims to perform prayers in unison during the last nights of *Ramaḍān* (A., *qiyām al-layālī Ramaḍān*) something that had never been done by the Prophet during his lifetime. 'Umar noted that this practice as favourable *bid'ah* (A., *ni'mat al-bid'a hādhihi*). According to the proponents of *Majlis Dhikr*, it can be inferred from this statement that 'Umar admitted that some *bid'ah* are favourable and some are not. Based on 'Umar's saying, Imām Shāfi'ī held the opinion that new practices can be categorized as praiseworthy (A., *bid'ah maḥmuda*) (Badruzzaman 2003: 39-40).

In regard to misleading *bid'ah,* Imām Shāfi'ī was reliant on the Prophetic hadith which reported that whoever performs misleading *bid'ah* not preferred by God and His Prophet, will incur sin. Therefore, Badruzzaman argued that based on 'Umar's saying, it can be inferred that not all *bid'ah* can be categorized as misleading as argued by the Salafi. In his view, if all *bid'ah* are considered as misleading, the Prophet would not have specifically mentioned only those who practised misleading *bid'ah* as sinful. As argued by Badruzzaman, it can plausibly be inferred that along with misleading *bid'ah,* there must be non-misleading *bid'ah* (Badruzzaman 2003: 39-40).

In addition to Imām Shāfi'ī, al-Ghazālī (d.1111) argued that not all *bid'ah* is prohibited. The *bid'ah* which is prohibited is only that which clearly contradicts the hadith and rejects the prescriptions of Islamic law. Something categorized as *bid'ah* can become obligatory under particular conditions providing that there is a condition which causes the change (Hasan 2006:236).

In addition, the proponents of *Majlis Dhikr* also refer to the view of 'Iz al-Dīn ibn 'Abd al-Salām (d.660/1262) who classified *bid'ah* according to a legal classification on a scale from one to five: 1) mandatory innovation (A., *bid'ah wājibat*), 2) prohibited innovation (A., *bid'ah muḥarramat*), 3) recommended innovation (A., *bid'ah mandūbat*), 4) reprehensible innovation (A.,*bid'ah makrūhat*), and 5) permissible innovation (A., *bid'ah mubāḥa*). In other words, new practices should be weighed in the light of these five principles. In this case, if practices can be considered as recommended innovation, they can be practised by Muslims and cannot be considered as *bid'ah* in its negative sense. In contrast, if these new practices are categorised as prohibited innovation, Muslim are prohibited to practise them and as result, this innovation can be considered as negative. Therefore, for the proponents of *Majlis Dhikr*, based on these categories, the practice of reciting vocal *dhikr* in unison cannot be categorized as *bid'ah* in its negative sense because it is sanctioned by the

Qur'an and hadith (Badruzzaman 2003:42-43). This ritual practice might fall to the categorization of recommended innovation or even mandatory innovation as proposed by 'Iz al-Dīn ibn 'Abd al-Salām.

For the proponents of *Majlis Dhikr*, if every novelty is regarded as *bid'ah*, then everything that has resulted from the well-established process of legal decisions through the independent interpreting of legal sources (I., *ijtihad*, A., *ijtihād*) should be regarded as *bid'ah* because it is not clearly mentioned in the Qur'an and hadith. If this is the case, they question the significance of *ijtihad* which was strongly urged by the Prophet upon his Companions in the situation where there is no clear text to be found. If the result of *ijtihad* is regarded as *bid'ah*, it would contradict the Prophetic tradition which reported that if a judge passes judgment and makes use of *ijtihad*, and he is right, then he will have two rewards, whereas if he makes a mistake, there will be only one reward. In this regard, the proponents of *Majlis Dhikr* give an example of the practice of almsgiving (I., *zakat*). In this matter, as a result of their interpretation (*ijtihad*), Muslim scholars have required every Muslim to pay their *zakat* on rice, banknotes (I., *uang kertas*), and cows (cattle), even though paying *zakat* on these things was not known during the lifetime of the Prophet. Nevertheless, this new practice has been accepted by Muslim scholars without deeming it as *bid'ah* (Badruzzaman 2003:51-52).

The argument put forward by the proponents of *Majlis Dhikr* on the matter of *bid'ah* is similar to that of *Kyai* Hashim Ash'ari, the founder of Nahdlatul Ulama'. Quoting the view of Syaikh Zaruq, *Kyai* Hashim Ash'ari said that when authoritative Muslim scholars put forward their views, these views cannot be considered as *bid'ah* because they deduce law by conducting *ijtihad* without transcending the limit (Asy'ari 2005:168). Therefore, according to the proponents of *Majlis Dhikr*, all legal matters that come under the category of *ijtihad* cannot be categorized as *bid'ah*. If they should be considered as *bid'ah*, they have to be conceived of as praiseworthy *bid'ah*.

2.2. Theological Debates on *Dhikr* Ritual

The strong criticism put forward by Indonesian Salafi has mainly been addressed to the reciting of vocal *dhikr* ritual in unison (I., *berjamaah*) conducted by *Majlis Dhikr* groups in urban areas, especially in Jakarta. Currently, the growth of these groups is apparent in the Indonesian capital city. Among these groups, one of the best known are the *Majlis Dhikr* group *Al-Zikrah* led by Arifin Ilham, the *Dhikr* healing group (I., *Majlis Dhikr Penyembuhan*) established by Ustadz Haryono, and *Manajemen Qalbu* guided by the popular Indonesian preacher, Abdullah Gymnastiar, known as AA Gym (Watson 2005:776).

The prominence of these *Majlis Dhikr* groups is evident in the current landscape of Indonesian Islam due to the intensive publicity of Indonesian electronic and printed media which regularly report on their activities. During my research, most Indonesian TV stations had at least one program on their schedule for Islam that dealt with the activities of these groups. In addition, books, cassettes and CDs produced by these groups are readily available in both large and small bookshops throughout Indonesian cities. Several bookshops, like Gramedia and Gunung Agung, set up special display tables for AA Gym's works.

AA Gym's and Arifin Ilham's activities have specifically attracted criticism from the Salafi. To criticize the *dakwah* strategy of AA Gym and Arifin Ilham's *dhikr* groups, Indonesian Salafi have written books which have been widely circulated in many Indonesian cities. For instance, Abdurrahman Al-Mukaffi wrote a book entitled *Rapot Merah AA Gym, MQ (Manajemen Qalbu) di Penjara Tasawuf* (A Red Report on AA Gym, MQ [The Management of the Heart] in the Prison of Sufism) which has become a bestseller and has been reprinted six times. This book is mainly intended to criticize the *dakwah* themes and spiritual experiences presented by AA Gym which the author considers as part of the misleading *bid'ah* that has contaminated the purity of Muslims' belief. The book, whose foreword was written by Hartono Ahmad Jaiz, an outspoken proponent of DDII was published by Darul Falah, one of publishing houses which specializes on publishing Salafi books.

In regard to the Arifin Ilham's *Majlis Dhikr* group, Abu Amsaka, one of the outspoken proponents of Indonesian Salafi group wrote a book entitled *Koreksi Dzikir Jama'ah M. Arifin Ilham* (Correction of M. Arifin Ilham's *Dzikir* in Unison). In fact, this book is aimed at responding to two books, the one entitled, '*Hikmah Dzikir Berjamaah* (The Benefit of Reciting *Dzikir* in Unison) written by M. Arifin Ilham and Debby M. Nasution, and the other, *Hakikat Dzikr, Jalan Taat Menuju Allah, Rahasia dan Kiat-kiat Mensucikan Jiwa dalam Upaya Meraih Hidup Bermakna* (The Essence of *Dhikr*, The Way of Obedience Toward Allah, Secrets and Methods to Purify the Soul in an Effort to Achieve a Meaningful Life) written by M.Arifin Ilham. Like Mukaffi's book, Amsaka's book is also published by Darul Falah. Like al-Mukaffi, Abu Amsaka rejects all ritual practised by Arifin Ilham and his group. Without conducting research on the activities of the group, the author personally accuses Arifin Ilham of using his group as a means to run his business and to achieve material interests

(Amsaka 2003:51-52). Abu Amsaka is convinced that the ritual of *Majlis Dhikr* conducted by Arifin Ilham and his group has no strong legal basis so that it can be considered *bid'ah* that should not be practised by good Muslims.

Several aspects of the rituals of *Majlis Dhikr* have fed a polemical debate involving the proponents of these groups and Indonesian Salafi. These aspects include the reciting of vocal *dhikr* (I., *zikir dengan suara*), the recitation of *dhikr* in unison (I., *zikir dengan berjamaah*) and the recitation of *dhikr* by crying (I., *zikir dengan menangis*). Here I present the responses of the proponents of *dhikr* group (A., *Jamaah Dhikr*) who have been accused by the Salafi of performing *bid'ah.*

The main objection of the Indonesian Salafi group toward *dhikr* ritual performed by Arifin Ilham and his group is related to the fact that the ritual of his *dhikr* is not only recited vocally (A., *jahr*) but it is also recited in unison (I., *berjamaah*). Abu Amsaka finds that neither the Qur'anic teachings nor the Prophetic tradition supports such practices. Therefore, in the interpretation of Abu Amsaka, such practices constitute a flagrant violation of divine law as prescribed in the two primary sources of law, the Qur'anic revelation and hadith (Amsaka 2003:24). Following his definition of *bid'ah,* Amsaka argues that such practices are considered as being misguided (I., *sesat*) and misleading (I., *menyesatkan*). Abu Amsaka doubts whether Arifin Ilham and his group have sincerity in performing such vocal *dhikr* ritual. He explains this as follows:

> ...that event exudes a smell of bid'ah, even though it has been attended by the highest status of religious teachers (I., *ustadz yang paling ustadz*) or the highest status Muslim scholars (I., *ulama yang paling ulama*); that event is full of bad odour for the purity of Islamic practices and the effort of following the Qur'an and Sunnah, even though the participants at the event have used the most fragrant and expensive perfumes; that event is far from deep sincerity with God, even though its participants' clothes are all white (Amsaka 2003:201-02).

In criticising Arifin Ilham, Abu Amsaka argues that Arifin Ilham and his colleagues made use of general Qur'anic verses on *dhikr* to legitimize their activities. Abu Amsaka maintains that those general verses need to be interpreted specifically in the light of other Qur'anic verses on the ethics of praying and *dhikr.* For Abu Amsaka, general verses should be interpreted by using specific verses; he believes that this is the best method to understand the meaning of the Qur'an. Without this interpretation, people cannot understand the meaning of the Qur'an properly. By this argument he considers what Arifin Ilham practises with his *dhikr* group is far from the true understanding and meaning of Qur'anic verses. To criticize Arifin Ilham's *dhikr* ritual, Abu Amsaka cites several verses of the Qur'an which according to him can be used to cast doubt on the ritual conducted by Arifin Ilham. For instance, Abu Amsaka cites the specific verses on the ethics of prayer and *dhikr* as follows,

> Call on your Lord with humility and in private: for God loveth not those who trespass beyond bounds. (7:55).

> And bethink thyself of thy Sustainer humbly and with awe, and without raising thy voice, at morn and at evening; and do not allow thyself to be heedless (7:205).

Abu Amsaka laments the fact that Arifin Ilham does not cite these verses in his book. Abu Amsaka accuses Arifin Ilham of unfairly dealing with the book of God (A., *kitabullah*) by hiding information about these verses intentionally. Those verses, Abu Amsaka argues, clearly mention that *dhikr* should not be performed loudly and in unison to be heard by other people or broadcast widely by TV stations (Amsaka 2003:80-83).

In explaining those verses, Abu Amsaka cites several authoritative exegetes (A., *mufassir*) such as Ibn Kathīr (1301-1373) in his *Tafsīr al-Qur'ān al-'Aẓīm* (The Noble Qur'an), al-Qurṭūbī (d.1273) in his *Al-Jāmi' Li-Aḥkām al-Qur'ān* (The Compendium of Legal Rulings of the Qur'an) and Jalāl al- Dīn al-Maḥallī (d.864/1459) and Jalāl al- Dīn al-Suyūṭī (849/1445-911/1505) in their book *Tafsīr al-Jalālain*(Tafsir of the Twin Jalals). Amsaka points out that, all of the exegetes (A., *mufassirun*) have interpreted the Qur'anic verses (7:55) to mean that praying (I., *do'a*) should be recited in the secrecy of one heart. Likewise, in order to interpret a particular verse (7:205), Abu Amsaka quotes the interpretation of the authors of *Tafsīr al-Jalālain*who argue that the meaning of the verse is that Muslims should remember God within their hearts secretly, humbly submissively and fearfully. Abu Amsaka also quotes Ibn 'Abbās who says that the meaning of the verse is that a person should recite *dhikr* which can only be heard by the reciter. Based on this interpretation, Abu Amsaka concludes that the methods and the ethics of reciting prayer (*do'a*) and *dhikr* should be conducted fearfully, humbly, and without reciting loudly (Amsaka 2003:96).

Moreover, Abu Amsaka criticizes Arifin Ilham who relies heavily on hadith rather than relying on the Qur'an to support his argument on the permissibility of performing vocal *dhikr* ritual in unison. In his book, Arifin Ilham uses the hadith attributed to one of the Prophet's Companions, Ibn 'Abbās, to support his vocal *dhikr* ritual (I., *dengan bersuara*). The hadith is as follows:

> 'Ibn 'Abbās said that in the time of the Prophet people recited vocal *dhikr* after prayers. He also said, 'I knew that they have finished prayers because I heard their voice of *dhikr* (narrated by Bukhari and Muslim).

Amsaka asks Arifin Ilham why he uses a hadith narrated by Ibn 'Abbās and ignores those verses which clearly mention the recitation of prayer and *dhikr* without raising one's voice. Without a doubt, Amsaka believes that the Qur'an which was revealed by God provides a stronger basis for ritual than a hadith which was narrated by a human. Therefore, in this matter, instead of using the hadith, he argues that the Qur'an should be used as the first authority and as a valid basis for any ritual (I., *ibadah*) before any hadith. Again, Amsaka explicitly accuses Arifin Ilham of involving personal interest to popularize his group by intentionally concealing those verses which are contradictory to his *dhikr* ritual practice (Amsaka 2003:99).

In regard to the hadith attributed to the Prophet's Companion, Ibn 'Abbās, used by Arifin Ilham as the basis of his *dhikr* ritual, Abu Amsaka makes a special comment. Quoting Imam Shāfi'ī, the text of the hadith should not be interpreted as if the Prophet regularly recited vocal *dhikr* after the five daily prayers. Instead, the hadith should be understood to indicate that the Prophet recited vocal *dhikr* for the purpose of teaching *dhikr* to his Companions and that he did not practice it as a habit. Therefore, Amsaka concludes that this hadith cannot be regarded as a theological argument for practising *dhikr* vocally and in unison (Amsaka 2003:105-106).

As a final argument that reciting vocal *dhikr* was not sanctioned and practised by the Prophet, Amsaka quotes the Prophetic hadith saying that the Prophet asked his Companions to lower their voice because they did not pray to a deaf man and someone invisible but to The Knower of All, The Hearer of All, and The Closest of All.

In addition to the fact that no Qur'anic verses or hadith sanction the reciting vocal *dhikr* in unison, Abu Amsaka believes that such vocal *dhikr* ritual practice is also susceptible to being a form of showing off (A., *riyā'*) which is strongly condemned by God. It will be even more susceptible if the ritual practice is broadcast by national television involving advertising and capital investment. In this regard, according to Abu Amsaka what Arifin Ilham performs with his group can be seen as a part of the commercialization of a product which needs to be advertised openly through the media based on consumer demand. This practice, as Abu Amsaka argues, is far from a pure and comprehensive Islamic practice (I., *Islam kaffah*) and it is not free from economical interests. Abu Amsaka regrets this strategy of *dakwah*(Amsaka 2003:167). In line with this,

Abu Amsaka argues that instead of urging Muslims to observe virtues openly, Islam gives emphasis to the merit of concealing virtues from others' sight. For Amsaka, concealing one's virtues is a necessary condition to allow Muslims to become sincere (I., *ikhlas*) (Amsaka 2003:169).

Apart from theological criticism of the *dhikr* ritual conducted by Arifin Ilham, Abu Amsaka also criticizes the cover of Arifin's book. Arifin Ilham has put his picture on the cover of his several books. Amsaka asks why Arifin Ilham does this. Amsaka was convinced that the reason is to expose Arifin's name, which is becoming famous, in order to obtain personal and business advantage. Abu Amsaka (2003:160) writes as follows:

> This is understandable, particularly from a business consideration, what is the best way to increase the product so that it can be easily accepted by consumers, purchased and spread, and then wait a return that can be put in the pocket. This is what we call the world of business, that is, the world of gaining advantage.[5]

In addition, from the perspective of pure Islamic theology, putting a picture on the front cover of a book can lead to the establishment of a cult surrounding Arifin Ilham which will eventually jeopardize the purity of the Islamic faith. Furthermore, Abu Amsaka worries that this picture will be treated just as the statue of Lata, one of the gods worshipped by unbelievers during the first period of the Islam in Mecca. Lata was a virtuous and generous person at that time. After he died, people put his statue next to the Ka'bah and they worshipped it (Amsaka 2003:162). Abu Amsaka urged that Arifin Ilham's picture should not be put on his books' covers, if he is really sincere in his *dakwah.* Amsaka adds that removing the picture from the cover would protect Arifin Ilham from the worst thing that can happen such as a personality cult, self admiration (A., '*ujb*) and showing off (A., *riyā'*). In this regard, Amsaka makes use of the concept of *sadd dhar'i,* that is, preventing evil before it materialises (Amsaka 2003:165).

Amsaka argues that putting a picture on the front cover of a book strongly contradicts the teachings of the Prophet. To support his argument, Amsaka cites a hadith reported by Bukhari and Muslim that the angels of God will not enter a house which has a painting or picture in it. Amsaka was convinced that this prohibition encompasses all kinds of representations either in the form of a statue, a painting, or a picture (Amsaka 2003:164).

---

5 Hal ini dapat dimaklumi, terutama dari pertimbangan market dan bisnis, bagaimana kiat yang jitu untuk mendongkrak produk agar dapat mudah diterima konsumen, menyebar luas, dibeli lalu tinggal menunggu berapa keuntungan yang masuk kantong. Inilah dunia bisnis, dunia untuk mencari keuntungan.

Another strong Salafi criticism of Arifin Ilham's *dhikr* ritual has to do with the weeping that occurs during the *dhikr* ritual. As far as this weeping is concerned, Abu Amsaka divides weeping into two categories. The first category is the weeping sanctioned by God which leads to an increase in the fear of God and the gentleness of heart, but not weeping which is intended for showing off to please others. The second category is pretentious weeping that is performed for the sake of gaining interest from other people (Amsaka 2003:187). In this regard, Abu Amsaka does not directly accuse Arifin Ilham and his group of performing pretentious crying. However, before judging the crying performed by Arifin Ilham and his group, Abu Amsaka gives the example of his friend who stopped weeping when he gave Friday sermons because he fear showing off to others. By comparison, Abu Amsaka adds, weeping shown during Arifin Ilham's *dhikr* ritual is intentionally conducted from the beginning of the ritual until the ritual concludes without any attempt made to stop it (Amsaka 2003:209). From the comparison Abu Amsaka makes, it can be inferred that he categorizes weeping in the *dhikr* ritual as pretentious crying rather than crying to increase a sense of the fear of God.

Two books have been written in response to criticisms made by Abu Amsaka. The first book, entitled 'Koreksi Zikir Keblinger: Kearifan Menilai Zikir *Berjamaah Dan Bisnis M. Arifin Ilham,* was written by Saefulloh M Satori and second book, entitled *'Zikir Berjamaah: Sunnah atau Bid'ah',* was written by Ahmad Dimyathi Badruzzaman. Satori admits that, instead of fulfilling Arifin Ilham's order, the aim of his writing is solely to clarify objectively the accusation of *bid'ah* made by the Salafi group toward *dhikr* ritual conducted by Arifin Ilham. Except for interviewing Arifin Ilham, the author had no previous contact with him. Therefore, Satori argues that his writing is far from subjective (Satori 2003:2-6). In contrast, Badruzzaman, one of the members of *Majlis Dhikr al-Dhikra*'s Supreme Islamic Council (I., *Dewan Syuriah*), wrote his book after he met Arifin Ilham who told him that there was a person who considered his *dhikr* ritual as illicit *bid'ah* which opens its participants to the threat of hell. With support from Arifin Ilham, Badruzzaman wrote the book to inform people about the status of *dhikr* ritual according to Islamic law; whether it should be categorized as illicit novelty (A., *bid'a ḍalāla*) or whether instead it can be considered relevant to the Prophetic tradition (A., *sunnat nabawiyyat*) (Badruzzaman 2003:vi). Therefore, the book was intended to reassure Indonesian Muslims that there is no fundamental problem with the ritual of reciting *dhikr* vocally and in unison.

Unlike Abu Amsaka who sharply criticizes Arifin Ilham, Badruzzaman calmly cites several arguments taken from the Qur'an, hadith, and from the views of Muslim scholars to support his belief in the permissibility of reciting *dhikr* vocally and in unison. He does so without personally criticizing Abu Amsaka. In relation to reciting *dhikr* in unison, Badruzzaman offers different views from the ones presented by Amsaka. Badruzzaman, a proponent of *Majlis Dhikr* ritual argues that the recitation of *dhikr* in unison is sanctioned by God for both male and female Muslims based on several Quranic verses and hadith. He identifies several of these Qur'anic verses which sanction *dhikr* ritual such as 3: 191, 33:41, and 33:35. All of these verses use the plural form of *dhikr* rather than a singular form to signify the order of the remembrance of God. As argued by Badruzzaman, this indicates that the recitation of *dhikr* in unison is lawful and cannot be regarded as misleading innovation (A., *bid'a ḍalāla*).

In order to support his argument on the permissibility of reciting vocal *dhikr* in unison (I., *berjamaah*) Badruzzaman goes on to make use of several hadith that endorse this practice. According to him, there are a lot of hadith that sanction this kind of ritual. However, in order to answer the accusation of the Salafi group, he mentions only ten hadith in his book. To make it clear his argument on this matter, I quote two hadith as follows:

> None of the group of people sitting at one gathering (A., *majlis*) in which they recite *dhikr* to God and then they stand up (after finishing reciting *dhikr*) except the Angels of God say to them: 'Stand up, indeed God has forgiven your sins and has replaced your bad deeds with good ones.'

> God will say in the hereafter, 'all groups will know which one is the most honourable. The Prophet was asked, 'Oh! Prophet, which one is the most honourable group?' He said, 'The group of dhikr gathering (A., *majlis dhikr*)'.

Badruzzaman argues that the word '*majlis*' and 'the group of people' mentioned in these hadith indicates that the reciting of *dhikr* was conducted in unison during the Prophet life (Badruzzaman 2003). Moreover, Badruzzaman also mentions one hadith in which the Prophet not only urged Muslim to practise *dhikr* but he also was actively involved in a *dhikr* gathering among his Companions (Badruzzaman 2003:69). Based on these hadith, he maintains that instead of being considered *bid'ah,* the reciting *dhikr* is unanimously recognized as part of the Prophetic tradition (I., *sunnah*). As a result, Muslims cannot charge someone who practises this kind of *dhikr* as an innovator (I., *pelaku bid'ah*) (Badruzzaman 2003:72-73).

In addition to Qur'anic verses and hadith, Badruzzaman also cites the views of well-known Muslim scholars about the permissibility of practising *dhikr* in unison. It is interesting to note here that Badruzzaman not only quotes the views of classical Muslim jurists and scholars but also quotes modern Muslim scholars on this matter. He, for instance, refers to Sayyid Sābiq, the Egyptian Muslim scholar and Hasbi Ash-Shiddieqy, the Indonesian 'reformist' Muslim scholar who frequently criticizes religious rituals practised by 'traditionalist' Indonesian Muslims and who promotes pristine Islamic ritual in all of his books. As cited by Badruzzaman, Sayyid Sābiq argues that the Prophet recommended his followers to sit in *dhikr* gatherings (I., *majlis dhikr*). Similarly, Ash-Shiddieqy points out that it was desirable (I., *sangat disukai*) to hold gatherings (*halaqa-halaqa*) to recite *dhikr* and to make people accustomed to the recitation of *dhikr* in these gatherings (Badruzzaman 2003:70-71). It is likely that Badruzzaman quotes these two scholars intentionally to show that such scholars, to whom most modernist Indonesian Muslims generally refer, consider the recitation of *dhikr* in unison as recommended ritual.

Another issue which becomes the main concern of Badruzzaman is the recitation of vocal *dhikr* (I., *dhikr bersuara*). With regard to those who deny the permissibility of this practice, like Abu Amsaka, Badruzzaman also make use of a Qur'anic verse, several hadith and the views of Muslim scholars to deal with this issue. He cites one verse in particular as follows:

> And when you have performed your holy rites, recite *dhikr* (by mentioning the name of God) as you remember your fathers, or yet more intensely. There are some people who say, 'Our Lord, give to us in this world'; such people will have no part in the hereafter.

In elaborating on this verse, Badruzzaman cites several exegetes. He, for instance, refers to Aḥmad Musṭāfa al-Marāghī (d. 1952) and Aḥmad al-Ṣāwī al-Mālikī (d.1825) who stated that after completing the pilgrimage, Muslims are urged to recite *dhikr* as they used to mention their fathers and even louder.

According to Badruzzaman, even though the verse mentioned above is particularly related to *dhikr* ritual conducted after performing the pilgrimage, nevertheless the meaning of the verse is not confined to the ritual during pilgrimage. In other words, the meaning of the verse can also be considered in a general context because the text used in the verse is general such as *fadhkurū Allāh*(you should recite *dhikr* by mentioning the name of God). In this regard, Badruzzaman bases his argument on the Islamic legal theory that 'the fundamental guide is the universality of text, not the particularity of text' (A., *al-Ibra bi umūm al-lafẓi lā biḥusūs al-sabāb*). With this theory, Badurzzaman argues that reciting *dhikr* with a raised voice is not only recommended for those who perform pilgrimage ritual (I., *ibadah haji*) but also recommended for those who do not perform pilgrimage ritual (Badruzzaman 2003:83). Apart from the verse, Badruzzaman also presents the argument taken from a hadith as explanation of the universality of the verse. In this regard, he uses the hadith attributed to Ibn 'Abbās who heard the Prophet recite *dhikr* after prayers. This hadith, Badruzzaman adds, indicates that the Prophet used to recite vocal *dhikr* at that time so that Ibn Abbas could hear it. It is based on this hadith that several Muslim jurists such as Ibn Hajjār al-'Asqalānī (d. 852/1448) and Abu Zakāriat Yaḥyā ibn Sharaf al-Nawāwī (w. 676/1277) considered the reciting *dhikr* with a voice as recommended practice (Badruzzaman 2003:84).

Another Prophetic tradition used by Badruzzaman is the one which mentions the Prophet asking Muslims to recite *dhikr* until hypocrites said they were showing off (*riyā'*) and another version which says until people regarded them as crazy. Badruzzaman interprets this hadith to mean that the Prophet urged his followers to recite *dhikr* vocally. This interpretation is based on the fact that the accusation of showing off and being crazy would not have been attributed to those who recited *dhikr*, if they recited silent *dhikr*. Therefore, Badruzzaman is convinced that the recitation of vocal *dhikr* is a unanimously recognized part of the Prophetic tradition. Badruzzaman, quoting al-Nawāwī's view, argues that Muslims should not stop reciting vocal *dhikr* and silent *dhikr* just because of fearing others' accusation of this practice as a form of showing off (Badruzzaman 2003:86).

After presenting his argument taken from Qur'anic verses and hadith, Badruzzaman specifically comments on a particular verse used by those who reject the permissibility of reciting a vocal *dhikr*. The verse, as quoted by Amsaka, is as follows:

> And bethink thyself of thy Sustainer humbly and with awe, and without raising thy voice, at morn and at evening; and do not allow thyself to be heedless (7:205).

This verse seems to prohibit Muslims from reciting vocal *dhikr* particularly as understood by the phrase *without loudness in words*. Badruzzaman maintains that it seems that this verse contradicts the previous hadith. Therefore, in this regard, referring to Islamic legal theory, Badruzzaman tries to arrive at a compromise between the verse and the hadith that recommends reciting vocal *dhikr* by arguing that complying with one of two seemingly different texts is better than complying with nothing (Badruzzaman 2003:88).

Like Amsaka, Badruzzaman uses an authoritative exegesis to interpret the verse. In this case, he quotes Ibn Kathīr (d. 774/1372) arguing that the word *without loudness in words* means that it is recommended to recite *dhikr* without shouting and with using an extremely loud voice. Based on this interpretation,

Badruzzaman points out that basically reciting vocal *dhikr* is recommended, and hence, there is no contradiction between the Qur'anic verse and hadith. Rather than prohibiting Muslims from reciting vocal *dhikr*, this verse, according to Badruzzaman only prohibits them from reciting *dhikr* in an extremely loud fashion (Badruzzaman 2003:90).

In addition, Badruzzaman goes on to respond to a hadith used by Amsaka to refuse the permissibility of reciting vocal *dhikr*. It was reported in the hadith that the Prophet asked his Companion to lower his voice because he did not pray to a deaf God. In elaborating on this hadith, Badruzzaman again cites the view of the Muslim scholar, Shihab al-Dīn al-Qaṣṭallānī (d. 923/1517) who argued that in the hadith the Prophet only prohibited his Companion from reciting excessively vocal *dhikr* (Baddruzzaman 2003:90).

In regard to crying during the recitation of *dhikr*, unlike Abu Amsaka and Ibn Mukaffi, Badruzzaman allows such practice providing that people cry because of fearing of God and out of admiration for the greatness of God. According to him, both the Qur'an and hadith endorse Muslims to cry when they recite *dhikr* and recite the Qur'an. In this regard, there are several Qur'anic verses and hadith together with the views of Muslim scholars that endorse the practice of crying while reciting the Qur'an and while reciting *dhikr*. According to Badruzzaman, all of these are enough to refute those who regard crying during *dhikr* as innovation and showing off. Accordingly, Badruzzaman strongly laments those who regard crying during *dhikr* recitation as conducted by Arifin Ilham as showing off. This accusation, according to Badruzzaman, is the result of prejudice (I., *prasangka buruk*) against other Muslims. Without doubt, negative thinking toward other fellow Muslims must be avoided by Muslims because it contradicts the teaching of the Qur'an and the Prophet (Badruzzaman 2003:101).

Badruzzam regards those who reject recommended practices conforming to the Prophetic tradition and regard them as illicit innovation as not in compliance with the teachings of the Prophet. As a result, these persons, according to Badruzzaman, cannot be regarded as followers of the Prophet. In line with this, he stresses that Muslims should not easily make the charge of practising *bid'ah* toward rituals practised by their fellow Muslims just because they themselves do not know that these rituals are recognised as a part of the Prophetic tradition.

Unlike Badruzzaman, Satori in his book, *Koreksi Zikir Keblinger, Kearifan Menilai Zikir Berjamaah dan Berbisnis M. Arifin Ilham* (The Correction of Confusing *Zikir*, The Wisdom of Valuing *Zikir* in Unison and The Business of M. Arifin Ilham) focuses on criticizing Abu Amsaka's views. Like Badruzzaman,

Satori is also responding to Amsaka's criticism by referring to arguments taken from the Qur'an and hadith. However, Satori, in his book, specifically focuses on criticizing an ideology held by the Salafi. According to the Salafi, the three generations who followed on after the death of the Prophet – the Companions (A., *ṣaḥabāt*), the Successors of his Companions (A., *tābi'īn*), and the Successors of the Successors (A, *tābi'it al-tābi'īn*) – are the best model for Muslims. These three generations are known in the Islamic literature as *Salāf al-Ṣāliḥ.* This interpretation is based on the fact that the Prophet mentioned that the best of his followers (*ummat*) were those of the three generations after his death. However, Satori argues, that several Muslim scholars have made a different interpretation of the meaning of this hadith particularly in regard to how many years are necessary to count as one generation. If one generation can live for one century, it would take three hundred years from the first generation to the third generation after the death of the Prophet. In Satori's view, the life of the Prophet's followers during the three hundred years after the death of the Prophet cannot be considered as ideal. This is partly because during this period different heretical sects appeared and there occurred the murder of some Companions. As a result, Satori points out that with their dark side, this period cannot be idealized as the best of all legal sources, as the Salafi believe. There is no clear argument in the hadith mentioning that this *salaf* period should be regarded as a reference in legal matters (Satori 118-123).

2.3. Conclusion

It is clear that the difference in the views regarding ritual practice between the Indonesian Salafi and the proponents of *Majlis Dhikr* can be traced back to their different interpretation of the concept of *bid'ah.* The Salafi believed that all rituals categorized as *bid'ah* should be considered to be misleading and their perpetrators should not be tolerated. For them, in order to be good Muslims, it is essential to avoid such *bid'ah* in worship (I., *ibadah*). In this regard, efforts should be made to purify Muslims from this *bid'ah* as part of *dakwah* which is strongly recommended by Islam (Al-Mukaffi 2003:xxvi). With this belief, the Salafi regard the practice of reciting vocal *dhikr* in unison as misleading *bid'ah* but also consider that its performers should be brought to the right path and to authentic Islamic teachings (Al-Mukaffi 2003:x). In contrast, the proponents of *Majlis Dhikr* believed that their vocal *dhikr* ritual in unison has a strong basis both in the Qur'an and hadith. For that reason, such ritual cannot be considered *bid'ah* because its theological basis can be found in both sources of Islamic conduct. For the proponents of *Majlis Dhikr,* rituals can be considered *bid'ah,* if the Qur'an, hadith, the practices of Prophet's Companions, and the consensus of Muslim scholars (I., *ulama*) neither support nor mention these rituals. In this context, the consensus of Muslim scholars also derives from their use of *ijtihad*, which is strongly supported by the Prophet.

In the matter of *dhikr*, both Salafi and the proponents of *Majlis Dhikr* similarly base their arguments on the Qur'an and hadith. Closer examination of their views shows that both Salafi and the proponents of *Majlis Dhikr* seem to agree that *dhikr* is recommended by God and the Prophet. However, one side considers that *dhikr* can be practised in unison, whereas the other side argues that *dhikr* can only be practised individually (I., *secara perorangan*). Differences among them on the way to recite *dhikr* are due to different interpretations of the Quranic verses and the texts of hadith. In the case of *dhikr*, we do not know exactly how the Prophet recited *dhikr*. All we know is that reciting *dhikr* was practised by the Prophet's Companions and the Prophet agreed with their practice. Therefore, I would argue that if people have different views on interpretable matters, they cannot be regarded as in violation of Islamic teachings nor considered to practise misleading *bid'ah* because of their understanding on these interpretative matters. The results of interpretation of religious matters categorised as interpretable cannot be regarded as an absolutely true. As argued by Quraish Shihab, the Qur'an and hadith cannot provide an absolute interpretation. Only God and His sayings are absolute, and only a few of the interpretations of these sayings can be regarded as absolute (Shihab 1996:497-98).

Chapter III: The Intellectual Response of Indonesian *Majlis Dhikr* Groups to Some Aspects of Their Ritual Practices

Although the *Majlis Dhikr* groups that I have studied cannot be categorised as recognized *tarekat* (*tarekat mu'tabarah*), their ritual practices have been strongly influenced by *tasawuf* teachings. For example, the *dhikr* ritual practised by these groups is similar to the ritual that has long been practised by other *tarekat* groups. It is important to note that the members and the leaders of these *Majlis Dhikr* groups claim that although the *dhikr* that they recite do not posses a chain of transmitters (A., *sanad*) like the *dhikr* ritual in other Sufi groups (I., *tarekat*), their aim is similar, namely, to attain close proximity to God and to gain tranquillity of heart. Moreover, they argue that the rituals practised by these groups have a strong basis in the Qur'an, hadith and the notions of Muslim scholars. Apart from the *dhikr* ritual, these groups also teach and practise some aspects of *tasawuf* which have been written and practised by earlier Muslim Sufi. Therefore, instead of accusing these groups of introducing innovation (I., *bid'ah*) within Islam and performing syncretic practices, I argue that they can be regarded as groups that still preserve and maintain the continuity of Sufi practices in Islam. As a result, their practices and rituals fall within the framework of Islamic Sufi practices and Islamic traditions. To support my argument, this chapter will explore how and to what extent these groups interpret and respond theologically to certain aspects of their ritual practices. Several topics discussed in this chapter will answer whether the belief and the ritual of *Majlis Dhikr* are relevant to the Islamic teachings and Islamic Sufi practices. Furthermore, these topics will give an understanding of the common ritual practised in the *Majlis Dhikr* groups.

3.1. *Ṣalawāt* As a Means to Approach God

In Islamic traditions, *taṣliyyat* or *Ṣalawāt* means the invocation of God's blessing upon the Prophet Muhammad. Some Muslim scholars argue that the word *Ṣalawāt* can be translated differently according to the subject of *Ṣalawāt*. For example, if the subject of *Ṣalawāt* is to God, *Ṣalawāt* implies that God will give His blessing and mercy. On the other hand, if the subject of *Ṣalawāt* is Angels, *Ṣalawāt* means they will pray and ask God to forgive the Prophet; while if the subject of *Ṣalawāt* is people, it could mean that they are asking God to give His blessing to Muhammad (Shihab 2006:333). More broadly, the word *Ṣalawāt* or *taṣliyyat* can be used to refer to the repetition of a blessing phrase, *sallawāhu 'alaihi wa sallam,* God bless him and give him peace. This blessing formula is always recited whenever the name of the Prophet Muhammad is mentioned (Robson 1936:365; Schimmel 1985). This practice is strongly recommended by the Prophet who said that those who do not recite the blessing formula when his name is mentioned can be regarded as extremely stingy (A., *bakhīl*).[1] As a result, Muslims recite the blessing phrase after the name of Muhammad is mentioned to avoid being regarded by their Prophet as not generous with their practice.

The place of *Ṣalawāt* among pious Islamic practices is important. Unlike other prayers, it is clearly mentioned in the Qur'an and is performed by God and His Angels for the Prophet Muhammad. The Qur'an says that God and His Angels send blessings to the Prophet, 'O! you who believe! Send your *Ṣalawāt* to Muhammad and salute him respectfully' (33:56). Based on this verse, even though there are thousands of prayers and poems intended to obtain Muhammad's intercession, the most efficacious is to ask God to bless Muhammad and his family by reciting the *Ṣalawāt* just as God and His Angels did. It is actually believed that a prayer to God without this invocation is useless.[2] In other words, *Ṣalawāt* is considered to be necessary for the granting of a prayer request.

There are numerous records of Prophetic sayings (*hadith*) that strongly stress the importance of reciting *Ṣalawāt*. For example, the Prophet said, 'He who sends blessings on me once, Allah sends blessings on him ten times and removes from him ten sins and raises him by ten degrees.' The Prophet also mentioned that the persons who will be closest to him on the Day of Judgment are those who give *Ṣalawāt* most to him. On another occasion, the Prophet said that whoever sends blessings to him ten times in the morning and ten times in the evening will have his intercession on judgment day. Moreover, the Prophet said that he will be able to hear someone's *Ṣalawāt* to him in his tomb, and God will support his worldly and other worldly affairs and the Prophet will be his witness and intercessor on the Day of Judgment.[3] These hadith all indicate that sending blessing to the Prophet will result in great rewards for the reciters.

---

1 قال " البخيل من ذكرت عنده .وأخرج أحمد والترمذي عن الحسين بن علي رضي الله عنه أن رسول الله صلى الله عليه وسلم فلم يصل عليّ.

2 إِنَّ الدُّعَاءَ مَوْقُوفٌ بَيْنَ السَّمَاءِ وَالأَرْضِ لاَ يَصْعَدُ مِنْهُ شَيْءٌ حَتَّى تُصَلِّيَ عَلَى نَبِيِّكَ

'Verily prayer will be jammed between heaven and earth and it cannot ascend at all until you give *Ṣalawāt* on your Prophet' (Narrated by Al-Turmudzî).

3 وأخرج البيهقي في الشعب والخطيب وابن عساكر عن أبي هريرة رضي الله عنه قال: قال رسول الله صلى الله عليه وسلم " من صلى عليَّ عند قبري سمعته، ومن صلى عليَّ نائياً كفى أمر دنياه وآخرته، وكنت له شهيداً وشفيعاً يوم القيامة ".

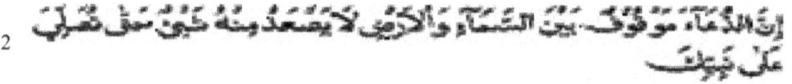

As far as these rewards are concerned, Muslim theologians have argued that they can be achieved by Muslims if they send blessings to the Prophet with sincerity and full consciousness (A., *khuḍūr al-qalbi*) and without neglect. In contrast, other Muslims theologians and Sufi, such as 'Abd Wahhāb al-Sha'rānī (b. 898/1493), pointed out that ten merits achieved as result of sending blessings to the Prophet could also be achieved by those who recite *Ṣalawāt* with neglect. Nevertheless, those who recite *Ṣalawāt* with full consciousness will obtain many more rewards known only by God (al-Nabhani,n.d.: 57).

However, the importance of *Ṣalawāt* in the Islamic tradition prompted questions about the usefulness of sending blessings for the Prophet since his status was already perfect (al-Nabhani n.d.:44). Muslim theologians have responded differently to this question. Al-Nabhani argued that after *adzan* (the call to daily prayers) has been performed, the Prophet asked Muslims to pray for him so that God would give him eternal rights of intercession and raise him to the highest rank as God had promised. If this prayer is granted by God, al- Nabhani argued, then God will give the Prophet eternal rights of intercession and raise him to the highest rank. Therefore, al-Nabhani concluded, the Prophet will benefit from the blessings given by Muslims to him.

However, Aḥmad bin Mubārak argued that God commands Muslims to send blessings to the Prophet Muhammad for the benefit of themselves, not for the benefit of the Prophet. Mubārak likened this to a generous man who gives his servants a piece of land to cultivate without asking for any reward. All the harvest thus goes to the servants. In a similar way, all rewards of *Ṣalawāt* are for those who send the blessing, not for the Prophet himself. However, these rewards can only be achieved by the reciters of *Ṣalawāt* because of their pure faith (*imān*), which results from the Prophet's light (A., *nūr Muhammad*). In other words, all the rewards attained by Muslims come from the Prophet himself. Mubarak made an analogy to the ocean and rain. The process of rain begins with the evaporation of water from the ocean. Then, rain falls on the continent and flows back into the ocean via the rivers. The rain water flowing into the ocean does not, therefore, add to the volume of the oceans water (al-Nabhani, n.d.:45).

Another theme related to *Ṣalawāt* is whether it is lawful or not to add the word *sayyidinā* (our Lord) in the blessing phrase, such as *Allāhumma ṣalli 'alā sayyidina Muḥammad.* Ibn Taymiyyah (1263 – 1328) did not support the practice of adding the word *sayyidinā* before the name Muhammad, either in daily prayer or other prayers, because the Prophet never said that should be done. In contrast, other Muslim theologians, such as al-Suyūṭī (1445-1505), urged Muslim to add *sayyidinā* before the name of Muhammad. Al-Suyūṭī stated that even though the prophet, in his *hadith* prohibited his Companions from doing this, the prohibition was mainly due to his modesty. The Prophet expressed his dislike of arrogance in his *hadith* which stated, 'I am a *sayyid* of the sons of Adam and I am not arrogant.' As a result, when his Companions asked him how to send blessing to him, he taught them the blessing phrase without the word *sayyidinā* before his name. Nevertheless, al-Suyūṭī argued that one of the ways Muslims can show their respect for the Prophet is to send the blessings phrase to him by adding the word *sayyidinā* before his name. This is partly because God has prohibited Muslims to address the Prophet without a title. Al-Suyūṭi cited the verse of the Qur'an which said that, 'make not the calling of the Messenger (Muhammad) among you as your calling one of another (al-Nūr 24: 63). In addition to this verse, al-Suyūṭi also cited the well-known statement attributed to Ibn Mas'ud, the Prophet's Companion: 'Beautify your blessing to your Prophet' (al-Nabhani,nd: 39-40). Therefore, the use of the word *sayyidinā* in the blessing is supported by the Qur'an and the practices of the Prophet's Companions.

In addition to the text of the *Ṣalawāt* blessing taught by the Prophet, there have been various other versions throughout Islamic history, recorded not only by his Companions but also by other pious Muslims. Al- Nabhani categorized the first kind of *Ṣalawāt* as *Ṣalawāt ma'thūrat* that were taught by the Prophet as reported in his *ḥadīth,* while he categorized as *ghair ma'thūrat*all the texts of *Ṣalawāt* not taught by the Prophet (al-Nabhani,n.d: 344). Muslims theologians have questioned which of these two categories of *Ṣalawāt* conveys more rewards. Hasbi Ash-Shiddieqy (1904-1975), argued that all *Ṣalawāt* taught by the Prophet through his words are more valued than other texts because they have been taught directly by the Prophet. He maintained that these *Ṣalawāt* are more prominent than those composed by others. For Hasbi, other *Ṣalawāt* composed by other Muslims can be considered to be innovations (*bid'ah*) because they not only contain exaggerated adoration of the Prophet but are not mentioned in hadith. Therefore, if Muslims recite these kinds of *Ṣalawāt,* they cannot be regarded as reciting *Ṣalawāt* and thus will not be able to obtain any rewards and benefits from their recitation. To support his argument, Hasbi cited the view of al-Suyūṭī saying that the best *Ṣalawāt* to recite was the *Ṣalawāt* usually recited on the occasion of *tashahhud* (sitting position of the second unit of prayer). If people recite this *Ṣalawāt,* they can be regarded as having recited *Ṣalawāt* but if they recite anything else, it will be doubtful whether they have recited *Ṣalawāt* (Ash-Shiddieqy 1964:70). In other words, any texts of *Ṣalawāt* which were not taught by the Prophet cannot be regarded as *Ṣalawāt.*

Other Muslim theologians like al-Sakhāwī (831-902) were opposed to this view, arguing that the Prophet has taught many ways to send blessing to him as recorded in different hadith. According to his Companions and the Successors of His Companions (A., *tābi'īn*) this indicates that neither the way to send blessing nor the text of the blessing is confined to the texts taught by the Prophet. Therefore, al-Sakhāwī argued, those who have been endowed by God with eloquence of language are allowed to compose *Ṣalawāt* that describe the Prophet's dignity. In this matter, al-Sakhāwi based his opinion on the well known statement attributed to the Prophet's companion, Ibn Mas'ūd, who said, 'beautify the blessing upon your Prophet, because you do not perhaps know this blessing was offered to the Prophet' (al-Nabhani n.d: 346).

In explaining his agreement with al-Sakhāwi's view on this matter, al- Nabhani said that the objective of *Ṣalawāt* or sending blessings to the Prophet is to glorify him because he still needs the mercy and blessing of God, despite his highest rank in the eyes of God. In this sense, al-Nabhani argued that the texts composed by his Companions and other Muslim scholars (A., *ulamā'*) should contain exaltation and glorification of the Prophet to meet the objective of *Ṣalawāt*. Therefore, al-Nabhani believed that these texts of *Ṣalawāt* would indeed lead to an increase in reward because of the glorification as well as the recitation of the *Ṣalawāt*itself. When someone asked al-Nabhani which one of the two kinds of *Ṣalawāt* lead to more rewards, he answered that this question was difficult to answer categorically because both are likely to provide rewards. Both have their own merits. According to al- Nabhani, one of the benefits of sending *Ṣalawāt* composed by the Prophet's Companions and Muslim scholars is to increase the eagerness of reciters to glorify the Prophet as well as to remember his beautiful characteristics. Al-Nabhani considered that this eventually would lead the reciters to increase their reciting of *Ṣalawāt* to the Prophet as well as their love of the Prophet. According to al-Nabhani, these are the greatest benefits of reciting those texts of *Ṣalawāt*. Moreover, most of the texts composed by Muslim scholars (A., '*ulamā'*) were dictated by the Prophet in visions either in their dreams or while awake. Al-Nabhani pointed out that because the Prophet had guaranteed that people can have dreams about him and that if they see the Prophet in a dream, he must be the real Prophet because Satan is unable to resemble him, the texts of *Ṣalawāt* dictated by him in dreams are legitimate because they must be from him (al-Nabhani, n.d: 347).

The recitation of *Ṣalawāt* also has a significant role in Sufi practices. It is believed that the blessing phrase of *Ṣalawāt* can be used as a means for Muslims to attain *wusul* or *ma'rifatullah* (the knowledge of God) and to obtain spiritual experiences. As mentioned by 'Abd al-Raḥmān ibn Musṭafā al-Idrūs, 'it is difficult to find authoritative Sufi masters (A.*murshīd*) who are able to help disciples (I., *murid*) to attain *wusul* or *ma'rifatullah* at the end of this age.' For al-Idrūs, the only possible way for Muslims to achieve *wusul* is by reciting

Ṣalawāt. Al-Idrus argued that unlike other virtues, which might be granted or might not be granted by God, requests made by reciting *Ṣalawāt* must be granted by God; the Prophet will reply with the same prayer whether it is recited in a conscious or an unconscious state (Sa'id 2004:6). Moreover, like reciting the Qur'an, the reciting of *Ṣalawāt* can give rewards to its reciters even if they do not understand the meaning of the text. Ahmad Ṣāwī stated that *Ṣalawāt* can be used as a means to approach God without any particular masters or transmitters (A., *isnād*) because the master of *Ṣalawāt* and its transmitter is the Prophet himself. By contrast, litanies such as *dhikr* and *wirid*, which are recited with the purpose of approaching God in some Sufi orders require the guidance of masters who have attained the highest Sufi states. If these *dhikr* are recited without the guidance of a master, the devil will interfere, so people will not derive any benefit from the practice at all (Sawi n.d:287).

3.1.1. *Majlis Dhikr* Groups' Understanding of *Ṣalawāt*

The members of *Majlis Dhikr* groups in Indonesia also believe that it is obligatory for Muslims to recite *Ṣalawāt* as an expression of their love and their gratitude to the Prophet. For them, the Prophet has sacrificed his life and time bringing his followers from the age of darkness (A., *jahiliyyat*) to the age of lightness and in bringing them from sadness to happiness in this world and the hereafter. In other words, according to them, the Prophet was the most loving person toward his followers. Moreover, they argue that if it was not for him, there might be no other lives in this world. As a result they feel that they are immeasurably in debt to the Prophet. This notion arises from their understanding of a well-known statement attributed to God who said to Adam, 'If it were not for Muhammad, I would not have created you.' It is in this sense that they should ask blessing from God by reciting *Ṣalawāt* to the Prophet; rewards will then be given not only to the reciters of the *Ṣalawāt* but also to other people surrounding them as well as other creatures such as jinn.[4]

Therefore, for Indonesian *Majlis Dhikr* groups, the reciting of *Ṣalawāt* is not simply an oral recitation of the blessing phrase for the Prophet but should be seen as a means to communicate spiritually with the Prophet (*A., ta'alluq bi jānibi al-nabī*). For example, according to a member of the *Wāḥidiyat* group, communicating with the Prophet can be performed in two ways: *ta'alluq ṣūriyy* (outward relationship) and *ta'alluq ma'nawiyy* (spiritual relationship). The former can be achieved by, firstly, completely following what the Prophet has ordered and completely avoiding what he has forbidden as well as maintaining

4 Interview with Zainuddin, Kediri, August, 2004.

a good relationship with other people, and all human beings. Secondly, by experiencing the state of oneness in the love of the Prophet by reciting *Ṣalawāt*, continuously remembering the Prophet's fine qualities followed by love and longing and the recitation of the life stories of the Prophet together with poems which can help people to increase their love for him. The second way (*ta'alluq ma'nawiyy*) can be done, firstly, by visualizing the image of the Prophet. Of course, this way of communicating can only be done by those who have experienced a visionary dream of the Prophet or have met him when awake. Those who have not experienced this simply imagine his fine personality followed with full of passion and compliments. If they have performed the *hajj*, they can imagine historic places in Mecca and Medina where the Prophet used to teach his followers. After this, they should internalize the concept of *Biḥaqīqat al-Muḥammadiyah*, which means that the origin of all creatures is from the Light of Muhammad (*Nūr Muḥammad*). This notion is based on the statement attributed to God that 'I (God) created you (Muhammad) from My light and I created creatures from your light.' To internalize this concept, people should imagine that anything they smell, see, and touch consists of *Nūr Muḥammad*. If they fail to visualize this concept, it is believed their mind's eye must be veiled by the dirt of passion (I., *nafsu*). Moreover, for the *Wāḥidiyat* group in particular, the simplest way to implement the concept of communicating with the Prophet is by increasingly reciting the phrase, *yā sayyidī yā rasulullāh*, which helps people remember the Prophet (Anonymous 1999:36-40).

In order to show respect to the Prophet, the *Majlis Dhikr* groups add the word *sayyidinā*before the name of Muhammad when they recite the *Ṣalawāt* phrase. Some of them argue that it is considered stingy if Muslims mention the name of the Prophet of Muhammad without adding *sayyidinā*, whereas when they address the president, they always add his title before his name such as Mr. President (I., *bapak presiden*). They believe that adding the word *sayyidinā* before the name of Muhammad in the *Ṣalawāt* phrase is a courtesy (I., *sopan santun*), which is preferable to complying with the command. They also base their notion on the Prophetic tradition that Abū Bakr refused the order of the Prophet who asked him to lead prayers. In courtesy, Abū Bakr requested that the Prophet be the leader. Based on this story, members of Indonesian *Majlis Dhikr* groups add the *sayyidinā* before the Prophet's name, as a courtesy, ignoring the Prophet's prohibition of the practice.

From the perspective of Indonesian *Majlis Dhikr* groups, the recitation of *Ṣalawāt* is an important aspect of their ritual practices. They fully understand that *Ṣalawāt* is a necessary condition for the granting of a prayer request. In other words, every prayer directed to God without adding *Ṣalawāt* is considered to be meaningless. It is for this reason that those groups include the blessing phrase of *Ṣalawāt* in their ritual practices. Some *Majlis Dhikr* groups urge that *Ṣalawāt* be read hundreds of times. One group has even singled out *Ṣalawāt* for their practice, and believe that the *Ṣalawāt* is the easiest way to achieve *wusul* (*ma'rifa*) with God without requiring a perfect master (A., *kāmil al-mukammil*), especially in the current situation where a perfect master is difficult to find. Another reason to recite *Ṣalawāt* relates to the suggestion by Muslim scholars that *Ṣalawāt* removes intense emotion, while other litanies (*dhikr*), can result in intensifying the emotion of the reciters. Adding *Ṣalawāt* among other litanies according to these scholars, can therefore balance the effect of those other litanies.

As far as the benefits of *Ṣalawāt* are concerned, Indonesian *Majlis Dhikr* groups, in common with other Muslim scholars, consider that reciting *Ṣalawāt* can be used for worldly purposes and non-worldly purposes. More specifically, they argue that *Ṣalawāt* can be used as a means to ask for the Prophet's intercession in this world and the hereafter. In this world, the members of these groups ask for the Prophet's intercession so that the Prophet can help them to succeed in their worldly endeavours. In this respect, one *Majlis Dhikr* group composed *Ṣalawāt* for particular purposes and performed special rituals to obtain their particular needs. Moreover, they also believe that some *Ṣalawāt* composed by Muslim scholars have particular benefits. For example, *Ṣalawāt Nariyat* can be used to improve one's livelihood (I., *rizki*); while *Ṣalawāt Munjiyat* can be used for safety purposes. In the hereafter, they believed that the Prophet will give his *shafā'at* (intercession) to those who recite *Ṣalawāt* and hence save them from trials of the hell.[5]

In relation to the texts of *Ṣalawāt* that must be recited, the Indonesian *Majlis Dhikr* groups use and recite not only the texts of *Ṣalawāt* taught by the Prophet but also *Ṣalawāt* written by other scholars. Unlike some Muslim scholars who forbid Muslims from reciting the latter, the Indonesian *Majlis Dhikr* groups regard those *Ṣalawāt* as appropriate to follow the commands of God to send *Ṣalawāt* to His Prophet Muhammad. As a result, instead of regarding these *Ṣalawāt* as innovations (*bid'ah*) to Islam, they consider reciting any respectful kind of *Ṣalawāt* to be lawful. In this respect, *Kyai* Busyra Mughi, one of the members of those groups argued as follows:

> Since the meaning of *Ṣalawāt* itself is prayer or supplication, it cannot be considered to be *bid'ah* if Muslims compose texts of *Ṣalawāt* and recite the texts of *Ṣalawāt* which were not taught by the Prophet. Like prayer, the Prophet only asked Muslims to pray, but he did not ask them to pray any particular prayers. In other words, the Prophet gave them the freedom

5 Interview with *Gus* Latif, Kediri, September, 2004.

> to recite various prayers. Furthermore, none of the Prophet's hadith asked Muslims to recite *Ṣalawāt* as taught by the Prophet. God and His Prophet only asked Muslims to recite *Ṣalawāt*. The Prophet never asked them to recite only the texts of prayers from him. In this case, as long as they have ability, people can write their own beautiful texts of *Ṣalawāt*. However, I admit that the *Ṣalawāt* and prayer taught by the Prophet are more excellent than others.

Kyai Marzuki, a leader of a pesantren in East Java, shared Kyai Mughni's view on this issue. Kyai Marzuki argued that Muslims can pray by using either text of prayers taught by the Prophet or texts from others. His view was based on the fact that according to Islamic law, all things are permissible (A., ibāhah) unless there is evidence of prohibition. In line with this notion, composing Ṣalawāt and reciting of these texts are permissible because no hadith prohibits Muslims from doing so. In addition to this argument, Kyai Marzuki categorized religious affairs into two categories. The first is 'ibāda maḥdla, which means something ordained specifically by God in the Qur'an and by the Prophet in his sayings (hadith), including detailed instruction such matters as prayers, almsgiving, fasting during the Ramadhan month, and the pilgrimage (the hajj). The second is 'ibāda ghair *maḥdla,* which means something ordained by God and his Prophet in general, but without specific mention of how to perform and practice it. Examples of this latter category are *dhikr* (chanting religious litanies), reciting *Ṣalawāt*and reciting the Qur'an. God and the Prophet only asked Muslims to recite these, but how many times was not specified. Therefore, Marzuki argues that Muslims are allowed to recite various texts of *Ṣalawāt,* recite as many pages of the Qur'an as they like, and perform *dhikr* as many times as they like.[6]

It is clear that on the matter of *Ṣalawāt* and related topics, Indonesian *Majlis Dhikr* groups have based their arguments on what has long been pointed out by the Prophet through the interpretation of other Muslim scholars. While following these Muslims scholars' notions of *Ṣalawāt,* they also have creatively adapted those notions in relation to the context of their culture. The process of adaptation, however, cannot be regarded as a violation of the main teaching of Islam itself, since Indonesian *Majlis Dhikr* groups still refer to the Prophet tradition. What Indonesian *Majlis Dhikr* groups have done can thus be regarded as maintaining the Islamic tradition, a term used by Nashr to refer to

> something which incorporates both the message received by the Prophet Muhammad in form of the Scripture as well as that Islam, as a religion, absorbed according to its own genius and made its own through transformation and synthesis (Muhaimin 1995:13).

---

6 Interview with Marzuki, Malang, March, 2005

With this definition, they believe that what they practise is justifiable by the text of Qur'an and hadith.

3.2. The Concepts of Sainthood (*Walī*) and Miracle (*Karamah*)

The concepts of sainthood and *karamah* are another topic which has drawn Sufi groups and Muslim scholars into vigorous debate. Despite strong criticism from reformist Muslims toward these concepts, they have had an important meaning in Muslim religiosity. In order to look at their significance, this section will discuss these two concepts among Sufi theorists and Muslim scholars, and how Indonesian *Majlis Dhikr* groups have responded to and applied these concepts in their religious practices.

Radtke (1996:124) has argued that the existence of a special category of saints (*waliyullah*) who have a close relationship with God is nowhere mentioned in the Qur'an and the hadith. Although it might be true to say that a coherent and systematic theory of sainthood cannot be found in either the Qur'an or in the Prophetic period. I would argue that the Qur'an and the explanation of the Prophet have inspired a clearly articulated Islamic doctrine of sainthood introduced by early Muslim Sufi. In other words, the comprehensive and systematic theory of saint and sainthood was developed several centuries after the death of the Prophet. Nevertheless, the Qur'an mentions the word *wali* in many places, with various meanings including friends, protectors, supporters and close relatives. This word, for instance, is not only applied to God, who is the believers' friend (7:196, 2:257 and 41:31), but also to Satan, whose attributes contrast with the attributes of God. The Qur'an also mentions the characteristics of *waliullāh* (friend of Allah) or *auliyaullāh* (pl. friends of Allah) who need not fear nor grieve (10:63). However, in the discussion of the concept of *wali* in Islam, some Muslim scholars seem to discuss only the definition and the meaning of the later, *auliyāullāh*.

To understand the meaning of the *waliullāh* as mentioned in the Qur'an, many Muslim interpreters of the Qur'an refer to the explanation of the Prophetic sayings (A., *hadith*) on this matter. For example, commenting on the word *auliyāullāh* in verse 10:63, al-Ṭabārī (d.310 H) in his book, *Jāmi' al-Bayān fī Tafsīr al-Qur'ān,* referred to two different hadith. Firstly, he noted that *auliyāullāh* (friends of God) are those who, when they are seen, cause people to think of God. Secondly, al-Ṭabāri pointed out that, when the Prophet's Companions asked the Prophet about the identity of the friends of God mentioned in the

Qur'an, the Prophet answered that 'they are servants of God who are envied even by prophets of God and martyrs. They love one another purely for God's sake without any consideration of material gains. Their faces will glow with the light of faith and they will be seated on the podium of *nur* (Divine light). They will be without fear and grief when all people will be steeped in fear and grief.' Then the Prophet recited the verse, 'Behold! the friends of Allah are such that they need not fear nor grieve' (10:62).[7] Other Muslims exegetes (A., *mufassir*) like Al-Zamakhshārī (d. 538) in his book *al-Kashshāf*, and Ibn Kathīr (d.774) in his book *Tafsīr al-Qur'ān al-Karīm,* followed the definition of *wali* given by al-Ṭabāri. In contrast, referring to 'Ālī ibn Abī Ṭālib, Al Qurtūbī (d.671), in his book *al-Jāmi' li Aḥkām al-Qur'ān* defined *auliyā'* (plural form of *wālī*) as people whose face is pale due to wakefulness, whose eyes look bleary because of crying, whose stomach is empty because of hunger, whose lips are dry because of chanting *dhikr.*

Based on their understanding of *waliyullah* derived from the Qur'an and the hadith, early Muslim Sufi specifically developed the idea of the friend of God (A., *waliullah*) in much detail. Al-Ḥākim al-Tirmīdhī (d. 898) is regarded as the first Muslim scholar to introduce the entire concept of the friend of God and friendship with God. Al-Tirmīdhi was convinced that the '*ulamā*'are responsible for preserving the validity of orthodox theology of Islam, while preserving the spiritual heritage of Islam has been entrusted to the saints of Islam (A., *auliyāu llah*). When the prophethood ended, the latter came to be considered as God's representatives on earth. According to Al-Tirmīdhī, God chose forty elected *auliyā'* who divided into *abdāl, ṣiddīqīn, umanā'* and *nuṣaḥā'* to administrate and control the world after the death of the Prophet. Through these *auliyā'* the world exists. Whenever one of them dies, another follows after him and occupies his position so the number remain at forty. This succession will continue until the end of this world (Radtke and O'kane 1996:109). These forty saints have a chief who has the seal of friendship (A., *khātim al-auliyā'*) from God. He is the highest and the most perfect among the friends of God (Radtke and O'kane 1996:101). Elaborating this concept, al-Tirmīdhī argued that God has chosen His prophets from His servants, and God has given preference to certain prophets over others. Among them, Muhammad is the seal of the Prophet (*khātim al-anbiyā'*). In this manner, God also has chosen one of His friends (*auliyā'*) above others. This concept of *khātim al-auliyā'*was new and had never been mentioned by previous Muslim Sufi, which made the work of Tirmīdhi famous in later centuries (Schimmel 1978:57). Al-Tirmīdhī's concept of *khātim al-auliyā'* was further developed by Ibn al-'Arabī.

7 http://www.altafsir.com/Tafasir.asp?tMadhNo=0&tTafsirNo=1&tSoraNo=10&tAyahNo=62&tDisplay=yes&Page=2&Size=1.

Al-Tirmīdhī defined two distinctive classes of friends of God, the *Walī ḥaqqullāh* and the *Walīullāh*. Those categorized as *Walī ḥaqqullāh* will be able to achieve nearness of God by undertaking worship of God and obedience to Him constantly without any intervening rebelliousness. In contrast, a *Walīullāh* is attracted to God by God and is a *majdhūb,* a person who is drawn from the place of divine closeness up to God Himself, to the highest of God's realms (Radtke and O'kane 1996:124). This definition is based on the Qur'anic verses that state 'And He takes possession of the righteous' (7:196). This latter class of saints is called *murād*(the sought). While, the former class is called *murīd*(the seekers). These two categories of saints, as Tirmīdhi argued, have different journeys to approach God. The ascent of *Walī ḥaqqullāh* will end at God's throne. They can approach God but not reach God Himself. In contrast, *Waliullāh* are able to reach beyond God's throne (Gibb 1996:110).

However, al-Qushayri (b.376/986) argued that a true saint must have two qualities. The saint has to fulfil completely obligations to God, while being under the continuous protection and safeguard of God in good and bad times. Therefore, although a *wali* is not sinless (A., *ma'ṣūm*), he or she is preserved from sin (A., *maḥfūẓ*). Based on this definition, al-Qushayri stressed the significance of Muslim saints acting in a manner that is not in conflict with the divine law (Dahlan n.d:16).

Muslim scholars such as al-Jurjānī (d.1413) and Ibn al-Mudābighī defined saints (*wali*) as those who have achieved the Gnosis of God (*ma'rifat*), worship constantly, and avoid disobedience, and lower desires (Dahlan n.d: 16). In line with this, al-Yusi pointed out that no one could achieve the position (*maqam*) of *wali* without meeting four conditions: Firstly, they have to understand Islamic theology so that they can distinguish between the creator (A., *khāliq*) and the created (A., *makhlūq*). Secondly, they should understand Islamic Law, either based on tradition or based on understanding of the Qur'an and the texts of Prophetic tradition. Thirdly, they should have good qualities such as sincerity (A., *ikhlāṣ*) and carefulness (A., *warā'*). Fourthly, they should be in a continual state of fear and never feel secure because they do not know whether they will be put in the group of fortunate people or unfortunate people in the hereafter.

It is clear from these conditions that saints should strictly observe the laws of *sharī'at*and other Islamic teachings. Therefore, if people claim to be *wali* but do not abide by *sharī'at*, most Muslim scholars do not consider them to be *wali.* For example, if such people were able to perform miracles, such as walking on water, flying in the air, travelling distances over the earth with supernatural speed (A., *ṭayy al-arḍ*), these miracles might be attributed to black magic and the assistance of jinn and the like (al-Hujwiri 1997:227). Of such people, the 12th century theologian, al-Ghazālī said:

> Undoubtedly, it is considered necessary to kill people who claim that they have a special relation with God which allows them to be free from observing the five daily prayers and allowing them to drink liquor and use the possessions of other people, as claimed by Sufi. Killing this type of persons is more preferable than killing a hundred infidels, because those people are much more dangerous than infidels (Bakri n.d:139).

One of the reasons why *wali* should abide by the laws of *sharī'at*is to warn people against those who pretend to be *wali* by performing miraculous deeds (A., *khāriq al-'āda*), showing fine manners and fine talk (Dahlan n.d: 16).

The discussion of sainthood in Islam raises the question of whether or not saints realize that they are saints. In his book, al-Qushairi mentioned the disagreement among Sufi as to whether or not people are able to know that they are *wali* or not, but did not clarify his view on this matter (Dahlan n.d:16). However, al-Tirmīdhi discussed the disagreement among Sufi and all of their arguments. In his own opinion, the friends of God are able to know that they are saints. He was strongly opposed to some Sufi who argued that it is not possible because if saints knew that they were *wali,* they would be sure of their salvation in the hereafter, which would result in a lack of willingness to worship. On this point, al-Tirmīdhi pointed out that believers (*mukminūn*) must know that they are believers but do not know whether they will be sure of their salvation. In the same manner, saints know that they are saints, but they are not sure of their salvation in the hereafter. Moreover, al-Tirmīdhi was opposed to those who asserted that saints did not know that they were *wali* because if they did, they would become victims of arrogance. On this matter, al-Tirmīdhi argued that because of their position as saints of God, they would be protected by God from falling prey to arrogance (al-Hujwiri 1997:224-225). Other Sufi have argued that saints must be able to know their sainthood because God endows sainthood on His servants. Therefore, sainthood is a blessing from God and may be known to the recipient to increase his gratitude to God (Kalabadzi 1985).

Sufi have also discussed the question of whether or not saints know each other. Abdullah Ibn Sahl argued that although saints are veiled from the eyes of the common people, they are supposed to know each other (Sa'id 2004:27). Schimmel maintained that they recognize fellow saints without ever having met them (1978:202). In line with this, Abdullah Ibn Sahl argued that God only gives information about people's sainthood to other saints and to those who are able to obtain benefit from those saints. As a sign of God's mercy to humankind, He veils His friends from the eyes of common people and keeps saints concealed from the public. This is not only because it is considered to be an infidelity if people recognize saints and then deny them, but also because it is considered sinful if people ignore saints after they recognize them (Sa'id 2004:27). In contrast to previous scholars, however, Abū Bakr claimed that no one is able to recognize people as saints of God during their life except God Himself. Nevertheless, Abū Bakr argued that people can be regarded as saints if during their life, those people have proper faith and show sincere conduct according to the Qur'an and Prophetic tradition, and die in a state of faith (*mukmin*). In addition, if such people perform miracles, they can be considered to be *wali* and Muslims should respect them (Abu Bakar 2004:21-47).

The hierarchical rank of saints is well known in the Sufi traditions. There are different numbers of saints in each rank, orders of rank in the hierarchy and names of saints in the hierarchy. Among some of the hierarchies discussed in the Sufi tradition are the 'outstanding' (A., *akhyār*), the 'substitutes' (A., *abdāl*), the 'devoted' (*abrār*), ' the poles' (A., *autād*), the 'chiefs' (A., *nuqabā'*) and the 'axis' or 'pole' (A., *qutb*), also referred to as the 'source of help' (A., *ghauth*). Sufi theorists agree that the highest saint in the hierarchy becomes the leader of the saints. In the Sufi tradition the highest ranking saint is called the *qutb* (plural: *aqṭāb*) or *ghauth* which some writers call *al-qutb al-ghauth*. He or she is the centre of the spiritual pole on whom other people depend. There is only one *qutb* or *ghauth* at anyone time. If that saint dies, he or she will be succeeded by another saint below him or her (Sa'id 2004). In this sense, the concept of *qutb* is similar to that of *khātim al-auliyā'*put forward by al-Tirmīdhī.

Abd al-Wahhāb al-Sha'rānī argued that the characteristic of this *qutb* is that his or her heart and mind always circles around (A., *ṭawāf*) God just as a pilgrim walks around the Ka'ba on a pilgrimage in Mecca. Moreover, he or she constantly witnesses God in every direction. However, this does not necessarily mean that God exists within this *qutb*. In addition, the *qutb* is believed to be the first person to face either calamity or receive the aid (I., *pertolongan*) given by God before it is given to the people. Al-Sha'rānī believes that the *qutb* bears such a heavy burden that he or she always has a headache. The *qutb* bears this heavy burden, distributes it among other saints below him, before it is finally distributed to other Muslims. As a result of this, people on this earth can exist. If the burden was not previously distributed by the *qutb* to his or her fellow saints and other Muslims, those who suffered from the calamity would vanish. Al-Sha'rānī's view on this matter derives from his interpretation of the Qur'anic verse saying 'And did not God check one set of people by means of another, the earth would indeed be full of mischief, but Allah is full of bounty to all the worlds (2:251) (Sa'id 2004:30-31).

Whereas the theory of the hierarchy of saints was developed in the Sufi tradition, Ibn Taymiyyah was strongly opposed to it, arguing that this theory is based on invalid Prophetic sayings (*hadith*). He claimed that this theory could be considered an innovation (*bid'ah*) within Islam that should not be tolerated. Therefore, Ibn Taymiyyah proposed a different classification of saints which is taken from the Qur'an (*al-Wāqi'at*chapter). According to his classification, there are two hierarchies of saints: the highest is *al-muqarrabūn* and the second is *aṣḥāb al-yamīn*. The first hierarchy includes those who are brought close by God. These saints always observe the worship of God, avoid His prohibitions, and perform all kinds of recommended deeds (A., *nawāfil*). The second category includes those who observe obligations and avoid God's prohibitions but do not pay attention to recommended deeds. Ibn Taymiyyah thus argued that *wali* could be drawn from Muslim scholars, workers, holy warriors (A., *sabīlillah*), traders and farmers as long as these people do not practise innovation (*bid'ah*) (Taymiyyah n.d-a:179).

The topic of saints in the Sufi tradition is closely related to the topic of miracles (I., *karamah*). Most Muslims theologians believe in the existence of *karamah* which encompasses supernatural deeds, miracles or extraordinary powers performed by saints who strictly observe the laws of *sharī'at*. In this sense, as Taylor argued, every *karamah* always demonstrates a dramatic transformation and fantastic occurrence which human beings cannot possibly perform without the intervention of God's power (Taylor 1998:128). However, Muslim theologians give different names to miracles performed other than by Muslim saints. For example, when such miracles or extraordinary powers are performed by prophets to support their mission, Muslim theologians classify them as *mu'jiza*. When such supernatural deeds are performed by pious Muslims, they call *ma'ūnah*. However, when such miracles are performed by those who do not abide by *sharī'at*, such as infidels, impostors or impious people, these miracles are called *istidrāj*. This last type of miracles is deliberately given by God in order to show that these people are on wrong path.

Ibn Taymiyyah argued that sainthood has nothing to do with extraordinary deeds (*khāriq al-'āda*) or miracles. Although it is possible for Muslim saints to perform *karamah*, not all saints have this ability. Some saints might not be able to perform and to possess such *karamah*, and God does not bestow the ability on them (Taymiyyah 1999:15). Therefore, the performance of *karamah* is not a prerequisite of sainthood in Islam. According to Abū Ḥasan al-Shādhilī, *karamah*cannot be sought either by chanting special *dhikr* or prayers; it is believed to be a blessing from God. In other words, saints are not the primary cause of miracles, but miracles can be performed with the intervention of God. In addition to this notion, if some one can perform *karamah*, this will not affect the status of a person's sainthood in the eyes of God. In other words, they do not necessarily achieve a higher status in the eyes of God than others who are unable to perform miracles. Some *wali* bestowed with this gift by God still feel cautious and ask God for refuge because this ability may make them subject to slander.

Most Sufi agree that instead of seeking *karamah,* people should make efforts to achieve steadfastness to improve their worship (A., *istiqāmat*). It is commonly accepted in the Sufi tradition that *istiqāmat* is better than a thousand *karamah.* According to al-Suhrawardi, for instance, seekers should accept this notion because many worshippers might be inclined to seek *karamah* because they have heard of the miracles performed by their predecessors as described in many hagiographical books. Sometimes, because they are unable to achieve *karamah,* they lose hope and begin to question the validity of their deeds. Al-Suhrawardi, therefore, argues that *istiqāmat* is very important in order to guide seekers to achieve the most essential objective of their worship and belief in God. In order to enhance the belief, God sometimes bestows miracles on His saints. However, al-Suhrawardi pointed out that it is probably because of their steadfastness, God unveils secrets and gives strong faith to seekers and saints, which can lead them to avoid passion (*nafs*) rather than giving them *karamah.* Miracles are therefore no longer needed because these saints have achieved the ultimate objective of their mystical path (Taymiyyah 1999:44-45).

3.2.1. The Concepts of Sainthood (*Wali*) and Miracle (*Karamah*) As Understood by *Majlis Dhikr* Groups

It is no exaggeration to say that the concepts of sainthood and miracles are an entry point to understand the practices of *Majlis Dhikr* groups in Indonesia. Like other Sufi groups, Indonesian *Majlis Dhikr* groups regard the concepts of sainthood and miracles as significant themes in their religious practice and belief. These two concepts have important meaning particularly in establishing the ritual and the teachings of these groups. Therefore, in order to understand *Majlis Dhikr* in Indonesia, people need to understand how these two concepts are understood by these *Majlis Dhikr* groups.

As argued by *Gus* Latif, a leader of *Majlis Dhikr* group *Iḥsāniyyat* in Kediri, East Java, believing in the existence of saints (*auliyā'*) is compulsory for Muslims, since God and his Prophet spoke about these saints and their miracles in the Qur'an and in hadith. For Indonesian *Majlis Dhikr, wali* are generally understood to be those who are loved by God and are entrusted to be His representatives on this world.[8] Abdul Latif Madjid, a leader of *Wāhidiyat*, pointed out that a *wali* is a person whose role is to improve the condition of this world. The heart of a *wali* is always connected to God. As a result, a *wali* is not only able to spread the light of God (A., *nūr Allah*) over the world but also to help others to approach God.[9]

Kyai Misbah, an older brother of *Gus* Latif from *Pesantren* Jampes, pointed out that *wali* can be divided into two categories. The first category is *wali* who are consistently devoted to God without the slightest indication of disobedience. The second category are *wali* who are protected by God. *Kyai* Misbah believed the former could be achieved by anyone through consistency of worship. In contrast, the latter cannot be sought because this status is given by God through His blessing. Such a person is sought by God to be His friend (A., *auliyā'*)[10] and is known as a *majdhūb*, a person who is drawn from the place of divine closeness up to God Himself, to the highest of God's realms. All such persons are chosen by God as *wali,* although they do not intend to become *wali.* With these categorizations, *Kyai* Misbah pointed out that saints are not limited to Muslim scholars; instead they may be chosen from farmers, traders and other ordinary Muslims, as long as they abide by Islamic laws. Consequently, people should not disparage other people because they do not know whether they are *wali* or not.[11]

Like other Sufi, Indonesian *Majlis Dhikr* groups agree that the consistency of worship (I., *istiqāmat*) is a primary requirement for *wali.* As a result, Muslims who do not undertake active worship (I., *ibadah*) and who commit sins cannot be considered as *wali.* In other words, as pointed out by *Kyai* Misbah, a major indicator of sainthood is the extent to which Muslims abide by Islamic Law. If they fail to follow the law, Muslims cannot be considered to be *wali*, even if they are able to perform miracles. *Kyai* Misbah told me that this is explained by most *'ulamā'*in order to prevent people from wrongly identifying *wali.* For him, the appearance of *khāriq al-'āda* (lit. violates habits) and the popularity of a person but without constant worship cannot be regarded as signs of sainthood. *Kyai* Misbah stressed this important aspect because many people misunderstand *wali.* They think a *wali* is a person bestowed with supernatural powers whose guests ask for blessing. In addition to constant *ibadah, Gus* Latif added that people cannot be considered as true *wali* until they die with a *ḥusn al- khātimat*(a good ending). In line with this, *Gus* Latif argued that unlike prophets, the status of saint can be removed by God, if they do not abide by *sharī'at.* He stated:

---

8 Interview with *Gus* Latif, Kediri, January, 2005.

9 Interview with Abdul Latif Madjid, Kediri, February, 2005.

10 This is reminiscent of the two distinct classes of *wali haqqullah* and *waliullah* mentioned previously.

11 Interview with *Kyai* Misbah, Kediri, January, 2005

> The status of prophets cannot be lost because they have received their status as prophet from the time they were born and God protects them from sins (*ma'shum*). In contrast, since God does not protect *wali* from sins, God can remove their status. This can be described with this analogy: if I love someone, but he or she does not respect me, I will not love him or her anymore. The same is true if God loves or chooses persons as His *wali* (friends), but they never respect Him, God will not love those saints.[12]

Indonesian *Majlis Dhikr* groups strongly believed in the hierarchy of saints. Zainuddin, one of the senior leaders in *Wāḥidiyat*, believes that the highest level in the hierarchy is called *wali qutb* or *ghauth hādza al-zamān*. Although he could not name the *qutb* of his time, Zainuddin believed that these *qutb* have existed in every age. When one died, another saint will succeed him. However, Zainuddin believed that by practising particular prayers, Muslims might be able to know the identity of the *ghauth* of the age, depending on the purity of their heart. Moreover, *qutb* are considered to have received perfection (I., *kesempurnaan*) and a mandate from God so that they can perfect other people. They are so close to God that they are able to help other people who want to approach God. Zainuddin explained to me how these *ghauth* could bring people closer to God:

> The closest person to God is a *qutb* or *ghauth*. They are so close to God that they 'know' where God exists. This closeness is obviously not in physical terms. As a result, they can help others to be near to God. Therefore, as explained by Jalaluddin al-Rumi, it might take two hundred years for people to approach God. However, if people approach these *qutb* who are able to approach God, they may take only two days.[13]

Zainuddin argued that in order to help people to approach God, these *qutb* should not meet people directly. Despite never meeting, these *qutb* are believed to be capable of bringing people to approach God and to know God (*ma'rifa billah*). Zainuddin explained that if these *ghauth* live at the place of sunset and people live at the place of sunrise, the *ghauth* are still able to teach people how to approach God.

Zainuddin, and his *Majlis Dhikr* members generally believe that if those *ghauth* have disciples, they must be able to give their spiritual light (A., *nadrat,* I., *pancaran batin*) to their disciples (I., *murid*) without meeting them. However, in

12 Interview with *Gus* Latif, Kediri, January, 2005

13 Interview with Zainuddin, Kediri, November, 2004.

order to receive this *nadrat* (spiritual light), disciples should be ready to accept it, by reciting particular prayers taught by their master. Zainuddin described the process of spreading *nadrat* (spiritual light) as follows:

> Disciples are like those who turn on television, while *ghauth* is like a TV station. When the TV station broadcasts its programs, people can watch these programs if they turn on their television. If they sleep or turn off the TV, they will not be able to watch them.

The ability of the *ghauth* to give their *nadrat* is illustrated by the following story. Zainuddin told me that when he married his wife, Ima, he asked her to practise a specific ritual (I., *mujahadah*) for forty days, a precondition for any new member of the *Wāḥidiyat* group. However, his wife was unable to complete the forty days *mujahadah*. Later, she dreamed one night that Abdul Latif Madjid, a leader of *Wāḥidiyat*, visited her. In her dream, he asked Ima whether she had finished. She said that she had not yet finished the *mujahadah*. After this occurrence, Ima completed the forty days *mujahadah* because she was worried that Abdul Latif would ask again her about it. Zainuddin maintained that this event is evidence that Abdul Latif Madjid, who is believed by *Wāḥidiyat* member to be a *ghauth*, is able to give his *nadrat* to his chosen disciples. As well as helping people to achieve the Gnosis of God (*ma'rifat billah*), *ghauth* are believed, especially among *Wāḥidiyat* members, not only to be capable of attracting, lifting and strengthening people's belief but also of withdrawing and weakening people' belief.[14]

Furthermore, the *Majlis Dhikr* groups believe saints, even if they have died, are capable of providing intercession (A., *shafā'at*) to living Muslims. *Gus* Latif told me that this is possible because their task is to help prophets, so they can give their intercession to other people. It is even thought that in their tombs, saints can hear people praying because they are still alive. They have only moved from this world to another and are still alive in the other world. The evidence for this belief, as *Gus* Latif argued, is taken from the practice of the Prophet Muhammad. When he passed Muslim tombs, Muhammad always prayed and greeted those buried in the tombs. This proved that the dead persons could hear the voice of living persons.

When asked whether saints know that they are saints, *Majlis Dhikr* members have different views. Kyai Mughni believes that saints do not know that God has chosen them as His saints.[15] They do not realize that they themselves are saints. *Kyai* Mughni's counterpart, *Kyai* Misbah, believes a notion prevalent

14 Interview with Zainuddin, Kediri, September, 2004.
15 Interview with *Kyai* Mughni, Kediri, February, 2005.

in Sufi tradition that since sainthood is a secret matter, no one knows saints, including the saints themselves, except other saints of the same status. He quoted the familiar phrase: *lā ya'rifu al-walī illa al-walī*(No one knows a saint except another saint). This is a strong belief in the *pesantren* tradition. Kyai Misbah made the following analogy:

> No one knows *wali* except another *wali*. It is fair that students should be tested with students and car mechanics should be tested with other car mechanics.[16]

As a result of this, *Kyai* Misbah maintained that true *wali* never disclose their sainthood to anyone else. If they expose their sainthood, they can be considered as the extremely stupid. Since sainthood is the trusteeship from God, it should be kept secret and not told to anyone else.

In contrast, although he quoted the same phrase as *Kyai* Misbah cited, Zainuddin interpreted it differently. He argued that no one knows a saint except the saint himself or herself. Zainuddin based his view on the fact that some Muslim saints such as Shaikh 'Abd al-Qādir al-Jaylānī and Ibn 'Arābī knew that they were saints. According to him, some saints were even given the right to reveal their sainthood, some should conceal their sainthood, while others can choose either to expose or conceal their sainthood. Despite this, Hasyim Asy'ari, a founder of Nahdlatul Ulama, strongly condemned those who proclaimed themselves to be *wali* as happened in many Sufi orders. He maintained:

> One of the temptations which could ruin Muslims in general is self-announcement of *murshid*(I., *guru tarekat*) and self-announcement of saints of God, even *wali qutb* or *imam mahdi.* When people proclaim themselves as *wali,* but never abide by the Prophet's laws (*shariah*), they are liars. Those who proclaim sainthood are not real saints, they are only fake saints (J., *wali-walian*) because they reveal a specific secret (*sirr al-khusūsiyyat*) (Qomar 2002:49)

The discussion of sainthood among *Majlis Dhikr* members is inseparable from the discussion of *karamah.* Members of *Majlis Dhikr* are concerned with *karamah* because this term has often been linked with other terms such as *ilmu karamah, ilmu hikmah, kadigdayan karamah,* and *karamah sejati,* which have been used and advertised widely in particular Indonesian media. Responding to this issue, *Gus* Latif explained to me that there are two kinds of *karamah.* The first *karamah* is natural and is possessed by devout Muslims because of their intense devotion to God. This *karamah* happens merely because of God's

16 Interviw with *Kyai* Misbah, Kediri, January, 2005.

blessing and cannot be sought by Muslims. The second type of *karamah* is sought (I., *yang dicari*). For example, when devout Muslims practise and recite particular prayers and are then able to perform miracles (I., *ilmu putih*), this can be categorized as the second type of *karamah.* In contrast, if these miracles are performed by bad people (I., *orang yang durhaka*), this kind of miracle can be categorized as black magic (I., *ilmu hitam* or *ilmu musyrik*). Therefore, *Gus* Latif concluded that if those *karamah* discussed by the Indonesian media are sought and practised by good Muslims, then they can be categorized as *ilmu putih.*[17]

Based on this categorization, *Gus* Latif agreed with the general view of Muslim Sufi and theologians and argued that miracles (*karamah*) are not a prerequisite of sainthood. Unlike prophets equipped with *mu'jiza* to spread Islam (A., *tablīgh*) and to challenge unbelievers, saints do not have this task, so they do not need miracles (I., *karamah*). In other words, saints should not use *karamah* as a testament to their sainthood, while prophets should have *mu'jiza* as a testament to their prophethood. *Gus* Latif argued that many Muslim saints who cannot perform miracles still frequently achieve the highest level of sainthood. *Kyai* Misbah, senior teacher in Jampes and *Gus* Latif's older brother, pointed out that *karamah* is not the main objective of people's worship of God. *Kyai* Misbah gave an example of a person who was able to perform a miracle by changing rice into gold nuggets by touching it but he did not wish to have such miracle and prayed to God so that he would not have such miraclous ability. This indicates that performing miracles is not the main objective of the person. Like other Muslim scholars, *Kyai* Misbah agreed that since the consistency of worshipping (*istiqāmat*) is more important than *karamah,* people should seek *istiqāmat* instead of *karamah.*

It is clear that in regard to the concepts of sainthood and *karamah,* Indonesian *Majlis Dhikr* groups base their views on the interpretation of the Qur'an and hadith and the notions of Muslim Sufi and other theologians. Therefore in term of these important concepts, Indonesian *Majlis Dhikr* groups cannot be regarded as violating the teaching of *tasawuf.*

3.3. The Concept of *Tawassul*

Seeking mediation (A., I., *tawassul*) has become a significant practice in the rituals conducted by Indonesian *Majlis Dhikr* groups as well as within Indonesian *tarekat* in general. It is not an exaggeration to say that without

17 Interview with *Gus* Latif, Kediri, January, 2005.

understanding this concept, people might not be able to understand the essence of the rituals conducted by Indonesian *Majlis Dhikr* groups. As observed by Millie (2006:98-108) in West Java, *tawassul* is a constituent part of many of these groups' religious observances such as *manakiban,* the ritual reading of the signs of Allah's favour (A., *karamat*) upon 'Abd Qādir al-Jailānī, supplicating at graves (I., *ziarah*) and in some cases, religious study groups (I., *pengajian*). This concept has become a theological issue that has attracted hostile debates between proponents and opponents for centuries. Those who are opposed to the concept of *tawassul* vigorously attack and accuse the supporters of *tawassul* of practising *bid'ah* (innovation within Islam) and even, polytheism (A., *shirk*). In this section, I will explore how the concept of *tawassul* has been discussed and understood by its opponents and proponents. The understanding of *tawassul* among Indonesian *Majlis Dhikr* groups will also be discussed in order to reveal their intellectual and theological response to this concept.

The word *wasīlat* is mentioned twice in the Qur'an in chapter 5 verse 35 and chapter 17 verse 57 (al-Hilali 1996:124 & 320), and can be translated as 'a means that can be used to gain nearness to God.' Following this general meaning, *tawassul* or *tawassulan* means the use of *wasīlat* to obtain nearness to God. In fact, most Muslim theologians agree that a means (A., *wasīlat*) is needed in order to approach God. Nevertheless, when they come to the question of what kind of means can be sought, Muslim theologians cannot reach consensus. While the majority have agreed that in order to approach and invoke God, people are allowed to seek a means (*tawassul*) through their good deeds, including their prayers, fasting, and reciting of the Qur'an in hope of securing divine assistance, there is no consensus on *wasīlat* sought in other ways such as through the person of the Prophet himself, his dignity, or other pious Muslims (saints). More specifically, the debate on this matter revolves around the question of whether or not it is permissible to make the Prophet, after his death, the means of supplication with such phrases as *allāhumma innī asaluka bi-nabiyyika* (O Allah! I beseech You through Your Prophet), or *bi-jāhi nabiyyika* (By the dignity of Your Prophet), or even *bi-Haqqi nabiyyika* (For the sake of Your Prophet), and whether or not it is permissible to call on deceased pious Muslims or Muslim saints, other than Prophet, as the means of supplication.

Some Muslim theologians have denied the permissibility of seeking a means through the person of the Prophet himself after his death. Taqiyyu al-Din Ahmad Ibn Taymiyyah (1263-1328), his students, Ibn Qayyim al-Jauziyah (1292-1350), and the Salafi group, for example, regard this as *shirk* because no dead can be asked to invoke God. The case would be different if the Prophet were still alive. For Ibn Taymiyyah, to request the Prophet's prayer during his lifetime and seek a means (*tawassul*) through his prayer was a sign of good virtue and strongly recommended (Taymiyyah n.d-b:201-202). In this sense, Ibn Taymiyyah defines *tawassul* as seeking the Prophet's prayer during his lifetime and his intercession (A., *shafā'at*) in the hereafter as well as seeking a means through pious Muslims' prayer during their lifetime. Ibn Taymiyyah believed that this would not lead people to polytheistic behaviour because they would not worship the Prophet during his lifetime and he would forbid people from worshipping him. However, Ibn Taymiyyah worried that appealing to the Prophet, as a *wasīlat*to supplicate God after his death would lead people to make the Prophet the associate of God as well as the object of worship as Christians do when they worship Jesus Christ (Taymiyyah 1987:220-21). Ibn Taymiyyah was convinced that after the death of the Prophet, his Companions no longer sought a means to God through his person. To support his opinion, Ibn Taymiyyah presented the Prophetic hadith which said that 'Umar ibn Khaṭṭāb used to seek *tawassul* through the Prophet, but when the Prophet died, 'Umar ibn Khaṭṭāb sought *tawassul* through the prayers of 'Abbās.[18] Ibn Taymiyyah used this as evidence that *tawassul* can only be sought through the prayers of living persons, not through the prayers of deceased persons. If seeking *tawassul* through the person or the position of the Prophet was allowed, Ibn Taymiyyah argued, why did 'Umar seek *tawassul* through the Prophet's uncle, not directly through the Prophet whose status was higher than his uncle. (Taymiyyah n.d-b:201).

However, Ibn Taymiyyah still allowed people to supplicate God by mentioning the names of the Prophets, pious Muslims or saints whose dignity is high before God, providing that the petitioners emulate their pious deeds and follow instructions that are sanctioned by God. In this sense, Ibn Taymiyyah did not specifically require that those mentioned in supplication be living persons or dead persons. He pointed out that people are allowed to supplicate God by saying,' O Allah! I beseech You by Your Prophet, by the dignity of Your Prophet and by your saints.' However, Ibn Taymiyyah argued that God did not grant the supplication because of the position of these pious Muslims. Instead, mentioning the dignity of those people was only meaningful if the supplicants complied with their teaching, which derives from God (Taymiyyah 1987:79-80).

The same argument was put forward by the prominent Salafi scholar, Muḥammad Nāṣir al-Dīn al-Albānī (d.1999), [19] who strongly opposed seeking

18 Annas narrated: Whenever drought threatened them, Umar ibn al-Khaṭṭāb used to ask Allah for rain through the mediation of al-Abbas ibn Abd al-Muttalib. He [Umar] used to say: "O Allah! We used to ask you through the means of our Prophet and You would bless us with rain, and now we ask You through the means of our Prophet's uncle, so bless us with rain." And it would rain.

19 In addition to 'Abd al-'Azīz 'Abd Allāh bin Bāz (d. 1999), Muḥammad Nāṣir al-Dīn al-Albānī (d. 1999) was an influential Salafi scholar whose *fatwa* (legal advice) has been referred by the contemporary Wahhabi authorities and the Salafi group. For his autobiography and his works and legal opinion (A., *fatwa*), refer to his website, http://www.alalbany.net/albany_serah.php, viewed 25 December , 10:54 am.

a means through the person and status of the Prophet. Like Ibn Taymiyyah, al-Albānī defines *tawassul* as seeking a means through the prayers of living persons by requesting them to pray. Therefore, seeking a means through the Prophet after his death is not proper. For al-Albānī, the Prophet can no longer hear and answer his followers who request him to petition God because he has moved to a place whose situation is not the same as in this world (Al-Albani 1975:52-3). Although some hadith indicate that all the prophets of God are still alive in their graves and perform prayers, their place, according to al-Albāni, has particular laws and forms which do not follow the laws in this world and are known only by God. Therefore, al-Albāni claimed that the life of Prophet Muhammad before he died and after he died is different (Al-Albani 1975:60-1). Like his predecessors, al-Albāni used the Prophetic tradition to support his argument. Based on this, he argued that *wainnā natawassalu ilaika bi ammi nabiyyika* (Now we ask you through the means of the Prophet's uncle) a phrase in the hadith, must not be translated as seeking a means through the person or the status of the Prophet's uncle. Instead, the word should be added to make the last part of the phrase read: *bi (du'āi) ammi nabiyyika,* which means through the prayers of Prophet's uncle.

Al-Albāni also used the following Prophetic hadith to reject the permissibility of seeking *tawassul* through the person and status of the Prophet:

> A blind man came to the Prophet and said: "Invoke Allah for me that God help me." The Prophet replied: "If you wish I will delay this, which would be better for you, and if you wish I will then invoke Allah the Exalted (for you)." The blind man said: "Then invoke God." The Prophet said to him: *idhhab fa tawadda', wa salli rak̬atayn thumma qul* -- "Go and make an ablution, pray two rak̬at, then say: "O Allah, I am asking you (*as'aluka*) and turning to you (*atawajjahu ilayka*) with your Prophet Muhammad (*bi nabiyyika Muhammad*), the Prophet of mercy; O Muhammad (*ya Muhammad*), I am turning with you to my Lord regarding my present need, I am asking my Lord with your intercession concerning the return of my sight (*inni atawajjahu bika ila rabbi fī hajati hadhih.* Another version has: *inni astashfi̬u bika̧ alārabbi fī raddi basarī*) so that He will fulfil my need; O Allah, allow him to intercede (with you) for me (*allahumma shaffi̬hu fiyya*)" (narrated by Turmudhī and Ibn Mājah).

For al-Albāni, this hadith can not be regarded as a basis for allowing supplicants to seek a means through the person of the Prophet, even though this hadith contains the term *binabiyyika Muhammad* (with Your Prophet, Muhammad). This phrase, al-Albani argued, should be read and interpreted as the prayers of the Prophet (*bidu'āinabiyyika Muhammad*) for several reasons. First, the blind man came to the Prophet to request his prayer to God on his behalf because he knew that the Prophet's supplication was much more powerful than others. If the blind man had intended to seek a means through the person or the status of Prophet, he would not have come to meet the Prophet; and it would have been better for him to stay at home. Secondly, when the Prophet gave options, the blind man chose to ask for the Prophet's prayer, as we can be read in the text of the hadith. Thirdly, the blind man again asked the Prophet to supplicate God for him. Fourthly, this hadith is commonly included by hadith scholars in a particular chapter on the miracles of the Prophet and his granting of prayers. Because of the Prophet's prayer to God, the blind man could see again. Therefore, al-Albāni claimed that the blind man could not have recovered because of his supplication alone without Prophet's prayer. If prayers alone were enough, other blind persons would use a similar prayer and be healed. However, the secret of the blind man's recovery was the Prophet's supplication (Al-Albani 1975:69-75).

Like his predecessors, Hartono Ahmad Jaiz, the proponent of the Salafi movement in Indonesia, argues that *tawassul* using the person of the Prophet is unlawful. Therefore, he condemns those who supplicate God by saying, 'O my Lord! with the Elect One (Muhammad) make us attain our goals, and forgive us for what has passed (*Ya rabbi bi al-mustafā balligh maqāṣidana, wa ighfir lanā mā maḍā yā wāṣi'a al-karami*). According to him, adding the phrase 'with the Elect one' (*bi al- muṣtafā*) can be regarded as taking an oath (I., *bersumpah*). Jaiz maintains that invoking created beings, such as angels, prophets and apostles, or places in making an oath while supplicating God is not permitted and can be considered as practising polytheism (A., *shirk*). Only the name of God should be used in taking oaths (Jaiz 1999:158).

By contrast, other Muslim scholars have supported the practice of seeking *tawassul* not only through the person of the Prophet but also by means of his dignity and the dignity of pious Muslims even if they have died. Ja'far Subhani, a Muslim scholar, for instance, wrote a whole book which focuses on defending *tawassul* practices from legal attacks conducted by Ibn Taymiyyah and Wahhabi groups. In this book, Subhani states unequivocally that seeking *wasilah* through the person of the Prophet and his dignity is lawful. Like the opponents of this kind of *tawassul,* Subhani used the hadith about the blind man to support his argument. He points out that the phrase in the hadith, 'with your Prophet Muhammad' (*bi nabiyyika Muhammad*) should be interpreted as meaning that the blind man sought a means through the Prophet, not through his prayer. To convince his readers of this, Subhani referred to another phrase in the hadith, 'I am turning with you to my Lord' (*Ya Muhammad innī tawajjahu bika ilā rabbī*). He argued that 'turning with you' can be used as evidence that the blind man used the person of the Prophet as a means of his *tawassul*(Subhani 1989).

The proponents of the notion that one can use the person of the Prophet as a means state unequivocally that although the Prophet has died, people are allowed to seek a means through his dignity and prayer to supplicate God. To support their argument, they present some examples of *tawassul* using the person of the Prophet that were conducted by the Prophet's Companions after his death. Al-Maliki (1946-2004),[20] an hadith scholar who lived in Mecca, for instance, cited hadith narrated by prominent Companions of the Prophet. One of the traditions cited states that when a person had difficulty seeing Uthmān ibn 'Affān, the fourth Caliph, a Prophetic Companion called Uthmān ibn Ḥunaif taught this person a prayer similar to the one taught by the Prophet to the blind man. The prayer is as follows (Al-Maliki 1993:70-1):

> O Allah, I am asking you and turning to you with your Prophet Muhammad, the Prophet of mercy; O Muhammad, I am turning with you to your God so fulfil my need...

After reciting the prayer, the person was able to meet the Caliph to convey his need. For al-Maliki this tradition suggested that people should still seek a means to supplicate God through the Prophet, even though he had died.

Another Prophetic Companion's tradition cited by al-Maliki is as follows:

> It is narrated by Mālik al-Dar, Umar's treasurer, that the people suffered a drought during the successorship of Umar, whereupon a man came to the grave of the Prophet and said: 'O Messenger of Allah, ask for rain for your Community, for verily they have almost perished.' After this the Prophet appeared to him in a dream and told him: 'Go to Umar and give him my greeting, then tell him that they will be watered. Tell him: You must be clever, you must be clever!' The man went and told Umar, who said: 'O my Lord, I will spare no effort except what is beyond my power!'

Al-Maliki was convinced that the transmitter of this tradition was regarded as sound by Ibn Ḥajr al-Asqalānī, a prominent hadith scholar whose reputation in this field is outstanding. Furthermore, al-Maliki gave more evidence from an hadith as follows (Al-Maliki 1993:76-7):

---

20 His full name is Sayyid Prof. Dr. Muḥammad ibn Sayyid 'Alāwī ibn Sayyid 'Abbās ibn Sayyid 'Abd al-'Azīz al-Mālikī al-Ḥasanī al-Makkī. He was born in Mecca in 1365/1946. He finished his PhD at the Al-Azhar University, Cairo. He taught in the King Abdul Aziz University and The University of Ummul Qura, Mecca. He resigned after several years teaching in these universities. He then opened class in his own house and established an Islamic boarding school. He provided free education for his students. He also received students from many *pesantren* in Indonesia, most of which were affiliated with NU. He was regarded as the important figure by *kyai* and *ulama* NU in Indonesia because he was not proponent of Wahabism.

> No sooner does one greet me than Allah sends back my soul so that I could return their greeting. (Narrated by Abu Hurarirah).

> My life is an immense good for you: you bring up new matters, and new matters are brought up for you. My death, also, is an immense good for you: your actions will be shown to me; if I see goodness I shall praise God and if I see evil I shall ask forgiveness of Him for you.

Al-Maliki regarded these two hadith and the companion tradition as evidence that seeking *tawassul* through the Prophet after his death is legal. Al-Maliki believed that the Prophet is not only alive in his grave but also is able to pray to God for the benefit of his followers and can reply to their greeting. To convince his readers about the life of the Prophet after his death, Al-Maliki cited the verse of the Qur'an relating to the life of martyrs' souls after their death. If people do not believe the Qur'anic verses about the life of the martyrs' soul, they must distrust the Qur'an. If they do believe in the life of the martyrs' souls, Al-Maliki said, why do they not believe that the Prophet and his Companions, whose status is much more higher than martyrs, are still alive (Al-Maliki 1993:117-8).

However, the vast majority of Muslim scholars warn people at the outset of their works not to believe that the Prophet himself can give benefit to, or harm others, in the same way as God while practising *tawassul*. Al-Maliki for example pointed out that to regard the Prophet as capable of this can be considered polytheism (Al-Maliki 1993:59). *Kyai* Hasyim Asy'ari (1871-1947), a leading Indonesian Muslim scholar and the founder of Nahdlatul Ulama, stated unequivocally that *tawassul* or *wasīlat* is just one of the ways to invoke God. *Tawassul* or *wasīlat* is mediation to approach God, and its ultimate purpose is to invoke God Himself rather than to invoke the object of *tawassul*(Asy'ari 2005:140). Similarly, Alā al-Dīn 'Alī ibn Dāwud al-'Aṭṭār (d.1324), a prominent Shafi'ite hadith scholar, pointed out that asking for God's help through the mediation and assistance of the Prophet is fine as long as people are careful not to ask the Prophet himself to resolve the problem because only God has the authority and power to do this (Taylor 1998:213). Even the supporters of *tawassul* state that people should not believe that the Prophet, with his own power and strength, can change the predestination of God (I., *takdir*)(Abu al-'Azayim 1981:24). Therefore, the proponents of this kind of *tawassul* warn that to prevent people from invoking a deceased person directly, laypeople should be guided by an expert to practise *tawassul* in a proper way.

From debates about *tawassul*, I can conclude that both sides base their ideas about the practice of *tawassul* in the Qur'an. To support their arguments, both sides also used similar hadith. However, they interpret the text of these hadith differently and, as a result, the conclusions derived from the text differ. In these debates the proponents of *tawassul* through the person and the dignity of the Prophet also cite particular hadith which they regarded as sound, while the opponents of such *tawassul* regarded these same hadith as weak.

3.3.1. Understanding the Concept of *Tawassul* Among *Majlis Dhikr* Groups

Indonesian *Majlis Dhikr* groups are familiar with the concept of *tawassul* discussed by those Muslim scholars. For example, *Kyai* Zainuddin, one of the leaders in the *Wāḥidiyat* group, gives a similar definition of *tawassul* to the one pointed out by other Muslim theologians. He is also well aware of the different interpretations of *tawassul* or *wasīlat*and the argument about whether this should be practised only through living persons and pious acts or also through deceased persons. Zainuddin is the proponent of the latter notion. For him *tawassul* is a means to approach God either using pious acts (I., *amal saleh*), the person of the Prophet, or other pious Muslims.

In the discussion with me in his office about this topic, Zainuddin criticized those who have rejected *tawassul* through the dead. On this matter, he cited the Prophetic hadith relating to Adam who asked God for forgiveness by seeking a means through the Prophet Muhammad long before he was born.[21] Zainuddin asked why people rejected the permissibility to seek a means through the Prophet after his death, while the Prophet Adam himself performed *tawassul* through the Prophet Muhammad, even though the Prophet Muhammad did not yet exist. Zainuddin maintained that Adam sought his *tawassul* through Muhammad's spirit (I., *ruh*) not through his body. He thus stated unequivocally that this implied that the spirit of the Prophet Muhammad was alive both before his birth and after his death. Therefore, Zainuddin argued, following the practice of Adam, *tawassul* can be performed through the spirit of the Prophet after his death, even though his body no longer exists.

Zainuddin also criticized those who have confined *tawassul* to pious acts and have rejected *tawassul* through the person of the Prophet and his dignity. In his

---

21 The Prophet said on the authority of ʿUmar: 'When Adam committed his mistake he said: O! my Lord, I am asking you to forgive me for the sake of Muhammad. Allah said: O! Adam, and how do you know about Muhammad whom I have not yet created? Adam replied, O! my Lord, after You created me with your hand and breathed into me of Your Spirit, I raised my head and saw written on the heights of the Throne: *La Ilaha illa Allah Muhammad al-Rasulullah* I understood that You would not place next to Your Name but the Most Beloved One of Your creation. Allah said: O! Adam, I have forgiven you, and were it not for Muhammad I would not have created you.'

view, people seek *wasīlat* through the person of the Prophet because of their love of him. Since, love (A., *mahabbat*) of the Prophet is a pious act, Zainuddin argued that seeking *wasīlat*through the person of the Prophet is similar to performing *tawassul* through a pious deed (I.,*amal saleh*).

Zainuddin strongly supported such *tawassul* because this is the main practice of his *Majlis Dhikr* group. *Tawassul* practised by this group, he noted, is to ask the intercession (A, *shafā'at*) of the Prophet Muhammad either in this world or in the hereafter, and to ask him to supplicate God on behalf of the supplicant. This practice of *tawassul* is performed in the group by reciting the following phrase: '*Yā Sayyidī yā Rasulallāh'* (Oh My Lord and Prophet of God). For Zainuddin, the purpose of this exclamation is to seek the intercession of the Prophet because he is the person created by God as the place to call on (I., *mengadu*). Zainuddin described the process of *tawassul* as follows:

> According to an hadith, the Prophet said: 'God has chosen a servant to become a place to call on, and the Prophet is the perfect person to be called on. He said that,'I will give my intercession to my *umat* who always call me.' Calling the Prophet does not mean that we worship him and the supplication is not being made to the Prophet whose name is invoked, but to Allah. Just as when people come to a *kyai* asking him to supplicate God on their behalf. In this case, we do not consider the *kyai* whom we asking to be God.[22]

According to Zainuddin, practising such *tawassul* cannot be considered as superstition or polytheism because it is strongly recommended in the Qur'an. Zainuddin pointed out that people can only be accused of polytheism if they believe in the existence of another God. Zainuddin believed that as long as people practice *tawassul* under this framework: seeking the help of Allah through the Prophet without regarding him as God, they cannot be regarded as polytheist. Zainuddin believed that seeking a means through the Prophet or pious Muslims will make it more likely that supplicant's prayer will be speedily answered by God. *Gus* Farih, a leader of *Dhikr al-Ghāfilīn* group, supported this view. He argued as follows:

> What is meant by *wasilah* here is that we believe that only God will help us and so we ask only Him for help. If we do not have such a conviction, our *tawassul* can be considered as idolatry (*shirk*). Therefore, if people say that asking Allah through dead persons is regarded as *shirk,* I would say that asking living persons can be considered as *shirk* too if we believe that these persons have the power to help. For example, when we ask a doctor to cure our sickness and we believe that the doctor, not God, can heal the sickness,

22 Interview with Zainuddin, Kediri, November, 2004.

> this conduct can be considered as *shirk* too. Therefore, in *tawassul* we never regard people we use as a means in *tawassul* or as agents who can give help or assistance.

Asked why people still need a means to approach God if He is closer to people than their jugular vein, Zainuddin told me that although God is the Most powerful, He still relies on Angels and the Prophet to deliver His teachings.[23] However, Zainuddin was reluctant to give this answer to support his notion of the permissibility of *wasīlat* through the Prophet because this argument opens endless debate (I., *debat kusir*). Therefore, Zanuddin believed that if Islamic law (*sharī'at*) acknowledges such *tawassul* practice, Muslims should accept and practise it, even though there are some different opinions on this matter.

Similarly, *Gus* Latif, one of the leaders of *Majlis Dhikr* in Kediri, also supported the practice of *tawassul* through the person of the Prophet and other pious Muslims after their death. He cited previous hadith that support the permissibility of such *tawassul*. He also pointed out that *tawassul* is needed in the supplication to God since this means that one's prayer to God will be more easily granted than if no intermediaries are used. For him, this practice is important because those persons whose names are mentioned in *tawassul* posses high status, dignity, and respect in Allah's eyes. By mentioning their names in the supplication, God will therefore give much more attention to one's prayer. *Gus* Latif also said that since the Prophet, his Companions, Muslim saints (A., *auliyā'*) and other pious Muslims are the most beloved persons of God, if people love these persons by mentioning their names in their prayer, in return God will love those supplicants. In this sense, *tawassul* is closely related to the concept of *barakah* (blessing), since *Gus* Latif believed that these pious persons are able to spread *barakah* because they are the most beloved persons of God. This is similar to the notion put forward by *Kyai* Hasyim Asy'ari who interpreted the Prophetic tradition as follows, 'People who love someone will be gathered [in the hereafter] with someone they love.' For *Kyai* Hasyim Asy'ari, this hadith can also mean that people whose pious acts are relatively few who love someone whose pious acts are perfect will be gathered [in the hereafter] with the that person (Asy'ari 2005:27).

Although most leaders of *Majlis dhikr* groups are familiar with the concept of *tawassul* as described by Muslim theologians, some of their practices of *tawassul* are different from those of the theologians. During my attendance at the *dhikr* rituals held by these groups, I never heard the *tawassul* phrase such as *Allāhumma innī atawassalu bijāhi nabiyyika an taqḍī ḥājātī* (God, verily I seek a means by the dignity of your messenger, fulfill my needs) used when those

---

23 In this context, Zainuddin said that God relies on Angels and the Prophet to deliver His teachings.

Majlis Dhikr groups performed *tawassul.* I only found one passage in the last part of a prayer in the *Ṣalāwat Wāḥidiyat* group that could be categorized as a *tawassul.* This passage was:

بِسْمِ اللهِ الرَّحْمٰنِ الرَّحِيْمِ. (اَللّٰهُمَّ بِحَقِّ اِسْمِكَ الْاَعْظَمِ وَبِجَاهِ سَيِّدِنَا مُحَمَّدٍ صَلَّى اللهُ عَلَيْهِ وَسَلَّمَ وَبِبَرَكَةِ
غَوْثِ هٰذَا الزَّمَانِ وَاَعْوَانِهِ وَسَائِرِ اَوْلِيَائِكَ يَا اَللهُ يَا اَللهُ يَا اَللهُ رَضِيَ اللهُ تَعَالٰى عَنْهُمْ ×٣)(بَلِّغْ جَمِيْعَ
الْعَالَمِيْنَ نِدَاءَنَا هٰذَا وَاجْعَلْ فِيْهِ تَأْثِيْرًا بَلِيْغًا ×٣)(فَاِنَّكَ عَلٰى كُلِّ شَيْءٍ قَدِيْرٌ وَبِالْاِجَابَةِ جَدِيْرٌ ×٣)

In the Name of Allah the Beneficient and the Merciful. O Allah! For the sake of Your greatest name and with the dignity of Muhammad peace and blessings be upon him and with the blessings of ghauthi hādha al-zamān and his helpers and the rest of your saints OAllah! O Allah! O Allah! May Allah be pleased with them, may God deliver our call to the whole of universe and may God make deep impression on it. Verily, You are able to all things. And verily You are the Most deserved one to grant a request.

The phrase categorized as tawassul in the passage is: 'For the sake of Your greatest name and with the dignity of Muhammad' and the word 'with the blessings of ghauthi hādha al-zamān and his helpers and the rest of your saints .' Instead of using a tawassul phrase, other groups performed tawassul by reciting the names of people followed by the recitation of al-Fātiḥat (the first chapter of Qur'an), for the benefit of the parties named. For example, in the dhikr ritual that I attended in one Muslim graveyard complex, the leader of the group Majlis Dhikr al-Ghāfilīn recited the following:

> To the presence (*ilā ḥaḍrati*) of the Prophet Muhammad, peace and blessing be upon him, next to the presence of my lord Syaikh 'Abd al-Qādir al-Jailānī and Syaikh Abū Ḥāmid Muḥammad al-Ghazālī, and my lord al-Habīb 'Abd Allah ibn 'Alwi al-Haddād, may God be pleased with them: *al-Fātiḥat* .

After this, the gathering recited the first chapter of the Qur'an in unison. The leader of *Majlis Dhikr* then continued to mention other names followed by reciting *al-Fātiḥat.* However, Marzuki, a Muslim scholar in the State Islamic University in Malang, argued that reciting *al-Fātiḥat* for the benefit of deceased persons obviously could not be regarded as the practice of *wasīlat.* Instead, this practice can be categorized as paying respect to fellow Muslims and the most respected people, including the Prophets of God, Muslim saints, parents, teachers, and others. For him, according to Islam, respect for those people is not confined to their life but also continues after their death by sending them *al-Fātiḥat* for the benefit of the people named. Muslim theologians have widely discussed this practice within the context of giving presents to deceased persons by sending them *al-Fātiḥat*.[24]

It is clear that on the matter of *tawassul,* Indonesian *Majlis Dhikr* groups do not confine the concept of *tawassul* to living persons, their prayers and through pious acts. *Tawassul* can also be conducted through deceased persons who are considered to occupy a position of favour with, or close proximity to, God. It is for this reason that *Majlis Dhikr* groups conduct their rituals at Muslim tomb sites and other Muslim saints' graveyards whose occupants are considered to have close proximity to God.

3.4. Sending the Merit of Pious Deeds to Deceased Persons

This topic is related to matters discussed within Islamic jurisprudence (I., *fiqih*) especially regarding the question of whether deceased persons can obtain benefit from the deeds of others. This question generates other questions. For example, can the living give the merit of their good deeds, such as reciting the Qur'an, charity (A., *shadaqat*), sacrifice (I., *kurban*), performing pilgrimage to Mecca (*haji*) and fasting, to deceased persons, and are deceased persons able to receive the merit of such pious acts. Within Islamic jurisprudence, this topic is categorized as a disputed matter (A., *khilāfiyyat*), and has been the subject of debates among religious scholars. Therefore, not all Muslims jurists (A., *fuqahā*) agree on the permissibility of such practice.

This topic is important to discuss further in order to understand the ritual practice of *Majlis Dhikr* groups in Indonesia because most of their rituals are concerned with giving the merit of pious acts (I., *amal saleh*) to deceased persons. Therefore, this section will focus on how these groups elaborate and approach this topic with reference to previous debates involving Muslim jurists.

The majority of religious scholars have argued that dead persons cannot benefit from the merit of others' good deeds. They base their argument on the following verses from the Qur'an.

> That no burdened person (with sins) shall bear the burden (sins) of another (53:38).And the man can have nothing but what he does (53:39).

24 Interview with Ustadz Marzuki, Malang, November, 2004.

> On this Day (Day of resurrection), none will be wronged in anything, nor will you bte requited anything except that which you used to do (36:54).

> ...He or she gets reward for that (good) which he or she has earned, and he or she is punished for that (evil) which he has earned (2:286).

The meaning of these verses is that people cannot bear the burden of another and people can only be rewarded because of the good deeds they have carried out themselves. For the supporters of this argument, these verses indicate that God is just toward His servants because He never punishes people for something that they have not done, and He will only reward people for their own good deeds. In the light of those verses, Imam Shāfi'ī, as cited by Ibn Kathīr (d.774 CE), pointed out that the merit of reciting the Qur'an for the deceased cannot be received by them because it is not recited by those deceased themselves, but by others. Therefore, Imam Shāfi'ī argued, even though reciting the Qur'an is considered to be a religious virtue, sending its merit to deceased persons was never sanctioned by the Prophet and his Companions.[25]

How about the hadith of the Prophet that 'When a person dies all his deeds are cut off except three; an ongoing charity (I., *amal jariyah*), beneficial knowledge, and a righteous child who prays for him or her' (the deceased). Does this hadith acknowledge that deceased persons can benefit from prayers supplicated by others? In response to this, Ibn Kathīr argued that all of the three kinds of deeds mentioned in the hadith are actually a result of the deceased persons' own deeds when they were still alive, not a result of others' deeds. For example, the decision to establish an ongoing charity (I., *amal jariah*) such as a mosque or a school was actually made by the deceased persons before they died, so they are still able to receive the merit of their own deeds even though they have passed away.[26] Likewise, persons who write a book from which others can obtain benefit are able to keep receiving the merit of their own deeds although they have died. Similarly, parents who educate their children to be righteous are able to benefit from the prayers of their children. In short, these kinds of deeds are a result of the deceased persons' deeds when they are still alive. The hadith cited indicates that other than these kinds of deeds, deceased persons cannot benefit from the actions of others.

Another argument against the ability of a deceased person to benefit from the merit of others is based on a logical argument rather than the text of hadith or

25 Ibn Kathīr 2006, Tafsīr al-Qur'ān al-Karīm , Jordan : Aal al-Bayt Institute for Islamic Thought, viewed 14 July 2006, 10:45 am: http://www.altafsir.com/Tafasir.asp?tMadhNo=0&tTafsirNo=7&tSoraNo=10&tAyahNo=62&tDisplay=yes&UserProfile=0.

26 *Ibid.*

the Qur'an. It is argued that God's commands to His servants are part of an obligation that should be fulfilled by each person. This obligation cannot be transferred and fulfilled by others. For instance, God will not accept someone's prayer if it is performed by others. Similarly, God will not accept someone's repentance if it is performed by others. Those who support this argument draw the analogy of sick persons who cannot benefit from someone else taking a tablet on their behalf, or a thirsty person, whose thirst cannot be quenched if others drink on his behalf (al-Jauziyah 1999:211)

Moreover, it is argued that not all pious acts necessarily generate merit, and only God can determine their worth. In other words, merit depends on God's gift. If God wishes, He will give the merit to anyone whom He wishes, but if He does not wish, He will not give the merit to anyone. If this is the case, how can people force God to give the merit of their pious acts to someone else. In other words, people cannot deliver the merit of their pious acts to deceased persons because that merit is fully in the power of God (al-Jauziyah 1999).

Other Islamic scholars have divided pious acts into two categories: the first, whose merit cannot be received by deceased persons, and the second which can. Examples of the first type include prayer, reciting the Qur'an and fasting. The merit of such deeds can only be obtained by their practitioners and such merit cannot be delivered to others. The second category includes returning deposited goods to the owner, paying a debt, charity, and making a pilgrimage to Mecca. The merit of such good deeds can be delivered to deceased persons because such deeds can be performed by others on behalf of people who are not able to perform them in person.

In contrast, other Muslim scholars such as al-Maliki, have responded that deceased persons can obtain benefit from the merit of others' pious acts such as reciting the Qur'an, charity, fasting, and the *hajj*. He pointed out that the hadith cited above could not be used as an argument to decide which kinds of pious acts can deliver merit to deceased persons, and which cannot. Instead, al-Maliki agreed that it is true that deceased persons are cut off from performing certain actions that living persons do. He argued, however, that the text of hadith does not indicate that a deceased person is cut off from obtaining the merit of others' deeds. For him, a pious deed is owned by the person who carries it out. If he or she gives the merit of this deed to another, the recipient will obtain benefit from it. Thus within Islamic jurisprudence, for example, if people die and they are in debt to others, their heirs can settle the debt on behalf of the deceased persons (Al-Maliki n.d:15).

Similar to al-Maliki, al-Jauziyah, a student of Ibn Taymiyyah, strongly criticized those who rejected the possibility of deceased persons benefiting from others' deeds. He specifically countered the argument of those who said that since an obligation imposed by God is part of an individual's responsibility, people cannot fulfil others' obligation. For al- Jauziyah, this notion does not prevent God from allowing Muslims to give the merit of pious acts to other people because this is part of God's grace for His servants. This is why, although the pilgrimage to Mecca and fasting are categorized as obligations for individual Muslims, the Prophet allowed Muslims to fulfil these obligation on behalf of others who could not do so including deceased persons. In al- Jauziyah's opinion, transmitting the merit of deeds and giving benefit to those who are in need are religious virtues sanctioned by God. Therefore, he argued, transmitting the merit of pious deeds to deceased persons, who are cut off from doing such deeds and are thus most in need of others' help, is even more beloved by God (al-Jauziyah 1999:225-6). To prove his point, al-Jauziyah cited two hadith which report that the Prophet allowed a man to fast on behalf of a deceased person who had fasting to make up. Another hadith cited by al-Jauziyah is a reliable hadith in which some one is reported to have asked the Prophet about a month's fasting his mother had missed before she passed away. The man asked the Prophet whether he should make up the fasting that his mother missed. The Prophet asked the man, 'If your mother had a debt would you settle it for her?' The man said that he would. The Prophet then said to the man that the debt to Allah has a greater right to be fulfilled (al-Jauziyah 1999:205).

Moreover, to convince his readers that deceased persons can obtain benefit from living persons, al- Jauziyah quoted another hadith which reported that the Prophet assumed that the dead could hear the greetings of the living because when they were addressed the spirits of the dead were returned to their body (al-Jauziyah 1999:15-6). He pointed out that if the deceased cannot hear the living, why did the Prophet ask Muslims to greet them when they visited Muslim tombs. al-Jauziyah argued that if people want to visit tombs, they should come bearing a gift dedicated to the dead, such as a supplication for the dead, alms offered on their behalf, or a righteous act bringing one closer to God. All of these acts can increase the dead's happiness just as the living are pleased when a visitor arrives bearing a gift (Taylor 1998:189).

With regard to the division of pious deeds into those which can bestow merit on deceased persons and those which cannot, al-Jauziyah argued that this division finds no sanction in the Prophetic tradition. To prove this, he cited several hadith containing examples of pious acts which can be performed by people on behalf of others. In addition, he also quoted AbūHanīfah's opinion that Islamic law (A., *shari'at*) allows pious acts conducted by their doers to be delivered to others. AbūHanīfah argued that discouraging Muslims from giving the benefit and merit of their virtues to their parents and Muslim fellows in a time when they are in need could not be regarded as compatible with Islamic law (al-Jauziyah 1999:228).

It is interesting to note here that al-Jauziyah's view on the legitimacy of deceased persons benefiting from the merit of pious deeds performed by living persons is not popular among Indonesian Muslims reformists such as Muhammadiyah, PERSIS (*Persatuan Islam*) and the Salafi groups. However on issues other than the issue of sending the merit of pious deeds to the dead, these groups invariably rely heavily on the opinion of both Ibn Taymiyyah and his student, al-Jauziyah. Both scholars are often referred by these groups when they criticize religious practices conducted by the members of Nahdlatul Ulama and PERTI (*Persatuan Tarbiyah Islamiyah,* The Association for Muslim Education), and al-Washliyah[27] and accuse them of practising illegitimate innovation within Islam (A., *bid'ah*) and idolatry (A., *shirk*). In contrast, al-Jauziyah's view on this matter has been widely accepted by Indonesian Muslims groups such as Nahdlatul Ulama, al-Washliyah and PERTI.

3.4.1. The *Majlis Dhikr* Groups' Understanding of Sending the Merit of Pious Deeds to Deceased Persons

Most of the leaders of *Majlis Dhikr* well understand that Muslim jurists have different views on the possibility of deceased persons receiving merit from others' pious acts. Responding to this matter, *Kyai* Misbah cited the hadith and the verses used by those who reject this possibility. Like al-Maliki, *Kyai* Misbah based his interpretation of the texts of the hadith on common sense: deceased persons are no longer able to conduct any kind of deeds, whether pious or sinful, because they have passed away. Therefore, according to him, the content of the hadith describes deceased persons who are not able to do anything. However, the hadith implies that living persons are still able to send the merit of their pious acts to the deceased. Asked about the hadith stating that a righteous child (I., *anak saleh*) who prays for his or her deceased parents can bestow benefit on their parents, *Kyai* Misbah said that term 'righteous' was the main factor. As a result, only righteous children can assist their deceased parents with their prayers. In other words, if their children are not righteous, the parents cannot

27 This Minangkabau-based traditionalist association was established in 1930. After Independence PERTI transformed itself into a political party. But today this organization is no longer a political party.

obtain any benefit from their children's prayers. However, if others who do not have any familial relationship with the deceased are righteous and pray for the deceased, the latter can benefit from their prayers. Likewise, only charity accompanied with sincerity (I., *ikhlas*) can benefit its doer after they have died.[28]

Regarding the text of the verse, 'and the man can have nothing but what he does (53:39),' *Kyai* Misbah pointed out that this verse is right in the sense that deceased persons can only take their own deeds to the grave. However, for him, this verse does not prevent living persons from sending the merit of their good deeds to deceased persons. To illustrate this point, *Kyai* Misbah made the following analogy: although I had come to his house to interview him with only a pen and a notebook and have not brought a tape recorder, my brother could send me a tape recorder later.

Gus Farih, one of leaders of the *Dhikr al-Ghafilin* group, is also convinced that deceased persons can obtain benefit from prayers offered on their behalf. To prove his claim, *Gus* Farih also uses a method of reasoning by analogy (A., *qiyās*), quoting one of the Qur'an's verses in which Abraham asked God for forgiveness for his parents and other believers until the day of Judgment. For *Gus* Farih, this verse indicates that Abraham asked God's pardon not only for living believers during his time but also all believers after his time until the Day of Judgment, including all those who had died. He further argued that if the prayer of Abraham did not benefit deceased persons, God would not have revealed the verse. In addition, *Gus* Farid used another example to support his claim which he explained to me as follows:

> One day the chairman of Muhammadiyah Youth Association in Kediri (*Ikatan Pemuda Muhammadiyah*) asked me whether our prayer can be received by deceased persons. The chairman asked me again, 'If the prayer can be received by the deceased persons, can you show me the hadith which justifies that practice?' I knew this young man wanted to ask me about the legitimacy of *tahlilan* [special ritual by reciting the phrase *lailaha illa Allah* person in unison for a deceased] that I practise. I said to him, if we have found evidence (I., *dalil*) justifying this view in the Qur'an, I think we do not need to find another *dalil* from an hadith, even though we can find another *dalil* from an hadith. As mentioned in the Qur'an, God teaches the Prophet to pray for his Muslim brothers who have preceded him. The prayer is as follows, *rabbanā ighfir lanā wa liikhwāninā al-lazdīnā sabaqūnā bi al-imān* [Our Lord! Forgive us and our brethren who came before us into the Faith] (59:10).If the prayers of living person could not be received by deceased persons, God would not have taught this prayer to his Prophet. Meanwhile, argument from the hadith can also be found in the hadith narrated by Imam

28 Interview with *Kyai* Misbah, Kediri, November, 2004.

> Muslim and Bukhari relating to the occasion when the Prophet visited *Uḥud*and *Baqi's* grave site. Firstly, the Prophet greeted the personages in those graves, saying *assalāmu'alaikum,* and the Prophet prayed for them. The word *assalāmu'alaikum*indicates that the Prophet chatted with the deceased persons and the prayer supplicated by the Prophet could be heard and its merit could be received by the deceased persons.

The members of the *Wāḥidiyat*group even believe that the merit of charity performed by living persons can benefit deceased persons. This can be seen from the courtesy (*adab*) of giving donations imposed by the group on its members. One of the *adab* is that before putting money into a donation box, members of this group should intend to give the merit of the donation to their families who are still alive or dead. This is due to the belief that donating to the *Wāḥidiyat* group can cause happiness and perfection of gnosis for living families and deceased families (Anonymous 1423:31-2). One of the members of this group, Dedey Firmansyah, a member of the group from Lampung, told the following story about the importance of delivering the merit of putting a money in a donation box (I., *kotak amal*) for his deceased father.

> This story took place when I ignored the significance of putting money into a donation box for the *Wāḥidiyat* group. One day, I dreamed my father, who had passed away, came to me. His face looked sad. He was silent but tears dropped from his eyes. In that dream, I was extremely sad too. The more I approached my father, the louder he cried. Then I asked him, 'Why are you crying?' He did not reply to my question and kept crying. While he was crying, he answered my question, 'Currently, I no longer receive your charity; pointing his finger to a donation box. Now, I feel tired. Do you leave me with this tiredness? (Rohani 2004:143).

There are many other stories told by the members of this group relating to the significance of putting some money into a donation box for deceased persons. These stories are stressed within the *Wāḥidiyat* group to encourage its members to donate more to the group.

3.5. Seeking Blessing (*barakah, tabarruk*)

The word *barakah* is an Arabic word meaning 'divine blessing'(Colin 1978:1032). According to the Qur'an, God can bestow blessings on particular people, places or times. For example, God blessed the persons of his prophets and his saints. In the Qur'an, God regards the night when the Qur'an was firstly revealed as a blessed night (A., *lailat al-mubārakat*). Moreover, places such as the Ka'ba and Jerusalem are considered blessed places. In other words, *barakah* can be in persons, places, and time. Meanwhile, from the same root as *barakah* derives the word *tabarruk* which means seeking divine blessing by means of someone or something which has been blessed by God. Seeking *barakah* (J., *ngalap berkah,* A., *tabarruk*) is a popular practice among *Majlis Dhikr* in Indonesia and among *Nahdliyyin,* a term referring to members of Nahdlatul Ulama. In this section, I will discuss this practice by referring to Muslims' interpretation of two sources of Islamic teachings, the Qur'an and hadith, and how this concept is interpreted and practised by the Indonesian *Majlis Dhikr* groups.

For the Salafi group, according to hadith and the Qur'an, *barakah* can be divided into two kinds: firstly, the *barakah* of physical essence (A., *dhat*) and secondly the *barakah* of righteous action and following the Prophet. For this group, the first kind of *barakah* is exclusively bestowed by the Prophet, including anything that is left from the body of the Prophet. It is argued that this type of *barakah* did not continue after the death of the Prophet. Therefore, none of his followers, including his Companions, had such *barakah.* However, according to this group, Muslims can still obtain his *barakah* by adhering to the Prophet's commands and avoiding his prohibitions. In addition, after his death, everything that remains of the Prophet's physical essence such as his hair can generate *barakah.*

Every Muslim can obtain the second type of *barakah,* if they act as commanded and avoid prohibited things following the example of the Prophet acted. In this sense, Salih (2007) argues that this second type of *barakah* comes not from the Prophet's physical body but from following the Prophet's guidance.[29] In other words, as Ibn Taymiyyah argued, people can obtain this second type of *barakah* if they strictly follow the guidance of the hadith and the Qur'an as the Prophet has taught and ordered them. Therefore, the extent to which people can obtain this type of *barakah* is determined by the extent to which they abide by hadith and the Qur'an (Al-Maliki 1993:179-80). In other words, Muslim can obtain growth and increase in the reward of their actions because of following the guidance of the Prophet. For this group, the source of both types of *barakah* is God. No one can be blessed unless God gives a blessing. Therefore, people cannot decide if something or someone is blessed. In order to regard something as having *barakah,* as an Indonesian Salafi preacher, Abdul Qadir Djaelani noted, people should refer to God and his Prophet (Djaelani 1996:218).

In line with these types of *barakah,* Imran, a proponent of the Salafi movement in Indonesia, has argued that since only the Prophet has *barakah* of physical

---

29 Salih bin Abdul-Aziz bin Muhammad Aal ash-Shaikh 1995, The Understanding of Tabarruk with Ahl al-Sunnah: Salafi Publications, viewed 2 January 2007, 11:04 am, http://www.spubs.com/sps/sp.cfm?subsecID=TAW04&articleID=TAW040001&articlePages=1.

essence (*dhāt*), and this *barakah* was cut off after his death, no one after his death can obtain this *barakah*. Seeking blessing (A., *tabarruk*) through the physical essence of the Prophet only happened when the Prophet was alive. After his death, Imran noted, none of his Companions practised such *tabarruk*. For example, after his death, none of his Companions sought blessing from his family, tomb, hair, or the water collected after washing his corpse. Therefore, Imran pointed out that if Muslims today seek *barakah* from Muslim saints such as Syeikh Abd al-Qādir al-Jailānī, his tomb and the tombs of other Muslims, this can be considered *bid'ah* because it has no sanction in the hadith and the Qur'an (Imran 1990:61-2). Abdul Qadir Djaelani, another proponent of the Salafi movement in Indonesia, even regards this practice as extremely reprehensible form of innovation (A., *bid'at ḍalālat*) which can lead its doer to infidelity. As a result, Muslims should repent if they practice such *tabarruk*(Djaelani 1996:220)

Further, since the *barakah* of physical essence is exclusive to the Prophet, Muslims cannot obtain *barakah* from the physical essence from people other than the Prophet including righteous persons. However, Muslims can only obtain *barakah* from the virtuous actions of righteous persons (I., *orang saleh*), not from their physical essence. In other words, the *barakah* of the righteous persons arises from their righteous actions, and it is because of these actions that other people can feel their blessing. An example of such righteous actions is calling people to goodness, and invoking God for them. Therefore, Salih regards the practice of kissing the hands of righteous persons in the belief that they contain physical blessing as a practice forbidden in Islam .

In contrast, al-Maliki recognized *tabarruk* as a practice in Islam which has long been a subject of debate among Muslim theologians. In his opinion, some Muslim theologians regard incorrectly those who practise *tabarruk* with the Prophet, his remains, his family, Muslim saints and Muslim scholars as practising polytheism (*shirk*). Al-Maliki defined *tabarruk* as the same as performing *tawassul* toward God by means of places, persons and their remains. Therefore, for al-Maliki, when performing *tabarruk*, Muslims should believe that because of their closeness and their high status before God, Muslims can obtain blessings from others. At the same time, Muslims should not believe that anyone can bring goodness and reject evil without the will of God (Al-Maliki 1993:158).

In contrast to those who regard *tabarruk* as polytheism, al-Maliki, based on his understanding of the Prophetic traditions, considered *tabarruk* as a permissible practice, even as a legitimate practice (A., *mashrū'*). For him, the greatest *tabarruk* is the one possessed by the Prophet Muhammad. To support his notion, al-Maliki quoted many hadith reporting that everything pertaining to the

Prophet, such as his hair, blood, sweat, saliva, and the water from his ablution was able to generate *barakah.* It is reported in the hadith that the Prophet's Companions used to seek blessing through those things. For al-Maliki, seeking *barakah* through the Prophet was not confined to his lifetime. In contrast to the Salafi groups' notions, al-Maliki cited several traditions of the Prophet's Companions proving that after his death, they still sought *barakah* by means of the Prophet's grave, podium, his house, his robe and places the Prophet touched (Al-Maliki 1993:167-77).

In support of this view, Imam Muslim (821-875), a prominent early hadith collector, narrated examples of *tabarruk* performed by 'Umar Ibn Khaṭṭāb. One of these was that he kissed the Black Stone (A., *Ḥajr Aswad*) located in one of the corners of the wall around the Ka'ba[30] because he saw the Prophet do it. When kissing the stone, 'Umar said, 'you are just a stone, if the Prophet had not done it, I would not have done it.' On another occasion, Imam Bukhārī (810-870), a prominent hadith scholar, reported that when 'Umar Ibn Khaṭṭāb was about to die, he told his son, Abdullah, to ask permission from 'Āishat (the widow of the Prophet) to let him be buried beside the tombs of the Prophet and Abū Bakr (Al-Maliki 1993:158-81). Other Muslim scholars such as al-Ghazālī, al-Subkī, 'Alā al-Dīn also supported the permissibility of seeking *barakah* through the Prophet after his death. They based this on the belief that God bestowed blessing on the Prophet so that his body could not physically perish in the grave (Taylor 1998:213).

For al-Maliki seeking blessing through the relics of the righteous and the Prophets is lawful because the Prophet practised it. To support his claim, al-Maliki cited the hadith narrated by a reliable hadith scholar, Imam Muslim, in which the Prophet was reported to have travelled with his Companions and stopped to take a rest at a place known as al-hijr, which used to belong to the community of Thamūd, a community who lived during the time of Prophet Ṣāliḥ (Shelah). The Prophet's Companions prepared a meal and took water from that place. Then, the Prophet asked his Companions to throw away the water taken from the well at al-hijr and to give the meal to their camels. Instead, he asked his Companions to take water from the well from which the Prophet Ṣaliḥ's camel used to drink (Al-Maliki 1993:178). In this hadith, the Prophet was reported to be seeking barakah through the well of the Prophet Ṣalih rather than through Thamud's well because the Thamud were known as a group of people who opposed Prophet Ṣaliḥ. This hadith, as argued al-Maliki, can be used to support the permissibility of seeking barakah through the relics of righteous persons (I., orang saleh) (Al-Maliki 1993:178).

---

30 Ka'ba is situated almost in the centre of the great mosque in Mecca (*masji al-haram*). All Muslims in the world should direct themselves to the Ka'ba when they perform prayers.

3.5.1. The Concept of *Tabarruk* As Understood by *Majlis Dhikr* Groups

In relation to *tabaruuk,* Indonesian *Majlis Dhikr* leaders define *barakah* as 'increase' (A., *ziyādat*) or 'growth' (A., *namā'*). In other words, Muslims who perform *tabarruk* are seeking an increase or growth in something such as their possessions, wealth, offspring or success. In line with this definition, *Kyai* Misbah, a senior leader among *Majlis Dhikr* groups in Jampes Kediri, told me that *barakah* is a quality that can lead to an increase in other qualities. However, for him, some qualities cannot grow or increase, as he explained in the following:

> For instance, some people have mastered many kinds of Islamic knowledge. Nevertheless, the knowledge they have does not contain *barakah* because they use the knowledge for the benefit of themselves. They never spread and teach the knowledge for the benefit of other Muslims, such as teaching the knowledge to other people. Another example of *barakah* is someone who has a rice field. Even though the rice field is not large enough, these people can share their harvest with the needy. In this case, this rice field can be regarded as having *barakah.*

In this sense, something can be regarded as having *barakah* if it can generate further qualities and benefit for other people.

According to *Kyai* Misbah, there are two kinds of *barakah.* The first is a *barakah* which is dependent (I., *disandarkan*) on humankind. This type of *barakah* is similar to *wasīlat*; hence a person who becomes the object of *tabarruk* serves as a means to ask God. In this sense, when people seek *barakah* from righteous dead persons, they should not ask the persons in the grave because the source of the *barakah* is God. Like the Salafi groups, *Kyai* Misbah pointed out that since it is only God who has the authority to give *barakah* to someone, people should ask for *barakah* to God rather than through righteous persons who do not have the authority to spread blessing. To further explain this, *Kyai* Misbah gave the analogy of people who ask for money from a particular person who does not have money. Even though that person is asked to give money, he or she will not be able to, because he or she does not have any. The same is true of righteous persons who cannot give *barakah* because they do not posses *barakah* since the source of *barakah* is in the hands of God. *Kyai* Mughni, another senior *Kyai* in Jampes, gave the following example of this kind of *tabarruk*:

> Seeking *tabarruk* through pious persons is similar to *tawassul.* We just recite a prayer and send the merit of the prayer to the deceased pious persons with the hope that by our reciting we can obtain *barakah* from God. For example,

> someone with difficulty in seeking a livelihood can easily gain a livelihood because of prayers recited at the tomb of those righteous persons. In this case, we do not invoke those persons for *barakah* because they have passed away and they cannot do anything; instead, we invoke God. In other words, in this practice, we only approach the most beloved persons of God and by this practice we can obtain *barakah* from God, not from those persons we have visited. Unfortunately, lay people have misunderstood this practice. They practise *tabarruk* by seeking *barakah* directly from the personage lying in the graves.

The second type of *barakah* is dependent on God. For *Kyai* Misbah this type of *barakah* is the best *barakah* to seek. Therefore, *Kyai* Misbah urged Muslims to ask God for *barakah* directly either in mundane matters (I., *masalah duniawi*) or heavenly matters (I., *masalah ukhrawi*). For example, in mundane affairs Muslims can ask *barakah* from God for their children to become righteous persons. Moreover, Muslims can invoke *barakah* from God for their wealth so that, even though it is not much, they can use it for useful purposes. Invoking *barakah* for wealth is stressed by *Kyai* Misbah because if the wealth does not contain *barakah,* even though it is much, it will not benefit the owner and others. For instance, people may spend their wealth on wasteful things (I., *hura-hura*), in which case, *Kyai* Misbah said, it is not useful. In heavenly matters, Muslims can ask God for *barakah* to increase the quality of their pious acts by imbuing them with sincerity. *Kyai* Misbah also argued that even though a pious act may be small, it can produce *barakah* if it is sincere.

Asked why people should seek *barakah* through righteous persons before and after their death, the Indonesian *Majlis Dhikr* leader referred to similar practices performed by the Prophet and his Companions. Another reason for such a practice is that righteous persons, such as *'ulamā', wali,* and *kyai* have a high status before God.[31] With their high status and their closeness, they deserve to be approached. For *Kyai* Misbah, seeking *barakah* through these righteous persons is conducted with the hope that God will bless supplicants so they may be able perform the same righteous acts as those pious persons. However, Tholhah Hasan, a Muslim scholar from Nahdlatul Ulama has warned that people should not incorrectly seek *barakah* through anyone whose righteousness is in dispute. Consequently, Muslims are not allowed to seek *barakah* through sacred sites where guardian spirits (I., *pundhen-pundhen keramat*), *dukun-dukun* or sacred things (I., *benda-benda keramat*) are worshipped (Hasan 2006:287).

31 The high status of '*ulamā'*, for example is shown in the hadith where they are described not only as heirs of the Prophet but also as trustworthy persons of God for His people.

Like *Kyai* Misbah, *Gus* Fahri defined *barakah* as increasing qualities (J., *tambahe keapian*) and gave the following example:

> My grandmother used to be a fabric seller. She had many customers. However, she went bankrupt because the customers cheated her. They took material from her shop and promised to pay later, but they never returned to pay. Since all the stock in her shop was borrowed from her boss (J., *juragan*), the supplier, she had to pay him for all the stock. Unfortunately, she did not have enough money to pay her boss. She was very upset. She remembered that she had a piece of land in Ponorogo, which was given to her by her deceased parents as inheritance. She wanted to sell the land so that she could pay her boss. Even though she advertised the land, no one was interested in buying it. She remembered that the land used to belong to the late Mbah Muharram, so, she visited the tomb of Mbah Muharram and recited a whole chapter of the Qur'an. Before finishing the last part of the Qur'an she received a spiritual experience and could see the personage lying in the grave. One day later, she offered the land to Haji Maemun, a cow seller and the owner of land beside her land. Haji Maemun agreed to buy the land.

In his example, *Gus* Fahri described *barakah* as increasing a quality in the sense that his grandmother obtained *barakah* by reciting the Qur'an. As a result, she could obtain another quality, namely, she succeeded in selling her land.

According to *Kyai* Mughni, *Kyai* Misbah's brother-in-law, seeking *barakah* through the Prophet and his relics was not confined only to his lifetime but also continued after his death. As *Kyai* Mughni explained to me that one can seek *barakah* through the Prophet after his death, for example, by reciting a blessing phrase (*Ṣalāwa*) to him. Since the meaning of *barakah* is growth, reciting a blessing for the Prophet can lead to an increase in a quality. In addition, one can seek *barakah* through his relics praying in three mosques, namely the al-Ḥarām mosque in Mecca, the al- Nabawī mosque in Medina, and the al-Aqṣa mosque in Jerusalem. *Kyai* Mughni said that it is mentioned in a Prophetic hadith that by performing prayers in those mosques, God will increase the merit of the prayers a hundred thousand times compared to other mosques. Those three mosques, said *Kyai* Mughni, are regarded as blessed places and more efficacious than others because they are the places where the Prophet prayed. Since the source of *barakah* is God, *Kyai* Mughni argued that people could seek *barakah* through these mosques by invoking God directly, but not the Prophet.

3.6. Conclusion

It is clear that in some aspects of practical Sufism, *Majlis Dhikr* groups in Indonesia follow similar notions to those articulated by prominent Muslim scholars, Sufi and theologians. Leaders of Indonesian *Majlis Dhikr* groups attribute their notions to similar practices conducted by the Prophet himself, his Companions (A., *ṣaḥabāt*), the Successors of his Companions (A., *tābi'īn*), and the Successors of the Successors (A, *tābi'it al-tābi'īn*). Therefore, the Indonesian *Majlis Dhikr* groups cannot be regarded as practising polytheism (*shirk*) or making innovation (*bid'ah*) because what they practise can be related to their interpretation of the main sources of Islamic law (A., *sharī'at*), the hadith and the Qur'an, and the practice of the Prophet's Companions. If this interpretation differs from that of other groups of Muslims, one interpretation cannot be judged by another. Moreover, I argue that interpretations can be regarded as under the field of *ijtihad,* which means the use of all the capabilities of reason by particular Muslims in deducing interpretations from evidence from the Qur'an and hadith. If this is the case, one can expect different results of *ijtihad* among Muslims scholars. Muslims should not therefore claim that their own results of *ijtihad* are deemed to be true, while others' *ijtihad* are false, because all of these will be justified later in the hereafter. If the result is true according to the meaning and purpose of God and the Prophet, then it will have two rewards. In contrast, if the result is wrong because it does not agree with God's and the Prophet's purpose, it will have only one reward.

> Those who practise Sufism without tarekat only attain the experience of *'ilm al-yaqīn*. They never reach *'ain al-yaqīn* and *ḥaqq al-yaqīn*. This is because they only believe (I., *yakin*) based on their theoretical philosophy. They do not believe practically (I., *secaraamaliah*), even though they claim that they believe *secara amaliah*. In fact, this belief happens only in their imagination, as if they believe *secara amaliah*.

Chapter IV: 'Turn to God and His Prophet': The Spiritual Path of the *Ṣalawāt Wāḥidiyat* Group

This chapter examines a *Majlis Dhikr* group that defines itself not only as an alternative mystical path among other recognised Sufi orders but also as part of legitimate ritual practice in Islam. An assessment of how this *MajlisDhikr* group known as *Wāḥidiyat* does this requires assessment of its history and the sources and the arguments from which the doctrine and the ritual practices of this group are taken, as well as the way this group disseminates its teachings to others. What I hope to show here is that although this *Majlis Dhikr* group is not regarded as a *tarekat mu'tabarah* (a recognised Sufi group) by Nahdlatul Ulama, it still belongs in the frame of the Sufi teachings practised by other international Sufi groups. Moreover, despite the fact that this *Majlis Dhikr* group has developed from classical Sufism, it is not identical with it, and offers a world view and ritual that distinguishes it from other Sufi groups in Indonesia.

4.1. The Foundation of *Ṣalawāt Wāḥidiyat*

The word *Ṣalawāt* originally means 'blessing' or 'grace' of God. But according to Islamic tradition, the word *Ṣalawāt* refers to particular prayers or blessings to the Prophet Muhammad, which are therefore often followed by the word*al-Nabī* (the Prophet). The reciting of*Ṣalawāt* is part of Islamic teachings since it is revealed in the Qur'an and hadith. The recommendation to recite *Ṣalawāt* is primarily found in the Qur'an (33: 56) and hadith as follows:

> Undoubtedly Allah and His Angels send blessings on the Prophet. O' you who believe! Send upon Him Blessings and salute Him with all respect. (33:56)
>
> On the Day of Judgment the nearest person to me, from amongst the people, would be the one who would have recited *Ṣalāwat* the most in this (mortal) world. (Tirmidhi)

There are many other hadith which stress the importance and the benefit of reciting Ṣalawāt to the Prophet. Although the Prophet mentioned only one particular kind of Ṣalawāt which is well known as al-Ṣalawāt al-Ibrāhimiyyat[1], according to one informant this does not necessarily mean that he forbad his followers from composing other *Ṣalawāt.* As a result of this, it is believed that every person is allowed to compose the text of a*Ṣalawāt* as long as it is dedicated to the Prophet. In this sense, there are a number of*Ṣalawāt* composed by Muslim scholars. Some of these are named according to the use of the *Ṣalawāt,* others according to their composer. For example, *Ṣalawāt Nāriyat* or *Kāmilat,* composed by Sidi Ibrahim al-Nāzi,[2] is believed to be able to make livelihood easier for those who recite it four thousand times (Shihab 2006:363). Another *Ṣalawāt* is called *Ṣalawāt Munjiyāt* since it is used to avert danger. Yet another*Ṣalawāt* is called*Ṣalawāt Maṣīṣiyah* since it was composed by 'Abd al-Salām Ibn Maṣīṣ (d.1228), whose tomb in Morocco is an object of visitation and veneration. Other examples of this kind of *Ṣalawāt* are *Ṣalawāt Bakariyyat, Dardiriyat,* and *Mirghaniyat* (Shiddieqy 1964:70). Therefore, it is commonly asserted by *Wāḥidiyat* board members that there are two categories of *Ṣalawāt*: the first is *Ṣalawāt Ma'thūra,* which means that the text of the *Ṣalawāt* derives directly from the Prophet, and the second is *Ṣalawāt Ghairu Ma'thūra* meaning thet the text was not taught by the Prophet, but it was composed by the Prophet's Companions and Muslim '*ulamā*' (Anonymous 1999b:63-71). *Ṣalawāt Wāḥidiyat,* therefore, can be added as an example of *Ṣalawāt* in this latter category since its text was composed by a Muslim scholar (I., *ulama*).

The origin of *Ṣalawāt Wāḥidiyat* is closely connected with the figure of the late K.H Abdul Madjid Ma'ruf, often called *Kyai* Madjid. He was not only the author of the *Ṣalawāt Wāḥidiyat* but also the leader of a *pondok pesantren* (Islamic boarding school) in Bandar Lor village, Mojoroto, in the city of Kediri, East Java. Among his followers he was regarded as 'the source of help of his age' (*ghauth hādza al-zamān*), a title accorded to the highest leaders of the Sufi hierarchy who govern the universe. An informant described his saintship like this:

---

1 *Al-Ṣalawāt al-Ibrāhimiyyat* is a text of the *Ṣalawāt* which was directly taught by the Prophet. This *Ṣalawāt* is called *Ibrāhimiyyat* because its text contains praise not only for the Prophet but also for Abraham. Many different Hadith texts mention the text of the *Ṣalawāt* narrated by different figures (Muslim and Abū Dāwud, Muslim and Abī Mas'ūd, Al-Bukhārī from Abū Sa'īd) but all of them contain praise for Abraham. The text of the *Ṣalawāt* is as follows: Blessings be upon Muhammad and Muhammad's family just as You blessed Abraham's family and sanctify Muhammad and Muhammad's family just as You sanctified Abraham's family.

2 In Morocco, this *Ṣalawāt* is known as *Ṣalawāt al-Nāziyyat.* This name is much more appropriate than *Ṣalawāt Nāriyat* since there is no word in the text of this *Ṣalawāt* signifying the word *nār* meaning fire.

> The sainthood of *Kyai* Madjid Ma'ruf can be obviously seen from the light of faith shining from his works of *Ṣalawāt.* As noted by Shaikh Musthofa al-Thomum in his book entitled, *Manaqib al-Sayyid Muhammad Sirr al-Khatami al-Mirghoni,* indeed, the secret of the saint is within his *hizb* (litany, special prayer formula) and his station (*maqam*) can be seen from the composition of his *shalawat* (exaltation) on the Prophet (peace be upon him). And the attributes of the Prophet written in the composition of his *Ṣalawāt* constitute a degree and a station of such saints.

The sainthood of *Kyai* Abdul Madjid Ma'ruf was also been supported by some well-known *kyai* (religious leaders) in Kediri. For example, after looking for God's guidance in the course of forty days' meditation and eating only white rice (I. *puasa mutih*), *Kyai* Mubashir Mundir, who was himself known as a *wali* (saint) in Kediri, received an unseen whisper (I. *bisikan gaib;* A. *ḥātif*) saying that *Kyai* Abdul Madjid Ma'ruf was 'the source of help of his age' (A, *ghauth al-aqtāb hādza al-zamān*). Another figure who acknowledged the sainthood of *Kyai* Abdul Madjid Ma'ruf was *Kyai* Hamim Jazuli or Gus Mik, the founder of *Majlis Dhikr al-Ghāfilīn.* He said that *Kyai* Madjid Ma'ruf was the *rāis al-'ārifīn* (the leader of the Gnostics and Saints). He even said that if Shaikh 'Abd al-Qādir al-Jaylānī (1078-1166)[3] was still alive; he would have practised *Kyai* Abdul Madjid's *Ṣalawāt* (prayer).

Other support was given by *Kyai* Abdul Wahab Hasbullah, one of the founders of Nahdlatul Ulama (NU). When *Kyai* Madjid offered people the *Ṣalawāt Wāḥidiyat*, the entire audience invited for his son's circumcision ceremony accepted the *Ṣalawāt,* including *Kyai* Wahab Hasbullah. He was reported as saying to the audience, '*Kyai* Madjid's knowledge is very deep, like a well which is ten metres deep, while my well is only one to two metres deep.' He continued to say 'I will practise his *Ṣalawāt*.' These acknowledgments gained from those who had high spiritual standing among the Muslim *ummat* were utilized by the newly born *Wāḥidiyat* to achieve legitimacy among its followers. These acknowledgments were documented in a book, and the followers of *Wāḥidiyat* are reminded of them at every official ritual so that their belief and surrender (A. *taslīm*) to the *Kyai* Madjid Ma'ruf can be improved. Another reason for this might be to give the impression that not all *kyai* or *'ulamā'* in Kediri disagreed with the founder of *Wāḥidiyat*; in fact, one of them who held a high position in the Nahdlatul Ulama organization accepted and practised the *Ṣalawāt*. This was particularly needed when *Wāḥidiyat* faced vigorous criticism from *Kyai* Machrus, the guardian of the *Pesantren* Lirboyo, Kediri.

Kyai Madjid's father, *Kyai* Ma'ruf (b. 1852), was a charismatic and well-known religious scholar (*'ulamā'*) in Java. Among the followers of *Wāḥidiyat,* he was

3 He is the founder of the oldest of the Muslim Sufi group called Tarekat Qadiriyah.

regarded as a *wali,* whose tomb in *Pesantren* Kedunglo has been an object of visitation and veneration. Although he was a scholar who mastered various disciplines of religious knowledge, he was well known among many *pesantren* communities as a *kyai* who possessed supernatural qualities (I., *karamah).* One of his reported supernatural qualities was that instead of praying in Arabic, he prayed in the Javanese language; but his prayer was powerful. The story about his extraordinary power was widely known in *pesantren* circles. He was a founder of *Pesantren* Kedunglo after studying in many *pesantren,* such as *Pesantren* Cepoko Nganjuk, *Pesantren* Langitan Tuban and *pesantren* of *Kyai Shaikhanā* Cholil Bangkalan, Madura. He also studied in the Holy City of Mecca under the supervision of the great Indonesian Muslim scholars who taught there such as Shaikh *Kyai* Nawawi al-Bantani from Banten, Shaikh Ahmad Khātib al-Minangkabawi from West Sumatra, and Shaikh Mahfudz al-Tirmīsī from Pacitan East Java (Vety 2001:54-61). It is clear that *Kyai* Abdul Madjid Ma'ruf had a well respected genealogy ('blue blood'). His status and religious authority was derived from his family tree as well as from the depth of his own religious piety. The *kyai*'s genealogy obviously played a part in building up his authority among his followers.

As the son of a *kyai, Kyai* Abdul Madjid Ma'ruf (1918-1989) learned religion firstly with his father *Kyai* Ma'ruf. Then he undertook further study in several *pesantren.* The first *pesantren* where he studied was *pesantren* Banjarmelati, in Kediri, under instruction of *Kyai* Shaleh, his grandfather. This *pesantren* is regarded as the oldest *pesantren* from which some large *pesantren* such as *Pesantren* Lirboyo and *Pesantren* Jampes are linked. He then moved to study in *Pesantren* Kemayan, twelve kilometres south of his home, where he spent about three years. As well as his study in these *pesantren,* he was said to have studied in a secular school until secondary level (Bawani 1981:1-31).

In 1959, his followers believed that *Kyai* Abdul Madjid Ma'ruf, as he was usually called, experienced the highest of spiritual moments when he received an invisible order (I., *perintah gaib*) or invisible caller (A., *ḥatif*) to improve and rebuild people's morality by means of a spiritual path that would bring them to the consciousness of God and the prophet. The invisible order, which was to affect his spiritual life, convinced him that people have suffered increasingly serious moral problems. This spiritual order is believed by his son, Abdul Latif Madjid in particular and by *Wāḥidiyat* members in general to have come from the Prophet Muhammad, who appeared to *Kyai* Abdul Majid Ma'ruf when he was awake (Madjid 2001). However, on another occasion his son has said that his father met the Prophet in a sleeping state (*ru'yat al-sāliḥat).* His son was convinced that only those who had reached the highest spiritual state can experience a vision of the Prophet (Madjid 1999:10).

Kyai Abdul Madjid Ma'ruf was considered by his followers not only as *ghauth hādhā al-zamān* but also as the reformer (A., *mujaddid)* of his age. His followers believed that such reformer of Islam comes at the end of every century to revitalize Islam and save society from moral and spiritual decadency. This belief is based on a Prophetic hadith. In line with this hadith, his followers maintain that after the death of *Kyai* Abdul Madjid Ma'ruf no other man can claim to be a saint (*wali*).

What *Kyai* Abdul Madjid Ma'ruf experienced with divine inspiration was not novel for Muslim reformers. Other reformers in previous centuries such as Shah Wali Allah of Delhi (1703-62) and Usuman dan Fudio of West Africa (1754-1817) received visionary dreams before reforming religious practice in their societies. Shah Wali Allah, for example, experienced a visionary dream in which he met the Prophet's grandsons, Ḥasan and Ḥusain. It was said that Ḥasan and Ḥusain appeared to him, gave him a pen and clothed him in the Prophet's mantle. Likewise, Usuman dan Fudio dreamed that 'Abd al-Qādir al-Jaylānī, a great saint, in the company of the Prophet brought a green robe embroidered with the phrase, 'There is no god but God and Muhammad is his Messenger'(Sirriyeh 1999:5). For these reformers, these spiritual experiences gave a divine power so that their religious reformation would find firm legitimation. By the same token, the spiritual order from the Prophet experienced by *Kyai* Abdul Majdid gave a strong impression and justification to his followers that what he taught and wrote was actually permitted, and requested directly by the Prophet, not of the *kyai*'s own free will and decision. As Gilsenan (1973: 35) has observed 'it is not uncommon for the foundation of a brotherhood to arise out of such a truth vision (A.,*ru'ya al- ṣadiqa*).' As a result, *Kyai* Abdul Madjid Ma'ruf did not face questions of legitimacy among his followers.

Through this spiritual experience, *Kyai* Abdul Majid Ma'ruf reportedly developed a deepening spiritual relationship with God and the Prophet and spent much time in contemplation and recitation of many kinds of *Ṣalawāt* such as *Ṣalawāt Badawiyah, Ṣalawāt Nāriyat,* and *Ṣalawāt Massisiyah.* In addition, he made an effort to focus his spiritual power on praying for the betterment of the Islamic life of Muslim community.

In 1963, *Kyai* Abdul Madjid Ma'ruf experienced another spiritual event. This invisible order urged him to do the same things. As a result of this, he endeavoured to improve his praying and proximity (A., *taqarrub*) to God. This resulted in a physical health problem, but he did not let this prevent him from continuously communicating with God.[4] Not long after the second order, he received another spiritual command which was harder and accompanied with

4 Interview with Zainuddin, Kediri, November, 2004.

a threat. The threat was so great that he trembled with fear. This critical event shaped *Kyai* Majid's commitment to begin to write litanies which would be useful for his society. He, then, wrote the text of the litanies that are called *Wāhidiyyat* The first litany he wrote is as follows:

اللهم كما انت اهله . صل وسلم وبارك على سيدنا ومولانا وشفيعنا وحبيبنا
وقرة أعيننا محمد صلى الله عليه وسلم كما هو اهله . نسألك اللهم بحقه ان تغرقنا في لجة
بحر الوحدة . حتى لا نرى ولا نسمع ولا نجد ولا نحس ولا نتحرك ولا نسكن الا بها .
وترزقنا تمام مغفرتك يا الله وتمام نعمتك يا الله وتمام معرفتك يا الله وتمام محبتك يا الله
وتمام رضوانك يا الله وصل وسلم وبارك عليه وعلى آله وصحبه . عدد ما أحاط به
علمك واحصاه كتابك . برحمتك يا ارحم الراحمين والحمد لله رب العالمين ٧×

> O! Lord as You are the right one, exaltation, peace, and blessings upon our Lord, and our intercessor, our beloved, our heart, Muhammad (peace be upon him) just as he is the qualified. We ask you O! Allah by his right to immerse us in the depth of sea of the oneness so that we cannot see, hear, feel, move and rest except with it. And we ask your perfect forgiveness O! Allah, your perfect amenity O! Allah, we ask for my perfect gnosis of you , and my perfect love to you, my perfect consent to you O! Allah. And exaltation, peace, and blessings be upon Him and His relatives and His companions as many as the number of things which is encompassed by your knowledge and included in your book, by your mercy, O! The Most Merciful of merciful people, all praise is due to Allah, the Lord of the Worlds.

Kyai Madjid Ma'ruf called this prayer *Ṣalawāt Ma'rifat* (The Gnosis Supplication), without explaining the meaning of *ma'rifat.* He intended that those who read the prayer would be able to reach the state of *ma'rifat,* which, according to Sufi scholars, is the highest station achieved by a Sufi. After writing the prayer, he asked some people to read it continuously. Among those whom he asked were Abdul Jalil, a senior person of Kampung Jamsaren, Muhtar, a market trader, and Dahlan, a *Pesantren* Kedunglo student from Demak, Central Java. After practising and reading the prayers, they admitted that they were blessed with a feeling of calmness and were much more conscious of God.

Within the same year, *Kyai* Abdul Madjid Ma'ruf composed another *Ṣalawāt* prayer. Although the composition of this prayer was shorter than previous one, it was believed that it can give more positive effects to its readers by improving their consciousness of God and the quietness of soul. The prayer is as follows:

اللهم يا واحد يا احد . يا واجد يا جواد . صل وسلم وبارك على سيدنا محمد وعلى
آل سيدنا محمد في كل لمحة ونفس بعدد معلومات الله وفيوضاته وامداده ×١٠٠

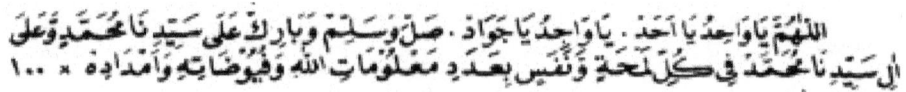

> O! God O! The oneness, the One, O! the Finder, the Most generous. Exalt, peace, blessing upon our Lord Muhammad and his family in every glance of the eye and in every breath with as many as the knowledge of God and His stream of grace and His assistance (100 times).

He gave this prayer publicly to those who visited him regardless of their social background, asking them not only to read it but also to disseminate it to other people. Apart from this, he asked one of his students to write the *Ṣalawāt* and send it to other Muslim scholars (*kyai*) together with a letter recommending that this prayer be read by local people. In addition to his religious and preaching motives, he sent the prayer to many *kyai* perhaps because he needed them to assist in the dissemination of the prayer as widely as possible. This is understandable since *kyai* are regarded not only as teachers but also as living saints who are responsible for the spiritual training of people. In other words, as Woodward has argued, *kyai* play an important role in the religious lives of lay Muslims (Woodward 1989).

Pesantren Kedunglo held its weekly public instruction (*pengajian umum*) on Sufi doctrines and practices on Thursday night. The Sufi text used as a reference in the instruction was *Kitāb al-Ḥikam*written by Ibn 'Athāillah al-Iskandārī (d.1309). The reason why this Sufi book was more often chosen than the Sufi treatise such as Al-Ghazālī's *Iḥyā' 'Ulūm al-Dīn,* is because the book contains teaching about the struggle against *nafs* (lower soul) which is in line with *Wāḥidiyat*teachings. The participants in this instruction ranged from students to local people. *Kyai* Abdul Majdid Ma'ruf used the instruction as a means to introduce and explain his teachings on *Ṣalawāt*. On such occasions, *Kyai* Abdul Madjid Ma'ruf also explained in detail some aspects of Sufi doctrines which later become a pillar of his teachings. Not long after releasing the second *Ṣalawāt,* in 1963 at the weekly *pengajian, Kyai* Abdul Madjid Ma'ruf launched a third *Ṣalawāt* that he called *Ṣalawāt Thalj al- Qulūb*(The Cooling of the Heart prayer). He wrote the prayer as follows:

يا شافع الخلق الصلاة والسلام ∴ عليك نور الخلق هادي الأنام
وأصله وروحه أدركني ∴ فقد ظلمت أبدا وربني
وليس لي يا سيدي سواكا ∴ فإن ترد كنت شخصا هالكا

> O! The Prophet, intercessor to creatures, blessing and peace of God is upon you, O! The light of creatures, O! The guidance of mankind, O! The source of mankind and O! the spirit of mankind, guide me and teach me because I am really a wrongdoer, I am meaningless without you, if you leave me I will be a destroyed person.

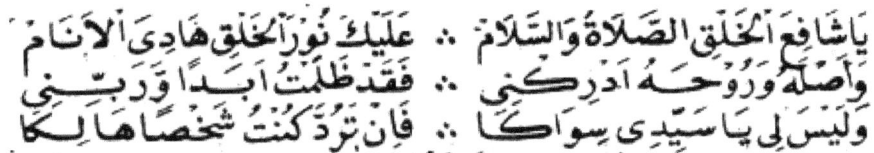

It was reported that he composed the *Ṣalawāt Thalj al- Qulūb* because after practising the *Ṣalawāt Ma'rifat* a number of people experienced *jadhba* (J., *jadhab,* attraction), a high spiritual experience in which a person can be exalted into a state of ecstasy and of union. The people who experienced *jadhba* or *majdhūb* (attracted) behaved in an uncontrolled way just like crazy people because of the overwhelming shock of 'the unveiling' (Schimmel 1978). But in the case of *Wāḥidiyat,* they wept all the time after practising the *Ṣalawāt Ma'rifat*(Madjid 2001:21-27).

Kyai Abdul Madjid Ma'ruf then called those three prayer compositions *Ṣalawāt Wāhidiyat.* As implied in the first *Ṣalawāt*, the name *Wāhidiyat* was derived from *al-Wāhid,* one of the names of God (*Asmā al- Husnā)* which means The One (Qomari 2003:31-32). *Kyai* Abdul Madjid Ma'ruf used the name because, according to Muslim scholars, *al-Wāhid* has many purposes, namely to get rid of a feeling of confusion and anxiety and to increase a feeling of fear of God rather than of God's creatures. Another reason might be that the use of God's names in praying is strongly recommended by the Qur'an and the Prophet tradition so that God may grant the prayer. This is revealed in the Qur'an as follows:

> And Allah's are the best names, therefore call on Him thereby, and leave alone those who violate the sanctity of His names; they shall be recompensed for what they did. (7:180)

At the end of 1963, *Kyai* Abdul Madjid Ma'ruf invited many *kyai* and other notable figures who practised *Ṣalawāt Wāhidiyat* to discuss a topic related to *Ṣalawāt Waḥidiyat.* The meeting, chaired by *Kyai* Abdul Madjid Ma'ruf, produced several decisions including the composition of the text of *Ṣalawāt* , the method of reciting the *Ṣalawāt,* and the guarantee which was that: 'If the *Ṣalawāt* is recited for forty consecutive days and there is no effect on heart at all, (the author) can be called to account in the world and the hereafter.'[5] All of this were printed as a pamphlet. It was not clear why *Kyai* Abdul Madjid Ma'ruf proposed putting this guarantee in the pamphlet. Qomari Mukhtar (2003), a member of *Wāḥidiyat,* argues that the guarantee from *Kyai* Abdul Madjid Ma'ruf should be seen as a part of his guidance to his followers in order to take responsibility for any matters that they have done. Mukhtar maintains that this guarantee should not be interpreted as if *Kyai* Abdul Madjid Ma'ruf guarantees paradise to his followers in the hereafter. However, others might argue that the guarantee could be seen as a part of an advertisement for the power of the prayer. As a result, the guarantee would convince the readers and the followers that the *Ṣalawāt Wāḥidiyat* can be a panacea for any problems

5 *'Menawi sampun jangkep 40 dinten boten wonten perubahan manah, kinging dipun tuntut dunyan wa ukhron.'*

they face, if it is recited continuously for forty days. However, the guarantee is not found in the new printed text of *Ṣalawāt.* This might be due to the fact that the guarantee has prompted criticism from many *kyai* (religious leaders) in Kediri.

It took eighteen years to complete the composition and the ritual of *Ṣalawāt Wāhidiyat.* This was not a short time to accomplish the teaching and the composition of *Ṣalawāt Wāhidiyat.* In 1964, the first of a series of one week *Wāhidiyat* camps was held bringing many delegations from cities in East Java such as Kediri, Blitar, Nganjuk, Jombang, Mojokerto, Surabaya, Malang, Madiun, and Ngawi. Activities were guided directly by *Kyai* Abdul Madjid Ma'ruf who gave a series of lectures about *Ṣalawāt Wāḥidiyat* for new preachers of *Wāḥidiyat (da'i).* As described by Mukhtar (1997), the first *Wāḥidiyat* camp was attended by many *'ulamā'*and *kyai.* However, not every participant came with the intention of learning the teachings of *Wāḥidiyat.* Some of them joined the camp just to test *Kyai* Abdul Madjid Ma'ruf on matters to do with the teachings of *Wāhidiyat.* If *Kyai* Abdul Madjid Ma'ruf could give a satisfactory answer, then they would submit to him.

On the final day of the camp, *Kyai* Abdul Madjid explained the qualifications that disciples (*murīd*) and spiritual guides (*murshid*) should have. As retold by Mukhtar, *Kyai* Madjid described these as follows:

> A *murshid* should posses qualifications needed such as the capability to teach *(tarbiyah)* his *murīd,* although they are in a very distant place. For example, if the *murid* stays at the sunset place and the *murshid* stay at the sunrise place, the *murshid* can teach them. In addition, the *murshid* should not hope for a *murīd*'s possessions. Meanwhile, a *murīd* should behave like a dead body (*kalmayyit*), and surrender completely to the master. Whatever a *murid* possessed should be given absolutely to the master, including the mind, time, energy, wife or husband (Mukhtar 1997:45).

Instead of accepting the title of *murshid* given by his disciples, *Kyai* Abdul Madjid Ma'ruf asked them, together with him, to come close to God, the Prophet and the Muslim saints (*ghauth hāzda al zamān*) because he did not posses the qualifications to become either a *m–urshid* or *murīd.* Although he refused the title of *murshid* from his disciples, his disciples still awarded it to him. Furthermore, the followers of *Wāḥidiyat* (I., *pengamal Wāḥidiyat*) believed he was the only one who was able to bring them to the experience of *ma'rifat* (gnosis), intuitive knowledge of God (Yusuf 2003:2). In order to complete the *Ṣalawāt*, *Kyai* Abdul Madjid Ma'ruf introduced an exclamation phrase to the participants of thet camp, and included it in the body of the text of the *Ṣalawāt Wāḥidiyat.* This exclamation was as follows: '*Yā Sayyidī yā Rasūl Allah*' (O

بسم الله الرحمن الرحيم

الصلوات الواحدية : فائده منجرنهكن هات دان معرفة بالله ورسوله صلى الله عليه وسلم ∴

ماريله سكنف فرهاتيان، كيت فوستكن مغهدف حضرة الله سبحانه وتعالى دان مراسا سفرتي بنار بنار برادا دهدافن جنجوغن كيت رسول الله صلى الله عليه وسلم دغن ادب ظاهر باطن تعظيم محبة سبائيك بائيك ڤ سمتا تامتا مغبديكن ديري كفد الله دغن إخلاص تنفا فامفريه أفا فون جوك (لله)، دان نية مغيكوتي تونتونن رسول الله صلى الله عليه وسلم (للرسول).

ماريكيت سداري سوغكه سوغكه بهواكيت ملاكوكن اين سموا اداله سمتا تامتا كرنا فضل دار الله أتس تيته الله (بالله)، دان أتس شفاعة أتو جاسا رسول الله صلى الله عليه وسلم (بالرسول) كيت سما سكالي تيدك ادا كممفوان أفا أفا.

ماركيت مغاكوي دغن جوجر بهواكيت اين فنوه دوسا دان سلالو بربوات ظالم، بائيك ترهداف الله تعالى ورسوله صلى الله عليه وسلم، ترهداف اورغ توا، ترهداف كلوارك دان ترهداف أمة دان مشركة . ساغت ممبوتوهكن مغفرة فغامفونن، هداية، توفيق الله تعالى . ممبوتوهكن شفاعة تربية رسول الله صلى الله عليه وسلم دان بركة كرامة دعاء رست غوث هذا الزمان وأعوانه وسائر أولياء الله رضي الله تعالى عنهم.

إلى حضرة سيدنا محمد صلى الله عليه وسلم الفاتحة × ٧
وإلى حضرة غوث هذا الزمان وأعوانه وسائر أولياء الله رضي الله تعالى عنهم الفاتحة × ٧

اللهم يا واحد يا احد . يا واجد يا جواد . صل وسلم وبارك على سيدنا محمد وعلى آل سيدنا محمد في كل لمحة ونفس بعدد معلومات الله وفيوضاته وامداده × ١٠٠

اللهم كما انت اهله . صل وسلم وبارك على سيدنا ومولانا وشفيعنا وحبيبنا وقرة أعيننا محمد صلى الله عليه وسلم كما هو اهله . نسألك اللهم بحقه ان تغرقنا في لجة بحر الوحدة . حتى لا نرى ولا نسمع ولا نجد ولا نحس ولا نتحرك ولا نسكن إلا بها . وترزقنا تمام مغفرتك يا الله وتمام نعمتك يا الله وتمام معرفتك يا الله وتمام محبتك يا الله وتمام رضوانك يا الله وصل وسلم وبارك عليه وعلى آله وصحبه . عدد ما أحاط به علمك واحصاه كتابك . برحمتك يا ارحم الراحمين والحمد لله رب العالمين × ٧

يا شافع الخلق الصلاة والسلام ∴ عليك نور الخلق هادي الأنام
وأصله وروحه ادركني ∴ فقد ظلمت ابدا وربني
وليس لي يا سيدي سواكا ∴ فإن ترد كنت شخصا هالكا
× ٣

ياسيدي ... يا رسول الله × ٧

يا أيها الغوث سلام الله ∴ عليك ربني بإذن الله
وانظر إلى سيدي بنظرة ∴ موصلة للحضرة العلية
× ٣

يا شافع الخلق حبيب الله ∴ صلاته عليك مع سلامه
ضلت وضلت حيلتي في بلدتي ∴ خذ بيدي ياسيدي والأمة
× ٣

ياسيدي ... يا رسول الله × ٧

يا ربنا اللهم صل سلم ∴ على محمد شفيع الأمم
والآل واجعل الأنام مسرعين ∴ بالواحدية لرب العالمين
يا ربنا اغفر يسر افتح واهدنا ∴ قرب وألف بيننا يا ربنا
× ٣

اللهم بارك فيما خلقت وهذه البلدة يا الله، وفي هذه المجاهدة يا الله × ٧

إستغراق (ديم تيدك ممباچ أفا أفا . سكنف فرهاتيان ظاهر باطن، فكيران دان فراساأن دي فوستكن هڽ كفد الله . تيدك ادا اچارا سلائن الله) - الفاتحة - الدعاء :

بسم الله الرحمن الرحيم . (اللهم بحق اسمك الأعظم وبجاه سيدنا محمد صلى الله عليه وسلم وبركة غوث هذا الزمان وأعوانه وسائر أوليائك يا الله يا الله يا الله رضي الله تعالى عنهم × ٣) (بلغ جميع العالمين نداءنا هذا واجعل فيه تأثيرا بليغا × ٣) (فإنك على كل شيء قدير وبالإجابة جدير × ٣) ففروا إلى الله × ٧ ، وقل جاء الحق وزهق الباطل إن الباطل كان زهوقا × ٣ - الفاتحة ∴

Plate 4.1: The text of *Ṣalawāt Wāḥidiyat* and its instruction how to recite it

My Lord and Prophet of God). The exclamation is believed by the member of *Wāḥidiyat* to have many purposes such as to purify one's soul and to increase the calmness of the soul. In addition, members in the formal congregation who are unable to recite the whole text of *Ṣalawāt Wāḥidiyat* can recite the exclamation phrase, provided that they recited it for about the same period of time as the recitation of the whole text of the *Ṣalawāt*.

The exclamation phrase is familiar to the followers of *Wāḥidiyat*and has become their mark of identity. They usually use this phrase to welcome people. It is not only used as a part of the formal ritual of *Wāḥidiyat,* but also as a part of daily activities, either in the *Wāḥidiyat* headquarters or in *Pesantren Wāḥidiyat.* For example, if a student has a call from his or her parents or others, the operator will announce it through the loudspeaker first by reciting the exclamation phrase. The exclamation can be found on a small printed card or a sticker supplemented with the following advice:

> Always read this phrase *Yā Sayyidī yā Rasūl Allah* orally or internally wherever you are every day for thirty minutes. This phrase can be used for various kinds of purposes, especially for purifying the soul and it can be practised by anyone. [6]

This card is distributed to people who attend to the formal ritual held in the *Pesantren* Kedunglo or when a member board of *Wāḥidiyat* makes an official journey to the branches of *Wāḥidiyat* throughout Indonesia.

Plate 4.2: Sticker of Wāḥidiyat displaying the logo of the group and Nidā' Yā Sayyidī yā Rasūl Allah (the exclamation).

In 1965, another prayer was introduced to the participants of the second *Wāḥidiyat* camp. This prayer consisted of a supplication for all the leaders of the saintly hierarchy, namely all 'the help' (*ghauth*) and 'the axis' (*qutb*), who have died. *Kyai* Abdul Madjid believed that although the *ghauth* has died, if God is willing, he can continue to give spiritual guidance and education to

6 *'Bacalah selalu dengan lisan atau dalam hati di mana anda berada kalimat Ya Sayyidi Ya Rasulallah; usahakan dibaca setiap hari 30 menit. Dapat digunakan untuk segala macam kebutuhan terutama kejernihan hati dan ketentraman jiwa boleh diamalkan oleh siapapun tanpa pandang bulu.'*

those who seek guidance. As a result, the *ghauth* will be able to help people to reach (A.,*wuṣūl*) God. The belief in *ghauth*'s existence, is strong among the followers of *Wāḥidiyat,* and it is one of the teachings of *Wāḥidiyat*. The prayer was known among the followers of *Wāḥidiyat* as *istighāthah* (appeal for aid). The prayer was as follows:

يا أيها الغوث سلام الله ∴ عليك ربني بإذن الله
وانظر إلي سيدي بنظرة ∴ موصلة للحضرة العلية

> O! *Ghauth* peace of Allah is on you; teach me by God's will, and O! My Lord radiate on me the radiation which can reach to His Highness.

In 1965, *Kyai* Abdul Madjid Ma'ruf also created another exclamation and asked his followers to recite it at the end of the prayer above. At that time he did not give any reason why this should be recited after the prayer. One of the followers believed that the only one who knew the reason and the secret of the exclamation was the author. At the beginning, this exclamation was not included in the printed text of *Ṣalāwa Wāhidiyat*. But, eight years later, not only was this exclamation included in the text, but it was also recited loudly while facing all four directions in turn. In fact, the exclamation was taken from the verses of Qur'an (17:8 and 51:50). Part of this exclamation phrase, 'therefore turn to Allah', was then taken as a symbol of this organization. The exclamation was as follows:

> Therefore, Turn to Allah, and say: Truth has come and falsehood has vanished; surely falsehood is a vanishing (thing).

Two years later *Kyai* Abdul Madjid Ma'ruf launched another *Ṣalawāt,* which he did not name at the time. The new *Ṣalawāt*is as follows:

يا ربنا اللهم صل سلم ∴ على محمد شفيع الأمم
والآل واجعل الأنام مسرعين ∴ بالواحدية لرب العالمين
يا ربنا اغفر يسر افتح واهدنا ∴ قرب وألف بيننا يا ربنا

> O! Our God exaltation and peace be upon Muhammad, the intercessor of people, and His followers, make people immediately to be aware of the Lord of the Worlds. O! Our Lord, forgive our sins, ease our concerns, open our mind, and guide us, strengthen our brotherhood, O! Our Lord.

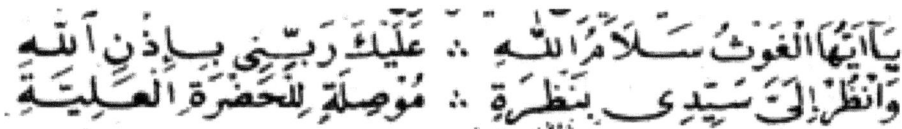

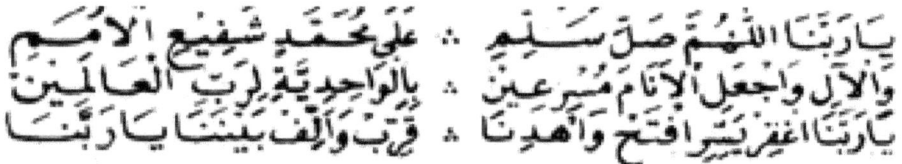

In 1971, before the first general election was held in the New Order era, he composed a new *Ṣalawāt* without giving a name to it. This new *Ṣalawāt* was similar to the previous one, but had a contextual meaning related to the political situation. In other words, this *Ṣalawāt* was composed in response to the disastrous political changes affecting the lives of the Indonesian people and Indonesian Muslims, in particular. By reciting the *Ṣalawāt* his followers were expected to be able to pass successfully through this difficult time. It was not clear whether political motives stimulated *Kyai* Abdul Madjid Ma'ruf to compose the *Ṣalawāt*.[7] But, according to an informant, the*Ṣalawāt Wāḥidiyat* group was not involved in political activities and was not affiliated to any particular political party. The new *Ṣalawāt* was as follows:

يَاشَافِعَ الْخَلْقِ حَبِيْبَ اللّٰهِ ∴ صَلَاتُهُ عَلَيْكَ مَعْ سَلَامِهِ
ضَلَّتْ وَضَلَّتْ حِيْلَتِيْ فِيْ بَلْدَتِيْ ∴ خُذْ بِيَدِيْ يَاسَيِّدِيْ وَالْأُمَّةِ

> O! The intercessor of people and the Beloved of Allah, His exaltation and peace is on you, my efforts have been stuck, in my country. O! My Lord, take my hand and people (*ummat*).

In order to complete the *Ṣalawāt Wāḥidiyat,* he composed two more prayers consecutively in 1972 and 1973, adding them to the final part of the *Ṣalawāt Wāḥidiyat.* From 1972 to 1981, he made a number of revisions to the *Ṣalawāt Wāḥidiyat,* before he decided to reprint it using Arabic script. According to the statutes of the organization (Chapter I: 1), *Ṣalawāt Wāḥidiyat*is the name given to these prayers written by *Kyai* Abdul Madjid Ma'ruf, as printed in the *Ṣalawāt Wāḥidiyat*pamphlet, including their method of recitation (Penyiar Shalawat Wahidiyah n.d:3).

It was believed by his followers that the many revisions and alterations of the *Ṣalawāt Wāḥidiyat* made by the author contained particular spiritual mysteries (*asrār*), which were known only by their author and those particular people who had been given spiritual knowledge by the author.

4.2. External Conflict in *Wāḥidiyat*

When the founder of the *Ṣalawāt Wāḥidiyat* was still alive, there was no little serious internal conflict among the board members of *Wāḥidiyat* which might threaten the unity of the organization. At that time, serious conflict

7 Interview with Zainuddin, Kediri, September, 2004.

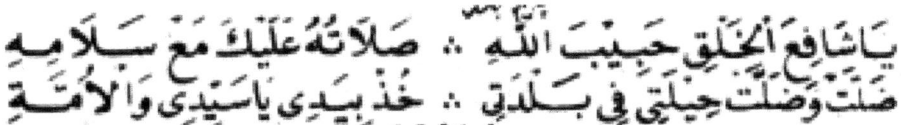

only occurred between the members of *Wāḥidiyat* central board and outsiders who questioned and criticized the validity of *Ṣalawāt Wāḥidiyat.* In dealing with these critics, the members of the central board answered the criticism by finding arguments derived either from the Qur'an or hadith.

The most vigorous criticism faced by *Wāḥidiyat* during its formative years was from *Kyai* Machrus Aly, one of the members of East Java's Provincial Supreme Religious Council (*syuriah*) in Nahdlatul Ulama, and the guardian (*pengasuh*) of *Pesantren* Lirboyo, the biggest *pesantren* in Kediri. Although the founder of *Pesantren* Lirboyo and that of *Pesantren* Kedunglo had a familial relationship, the short distance between *Pesantren* Lirboyo and *Pesantren* Kedunglo sparked heated conflict between the two *pesantren* leaders. According to an informant, *Kyai* Machrus prohibited his students from reciting and practising the *Ṣalawāt Wāḥidiyat.* The prohibition is still on display, written in Javanese-Arabic script on a large wooden plank on the wall above an entrance door of the *pesantren* mosque so that students of the *pesantren* can easily read the notice. The prohibition signed by *Kyai* Machrus Ali and *Kyai* Mazuqi Dahlan is as follows:

> (1). All students are prohibited from reciting *Ṣalawāt Wāḥidiyat,* (2) and from studying the books which are not suitable for their degree. (J., *1.Para santri dipun larang miridaken shalawat Wahidiyah, 2. Ngaos kitab ingkang diring pangkatipun*)

I tried to ask the students about the reason behind the prohibition; however, they did not give me a satisfactory answer.

Few people know the reason behind the prohibition. However, one of the *Wāḥidiyat* board members argues that it was to do with the political preference of *Kyai* Mahrus. He continued to say that since *Kyai* Machrus's political party preference was Nahdlatul Ulama (NU was a political party until 1973), so he wished to include *Wāḥidiyat*, which had attracted many followers, as part of the NU party. Yet, he was not successful because *Kyai* Abdul Madjid Ma'ruf did not agree. As a result, *Kyai* Machrus banned his students from reciting and practising *Ṣalawāt Wāḥidiyat.* However, this argument seems too subjective. It is unlikely that *Kyai* Machrus, who was known as a man of integrity, had such an intention. There could be a deeper reason for *Kyai* Machrus's ban.

An official of the Branch of the Religious Affairs Department in Kediri argues that the ban was issued due to the fact that, according to *Kyai* Machrus, practising and reciting of *Ṣalawāt Wāḥidiyat* could interfere with the students' concentration in studying in the *pesantren.* This is partly because reciting and practising the *Ṣalawāt Wāḥidiyat* not only takes a long time but it is recommended that it should be recited at each of the five daily prayers.

One of *Kyai* Machrus's sons, *Kyai* Kafabi, agrees with this argument, saying that his father banned his students from practising *Ṣalawāt Wāḥidiyat* because the main duty of the students was to study and learn rather than to deal with other issues. From the perspective of *Kyai* Machrus, learning and studying can be regarded as '*tarekat*' (the way, path), possibly the best path.[8]

Another reason for the ban had to do with the guarantee given by the author of *Ṣalawāt Wāḥidiyat.Kyai* Machrus continued to say that the author of the *Ṣalawāt Wāḥidiyat, Kyai* Madjid, was convinced that those who recited his *Ṣalawāt* for forty days consecutively would be guaranteed paradise. For *Kyai* Machrus, such a guarantee violated Islamic teachings since the Prophet himself was unable to guarantee that his followers would reached paradise. Another informant[9] explained *Kyai* Machrus's ban by saying:

> As a matter of fact, the author of *Ṣalawāt Wāḥidiyat* is still a relative of *Pesantren* Lirboyo itself... at the first time *Kyai* Madjid Ma'ruf who was younger than both *Kyai* Machrus and *Kyai* Marzuki, suddenly shocked many '*ulama*' who lived in Kediri with his *tarekat.* At first, the *tarekat* was legally accepted by those *ulama'* since its teaching was to spread the reciting of *Ṣalawāt.* Preaching the reciting of *Ṣalawāt* is recommended and is not prohibited. But the thing that was not be accepted by *Kyai* Machrus in particular, and *Pesantren* Lirboyo in general, was related to the other added information which was characterized as lying (*iftira'*). For example, whoever recites for a certain number of days would be able to gain gnosis. Where does such information come from? This is only *iftira'* (lying). Can we accept this information? Moreover, at that time there were many people who became mad after practising and reciting *Ṣalawāt Wāḥidiyat* ...furthermore, *Kyai* Madjid Ma'ruf was said to have seen the real Prophet, just as a live person, not in a dream. We did not have any evidence of this event. And if someone experiences visionary dreams of the Prophet, the dream, according to Islamic Law, cannot be used as an argument (*ḥujjat*), since it cannot be proven. If he believed that the dream of the Prophet is right, it is his right to say that. Yet, the dream cannot be delivered as a legal opinion (*fatwā*). ... Apart from that, the majority of *Wāḥidiyat* followers were lay people who had no deep knowledge of *sharī'at.* As a result, if such people were selected as a leaders in their hometowns, they would do anything that they wanted to do because they felt that they had achieved the highest spiritual stage and had been able to achieve *wuṣul* (*ma'rifat*) with Allah.

8 Interview with *Kyai* Kafabi, Kediri, February, 2005.
9 Interview with *Kyai* Idris Marzuki, Kediri, February, 2005.

The guarantee that *Kyai* Abdul Madjid Ma'ruf had printed in the first pamphlet of *Ṣalawāt Wāḥidiyat* told followers that if they recited *Ṣalawāt Wāḥidiyat* for forty consecutive days and there was no effect on their heart, *Kyai* Abdul Madjid Ma'ruf could be called on in the world and the hereafter. It is likely that this guarantee has been interpreted wrongly, as if the author was guaranteeing paradise for those who recite the *Ṣalawāt*for forty consecutive days. However, from the perspective of the *Wāḥidiyat* board members, this guarantee should be seen as an expression of the responsibility of the author. In fact, there are many reasons why the guarantee should have been given by the author. Firstly, it was issued on the basis of thinking well of God (A., *ḥusn al-ẓann*), trusting in God's kindness in response to the *Ṣalawāt* prayer of His servants. Secondly, the guarantee was based on *ḥusn al-ẓann,* to think well of the Prophet, that he would give intercession (*shafā'at*) to his followers. Thirdly, the guarantee was given as a result of*huṣn al-zann* toward the Angels of God that they would certainly ask forgiveness for those who recited the *Ṣalawāt*. Fourthly, the guarantee was based on thinking well of *Wāḥidiyat* followers, who tirelessly ask for the guidance and blessing of God. However, for Sufi who emphasize humility, the guarantee might be regarded as too exaggerated, therefore it raised strong criticism among *'ulamā'* in Kediri. Furthermore, as observed by Sodli (1990:29) the guarantee is opposed to the teaching of the Qur'an and hadith that people cannot take responsibility for others in the hereafter and they cannot guarantee happiness by practising a particular action. God alone will decide whether they will be bestowed with tranquility of heart or not. What people might do is to make every effort (Sodli 1990:29). However, the guarantee is no longer included in the current pamphlet. The removal of the guarantee was undertaken by the members board of *Wāḥidiyat,* probably due to the fact that many *'ulāma'* raised objections to the guarantee.

An additional objection of *Kyai* Machrus towards *Ṣalawāt Wāḥidiyat* had to do with its chain of transmission (A., *isnād*). This objection might be based on the knowledge of Prophetic traditions. According to this, a Prophetic tradition can only be regarded as a valid tradition if it has an unbroken chain of narrators or transmitters who are authoritatively linked directly to the Prophet. According to *Kyai* Machrus, *Ṣalawāt Wāḥidiyat* did not posses a proper chain of transmitters (A.,*isnād min al-adillat*) linking the author of the *Ṣalawāt Wāḥidiyat* to the Prophet. *Kyai* Machrus argued that the transmitter of the *Ṣ alawāt Wāḥidiyat* was the author himself. Therefore, *Ṣalawāt Wāḥidiyat* could not be considered as a valid *Ṣalawāt*and it could not be practised by others.[10]

In order to answer this criticism, the members of *Ṣalawāt Wāḥidiyat* board maintain that an authoritative transmitter (A., *isnād min al-adillā'*) is not

10 Interview with *Kyai* Kafabi, Kediri, July, 2004.

needed for every kind of *Ṣalawāt,* since the *isnād* is through the Prophet himself. In other words, every person who has the capability to compose a *Ṣalawāt* can also teach the *Ṣalawāt*to others without having an authoritative transmitter. This argument is frequently cited by the current leader of *Ṣalawāt Wāḥidiyat.* Furthermore, in order to answer the problem of transmitters in *Ṣalawāt Wāḥidiyat,* another member also published a family tree of the author that shows genenalogical connection to the Prophet. *Kyai* Mundir, who is regarded as a respected *wali* (Muslim saint) in Kediri, created this family tree, but little is known about the method he applied to trace the genealogy of

the author's family. An informant told me that *Kyai* Mundir created the family tree on the basis of a divine inspiration.[11] Therefore, the evidence for the family tree is not based on historical methods. The list of author's genealogical descent from the Prophet is given as follows:

1. Faṭimat ibn Muḥammad
2. Ḥasan Ibn 'Alī
3. 'Abd Allah Ṣadiq
4. 'Alwī
5. Muḥammad 'Abd Allah
6. Aḥmad 'Abd Allah
7. Ḥafiẓ Ilyās
8. 'Alī Raḥmat 'Abd Allah
9. Muhammad Abu Ḥasan
10. Uthmān Karīm
11. 'Alī Ṣodīq 'Abd Allah
12. 'Alwī 'Abd Aillah
13. 'Abd Allah 'Alwī
14. Mālik Musṭafā
15. 'Abd al-Raḥman Karīm
16. Ģazālī Ilyās
17. 'Abd Allah Ģazālī
18. 'Abd al 'Azīs 'Abd Allah
19. Iḥsan Nawāwī
20. Hanafī Mūsā
21. 'Abd al-Mālik Karīm
22. Zayn al-Dīn

11 Interview with Qomari Mukhtar, Kediri, July, 2004.

23. 'Abd Allah Mūsā
24. 'Abd al-Raḥman
25. Syāfi'ī
26. Ṣālih
27. 'Abd al-Razzāq
28. Syāfi'ī
29. 'Abdul Madjīd
30. Ma'rūf
31. Kyai 'Abdul Madjīd

The purpose of presenting this family tree, is perhaps to convince others that the author was an authoritative person who could compose and teach the *Ṣalawāt Wāḥidiyat* since he was a descendant of the Prophet. The reason for this is because within the *pesantren* tradition, the *'ulamā'*s authority and status is heavily derived from his family genealogy. In addition to this, the family genealogy can add to the authority of the author among his followers. As described by Woodward (1989:145) 'a clear line of educational descent from the Prophet is one of the most important criteria for establishing a claim to the title of *kyai.'* Nevertheless, a family genealogy is not relevant to answer the problem of *isnād* since it indicates only the genealogical ties of the author, while an *isnād* is related to the list of authoritative people who hear and receive messages from one to another linking back to the Prophet. The preservation of family trees linked to the Prophet is usually more emphasized among Arab families (*sharifian* families) in Indonesia.

Another objection to*Ṣalawāt Wāḥidiyat* from many *kyai* in Kediri, and *Kyai* Machrus in particular, was that the author of the *Ṣalawāt* reported that he received it from the Prophet Muhammad when he experienced a mystical dream. In such a case *Kyai* Machrus said that a dream cannot be regarded as an argument (A., *ḥujjat*) nor can it be delivered as a legal opinion (A., *fatwā*) for others. However, if the dreamer practises by himself what he received in the dream, Islamic law will guarantee it. To deal with this objection, the official board of *Wāḥidiyat* has written a history of *Ṣalawāt* and put it in the statutes of the organization. It explains that the author received the order to write the *Ṣalawāt Wāḥidiyat* when he was awake, not in a dream. However, some followers are convinced that the author of *Ṣalawāt Wāḥidiyat* was asked by the Prophet Muhammad to compose the *Ṣalawāt*.

As far as the visionary dream of the Prophet is concerned, *Kyai* Ali Mashuri, a Muslim scholar from Sidoarjo, argues that people should be careful about such dreams. In fact, the Prophet guaranteed that people can have dreams about him and that if they see the Prophet in a dream, he must be the real Prophet since Satan is unable to resemble him. Therefore, having a dream about the Prophet can be justified in Islam. Nevertheless, despite the Prophet's guarantee, one should be concerned about how far the dreamer has observed the normative piety of Islam (*sharī'at).* For example, if people claim to have met the Prophet in a dream but they have not observed the *sharī'at* properly, the dream cannot be regarded as a truth. Although dreams of the Prophet are possible for those who are pious and have the *maqām* (particular station in Sufism), the dream should not be told to others, even their wives, let alone to others for the sake of popularity.[12]

The spiritual dream of the Prophet has been used by *Wāḥidiyat*, as *Kyai* Ali Mashuri argues, as an icon to spread its teachings and attract other followers. Although the aim of the *Ṣalawāt* is to achieve the knowledge of God and His Prophet (*ma'rifat billāh wa rasūlihi*), *Wāḥidiyat* regards the spiritual experience (I., *pengalaman ruhani*) either in a dream or in a waking state as an important achievement for its followers. As a result, this spiritual experience is emphasized, and if followers have experienced it, they can tell others about the experience. With their consent, board members of *Ṣalawāt Wāḥidiyat* have collected these spiritual experiences and published them in a book and in a magazine so that other followers can not only read the stories but also improve their reciting of *Ṣalawāt Wāḥidiyat*, so they can achieve similar experiences.

When *Kyai* Ali Mashuri was asked about his opinion of *Wāḥidiyat,* he argued that since the founder of *Ṣalawāt Wāḥidiyat* did not regard *Wāḥidiyat* as a *tarekat* (Sufi order), the existence of the *Ṣalawāt Wāḥidiyat* organization is acceptable as long as it intends to spread the teaching of *Ṣalawāt* reciting among people and also to improve the proselytization of Islam (*da'wat wa al-irsyād).* Although he agrees with the spreading of *Ṣalawāt* performed by *Ṣalawāt Wāḥidiyat* group, he is opposed to the formal loud weeping ritual, which is commonly practised by many followers of *Ṣalawāt Wāḥidiyat* using a loudspeaker. In his opinion, although crying while praying is sanctioned by Islam, and even recommended in some cases, such weeping should only be performed in quiet situations when people pray and practise ritual meditation individually.[13]

In contrast, the practice of weeping has become a symbol of the ritual practice of *Ṣalawāt Wāḥidiyat* and it is emphasized in every ritual. According to *Wāḥidiyat* teachings, weeping is allowed in Islam since it was practised by the

12 Interview with *Kyai* Ali Mashuri, Sidoarjo, January, 2005.

13 *Ibid.*

Prophet Muhammad and Adam. The Qur'an and hadith even condemn those who are unable to weep (53:59-61). The Qur'an and the Prophetic tradition *(hadith)* speak about crying as follows:

> And they fall down on their faces weeping, and it adds to their humility. (17:109)
>
> These are they on whom Allah bestowed favors, from among the prophets of the seed of Adam, and of those whom We carried with Nuh (Noah), and of the seed of Ibrahim (Abraham) and Israel, and of those whom We guided and chose; when the communications of the Beneficent God were recited to them, they fell down making obeisance and weeping. (19:58)
>
> Oh! Mankind cry, if you cannot cry, try to cry (narrated by Abū Dāwud from Anas)
>
> The Prophet says: 'two kinds of eyes which will not touch the fire of the hell are eyes which are crying due to fear of Allah, and eyes which are awake all night for the sake of fighting in the way of God (*Sabīlillah)* (narrated by al-Ṭabrāniy).

It is argued that the weeping practised by *Wāḥidiyat* followers in formal *Wāḥidiyat* rituals is the kind of weeping that is intended for God and the Prophet. This crying has nothing to do with the loss of things. They cry because they feel that they have sinned against God, the Prophet, parents, relatives, teachers, leaders, and other creatures, and they are struggling for the consciousness of God and the Prophet (Anonymous n.d.-a:198-203).

However, the arguments derived from both the Qur'an and hadith above do not indicate how and where the weeping should be performed. In the case of *Wāḥidiyat*, the weeping is performed collectively and can be heard from distant places since it is broadcast by a loudspeaker facing in four directions. Opponents of this group always question whether the weeping is sincere and why it is necessary to weep collectively using a loud speaker. It is also likely that some objections to this broadcast weeping are based on the opinion that it can disturb the tranquility of public life.

Similar opinions have been voiced by Sayyid Rashīd Riḍā (1865-1935) who is known as a vigorous opponent of unlawful innovation (I., *bid'ah*). Citing Riḍā's view, Rakhmat explained that weeping cannot be regarded as part of *bid'ah* if it is carried out to improve the humility of praying. He bases his view on the Prophet's statement that 'indeed, the Qur'ān was derived in sadness and pain. If you recite it, cry. If you are not able to cry, try to cry.' Riḍā further argues that weeping will become a bad thing if it consists of *riyā'* (showing off) . In other words, people weep because they want to be regarded by others as having a deep sense of humility (Rakhmat 1998:111).

During the early years, *Ṣalawāt Wāḥidiyat* received criticism not only from religious leaders but also from lay people. Examples of the criticisms include the following: that *Ṣalawāt Wāḥidiyat* is a new teaching which is not sanctioned by the Qur'an and hadith, *Ṣalawāt Wāḥidiyat* involves practices obtained from a jinn and the Nyai Roro Kidul[14], *Ṣalawāt Wāḥidiyat* and its teachings is not based on the *Ahlussunnah wal Jama'ah*, the author of the *Ṣalawāt Wāḥidiyat* has guided his followers to make a cult of the Prophet, and the ritual of weeping in *Ṣalawāt Wāḥidiyat* is not part of Islamic teachings. These examples of criticisms can seen as evidence that *Wāḥidiyat* faced the problem of legitimation at the time of its founding.

4.3. Internal Conflict in *Wāḥidiyat*

Internal conflict among the board members of Ṣalawāt Wāḥidiyat happened when this organization held its first major gathering in 1985. From 1964 to 1985 the Ṣalawāt Wāḥidiyat had only a single organization, that is The Centre of Ṣalāwat Wāḥidiyat Preaching (Pusat Penyiaran Ṣalawāt Wāḥidiyat). This body was established to decide on organizational policy and to practise, spread, and develop the Ṣalawāt Wāḥidiyat, to print the pamphlets of Ṣalawāt Wāḥidiyat, and to arrange weekly teaching of al-Ḥikam[15] in the pesantren. Until the Indonesian government issued Law Number 8 (1985) about mass organizations and Pancasila as a sole foundation (azas tunggal), Wāḥidiyat did not have the same statutes that other organizations had. However, according to Law Number (8) 1985, chapter II, article 2, all mass organizations had to be based on Pancasila as their sole foundation. Article 4 of this chapter stated that all mass organizations were required to mention this base, as described in article 2 in their statutes (Anonymous 1985:468). In order to meet the Law, Wāḥidiyat held its first gathering to establish a new board and the statutes of the organization. Decisions made at this meeting included the determining of the organization's statutes, the election of the members of Wāḥidiyat Struggle Advisory Board (Dewan Pertimbangan Perjuangan Waḥidiyat or DPPW), which was later changed to The Wāḥidiyat Judgment Assembly (Majlis Pertimbangan *Wāḥidiyat*), and the election of The Centre of *Ṣalawāt Wāḥidiyat* Preaching Board (*Pusat Penyiaran Ṣalawāt Wāḥidiyat*, or PPSW) which was

14 A legendary goddess who is believed by Javanese to live in the Indian Ocean.

15 A famous Sufi book written by Ibn Athaillah al-Iskandarī.

changed to The Committee of *Ṣalawāt Wāḥidiyat* Preaching Board Centre (Panitia Penyiar Shalawat Wahidiyah Pusat or PPSWP) and later changed to The Central *Ṣalawāt Wāḥidiyat* Preaching Board (*Penyiar Shalawat Wahidiyah Pusat* or PSWP). The first board functioned to develop, guide, direct, advise and supervise the activities of The Centre of *Ṣalawāt Wāḥidiyat* Preaching. The board was chaired by Abdul Latif Madjid, the son of *Kyai* Abdul Madjid Ma'ruf and the second board was chaired by *Kyai* Muhammad Ruhan Sanusi, the senior *kyai* in *Wāḥidiyat.*

Internal conflict emerged after the establishment of these two authoritative boards. Although the DPPW functioned to guide and supervise the PSWP, members of the latter thought the DPPW intervened too much in the practical affairs of the PSWP. The position of Abdul Latif Madjid Ma'ruf as the chairman of DPPW as well as the son of *Kyai* Abdul Madjid Ma'ruf, the author of the *Ṣalawāt,* gave him more authority and power to build up and direct PSWP. It was reported by an informant that Abdul Latif Madjid seemed to aspire to lead *Wāḥidiyat* at that time. As a result, the members of PSWP felt that they were not be free to implement the policies of the organization. On the 7th May 1986, to solve the conflict between the two boards, *Kyai* Abdul Madjid Ma'ruf established a 'team of three' to seek a possible solution to the problem within *Wāḥidiyat.* He, then, gave a solution to cope with the problem which is known as *Wasiat 9 Mei 1986.* In his *wasiat, Kyai* Abdul Madjid Ma'ruf stated:

> The struggle of*Wāḥidiyat* is like other Islamic struggles. *Wāḥidiyat* is not like an inheritance [which can be given to the son of the author]. It is part of your right to make a struggle for *Wāḥidiyat.* It is expected that all of you will be in unity until the Day of Judgment (*yaumil qiyāmat*). All members of *Wāḥidiy*at preachers and members of *Wāḥidiyat* Struggle Advisory Board [DPPW] and followers can be regarded as my representatives (*wakil). Al-Wākil Athīr al-Muwakkil.* Every word and deed which can cause slander should be completely removed. For a large event in *Wāḥidiyat* such as *Mujāhada Kubrā* and others, I asked that they be held in Kedunglo, if there is no obstacle.

However, this solution did not necessarily mean that the problem could be resolved. Instead, the tension between Abdul Latif Madjid and PPSW worsened when they had to decide whether or not *Wāḥidiyat* should be registered legally with The General Director of the Social and Political Office in Jakarta in accord with Law Number 8. Abdul Latif Madjid argued that the registration was not important, and in most cases would restrict the organization. In contrast, PSWP members were convinced that *Wāḥidiyat* would benefit from the registration since the government would not be suspicious of it. Registering the organization with the government and putting *Pancasila* as its sole foundation was inevitable not only for *Wāḥidiyat* but also for other organizations, otherwise the regime would ban those organizations by stigmatizing them as communist or as extremist Islam. Political analysts and observers at that time were convinced that the Law Number (8) 1985, which decreed this registration, was part of the overall strategy of the regime to weaken political rivals and dominate all aspects of Indonesian social life.

In order to resolve the problem, the two boards agreed to bring this case to *Kyai* Madjid. He, then, suggested that this problem should be resolved through a mechanism other than discussion (I., *musyawarah)*, namely by invoking God through *istikhāra* prayers. This is a special prayer aimed at seeking guidance from God when Muslims face difficult options. Like a dream, *istikhāra* prayer has traditionally been an important aspect in the *pesantren* tradition and Islamic belief in general because it is recommended by Prophetic hadith. In order to know the result of one's *istikhāra* prayers, after observing the prayer Muslims usually look for guidance by opening one page of the Qur'an and pointing randomly to one verse on the page. If the verse consists of goodness, it can be used as guidance. Alternatively, people can find the result of *istikhāra* prayers from a dream. For example, if they experience a good dream, then the dream can be the basis for a decision and action. The use of dreams as the basis of action for Muslims is possible because they believe that there is a distinction between false dreams and true dreams. According to the Prophetic sayings, false dreams are thought to be caused either by Satan or other evil spirits. In contrast, true or good dreams are thought to be caused by God or an angel.

Of thirty one people who were asked to perform the *istikhāra* prayer, nineteen people reported the result by putting their response in an envelope. The results were as follows: The response in one envelope could not be interpreted; one envelope was cancelled; four envelopes suggested that *Wāḥidiyat* should not be registered; six envelopes asked that *Wāḥidiyat* be registered; and seven envelopes were blank. Abdul Latif Madjid, however, refused to accept the result maintaining that the *istikhāra* prayer had to be repeated due to the fact that seven people did not receive guidance from God. Because of his son's objection, *Kyai* Abdul Madjid Ma'ruf asked the seven members of board who had not received the sign from God during their previous prayer as well as one member whose response could not be interpreted to carry out *istikhāra* prayer again. In the end, the result of the *istikhāra* prayer revealed that six people received God's guidance to register *Wāḥidiyat* with the Director General of Social Political Office, while two people received God's guidance not to register.

To implement the result of the *istikhāra* prayer, the organization of *Wāḥidiyat* was be registered with the government. On September 8th 1987, The Social and Political Director of East Java officially registered *Wāḥidiyat* as a social and religious organization and issued it with a registered number. However, according to Abdul Latif Madjid, the process of registration by PPSW violated an agreement made by the two parties. He actually agreed with the registration, but claimed that the registration carried out by the PPSW members was not only too soon after it had been decided at the meeting, but was done before the result of the *istikhāra* prayer was revealed. The tension, therefore, did not automatically cease, since Abdul Latif Madjid continued to oppose the registration by rejecting the statutes of the organization and wrote a letter to all branches of *Wāḥidiyat* asking them not to discuss the registration or the statutes since they had not been resolved by the central board members of the *Wāḥidiyat*. As a result of this, *Kyai* Abdul Madjid Ma'ruf issued a letter that suspended the members of PSWP or MPW and asked the general members to nominate people for a new structure for the *Wāḥidiyat* organization. In this new structure, those that had been involved in the conflict could still become members.

This incident shows that, the problem in *Wāḥidiyat* happened as a result of the dissatisfaction and rivalry between two factions. The establishment of the new organization did not contribute to reducing the tension as long as those people involved in the conflict were still elected for the new structure. This was evident, particularly when the founder and the author of *Ṣalawāt Wāḥidiyat* died in 1989 (Yusuf 2003). As a result, conflict between the two factions became even stronger and this contributed to the break up of the organization.

The conflict emerged again, even more strongly because the two factions found it difficult to agree on a successor to the founder. Abdul Latif Madjid was convinced that he was entitled to be the successor since he was the oldest son, although he was not the first child because he had other older sisters. In the *pesantren* tradition descent is important since knowledge and blessing are geneologically transmitted (Woodward 1989). In addition to this, his loyal followers were also convinced that he should succeed the founder, his father, although *Kyai* Madjid Ma'ruf did not clearly bequeath *Wāḥidiyat* to him. This conviction was based on the signs and gestures given by the founder, that could be interpreted as indicating that Abdul Latif Madjid would be his successor. For example, one informant told me that during the founder's last illness, *Kyai* Abdul Madjid Ma'ruf designated Abdul Latif Madjid to lead the prayers in his absence on the fourth day of *Mujāhada Kubrā*, a half yearly ritual in *Wāḥidiyat*, particularly the sunset prayer which *Kyai* Abdul Madjid Ma'ruf had always led during the *Mujāhada Kubrā*. This was the last *Mujāhada Kubrā* for the founder since he died ten days later.

This *Mujāhada Kubrā* was held for four consecutive days. From the first day to the third day, *Kyai* Abdul Madjid Ma'ruf's family voted for the candidate to lead the sunset prayer. The informant maintains that Abdul Latif Madjid was elected as the leader of the sunset prayer for the first day, while his brother, Abdul Hamid and his relative, Imam Yahya were elected leaders on the second and third day respectively, Abdul Latif Madjid thus succeeded the founder as leader on both the first and the last day of the *Mujāhada Kubrā*.[16] This could be interpreted as an indication that Abdul Latif Madjid should succeed the founder and was one way to convince followers that Abdul Latif Madjid was the most eligible person to succeed the founder of *Wāḥidiyat*.This event reminds us of the story of the succession to the Prophet. During his last illness, the Prophet designated Abū Bakr to lead prayer. Many took this gesture as an indication that Abū Bakr would succeed the Prophet. Upon the Prophet's death, he was elected the first Caliph, by the acclamation of the people present at the meeting of *Saqifat*.

According to the PSWP faction, before *Kyai* Abdul Madjid Ma'ruf was buried, his wife made an announcement at a meeting attended by the two factions. She explained that since the late leader had not given any last testament, two things had been left: first, the *pesantren* and second *Wāḥidiyat*. The female *pesantren* and the male *pesantren* would be given to Nurul and Abdul Hamid respectively, and the formal school of *Wāḥidiyat* would be given to Abdul Latif Madjid. Meanwhile, the organization of *Wāḥidiyat* would be run by all the children of the founder with the help of the members of the Central Board of *Wāḥidiyat*. All those in attendance agreed to the decision (Yusuf 2003:16-18). But according to another faction, Abdul Latif Madjid was not invited to the meeting. Therefore, he did not know about the announcement. Since the meeting was a family meeting, it was inappropriate that Abdul Latif Madjid was not invited, especially as he was the oldest son of the founder. The informant further said that in the meeting, Abdul Hamid was selected as the successor of the founder. This decision was valid for only a few hours since in the morning it was changed.[17]

Without involving other members of PSWP (the Central Board of *Wāḥidiyat*) a second family meeting was held, and it was decided that Abdul Latif Madjid would lead *Pesantren* Kedunglo. According to his supporters, if he was selected as the leader of the *Pesantren*, he was the successor of the founder in *Wāḥidiyat* as well. As a result of this, his brother, Abdul Hamid, disputed the decision because the election of Abdul Latif Madjid as the leader of *Wāḥidiyat* had not been mentioned in the letter given to him. Therefore, instead of supporting the

16 Interview with Zainuddin, Kediri, September, 2004.
17 Interview with Zainuddin, Kediri, September, 2004.

election, he was only willing to obey the *wasiat* from his father which meant he had to oppose his brother. However, it is clear that Abdul Hamid was opposed to his brother, not because he had to obey the *wasiat,* but because in the second familial meeting he was not elected as the successor to *Wāhidiyat.* If he strictly followed the *wasiat* of his father, he would have refused to be selected as the successor of the founder at the first meeting.

It is clear that the earlier decision was changed due to strong pressure from one of the members of the family, probably Abdul Latif Madjid, who was reportedly not involved in the first meeting. He wished to be the successor of the founder of *Wāḥidiyat,* and was entitled to succeed his father because he was the oldest son. As far as the election was concerned, he maintains that as a matter of fact his election had long been decided by his charismatic grandfather, *Kyai* Ma'ruf who was known as a *wali.* Abdul Latif Madjid recounted this in his weekly classes on *Kitab al-Ḥikam*many years after the death of *Kyai* Abdul Madjid Ma'uf, when he explained about God's promises which do not seem to be fulfilled. Quoting the words of *al-Ḥikam,*[18] he maintained that this does not necessarily mean that God does not grant them. God might be suspending his promise, and will fulfill it later at the right time. He described the story as follows.

> It was reported that before *Kyai* Abdul Madjid Ma'ruf died, Pak Joni (a newly coverted Muslim from Flores) living in Tulungagung was told by *Kyai* Ma'ruf in his dream, 'Jon, ask Latif and Yahya to see Madjid (the founder of *Wāḥidiyat*), and tell him that after Madjid Ma'ruf dies, Latif should become *kyai* in Kedunglo.' After *Kyai* Madjid Ma'ruf died, in the family meeting at 21.00 pm, I was not selected as the *kyai* of Kedunglo, But after the second meeting at 2.00 am, I was selected as the successor of Kedunglo. Thus, the promise of God through the *Kyai* Ma'ruf came true after a few four hours... This is a real story. It has a witness, Ask Mbah Nyai Madjid Ma'ruf (the wife of the late founder), Pak Yahya, and Pak Joni. All of them are still alive...That is the promise of God. In the first meeting His promise was not fulfilled, but four hours later His promise was fulfilled (Madjid 1425 34-37).

There are many other stories which confirm Abdul Latif Madjid as the successor of *Kyai* Abdul Madjid Ma'ruf, and most of them are based on followers' dreams (Rohani 2004). It is clear that in order to support his position, Abdul Latif Madjid not only used information taken from dreams but also borrowed an

18 Ibn 'Aṭāillah states: 'If what was promised does not occur, even though the time for its occurrence had been fixed, then that must not make you doubt the promise. Otherwise, your intellect will be obscured and the light of your innermost heart extinguished' ('Aṭāillah 1978: 48).

authoritative person as a means to legitimise his election as the successor of the founder. He needed to explain the story to his followers since at the same time another faction questioned the validity of his choice as the leader.

This other faction was convinced that since the founder stated on the 9th May 1986 that *Wāḥidiyat* was not something which could be inherited, the sons or the relatives of the late leader could not proclaim themselves successors of the founder. In other words, the founder of *Wāḥidiyat* never publicly appointed his successor. Based on this *wasiat,* this faction maintained that the successor of the *Wāḥidiyat* leader should be voted on through a formal election involving all parties. This faction further argued that if a son of the founder proclaimed himself the leader of *Wāḥidiyat*, this could be regarded as deviation from the true teaching of the founder (Yusuf 2003:4). However, this argument was not convincing since this faction then gave their strong support to Abdul Hamid to lead an informal forum which was known as *Milādiyat* forum (birth), a name derived from the birthday of *Kyai* Abdul Madjid Ma'ruf. If this faction had been committed to their view, they would not have supported Abdul Hamid to establish the forum. Since the birthday of the founder was on Friday *Wage* (Javanese calendar), this new forum was held every forty days. This forum, inevitably, opposed the claims of Abdul Latif Madjid. The faction gave support to Abdul Hamid since he was the only one who was able to oppose the dominance of Abdul Latif Madjid in *Wāḥidiyat*. Furthermore, Abdul Hamid had strong ties with the faction because one of the senior members was his father-in-law.[19] The establishment of this forum, therefore, sharpened the tenor of the factional rivalries. After that, *Wāḥidiyat* was filled with increasing tension and growing hatred between the factions. Each faction had its own loyal supporters. One informant told me that the conflict was so strong that it sometimes led to physical conflict among rival groups.[20]

However, the alliance between Abdul Hamid and the faction did not last. Internal conflict between Abdul Hamid and his faction resulted in a split of the alliance. One informant speculates that this happened because Abdul Hamid was not satisfied with his position in the forum when he realised he was just a symbolic leader and that the real authority was still in the hands of the forum members, notably the former board of PPSW. As a result, he left the forum, at the expense of his relationship with his father-in-law and established a new organization named *Milādiyat,* which was legally registered in the Department of Justice. The headquarters of his organization is situated directly beside the *Pesantren* Kedunglo.

19 Interview with Zainuddin, Kediri, September, 2004.
20 Interview with Khozin, Kediri, September, 2004.

Instead of joining the Abdul Latif Madjid faction, the remaining members of the forum, who were mainly former members of PSWP moved to the *Pesantren al-Taḥdhīb* in Ngoro, Jombang under the leadership of Ihsan Mahin, Abdul Hamid's father-in-law. The reason given for this was to save the teaching of *Wāḥidiyat*from corruption.[21] This faction, then, established a new organization but kept the same name, that is, *Penyiar Ṣalawāt Wāḥidiyat* (PSW). This name might have been deliberately used to give the impression that this was the true organization initially established by the founder of *Wāḥidiyat*. This group concentrated their activities in the *pesantren*. The organization also established many branches throughout Indonesia. Meanwhile, Abdul Latif Madjid succeeded his father and established a new organization named *Yayasan Perjuangan Wahidiyah dan Pondok Pesantren Kedunglo* (The Wahidiyah Foundation of Struggle and Kedunglo Islamic Boarding School), and occupied *Pesantren* Kedunglo.

The proponents of PSW believe that any organizations established after the death of the founder of *Wāḥidiyat*, irrespective of their names, are not in line with the teaching of *Kyai* Abdul Madjid Ma'ruf. Only the organization established by *Kyai* Abdul Madjid Ma'ruf, that is PSW has validity (Yusuf 2003:14). In other words, they argue that the true organization and the leadership in *Wāḥidiyat* is nothing but PSW, which has moved to Ngoro, Jombang. In order to assure its followers, one of the member of this group published a provocative book entitled *'Aku Pengganti Muallif Ṣalawāt Wāḥidiyat* (*I am the Successor of the Author of the Ṣalawa Wāḥidiyat*) written by Muhammad Djazuli Yusuf. In this book Yusuf claims that organizations other than PSW have been established just for the sake of material gain rather than to implement the teaching of the founder. In his opinion, those who are not following the teaching of the founder can be regarded as rebellious students, and as a consequence their repentance cannot be accepted. He regards those who established another organizations as Kharijites, the name of Islamic theological sect which was opposed to the four official caliphs in the Islamic history after the Prophet died (Yusuf 2003:14-15).

In addition, the proponents of PSW argue that although *Kyai* Abdul Madjid Ma'ruf had died, he is the only great teacher who can bring the followers of *Wāḥidiyat* to *wuṣūl*to God on the Day of Judgment. None of the *Wāḥidiyat* followers can equal *Kyai* Abdul Madjid Ma'ruf in his perfection as a *murabbi* (spiritual teacher). This means that although the followers of *Wāḥidiyat* are guaranteed to achieve a perfect level of spirituality within *Wāḥidiyat*, they have only achieved one aspect of *Kyai* Abdul Madjid Ma'ruf's qualities, and at the same time their position remains as students of *Kyai* Abdul Madjid Ma'ruf. As a

21 *Kyai*Djazuli Yusuf told me that ' To save the struggle of *Wāḥidiyat*(*perjuangan Wahdiyah*), the organization had to be moved to Ngoro.'

consequence, anyone who proclaims himself the successor of the author, should not be perceived as perfect as the author since it is impossible for an heir to inherit all the properties and qualities belonging to the late author. The heir, however, might have one quality that the author had. This is like the Muslim scholars who have been regarded in the Prophetic tradition as the inheritors of the Prophet. As heirs of the Prophet, they do not inherit all the Prophet's qualities and knowledge (Yusuf 1994:14-15). Yusuf put forward this view due to the fact that after the death of the author, following the emergence of several *Wāḥidiyat* organizations, many followers of *Wāḥidiyat* were confused about whom they had to entrust with their spiritual development. In this sense, the aim of this opinion was twofold; to give the impression to the followers that the new PSW established in Ngoro, Jombang was the official body to which they should submit to improve their spiritual qualities and to demonstrate that although the sons of the author led other *Wāḥidiyat* organizations, they were not equal to *Kyai* Abdul Madjid Ma'ruf in their qualities.

The impact of these conflicts were strongly felt by *Wāḥidiyat* followers in many regions. It was reported that many *Wāḥidiyat* followers in Sumenep, Madura, were divided into two factions: those who followed the older generation (PSW) which still maintained the authority of *Kyai* Abdul Madjid Ma'ruf while not submitting to Abdul Latif Madjid, and those mostly of a younger generation who followed Abdul Latif Madjid. This conflict thus resulted in confusion among people on which group to join (Anonymous 1999c:36).

It is clear that each faction made their own judgment on the validity of their organizations. The first faction made its judgment by relying on the genealogical family, while the other used the official structural organization established by the founder. These conflicts show that any religious organization can be vulnerable to conflict if one of the proponents of the organization emphasises his or her own interest rather than those of the organization. The internal conflict in *Wāḥidiyat* might not have happened if each faction had negotiated the quest for power by individuals without sacrificing the unity of the organization.

Plate 4.3: The Logo of Ṣalawāt Wāḥidiyat group and Pesantren Kedunglo (Yayasan Perjuangan Wahidiyah dan Pondok Pesantren Kedunglo) in Kediri.

Plate 4.4: The Logo of Ṣalawāt Wāḥidiyat group (Penyiar Sholawat Wahidiyah, PSW) in Ngoro, Jombang.

4.4. The Teaching of *Wāḥidiyat*

The doctrine and rituals of *Wāḥidiyat* practised by its followers were created by *Kyai* Abdul Madjid Ma'ruf, the founder of *Wāḥidiyat*. However, *Kyai* Abdul Madjid Ma'ruf did not write any book explaining the doctrines of *Wāḥidiyat*. The only reference which can be relied on is based on the transcript of his instructions on *Kitab al-Ḥikam* published by the *Wāḥidiyat* Foundation in a book entitled *Pengajian Kitab al-Ḥikam dan Kuliah Wahidiyah Ahad Pagi Oleh Al-Mukarrom Mbah KH. Abdul Madjid Ma'ruf Qoddasallohu Sirrohu Wa RA* (The Instruction of al-Hikam Book and the Sunday Morning *Wāḥidiyat* Lecture by Al-Mukarrom Mbah KH.Abdul Madjid Ma'ruf Qaddasallohu Sirrohu Wa RA, 2001). This book is available only in the *Wāḥidiyat* shop in Kediri.

According to the author of *Wāḥidiyat*, *Ṣalawāt Wāḥidiyat* is based on the Qur'an and hadith, the two basic sources of Islam, which consequently form the foundation of the teaching of *Ṣalawāt Wāḥidiyat*. What is meant by the teachings of *Ṣalawāt Wāḥidiyat* is the practical guidance for the inner life and the external life, drawing on aspects of Islamic law (*sharī'at*) and *ḥaqīqat* (the truth) in the improvement of faith (*imān*) and in the mystical knowledge of God (*ma'rifat*), the observance of *Islām*, the actualization of*iḥsān* (goodness)[22] and the implementation of morals (*akhlāq*).

It is clear from this definition that the teaching of *Wāḥidiyat* includes Islamic law (*sharī'at*), morality (*akhlāq*) and the transcendent truth (*ḥaqīqat* or *ma'rifat*). These three aspects of the teachings are similar to the tripartite path to God which is widely known in Sufi traditions, that is *sharī'at*, *ṭarīqat*, and *ḥaqīqat* or *ma'rifat*. These three aspects of *Wāḥidiyat* teaching are regarded as like an essence and its nature, or like sugar and sweetness, neither of which can be separated. Therefore, people cannot ignore one of these three aspects and stress the others (Madjid 2000a:20). According to *Kyai* Abdul Madjid, '*sharī'at* without *ḥaqīqat* is emptiness, while *ḥaqīqat* without *sharī'at* is invalid' (Madjid 1423a:20-25). On the basis of this definition, the ultimate aim of *Wāḥidiyat* teachings is to achieve *ma'rifat* or *wuṣūl* with God. However, instead of using the word *ṭarīqat* (the mystical path to God), the founder of *Wāḥidiyat* used *akhlāq* in his definition of the *Wāḥidiyat* teachings. He omitted the word *ṭarīqat* because *Wāḥidiyat* is not categorized as a *ṭarīqat* (*I.: tarekat*, sufi order) and he never regarded *Wāḥidiyat* as a *ṭarīqat*. Moreover, if the word*ṭarīqat* were mentioned in the teachings, it might raise objections from the leaders of established *tarekat*. Nevertheless, *Kyai* Abdul Madjid Ma'ruf argued that

22 *Ihsan* means beauty, goodness used by Sufis to refer to an ideal state of worshipping God.

Wāḥidiyat to some extent can be regarded as a *ṭarīqat* in its literal meaning, that is 'a path' to God, since it provides the way for those who seek closeness to God. He put it as follows:

> Some one asked *Kyai* Madjid, 'Excuse me *Kyai*, Is *Ṣalawāt Wāḥidiyat* able to be categorized as a *ṭarīqat*?' He replied, ' Reciting *Ṣalawāt* is reciting *Ṣalawāt*. If the word *ṭarīqat* refers to a *Jam'iyyat Ṭarīqat* (Sufi organization), *Ṣalawāt Wāḥidiyat* cannot be regarded as a *ṭarīqat*. However, it also can be regarded as a *ṭarīqat*, because to *wuṣul* (reach) God can be done through as many paths as a number of creatures'(Qomari 2003:101).[23]

In the guidance book of the principle teachings of Wāḥidiyat published by Yayasan Perjuangan Wahidiyah (Anonymous n.d.-b), Kyai Madjid Ma'ruf quotes a large number of verses from the Qur'an and hadith to support his teachings. As well, he refers to the thoughts of several famous Sufi such as Abu Ḥasan al-Shādhilī[24] (1196-1258), al-Ghazālī[25] (1058-1111) and Imam Ibn 'Aṭāillah al-Iskandārī[26] (d. 1309), whose teachings have also been widely recognised among Sufi orders in Indonesia. Ibn 'Aṭāillah in particular inspired and influenced Kyai Abdul Madjid Ma'ruf's views in establishing the teachings of Wāḥidiyat. By quoting these authoritative references, Wāḥidiyat cannot be regarded as a deviant group. In addition, this gives the impression that the teachings of *Wāḥidiyat* do not contradict the basic teaching of Islam, nor is it an addition to these teachings.

Indeed, *Wāḥidiyat* teachings have very strong roots in Islamic doctrine. This is important since *Wāḥidiyat*, as a new Islamic spiritual group, needed to clarify its position among other Islamic spiritual groups to avoid being regarded as deviant. This explanation was evidently effective because none of the Muslim organizations in Indonesia, including Nahdlatul Ulama and Muhammadiyah, the two biggest Muslim organizations, officially criticized the existence of *Wāḥidiyat*. In 1977, the conference of *Jam'iyyat Ṭarīqat Mu'tabara Nahḍiyyīn* (Federation of Recognised *Tarekat* of NU), the official Sufi order group established by Nahdlatul Ulama, decided that *Wāḥidiyat* could be practised by all members of *tarekat* as long as this was in accordance with Islamic law (Qomari

23 *Nyuwun sewu Romo, Shalawat Wahidiyah meniko punopo termasuk thariqot? Mbah Yahi dawuh,'Maos shalawat inggih maos shalawat, menawi ingkang dimaksudaken jam'iyah thorikot meniko sanes, nanging menawi dipun wastani tharikot inggih saget kemawon, sebab menuju wusul ilallah puniko marginipun sedoyo wilangane makhluk.*

24 This Sufi leader's full name was Abū al-Ḥasan 'Alī Ibn Abd Allah Ibn al-Jabbār al-Shādhilī. He founded the *tarekat* called Shadhiliyah. His teachings are widespread in North Africa and similarly present in the most of Islamic world, as far as Indonesia (Lewis 1971: 707-08).

25 Al-Ghazālī's full name was Abū Ḥāmid Muḥammad Ibn Muḥammad al-Ṭūsī al-Ghazālī. He was a prominent Muslim scholar, theologian, jurist, Sufi and religious reformer (Lewis 1965: 1038-40).

26 Among the works of this Sufi sage and scholar of 13th century Egypt, *Kitāb al-Ḥikam* is particularly noteworthy because of its universal value ('Ata'illah 1978:3).

2003:85). Furthermore, strong support was received from the government, which provided an official letter issued by the head of the Attorney General's Office (I., *Kantor Kejaksaan Negeri*) in East Java and Religious Research and Development Unit of the Ministry Relgious of Religious Affairs in Jakarta. The Unit of the Ministry of Religious Affairs maintained that *Wāḥidiyat* was allowed to be taught and spread to common people due to the fact that it is not part of *Islam Jama'ah,*[27] the name of a Indonesian Muslim organization which was officially banned by the Indonesian government. Strong criticism given to *Wāḥidiyat* onlycame from local Muslim scholars, the effect of which was not significant in the spreadof *Wāḥidiyat.*

To begin our discussion of these mystical teachings, we will consider the book entitled *Kuliah Wāḥidiyat Untuk Menjernihkan Hati dan Ma'rifat Billah Wa Bi Rasūlihi SAW* (The *Wāḥidiyat* Teaching For Purifying Soul and Gnosis of God and His Prophet). In this book *Kyai* Abdul Madjid Ma'ruf emphasizes the importance of the teachings of *Wāḥidiyat* including *Li Allāh, Bi Allāh, Li al-Rasūl, Bi al-Rasūl, Li al-Ghauth, Bi al-Ghauth, Yu'tī kulla dhī ḥaqqin ḥaqqah,* and *Taqdīm al-aham fa al-aham thumma al-anfa' fa al-anfa'.* He insists that these teachings should be implemented in the heart of *Wāḥidiyat* followers during every activity and deed categorized as *'ibādat* (worship).

Li Allāh (for God), the first doctrine of *Wāḥidiyat,* is considered the entry point for followers to practise the mystical path within *Wāḥidiyat.* According to *Kyai* Abdul Madjid, the meaning and the application of *Li Allāh* adheres to every inward and outward deed (I., *amal lahiriah dan batiniah*), either in the form of obligatory (A.,*wājib),* recommended (A.,*sunnat*) or permitted deeds (A.,*mubāh*), whether it has connection with God and His Messenger or is related to public affairs as long as it does not break the law of God and involves a pious intention (A.,*ikhlāṣ*) to worship God without expecting any worldly and eschatological reward. In other words, *Kyai* Abdul Madjid Ma'ruf here stresses the importance of pious intent in every devotion to God without expectation of obtaining paradise or in fear of hell (Anonymous n.d.-a:317). But, *Kyai* Abdul Madjid Ma'ruf argues that followers are still allowed to hope for paradise and to fear hell providing that the hope is within the context of worship. In this sense, sincere and pure intentions are required to transform activities into worship. In contrast, every deed that is not performed solely to worship God falls to the desire of the lower soul (A., *li al-nafs*). Hence, if Muslims' deeds are filled with this *nafs,* it will prevent them from obtaining the consciousness of God and His Prophet to which the *Wāḥidiyat* teachings are aimed. He argues that this first doctrine can be compared with the doctrine of *sharī'at,* the first

27 Because of the ban, this organization firstly changed its name to LEMKARI and then changed to LDII, *Lembaga Dakwah Islam Indonesia,* Indonesian Islamic Preaching Board.

of the tripartite path to God (Anonymous n.d.-a:381). With this explanation, *Kyai* Abdul Madjid Ma'ruf stresses the importance of *sharī'at* as the initial state for those who wish to enter the mystical path. His view on the importance of *sharī'at* is not unusual as most traditional *santri* in Java maintain that all the requirements of *sharī'at* should be fulfilled prior to entering upon the mystical path. Moreover, they argue that mystical path should be cultivated on the basis of outward piety (*sharī'at)* (Woodward 1989:81).

The second doctrine of *Wāḥidiyat* is *Bi Allāh.* What is meant by the doctrine *Bi Allāh* (because of Allah) here is that every person's outward and inward aspects are nothing but the creation and action of God. This definition is derived from the verse of the Qur'an stating that 'and God has created you and what you make' (37: 96). As a consequence, one cannot claim to have strength and power to act and to do either something good or bad, since the power and strength belongs to God Himself. This verse is not interpreted from the perspective of predestination, but from the Sufi point of view. In fact, this doctrine is practised as the implementation of the phrase, *'lā ḥaula wa lā quwwata illā bi Allāh*: There is no power and might save in God (Anonymous n.d.-a:98). Quoting Sunan Kalijaga, one of nine Javanese Muslim saints, Abdul Latif Madjid explains that according to this doctrine 'a human is like a puppet and the God is like a puppeteer' (Madjid 1423b:29-33). As far as bad deeds are concerned, *Kyai* Abdul Madjid Ma'ruf maintains that unlike good deeds, bad deeds should also be based on the doctrine of *Bi Allāh.* Therefore, one should keep in mind that every bad deed can only happen because of God. However, this does not necessarily mean that people are permitted to do bad deeds, even though they are performed through *Bi Allāh. Kyai* Abdul Madjid Ma'ruf defines this doctrine a *haqīqat*, another of the tripartite ways to God.

Kyai Abdul Madjid Ma'ruf's explanation of this doctrine largely follows Ibn 'Aṭāillah's mystical teachings on the importance of relying on the Divinity rather than people's own actions and deeds, as he explains in *al-Ḥikam.* In elucidating the doctrine, *Kyai* Abdul Madjid Ma'ruf maintained as follows:

> As a matter of fact, when we see, hear, feel, find, move, stay, imagine, think, and so on and so forth, we should feel within our heart that all of these can happen because of God's command…if all activities are based on *Li Allah-Bi Allah,* they will be regarded as worship. In contrast, if all activities, including prayers, *dhikr,* are not based on *Li Allah-Bi Allah,* they will be worthless. They are just like a dead body which cannot give any benefits or harm (Anonymous n.d.-a:98)

With this explanation, *Kyai* Abdul Madjid Ma'ruf argues that if this doctrine is absent from the heart of someone, they will tend to follow their own desire (*bi al-nafs).* As a result, they can easily claim that everything they do is because of their own strength and power. *Kyai* Abdul Madjid Ma'ruf is convinced that if this feeling increases everyday, people will become egocentric and proud (A., *'ujb,ananiyya*) which is believed to be the cause of moral decadence, deviation, hostility, and quarrels. In addition, people's reliance upon their own strength and power will lead them to commit hidden polytheism (*shirkkhāfīy*[28]) (12: 106). Therefore, he insists that it is incumbent upon every follower to purge the *nafs* of its evil attributes by applying the doctrine of *Li Allāh -Bi Allāh,* reciting *Ṣalawāt Wāḥidiyat* and striving (A., *mujāhada*) to ask forgiveness and guidance from God. He further maintains that once people manage to purge the *nafs* from their own deeds, they will come to a spiritual stage called *wuṣul* (union) and *ma'rifat* (gnosis), both of which are the ultimate goal of *Wāḥidiyat.*

The third doctrine of *Wāḥidiyat* is *Li al-Rasūl* which means that every deed categorized as worship must be preceded not only with the doctrine *li-Allah* but also with an intention to follow the Prophet's guidance. The aim of this doctrine is not only to improve the purity of intention *(ikhlāṣ),* but also to keep in touch with the Prophet. *Kyai* Abdul Madjid Ma'ruf is convinced that if people apply this doctrine, God will bestow the feeling of intimate relationship with the Prophet, enabling them to imitate the Prophet ethics (*takhalluq bi akhlāq al-rasūl)* in every situation. Moreover, since the essence of observance requires the understanding of the observed in every situation, such an intimate relationship will lead people to achieve the intended observance of the Prophet (Anonymous n.d.-a). Like the doctrine *Li Allāh*, this doctrine can be categorized as *sharī'at.*

The fourth doctrine of *Wāḥidiyat* is *Bi al-Rasūl* which means that every person's inward and outward deeds which do not violate the law of God have to be believed as result of the Prophet. Moreover, *Kyai* Abdul Madjid Ma'ruf explains that all the creatures in the world were created by God's mercy, which is given through the Prophet. Without him, the world would not have been created. The merit of the Prophet is not confined to the time during which the Prophet lived, but continues to the present. If the merit of the Prophet had stopped just for a second, people would have been nothing (Anonymous n.d.-a). This doctrine is basically elaborated from the concept of *Nūr Muḥammad* (the Light of Muḥammad), and it is also called *al-Ḥaqīqat al-Muḥammadiyyat,* which was first introduced by Ibn 'Arabī (1165-1240)[29] who developed more completely the doctrine of the pre-existence of Muḥammad before creation. According to

28 Associating partners with God.

29 Al-'Arabi's full name was Muḥyi al-Dīn Abū 'Abd Allāh Muḥammad Ibn 'Alī Ibn Muḥammad Ibn al-'Arabī. He was the greatest Sufi in Islam. He was the most prolific of Sufi writers. The number of his works number more than 239.

the *hadith qudsī*,[30] all creatures are created from *Nūr Muḥammad* which was created from the light of God (*khalaqtuka min nūrī wa khalaqtu al-khalqa mi al-nūrika*). Therefore, the world is a manifestation of that Light, and it emanated to Adam, the Prophets, and the *Aqtāb*, the axis, all of which are the perfect Man (*Insān al-Kāmil*). However, the concept of *Nur Muḥammad* in the *Waḥidiyat* is conceived only as a basis on which the followers of *Wāḥidiyat* should relate to the Prophet. In his attempt to explain the concept of *Nūr Muhammad*, *Kyai* Abdul Latif Madjid describes it as follows:

> *Wāḥidiyat* can be regarded as a Sufi group which follows the concept of *Nūr Muḥammad*. Not all Sufis, such as Hamka,[31] can receive the teaching of *Nūr Muḥammad*. In *Waḥidiyat*, it can be described as the connection of cotton, thread and fabric. The cotton is God, the thread is *Nūr Muḥammad* and the fabric is all creation. In fact the fabric is nothing without the thread and the thread is nothing without the cotton.

Unlike the application of the doctrine of *Bi Allāh*, the application of this doctrine is confined only to good deeds which are relevant to the law of God. In contrast, bad deeds which violate the law of God cannot be deemed to be the merit of the Prophet. *Kyai* Abdul Madjid Ma'ruf argues that the application of this doctrine, therefore, leads people always to feel that God and His Prophet will watch them, and as a consequence they will not dare to do something which violates the law of God (Anonymous 1999a). This teaching reminds us of the concept of *iḥsān* which means, according to traditions of the Prophet, 'that you worship God as if you see Him, for even though you do not see God, God always sees you.'

The fifth doctrine of *Wāḥidiyat* is *Li al-Ghauth* (for the saint). The definition of this doctrine is that every good deed should be based on *Li Allāh* and *Li al-Rasūl*, followed by an intention to follow the guidance of the *ghauth hādha al-zamān*. The application of this doctrine in *Wāḥidiyat* is confined to good deeds, not to bad deeds. This doctrine is derived from the verse of the Qur'an which is as follows:

> ...and follow the way of those who turn to me (in love): in the end the return of you all is to Me, and I will tell you the truth (and meaning) of all that ye did (31: 15).

---

30 A *hadith qudsī* is a tradition containing revelation from God phrased in the Prophet's own words (Saeed 2006:156).

31 Hamka's full name was Haji Abdul Malik Karim Amrullah (1908-1981) He was author of the book entitled *Tasawuf Modern*. He considered responsible for introducing Sufi teachings among Indonesian Muslim reformists.

Here *Kyai* Abdul Madjid Ma'ruf interprets the word 'those who turn to me (in love)' in this verse as the *Ghauth* (the Help), a friend of God and the highest spiritual authority possessed by saints. Although they have passed away, they are believed to be able to give spiritual guidance to people. However, the names of the *Ghauth* are not mentioned in this doctrine, so we do not know how many *Ghauth* exist in this world according to the doctrines of *Wāḥidiyat*. However, according to some followers, the *Ghauth* are *Kyai* Abdul Madjid and his son, *Kyai* Abdul Latif Madjid.

The next doctrine is *Bi al-Ghauth.* This is similar to *Bi Allāh*and *Bi al-Rasūl,* but also includes the belief that *Ghauth* gives spiritual guidance to Muslims, leading them to the consciousness of God and His Prophet, which in *Wāḥidiyat* is usually called*fafirrū ila Allah wa rasūlihī ṣalla Allāhu 'alaihi wasallam* ' (Turn to God and his Prophet, peace and blessing be upon him). This consciousness is inherent within the hearts of Muslims who cultivate the ethics of God and His Prophet in themselves (*takhalluq bi akhlāq Allah wa al-rasūl*). The application of this doctrine in *Wāḥidiyat* is intended not only to express gratitude to God but also to express gratitude to the *Ghauth* who transmits the grace of God to people. This is partly because the perfect expression of gratitude (A., *shukr)* to God requires the gratitude to those who cause the grace of God is be given. This teaching is based on the Prophetic tradition, 'Those who are unable to express gratitude to people, will not be able to express gratitude to God.' In this sense, a *Ghauth* is regarded not only as *waṣīlat* (intercessor) but also as *nāib al-rasūl* (a successor of the Prophet); and the Prophet is regarded as*waṣīlat al-'uẓmā* (the great intercessor) who brings people to *wuṣūl* (union) with God (Anonymous n.d.-a). In the case of *Waḥidiyat, Kyai* Abdul Madjid Ma'ruf as well as his son, Abdul Latif Madjid, are regarded by their followers not only as the *Ghauth* but also as perfect teachers (A., *kāmil mukammil)* who are able to be intercessors (A., *wasīlat*) towards God and the Prophet. In his speech on the occasion of *Mujāhada Kubrā*in 2000, Abdul Latif Madjid also regards himself as a point of intercession for *Waḥidiyat* followers. He said this as follows:

> Some one asked me, 'Uncle, I recited this litany, why has it not been successful?' I said to him,' Therefore you should take me as a mediator.' He answered: 'I did.' And I said to him, 'In that case, you have not given absolute submission to me. If you do not understand what total surrender means, simply recite this in the way I recite it '(Madjid 2000a).

If *Kyai* Madjid Ma'ruf and his son are considered to be *Ghauth,* their followers then have to submit absolutely to their guidance.

Another doctrine of *Waḥidiyat* is *Yu'tī kulla dhī ḥaqqin ḥaqqahu* (literally, meaning to accord rights to those who deserve them), which is interpreted to mean that people should give priority to fulfilling their obligations rather than in claiming their rights. The fulfillment of obligations will result in the fulfillment of other rights. For example, children must fulfill their obligations to their parents, and parents have to fulfill their obligations to their children without claiming their own rights. In fact, this doctrine is reminiscent of al-Ghazālī who defines justice as giving rights to those who possess those rights. According to *Kyai* Abdul Madjid Ma'ruf, this doctrine will give a balance between the esoteric life and exoteric life. He puts it this way:

> It is not enough for us just to study *imān musyāhada,* as the early Sufis who merely focused on their ascetic life *(zāhid)* and their isolation *(tajrīd)* so that they could not fulfil their duty as people of their nation (Anonymous 1425c:10-14).

The last doctrine of *Wāḥidiyat* is *taqdīm al-aham fa al-aham thumma al-anfa' fa al-anfa'*.This doctrine is described as giving priority to fulfilling the most important matters as well as the most useful matters. This doctrine applies especially when people are faced with two important options. In this case, they should choose which one is the most important. If both options are important, then one should choose the option which is more useful. According to this doctrine, everything that leads to the consciousness of God and His Prophet is regarded as most important (*aham*) and everything which gives benefits others is regarded as the most useful (Anonymous 1425b:30). This doctrine is derived from Islamic legal theories which state that preventing damage should be prioritized over seeking benefit *(dar'u al-mafāsid muqaddam alā jalb al-maṣāliḥ)* and that lesser injuries should be prioritized between two injuries (*fī al-ḍarārain akhdhu akhaffihimā*).

It is clear that the teachings of *Wāḥidiyat* stress the importance of the internal components of religious life as well as the necessity of observing the outward ritual forms of Islam and of avoiding *shirk khāfiy* (hidden polytheism). The first six doctrines are closely related to managing one's heart and intentions by emphasizing *dhawqiyyat* (mystical taste or sense), while the last two doctrines are concerned with daily activities which should also be fulfilled by *Wāḥidiyat* members. Practising the doctrines of *Wāḥidiyat* will not prevent them from being involved in social activities. Instead of encouraging passivity and withdrawal from worldly affairs, the followers of *Wāḥidiyat* are required to become involved in public life, not only by performing their daily tasks but also by spreading *Wāḥidiyat* to the community. In this sense, *Waḥidiyat* appeals to Muslim activism, since the fulfillment of worldly duties is seen as an integral part of its followers' progress in their spiritual journey.

In addition to *Wāḥidiyat's* main teachings, *Wāḥidiyat* followers are also introduced to philosophical and speculative aspects of Sufi teachings (*tasawwuf falsafiy*) such as *fana'* (annihilation), *mukāsyafat, musyāhadat* (vision), *'ilm al-yaqīn* (knowledge of certitude), *'ain al-yaqīn* (vision of certitude), *ḥaqq al-yaqīn* (the real certitude), and different stations in the Sufi path (*maqāmāt*) including *shukr* (gratitude) *iḥlāṣ* (sincerity), *ṣabr* (patience) *riḍā* (contentment) *maḥabba* (love), and *ḥusnu al-ẓann* (to think well of God). These stations are inspired mostly by al-Ghazālī's *Ihyā' al-'Ulūm al-Dīn* (The Revival of the Religious Sciences)[32] which has been widely used in many other traditional *pesantren* in Indonesia. However, not all the Sufi ideas maintained by al-Ghazālī are fully introduced to *Wāḥidiyat* followers, only those which are relevant to the teaching of *Wāḥidiyat* are taught to them.

4.5. The Ritual of *Mujāhada in Wāḥidiyat*: Spiritual Pilgrimage

Wāḥidiyat is a *Majlis Dhikr* group which focuses on the reciting of *Ṣalawāt* which is believed to be able to provide a shortcut for people seeking Gnosis of God (A., *ma'rifat bi-Allah*) and the purity of soul. For *Wāḥidiyat* to achieve *wuṣ ūl* (union) and *ma'rifat bi-Allah* is difficult for everyone, particularly without the guidance of a perfect master (A., *murshid*). Similarly, to find a perfect teacher (*kāmil mukammil*) is also not easy, particularly in this age. It is so difficult to attain *wuṣūl* and *ma'rifat billah* that some *'ulamā'* point out that only particular people who can do so. Nevertheless, *Wāḥidiyat* claims to offers the easiest way to achieve *wuṣūl* and *ma'rifat bi-Allah* , that is, by reciting *Ṣalawāt Wāḥidiyat* during the *mujāhada* ritual. Quoting the words of Muslim scholars in the book entitled *Sa'ādat al-Dārayni, Kyai* Abdul Latif Madjid explains:

> The easiest way to achieve *wuṣūl ma'rifat* to Allah particularly for those who have continuously committed sin, is by reciting *istighfār* (the forgiveness prayer) and *Ṣalāwa* (exaltation) towards the Prophet of God.

The practices and ritual of *Wāḥidiyat* focus on the continual recitation of *Ṣalawāt* based on *mujāhada.* In Sufism, *mujāhada,* which originally meant striving, refers to an intense spiritual effort that may lead to levels of spiritual ecstasy. Meanwhile, in the case of *Wāḥidiyat, mujāhada* is conceived as a method of reciting *Ṣalawāt Wāḥidiyat* in accordance with the methods and ethics taught by the author of the *Ṣalawāt,* including the implementation of

32 This book is the greatest work of al-Ghazālī both in size and in the importance of its content. It consists of four volumes. This book has been taught in Indonesian *pesantren* for centuries.

the doctrines of *Wāḥidiyat,* the imagination of the Prophet's presence, and the deep feeling of sinfulness towards God (Anonymous 1989). In other words, in *Wāḥidiyat,mujāhada* refers to an optimal effort to defeat passion (I., *nafsu;* A., *nafs*) in order to establish the consciousness of God and His Prophet (*ma'rifat bi-Allāh wa Rasūlihī* or *iman mushāhada*) and to achieve *wuṣūl* to God.

It is strongly recommended that members of this group should follow the *adab* (courtesy) that imposed by the group before practising *mujāhada* or reciting the *Ṣalawāt.* First, people should be purified either from *hadas besar* (major impurity)[33] or *hadas kecil* (minor impurity).[34] Second, they should face the direction of *Ka'ba* in Mecca (I., *kiblat*). Third, if people perform *mujāhada* together (I., *berjamaah*), they should form a circle facing each other. Fourth, this practice should be based on the teaching of *Wāḥidiyat.* Fifth, people should be inspired by the greatness of the Prophet by imagining that they sit in front of him. Sixth, people should feel full of sinful hoping for the God forgiveness and regretting their sinfulness. Seventh, people should be obedient to the Abdul Latif Madjid, the leader of the *Ṣalawāt Wāḥidiyat* group. Eighth, people should be inspired by the meaning of the text of *Ṣalawāt* while reciting it. Ninth, people should not be in a rush when recite the *Ṣalawāt.* When women menstruate, they are allowed to join the ritual and they can recite everything in the text of the *Ṣalawāt* but they should not recite the opening chapter of the Qur'an, *al-Fātiḥat* (Anonymous 1425a:23).

During *mujāhada,* the followers of *Wāḥidiyat* group, in Ngoro, Jombang are urged to visualize their master (A., *taṣawwur al-shaikh*), *Kyai* Abdul Madjid Ma'ruf. In contrast, I could not find the followers of *Wāḥidiyat* group in Kediri practise the visualization of their leader, *Kyai* Abdul Latif Madjid. This practice is very important to the Ngoro group, particularly to increase their love of the *murshid*(Yusuf 2003:61). This is partly because, although *Kyai* Abdul Madjid Ma'ruf has died, he is believed to be able to watch his followers as well as educate them spiritually. If the followers doubt the late founder's ability to watch and educate them, they will be prevented from receiving his blessing. By visualizing the *murshid,* the followers become conscious of his presence, which will save them from *nafs* (passion) and increase their spiritual achievement. However, the ritual practices of *Wāḥidiyat* do not determine the method for visualizing the *murshid.* Bruinessen (1992:85) points out that the visualization of the *murshid* is also practised by other international Sufi orders such as the Ni'matulla order in Iran, the Naqshabandiyah order, and the Shatariyah order.

---

33 An impurity that requires a Muslim to carry out a full ritual ablution (A., *ghusl*), as for example after having a wet dream or sexual intercourse with one's spouse.

34 An impurity that requires a Muslim to carry out a minor ritual ablution (A., *wuḍū'*), as for example after passing wind, urinating, or defecating.

Since *mujāhada* has bectome an important part of *Wāḥidiyat* rituals, it should be practised by those who want to join and those who have become members of *Waḥidiyat.* It is recommended that the number of one's *mujāhada* be increased when one has become a follower. This ritual practice of *mujāhada* is conducted in various ways. For example, those who are about to join *Wāḥidiyat* have to practise *mujāhada* for forty days consecutively. According to my informant, this kind of *mujāhada* constitutes the initial part of the *Wāḥidiyat* ritual. This can also be regarded as a dowry (*mahr*), a word used to refer to an obligatory payment given by a husband to his wife before marriage. Like *mahr,* the forty days of *mujāhada* is an obligation for new followers. If they cannot recite the whole of *Ṣalawāt Wāḥidiyat*, they must read part of the text. This allows those who cannot read Arabic fluently, to become followers of *Wāḥidiyat.* Unlike the ritual practice in a Sufi order (*tarekat*), to become a member of *Waḥidiyat,* the candidate does not undergo an initiation rite *bay'at* (a vow of allegiance) to his or her master.

Other rituals of *mujāhada* are conducted in *Waḥidiyat* on the basis of a set schedule, such as *Mujāhada Yaumiyyat* (daily), *Mujāhada Uṣbū'iyyat* (weekly) *Mujāhada Shahriyyat* (monthly, by the followers in each sub district, *kecamatan*), *Mujāhada Rub' al-Sanat* (quarterly, by the followers in each regency, *kabupaten*),*Mujāhada Niṣf al-Sanat* (half yearly, by all followers in one province), and *Mujāhada Kubrā* (the great *Mujāhada*). This last ritual is held twice a year at the centre of *Wāḥidiyat* to commemorate the birth day of *Wāḥidiyat* and the *Isra' Mi'rāj* (the night journey and the ascension of the Prophet) (Anonymous 1989). Apart from these kinds of *mujāhada,* there are other kinds of*mujāhada* which are conducted for particular purposes such as *Mujāhada Pertanian,* (*Mujāhada* for agricultural matters), *Mujāhada Pengobatan* (*Mujāhada* for healing) '*Mujāhada Kecerdasan* (*mujāhada* for increasing cleverness), *Mujāhada Keamanan* (*mujāhada*for security purposes), *Mujāhada Non-Stop* (24 hours *mujāhada,* for improving remembrance of God and His Prophet), *Mujāhada Pembangunan* (*mujāhada* for the inauguration of a building) and *Mujāhada Penyongsongan* (*mujāhada* for the success of an event). Another type of *mujāhada* is conducted for particular events, such as a general election, the commemoration of the revelation of the Qur'an (*nuzūl al-Qur'an*), Indonesian independence, and new year (Anonymous 1996).

These different uses indicate that the reciting of *Ṣalawāt Wāḥidiyat* through ritual *mujāhada* is like a panacea by which all problems faced by people can be resolved. For example, one informant mentioned that his old grandfather suffered from acute hepatitis. His doctor could not do anything to cure the ailment and asked the grandson to bring his grandfather home. The grandson then asked all the members of his family to practise *mujāhada* every night by asking a blessing of Abdul Latif Madjid's *karamah*. As a result, the health of his old grandfather gradually improved. There are many other stories about miracles of *mujāhada* that have been experienced by the followers of *Waḥidiyat*. These stories have been collected and published by *Pengalaman Rohani Team* (Spiritual Experience Team) either in the form of a book or magazine articles (Rohani 2004). These different forms of *mujāhada* are often used by *Wāḥidiyat* preachers to attract new followers.

Among *mujāhada* rituals conducted by members of *Wāḥidiyat* is the *Mujāhada Kubrā,* which is held twice annually. It is the most monumental event for all *Wāḥidiyat* followers. Since it is held at the central office of *Wāḥidiyat* in *Pesantren Kedunglo* where the tomb of the founder is located, it is to this *mujāhada* that all followers including men, women, youth and children flock to seek blessing and illumination (A., *barakat wa nadra*), either from *Kyai* Abdul Madjid, the founder of *Wāḥidiyat* or Abdul Latif Madjid. In order to seek blessing from the founder, the *Wāḥidiyat* followers usually visit his tomb and perform *mujāhada* there. The grave of the founder has become an important local pilgrimage site for his followers. Meanwhile, in order to seek *barakah* from Abdul Latif Madjid, they have to conduct a visitation (J., *pisowanan*). *Pisowanan* gives followers the opportunity to come and see the leader of *Wāḥidiyat*. Visitation is usually held in the morning after the dawn prayer. Before a *pisowanan* starts, all followers should sit in a long line so that they have a chance to shake hands with the leader and kiss his hand. Very often during *pisowanan* they cry hysterically and faint after succeeding in kissing the hand of their leader. Since both the late *Kyai* Abdul Madjid Ma'ruf and Abdul Latif Madjid are deemed to be saints (*wali*), for *Waḥidiyat* followers visiting the tomb of *Kyai* Abdul Madjid Ma'ruf, and shaking and kissing the hand of Abdul Latif Madjid offer intimacy with them. They convey a kind of blessing. As Werbner has argued, since a saint is regarded by Sufi followers as having divine sanctity which can irradiate them, to touch anything which is related to the saint is like absorbing his spiritual power (Werbner 2003).

Mujāhada Kubrā is a major event which involves followers from many regions throughout Indonesia and overseas as well. In order to avoid overcrowding, this event is divided into five sessions held over five days. The first session (Thursday evening) is for the preachers and board members of *Wāḥidiyat* from all levels of the organization, the second session (Friday evening) is for followers who are mothers, the third session (Saturday evening) is for followers who are young, the fourth session (Sunday morning) is for children, and the fifth session (Monday evening) is for followers who are fathers. Each session consists of a lecture on *Wāḥidiyat,* edicts (*fatwa*) and instructions (I., *amanah*) of the leader and the *mujāhada* ritual. Although *Mujāhada Kubrā* is divided into five sessions, each of which should be followed by particular people, most followers from cities outside of Kediri often participate in all sessions of *Mujāhada Kubrā*, regardless of the sessions. Those who join the ritual consist of different ages and genders (Anonymous 1999b). The fact that women can participate in the *mujāhada* ritual confirms Howell's observation that women are well represented in religious groups such as *tarekat* and are now active in the *Majlis Dhikr* groups (Howell et al 2001). This contrasts with previous times when the vast majority of those who joined *tarekat* were elderly people and men who had 'abandoned their worldly interest' (Dhofier 1999).

Plate 4.5: Female participants waiting for a pisowanan session

Plate 4.6: Female participants during a pisowanan session

Plate 4.7: Male participants at a Mujāhada Kubrā waiting for a pisowanan session

Plate 4.8: Male participants kissing their leader's hand during pisowanan session

Plate 4.9: The participants at a Mujāhada Kubrā praying at the tomb of Kyai Abdul Madjid Ma'ruf (the founder of the Wāḥidiyat group)

Plate 4.10: Children crying during Mujāhada Kubrā ritual in Pesantren Kedunglo,Kediri.

Plate 4.11: Female participants, including young girls, listening to fatwa during Mujāhada Kubrā ritual in Pesantren Kedunglo, Kediri.

The *Wāḥidiyat* lecture during *Mujāhada Kubrā* is usually given by an appointed preacher. The aim of this lecture is to increase the followers' understanding and strengthen their loyalty to *Wāḥidiyat.* It is in this lecture that the preacher usually persuades the followers of the importance of reciting *Ṣalawāt Wāḥidiyat* and *mujāhada,*telling of miraculous stories experienced by other followers. Only those who come early are able to sit near the stage to follow this lecture, others sit on mats outside the main location, where they can follow the lecture from a big video-link screen provided by the officials.

Unlike other Sufi orders which require their followers to have reached a certain age, in *Wāḥidiyat,* children are allowed not only to participate in *Mujāhada Kubrā* ritual but also to become *Wāḥidiyat* followers. Other Muslim groups object to this, arguing that the involvement of children in Sufi practice does not educate them since they are too young to experience and practise Sufi knowledge. As informed by Sodli, one of Muhammadiyah members compares the involvement of children in Sufism to asking a baby to eat hot chilli (Sodli 1990:28). In other words, it is argued that Sufi practices will harm the mental development of the children. In contrast, from *Wāḥidiyat's* point of view, this involvement of children in *Wāḥidiyat*practices aims to introduce them to the awareness of God and his Prophet at an early stage of their lives, and as such, it is expected that this awareness will endure when they have grown up.

Plate 4.12: Female students crying during a prayer session in Mujāhada Kubrā ritual in Pesantren Kedunglo, Kediri

The reciting of *Ṣalawāt Waḥidiyat* during *Mujāhada Kubrā* is conducted in unison (I. *berjamaah*) led by a leader (I., *imam*). It is interesting to note here that there are no qualifications for becoming an *imam* in the *Mujāhada Kubra.* Whether *imam* are men is not a big issue. Women can become *imam* for *Mujāhada Kubrā,* even though the participants of *Mujāhada Kubrā* are mostly male. Even adolescents and children can become *imam* as long as they can read the text of *Ṣalawāt Waḥidiyat* fluently. Followers are expected to weep as an expression of their deep repentance during the *mujāhada* ritual. The louder they weep, the deeper is their regret of their misdeeds. According to the teaching of *Waḥidiyat,* inability to weep during *mujāhada* ritual indicates that person suffers from 'stubbornness' (*kerasnya hati*) and this stubbornness is as a result of sins.

After reciting *Ṣalawāt*during*mujāhada,* the *mujāhidīn* (the participants of *mujāhada*) perform the*istighrāq* ritual. According to Sufi teaching, this term refers to 'the state of immersion in God' as a result of *dhikr*' (Trimingham 1971). In *Waḥidiyat,* the *istighrāq* ritual is a part of the*mujāhada* ritual where the followers should be silent. During this time they must practise three kinds of *istighrāq.* The first is *istighrāq wāḥidiyyat,* meaning that they have to concentrate and realize that everything in this world, including one's life, is created by God. The second is *istighrāq bi haqīqal al-Muhammadiyyat* which means that everything that was created by God including oneself is as a result of the light of Muhammad (*Nūr Muḥammad*). The third kind of *istighrāq* is *istighrāq aḥadiyyat* which refers to the state of immersion in God and the state of *fana' dhauqiyyat* (Madjid 2000b:25-31). In his attempt to explain the meaning of *istighrāq aḥadiyyat, Kyai* Latif quoted the definition of *maḥabbat* given by Junayd al-Baghdādī as follows:

> ...therefore those who love God (*maḥabbat*) are those who melt themselves within God which is called *fana'* not *manuggaling kawula marang Gusti* (the union of slaves with God). As a result, all of their movements are in fact God's movements...

At the end of reciting *Ṣalawāt* in the *mujāhada* ritual, all the participants are required to stand facing the four directions in turn while reciting loudly the word '*fafirrū ila Allah* (Turn to God). This ritual is performed to call humankind from all over the world to return to the path of God. This ritual follows a ritual conducted by the prophet Abraham. It was reported that when he finished building the holy Ka'bah, he then called humankind to perform pilgrimage (*hajj*) standing at the top of the hill *Qubays* and facing all four directions in turn.

After the *mujāhada* ritual finishes, the last part of each session in the *Mujāhada Kubrā* is edicts (*fatwa*) and instructions (*amanah*) presented by the leader of

Wāḥidiyat, Abdul Latif Madjid. The topic of the *fatwā* is chosen by Abdul Latif Madjid himself in accordance with the audience and the participants of *mujāhada*. He often delivers a speech which touches the heart of the audiences, leading them to weep. He very often comes to the location of the *mujāhada* after all the other parts of the ceremony have been completed. He walks from his house to reach the stage, followed by a group of people including his *pramu* (male assistants), official male members of *Wāḥidiyat,* male security guards in semi-military uniform and one person holding a lamp at the front of group, even though it is day time. This group is followed by *Ibu Nyai* (the *kyai's* wife) and his mother who are followed by *pramu wanita* (female assistants) and female security guards. When this group of people marches to the location, all the *mujāhada* participants are asked to stand in order to show respect for their leader. Most of them are weeping and shouting when they see their leader walk to the stage. The topic of his *fatwa* is not determined beforehand and as a result the audience does not know about the topic in advance.

Because *Mujāhada Kubrā* is a monumental event in *Wāḥidiyat*, most of other *mujāhada* are also conducted around this event. For example, *Mujāhada Penyongsongan* is held in the*pesantren* forty days before the *Mujāhada Kubrā* is held. This*mujāda* is conducted to ask God for the success of the *Mujāhada Kubrā* ritual. Other*mujāhada* are also held during the *Mujāhada Kubrā* such as *Mujāhada Keamanan* (*mujāhada* for security), *Mujāhada Non-Stop* (to keep remembering God), and *Mujāhada Keuangan* (*mujāhada* for raising money). The latter is held in order that this*Mujāhada Kubrā* can raise funding not only for the success of the *Mujāhada Kubrā,* but also for the preaching of *Wāḥidiyat*. It is in this*Mujāhada Kubrā* that the followers of *Wāḥidiyat*have a direct chance to contribute to the struggle for awareness of God and the Prophet within*Waḥidiyat*by putting some money into donation boxes (I., *kotak amal*). The places where these kinds of *mujāhada* are held are usually separated from the main hall of*Mujāhada Kubrā* and only those who are elected officially by the *Wāḥidiyat* board can participate in these *mujāhada.*

During *Mujāhada Kubrā,* the followers also have a chance to give a voluntary donation for the struggle of *Wāḥidiyat* by exchanging some money for a pack of sugar. The sugar, which is provided by the committee of *Mujāhada Kubrā* in the location, is believed to be efficacious for medical purposes. To use the sugar for medical purposes is very simple. One can add a teaspoon of sugar to water as a drink or mix sugar with food. The use of sugar as a means of healing (J., *suwuk*) is commonly practised in the local Sufi tradition. Other substances used for healing are water and salt. The sugar resembles normal sugar but it is provided by the committee after going through a process of special *mujāhada,* which is called *Mujāhada Gula* (*obat*) (*Mujāhada* for sugar medication). This *mujāhada* is conducted with particular prayers by individuals elected by the committee. It should be held for three consecutive days and nights without stopping.

Plate 4.13: The leader of Wāḥidiyat, Kyai Abdul Latif Madjid giving edicts (fatwa) in Mujāhada Kubrā.

Those who are involved in the *mujāhada* are not allowed to talk during the ritual. The *mujāhada* is divided into several phases, and each phase takes two hours and fifteen minutes. After finishing the *mujāhada*, the people involved in the ritual have to blow on sugar that they have been provided three times.

For *Wāḥidiyat* followers the *Mujāhada Kubrā* held at the *Wāḥidiyat* centre in Kedunglo can be seen as a pilgrimage which involves a process of 'spiritual renewal and a renewal of personhood through contact with a sacred highly structured and complex set of symbolic operations which bring about the desired transformation both in moral persona of a pilgrim, including his or her acquisition of the desired sacred substances to be taken back on the journey home, and of the community' (Werbner 2003). The annual *Mujāhada Kubrā* is regarded as the ultimate ritual in *Wāḥidiyat,* functioning not only as spiritual renewal but also as a renewal of *Wāḥidiyat* identity. In this sense, *Mujāhada Kubrā* can be compared with the great pilgrimage to Mecca. It is in such pilgrimage that Muslims from quite separate social backgrounds gather. As observed by Gilsenan (1993:17) in the pilgrimage 'the collective quest of pilgrims for blessing or knowledge was one that gave form and substance to the idea of the *umma*. These pilgrimages served as channels of information.' After returning from the pilgrimage, Muslims will feel that they have been born again in this world as a new person.

4.6. The Strategy to Preaching *Ṣalawāt Wāḥidiyat* (*Da'wah Wāḥidiyat*) in Implementing Sufi Tolerance: The Role of *Pesantren*

As Howell points out, 'the *pesantren* (Islamic boarding schools) have been both the loci of *tarekat* and important sources of recruitment for them, with former pupils returning later in life to their old *pesantren,* or to another in the *pesantren* network, to undertake more weighty spiritual regimes' (Howell 2001:705). This view might be valid only in the case of some *pesantren* which provide either the basics of Islamic teachings or the teaching of *tarekat* or a Sufi order. However, as Howell (2001), Zulkifli (2002) and Dhofier (1982) argue, although most *pesantren* in Java do not have a particular *tarekat* branch, the life in most *pesantren* still involves the practice of intimate aspects of Sufism such as reciting of *dhikr* and *wirid.* This is valid if Sufism is conceived not merely as the practices of a Sufi order but as ascetic and devotional practices that do not need to be involved with mystical way. Therefore, many students (*santri*) in those *pesantren* who join in the performance of collective *dhikr* and perform a particular *wirid* (chanting religious litanies) may not be members of a Sufi order.

This might be well explained by another expression that 'a follower of *tarekat* is also a Sufi, but a Sufi does not have to be a follower of *tarekat'* (Zulkifli 2001). *Pesantren* have thus played an important role in the maintenance of Sufi practices from the early days of *pesantren* in Indonesia.

Despite the fact that *Wāḥidiyat* is not a Sufi group, it nevertheless teaches and practises Sufi teaching as practised by other Sufi orders. In order to develop its teachings, *Wāḥidiyat* realizes that *pesantren* are a strategic means to disseminate its teaching. Therefore, *pesantren* are used not merely to teach basic religious knowledge, the Qur'an, law and theology, to mould *Wāḥidiyat* '*ulamā'* (Muslim scholars) who are the heirs of the prophets (A.,*warathat al-anbiyā'*) but also to create *Wāḥidiyat* cadres active in every aspect of life. To be more specific, the education system in the *pesantren* strives to mould *wali yang intelek, intelektual yang wali:* 'intellectual saints' (*wali* or *ārif* who also master secular knowledge), and 'saintly intellectuals' (scholars of modern knowledge who also have achieved *ma'rifat*). A similar vision is used particularly by *pesantren* which adopt a secular system of education as well as *salafi pesantren*[35] methods. *Pesantren Tebuireng* in Jombang, for example, aims to train its students to become *ulama intelektuil* and *intelektuil ulama* (Dhofier 1999).

To implement this vision, *Pesantren* Kedunglo offers two types of education. The first type is an educational system which is in cooperation with the Ministry of National Education (I., *Departemen Pendidikan Nasional*), and the Ministry of Religious Affairs (I., *Departemen Agama*) offering courses ranging from elementary level to university level (SD, SMP, SMU and *Sekolah Tinggi Ekonomi Wāḥidiyat* and *Sekolah Tinggi Agama Islam*). This system enables these various schools to receive educational subsidies from both the Ministry of National Education and the Ministry of Religious Affairs. The second type is a *diniyah* system which adopts *pesantren* methods. This system consists of several levels from *Taman Pendidikan Al-Qur'an* (TPA), *Madrasah Ibtidāiyat* (elementary school), through *Madrasah Thanāwiyyat* (secondary), to *Madrasah 'Āliyat* (high school). The characteristics of the *diniyah* system can be clearly seen from the texts used in the *pesantren.* Most of the texts are classical Arabic texts (I., *kitab kuning*) which are also widely used in many other *pesantren salaf* (traditional *pesantren*) and include Islamic jurisprudence (*fiqh*), Arab grammar (*Naḥwand Ṣaraf*), theology (*Tawḥīd*), and the study of the Prophetic tradition (*Ḥadīth),* the knowledge of*Ḥadīth* (*'Ulūm al-Hadīth*), Islamic history (*Tārikh),* and Islamic ethics (*Akhlāq*). The texts are given to students in evening class in accordance with their level of study. In addition to the texts, other local subjects

35 A *Pesantren Salafi* is a *pesantren* which still preserves the teaching of classical texts as essential education.

such as *kewahidiyahan* (*Wāḥidiyat* lectures) and public speaking (I.,*Praktek Khiṭābat* or *Pidato*) are taught at all levels of education in *Wāḥidiyat*. As argued by Abdul Mujib, a teacher in the *pesantren,* these two subjects, followed by the practice of the *mujāhada* ritual, give a firm grounding for students to achieve *ma'rifat,* the ultimate stage of Sufi practice and mould a cadre of *Wāḥidiyat* who can fulfil the proselytization of *Wāḥidiyat.*[36]

Although the *pesantren* has adopted the *diniyah* system, there is no segregation between female and male students in the classroom. Both are treated equally in terms of their rights to have an access to education. They are often involved together in *pesantren* activities such as sports, and Boy- and Girl- Scouts. Segregation is applied within *pesantren* only in the *mujāhada* ritual, the five daily prayers, and the weekly *al-Ḥikam*instruction (*Pengajian Mingguan Kitab al-Hikam).* In contrast, the segregation of female and male students is strictly applied at other neighboring *pesantren salaf*such as *Pesantren* Lirboyo, *Pesantren* Ploso, and *Pesantren* Jampes for most of the students' daily *pesantren* life.

In addition to the *pesantren,* another means used to cultivate the teachings of *Wāḥidiyat* is through the establishment of a central organization. The use of this organization to spread the teaching of *Wāḥidiyat* is considered important. This belief is inspired by the words of 'Alī ibn 'Abī Ṭālib, 'the truth (*al-ḥaq*) without organization will be defeated by the untruth (*al-bāṭil*) with organization.' Therefore, since its inception, the founder of *Wāḥidiyat* realized that the establishment of an organization was an important tool to facilitate the spread of his teachings. In the hands of his son, *Kyai* Abdul Latif Madjid, the management of the *Wāḥidiyat* organization has been increasingly improved. According to a recent report, *Wāḥidiyat* has established branches in seventeen provinces[37] and over 125 regencies throughout Indonesia, and it has 300 cooperatives (*koperasi Wahidiyah). Kyai* Abdul Latif Madjid claims that *Wāḥidiyat* also has several overseas agencies in Malaysia, Brunei, Singapore, Hong Kong, Thailand, Netherlands, England, Saudi Arabia, France, Peru, and Australia (Melbourne) (Madjid 2001:21-27). Nevertheless, the exact number of *Wāḥidiyat* followers and their social background are unknown because no official record has been made by the official board of *Wāḥidiyat,* nor are new followers officially registered.

---

36 Interview with Abdul Mujib, Kediri, September, 2004.

37 These seventeen provinces are: East Java, Central Java, West Java, Lampung, North Sumatra, South Sumatra, Jambi, Riau, Bali, East Kalimantan, South Kalimantan, Central Kalimantan, West Kalimantan, Gorontalo, NTT, Papua (Merauke), and South Sulawesi. [Interview with Zainuddin, Kediri, September, 2004].

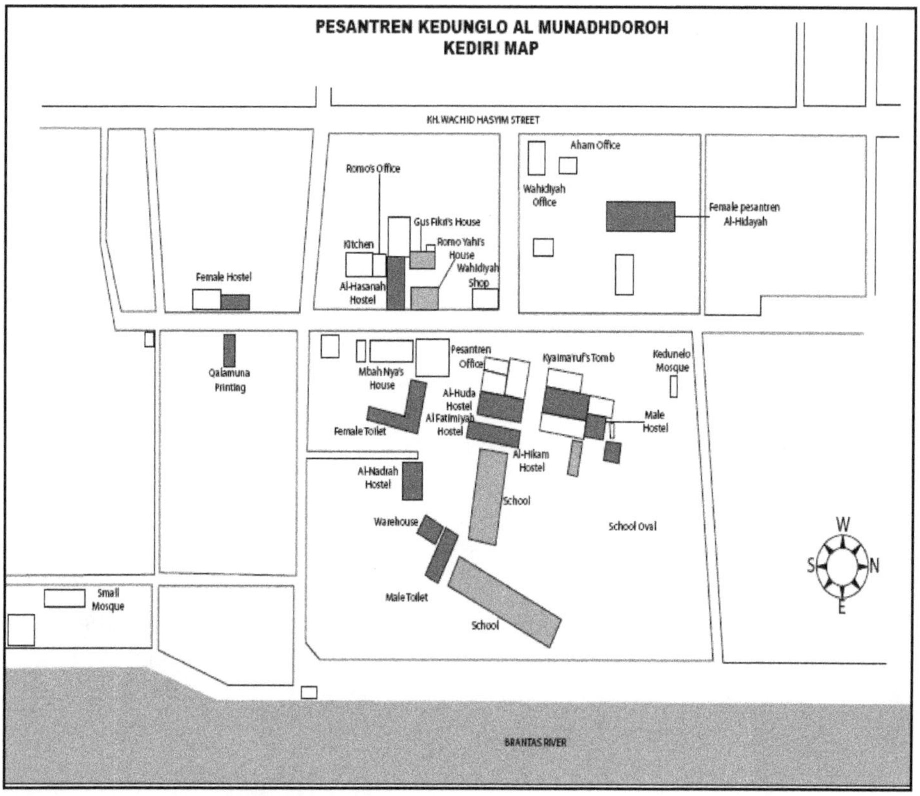

Map. 4. The Map of Pesantren Kedunglo, Kediri

The structure of *Wāḥidiyat*'s organization follows the typical structure of other Islamic organizations, such as Nahdlatul Ulama and Muhammadiyah. It consists of a central board office, representatives in provinces, regencies, sub-districts, and villages. The aims of this structure are to build strong ties among the followers, who cannot directly consult with the central board, and to help coordinate activities according to the level of the organizational structure. Since the structure of*Wāḥidiyat*involves a combination of organization and a foundation, the central board of *Wāḥidiyat* comprises the head of the foundation who is also the head of the central organization and the guardian of the *Wāḥidiyat* struggle (*pengasuh perjuangan*). It has a number of departments, including a department of regional affairs (*departemen urusan wilayah /daerah*), department of proselytization and development (*departemen penyiaran dan pembinaan*), department of women's development (*departemen pembina wanita*), department of adolescent's development (*departemen pembina remaja*), department of children's development (*departemen pembina anak-anak*), department of finance (*departemen keuangan*), department of cooperative (*departemen koperasi*), department of education and culture (*departemen pendidikan dan kebudayaan*), and department of equipment (*departemen perlengkapan*). These departments are headed by *pramu* who are appointed directly by the head of *Wāḥidiyat* as *pengasuh perjuangan* (The guardian of the struggle). The leader of *Wāḥidiyat* argues that the structure of *Wāḥidiyat* is derived from his concept of 'a state without land.' In other words, he has established a structure which is similar to that of a state government in its function and purpose. Such a structure requires officials to show responsibility towards the followers. In turn, like the people of a nation, the followers should take responsibility for supporting the struggle within *Wāḥidiyat*.[38]t

The highest authority and decision-making body in the *Wāḥidiyat* is, therefore, in the hands of *Kyai* Abdul Latif Madjid as the guardian of the *Wāḥidiyat's* struggle and as the head of the foundation and organization. He is called *Romo Yahi*[39] (the old *kyai)* among his followers. As *Romo Yahi,* for example, he can freely choose someone to be a *pramu* in a particular department, while at the same time he can replace one *pramu* with another if the *pramu* is regarded as an unsuccessful manager of his or her department. He also has the authority to set up new departments on the basis of the needs of the organization. Unlike other Islamic organizations in Indonesia such as Nahdlatul Ulama and Muhammadiyah, *Wāḥidiyat* does not have a board of advisors or a religious council which can control the head of the organization.

In order to support and run activities, the department of finance seeks and draws funding resources from many activities such as agriculture, cooperatives, printing, farming, stores, financial government assistance, as well as financial assistance from the followers. The financial assistance collected from the followers can be divided into three categories. The first category is income contribution (I., *sumbangan pendapatan*), that is, at least one percent of the followers' income is taken for the organization's funds every month. This can be taken from their daily income, monthly income or their occasional income. The second category is contributions taken from poll tax (I.; *zakat fitrah*), wealth tax (A., *zakat māl*), and charitable gifts (A., *ṣadaqat*). The third category is income from donations which are given voluntarily by followers on a daily basis. These three categories of funding are provided by all followers who earn their own income. The officials encourage the followers to increase their donations (Anonymous 1424b:30-31).

38 Interview with *Kyai* Abdul Latif Madjid, Kediri, January 2005.

39 *Romo Yahi* is the highest title in the *Wāḥidiyat* and given only to Abdul Latif Madjid as *pengasuh perjuangan Wāḥidiyat* (the guardian of *Wāḥidiyat's* struggle). His *pramu* cannot use this title. They can only be called as *kyai*. In contrast, in many other *pesantren salaf, kyai* is the highest title given to the leader of *pesantren*.

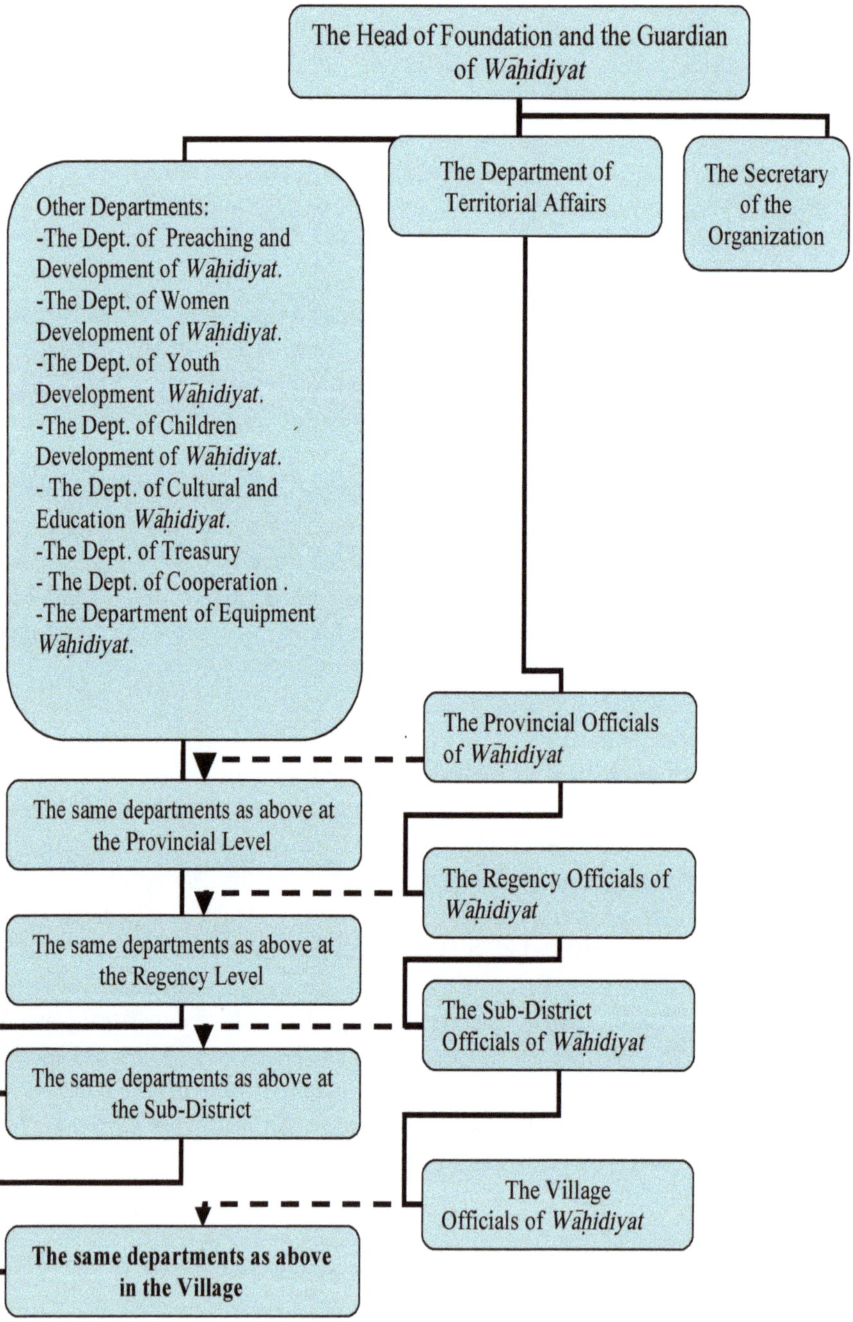

Figure 4.1 The Organizational Structure of Ṣalawāt Wāḥidiyat.

Source: Interview with Kyai Zainuddin, Kediri November 2004

At one time, ,*Wāḥidiyat* received financial aid from the government, even though with particular conditions, for example, that the aid should be free from any interest of government (at least, this notion was mentioned in the general program of the *Wāḥidiyat* organization in 1998).[40] In fact, government financial assistance is a big issue for *pesantren* particularly those categorized as traditional *pesantren.* As Pranowo observed, refusing to accept financial assistance from the government might be regarded as demonstrating a close-minded attitude. On the other hand, the refusal of the *kyai* leaders of *pesantren* to accept any governmental assistance for their *pesantren* can be described as part of 'a manifestation of the never-ending endeavor to achieve the self reliance, which is so essential to *santri* tradition' (Pranowo 1991:39-55). Furthermore, the refusal of *pesantren* to accept government assistance can be said to inculcate the value of *ikhlāṣ* (sincerity) which is part of Sufi teaching. It also avoids any intervention from the government, which might lessen the independence of the *pesantren.* Currently, the head of *Wāḥidiyat* does not want to receive any financial assistance from government. According to him, the reason is that no financial assistance from government can be free from corruption (I., *pungutan liar).* If *Wāḥidiyat* receives this assistance, it might be considered to be involved in such corruption. As a result, instead of receiving government donations, *Wāḥidiyat* has developed other resources.

According to informants, followers are not forced by the central department of finance to give alms and money to the central organization of *Wāḥidiyat.* Nevertheless, the followers are strongly encouraged to give donations, poll tax (*zakat fitrah*), and wealth tax (A., *zakat māl,* I., *zakat pendapatan*) for the struggle of *Wāḥidiyat.* The department argues that although it does not ask *zakat* and donation from the followers, it only represents the *Wāḥidiyat* organization's rights, which are in the hands of its followers. In order to implement this policy, the department has officially given detailed instructions to its representatives at all levels regarding the methods of collecting donations.

According to Islamic jurisprudence, there is no obligation for Muslims to give *zakat pendapatan* or *zakat māl* (wealth tax) to close neighbours. But, in the case of *zakat fitrah,* this should be distributed directly to the needy and the poor who live in the nearest place where the donors spend the first day of the month of *Syawal.* It is not to be given to an organization (Qardhawi 1995:411). To resolve this problem, the officials in *Wāḥidiyat,* particularly the department of finance, regard themselves as *mustaḥiq,*[41] so the followers can give their *zakat*

40 General Program of The *Wāḥidiyat* Foundation Struggle and Kedunglo Islamic Boarding School Kediri Regency , East Java Province (Program Umum Yayasan Perjuangan dan Pondok Pesantren Kedunglo Kodya Kediri Provinsi Jawa Timur (25 April 1998).

41 *Mustaḥiq* refers to people who are eligible to receive *zakat.* The Qur'an describes eight groups of people who are able to receive *zakat* including the poor (*miskīn*), the needy (*faqīr*), employees of *zakat* (*āmil*), those

fitrah to the department, which has representatives at all levels from provinces to villages (Anonymous 1423b). Of the eight groups of people who are eligible to receive *zakat (mustaḥiq),* the department defines itself as *sabīlillah bi sabīl al-khair* or *fīsabilillah,* rather than *'āmil* as commonly practised by other institutions. For this reason, the amount of money collected from *zakat* is used mainly to support the *Wāḥidiyat* struggle, not for other purposes.

Another method to collect financial support from followers is through collection boxes provided to followers by the financial department of *Wāḥidiyat*. This box should be put in front of followers' houses. It is highly recommended that the followers put some money into the box everyday with pure intention (I., *ikhlas*), regardless of the amount. The box will be collected by *Imam Jama'ah* (the village leader of *Wāḥidiyat*) on a weekly basis when the *Mujāhada 'Uṣbū'iyyat* (weekly *mujāhada*) is held in the village. Fifteen percent of the money collected from either *zakat* or *dana box* (box donation) is taken to to run the organization of *Wāḥidiyat* in the village, while the rest is kept by the *Imam Jama'ah Induk* (the main village leader of *Wāḥidiyat*). The *Imam Jama'ah Induk* is chosen from among the village leaders. The department of finance at sub-district level then collects the funds every month and passes them on to the department of finance at regency level. At the end of every month the funds should be given to the central department of finance after deducting the funds for the organization at the regency level (Anonymous 1423a:31-32)

The department of finance has an annual target of one hundred and twenty seven million rupiah (AUD$ 18,142,86) from *zakat fitrah,* twenty seven million (AUD$ 3,857,14) from *zakat mal* and one hundred fifty million (AUD$ 21,428,57)[42] from donations. However, this amount is just a target, and in fact the amount of money from those sources is frequently less than the target. This is because followers have different views of *zakat,* based on their own *madhab* (Islamic law school) back ground. This influences their acceptance of the obligation to pay *zakat* through *Wāḥidiyat.* Furthermore, the various degrees of loyalty and submission of the followers to the leader affect the level of contribution of *zakat* and the proportion of donations from followers' income (*sumbangan pendapatan*) given to the *Wāḥidiyat* (Anonymous 1424b).

According to one informant, the followers should give donations to the organization simply to express their gratitude, sacrifice and responsibility to help the organization in its efforts to bring Muslims to the consciousness of God and His Prophet. This is a hard task for the organization, which requires

who have just embraced Islam (*mu'allaf*), a debtor (*ghārim*), freed slaves (*riqāb),* those who struggle in the cause of Allah (*fīsabilillah*) and wayfarers (*Ibn sabīl*).

42 $AUD 1= Rp 7000

not only time, organizational management but also funds. Therefore, followers need to give financial assistance to the organization not only for the sake of the organization but also for the benefit of the followers themselves, particularly to improve their closeness to God and His Prophet. In other words, in order to achieve *ma'rifat bi-Allāh wa rasūlihi,* the followers of *Wāḥidiyat* should make an effort to use their ability, wealth, and knowledge to help the struggle of *Wāḥidiyat.* All of these efforts should be directed to follow the guidance of *Romo Yahi* (the leader of *Wāḥidiyat*). In this sense, sacrifice is strongly stressed within this group, and this has become a determining factor in measuring followers' submission (A., *taslīm*) to the leader of *Wāḥidiyat.*

All *Wāḥidiyat* followers have a responsibility to bring people regardless of their ethnic group, religious group or age, to the consciousness of God and His Prophet. In other words, they have a duty to spread the teaching of *Wāḥidiyat,* including the *Ṣalawāt Wāḥidiyat,* to other people including Muslims and non-Muslims. According to Slamet, a central *Wāḥidiyat* official, spreading the teaching of *Wāḥidiyat* to non-Muslims, is conducted without coercion. He added that, in many cases, they are interested in practising *Wāḥidiyat* ritual after they face a difficult problem and they ask *Wāḥidiyat* to solve it. In this case, Slamet pointed out that *Wāḥidiyat* officials never asked them to convert to Islam.[43] The opportunity to preach the teaching of *Wāḥidiyat* and the*Ṣalawāt* is to be given by the founder not only to the official board members but also to the followers and other people. As a result, those who have received and practised *Ṣalawāt Wāḥidiyat* can spread knowledge of the *Ṣalawāt* to others without asking for an *ijāza* (license) from the leader. With this feature, *Wāḥidiyat* is, in effect, a missionary group which strongly urges its followers to spread the teachings of *Wāḥidiyat* and the *Ṣalawāt* and to seek new followers. The missionary nature of *Wāḥidiyat* was clearly reflected by *Kyai* Abdul Madjid Ma'ruf. For instance, he suggested to his followers on the 25th anniversary of *Ṣalawāt Wāḥidiyat* that, 'Within a month, every *Wāḥidiyat* follower should recruit at least one new follower'(Anonymous 1989:70).

In contrast, other Sufi orders, such as Qodiriyah, Naqshabandiyah and Tijaniyah, require *bay'at* and *ijāza* for their followers. Only particular disciples who have received *ijāza* from their master are able to seek new followers. In line with this, there are three types of *ijāza*. The first is the lowest one given to disciples to practise *tarekat*. The second *ijāza* gives authority to disciples, as the representatives of their master, to guide others in practising Sufism. The third one is the highest *ijāza,* which authorizes the holder as Sufi master to offer initiation to novices (Bruinessen 1992:87).

43 Interview with Slamet, Kediri, September, 2004.

Despite the fact that all followers are responsible for spreading the teaching of *Wāḥidiyat* and the *Ṣalawāt*, the *Wāḥidiyat* organization has established a department of proselytization and development of *Wāḥidiyat* which focuses on spreading the teaching of *Wāḥidiyat*. This department is responsible for training *Wāḥidiyat* male preachers (A. *dā'ī*), female preachers (A. *dā'iyyat)* and cadres so that they can preach and offer true information concerning the teaching and the ritual of *Wāḥidiyat*. One of the activities of this department is to give short courses and regular upgrading training for preachers, members of board of the organization, and followers at all levels. Such activities not only enhance members' conceptual and practical understanding of *Wāḥidiyat* teaching, but also prepare them to become skillful cadres who are able to fulfil organizational tasks.

According to the book entitled *Bahan Up Grading Da'i Wahidiyah Bagian B* (Upgrading Materials for *Wāḥidiyat* Preachers Part B,n.d.), the importance of spreading the teachings of *Wāḥidiyat* can be compared with the duty to spread Islam (*da'wa Islāmiyyat*) itself. The rationale of this notion is that the teaching of *Wāḥidiyat,* in fact , contains an introduction to God and the Prophet which is also part of Islamic teachings. If that is the case, spreading *Wāḥidiyat* to other people can be considered as the same obligation as spreading Islamic teachings. It is, therefore, claimed that the spreading*Wāḥidiyat* among other people is sanctioned by the Qur'anic verses and the Prophetic tradition. In turn, those who do not spread the teaching of *Wāḥidiyat* can be regarded as violating Islamic teachings (Anonymous 1989:74). To support this argument, the following Islamic verses are quoted from the Qur'an and hadith:

> And from among you there should be a party who invites to good and enjoins what is right and forbids the wrong, and these it is that shall be successful (3:104).
>
> Those who are not concerned with Muslim affairs are not from their group (narrated by Ṭabrānī)
>
> Surely those who conceal the clear proofs and the guidance that We revealed after We made it clear in the Book for people, those it is whom Allah shall curse, and those who curse shall curse them too (1:159).

The first verse cited here implies that the spreading of *Wāḥidiyat* teaching is as obligatory as inviting others to be good, enjoining what is right and forbidding what is wrong (I., *amar ma'rufnahi munkar*). In contrast, the Prophetic sayings and the Qur'an verses quoted here show that those who do not want to spread the teaching of *Wāḥidiyat* can be likened not only to those who ignore other Muslims' affairs but also to those who hide the clear proof and guidance that God has revealed. However, some people object to the obligation to spread

Wāḥidiyat, particularly if it is justified by the texts from the Qur'an and hadith. They claim that the Qur'an and hadith text quoted here actually have a general meaning and do not therefore specifically refer to the spreading of *Wāḥidiyat*.

As a Sufi missionary group, *Wāḥidiyat* applies a strategy of preaching which draws its inspiration from the prophets' preaching. The prophets of God were equipped with miracles (A., *mu'jiza*) by which they proved their truthfulness. Whereas others were incapable of doing the same, *Kyai* Abdul Latif Madjid told me that the oldest strategy for preaching Islam is based on miracles performed by the prophets for introducing God to the people (A., *ummat*). Those miracles were given to the prophets in order to respond to people's needs. In line with this, the strategy of preaching in *Wāḥidiyat* is intended to meet people's needs, including all aspects of life such as the need to achieve *ma'rifat bi-Allāh,* quietness of heart, good health, and economic needs. Abdul Latif Madjid maintains that these are the main needs of human beings and they should be fulfilled by *Wāḥidiyat*.[44] Furthermore, he claims that *Wāḥidiyat* has responded to all of these needs and has thus succeeded in attracting rural as well as urban followers regardless of their social group, age, political party and religious background. He put it this way:

> All Praises are due to Allah. After practising *Wāḥidiyat*, we have been imbued with capacities. We easily love God, we easily apply *lillah* and *billah,* and easily perform worship. Furthermore, owing to *Ṣalawāt Wāḥidiyat*'s blessing (I, *berkah*) and the Prophet's mediation, according to our colleagues' reports, all praises are due to Allah, all of the people's problems can be solved: their economic problems, health problems or whatever their problems are, if they pray seriously, God will answer their prayers giving them [a solution] from unpredictable ways and predictable ways (Madjid 1423b:9).

Other strategies and methods to preach and advertise *Wāḥidiyat* include meeting people personally, explaining *Wāḥidiyat* at meetings involving many groups of people, writing letters of *dakwah,* and spreading *Wāḥidiyat* through newspapers, radio and television. Before applying these methods, all *Wāḥidiyat* preachers should perform a special *mujāhada* to ask God for success in their efforts. It is also suggested that every follower of *Wāḥidiyat* put such things as a *Wāḥidiyat* calendar, the *Wāḥidiyat* logo, the picture of *Kyai* Madjid Ma'ruf and *Kyai* Latif in their home and fly the *Wāḥidiyat* flag wherever a ritual of *mujāhada* is scheduled to be held (Anonymous 1425c:10-14). This will make *Wāḥidiyat* easily recognized.

44 Interview with Abdul Latif Madjid, Kediri, November, 2004.

The preaching of *Wāḥidiyat* as synonymous with the preaching of Islam does not prevent this group from being tolerant of other religious followers who wish to practise *Ṣalawāt Wāḥidiyat*. This group allows members of other religions to practise the *Ṣalawāt* without requiring them to convert to Islam. Other Muslim groups might object to this practice but it can be regarded as part of *Wāḥidiyat* strategy to spread the *Ṣalawāt Wāḥidiyat* while demonstrating the tolerant nature of Sufism in general toward other religious faiths. In this sense, Abdul Latif Madjid argues that members of other religions are not compelled to convert to Islam by practising *Ṣalawāt Wāḥidiyat*, but they are only asked to approach God. For him, the most important thing is that they want to recite *Ṣalawāt Wāḥidiyat*. When asked whether their good deeds (I. *amal saleh*) will be accepted by God if they were not Muslim, he replies that one should distinguish between the good deeds and prayers (A. *du'ā*) in relation to God. Good deeds are a matter of *fiqh* (Islamic jurisprudence), while prayers (*du'ā*) or *Ṣalawāt* do not belong under *fiqh* rules. According to *fiqh* rules, good deeds (I., *amal saleh*) will only be accepted by God if they are performed by Muslims, not by other religious believers. However, since prayers are not under *fiqh* provisions, the prayers invoked by other religious followers can be granted by God, even though they are not Muslims. They may even be infidels (I., *kafir*). Abdul Latif Madjid gives the example of a Javanese man who did not perform ritual prayers or other religious acts but who came to a *kyai* to study the knowledge of invulnerability (I., *ilmu kekebalan*). After some years, the man was able to master the *ilmu kekebalan* and became an expert (I., *jawara*). This example, according to Abdul Latif Madjid, can be regarded as evidence that the man's prayers were granted (A., *ijabah*) by God although he was not a committed Muslim. *Kyai* Abdul Latif Madjid, further argues that to become a Muslim is matter of divine guidance (I., *hidayah*). Since it is a matter of *hidayah*, people cannot compel other religious faiths to convert to Islam. For Abdul Latif, people's willingness to recite and practise *Ṣalāwa Wāḥidiyat* is also a result of guidance (I., *hidayah*) (Madjid 2001:25). It is for this reason that after practising the forty days *Mujāhada*, seventy Balinese Hindu followers were also able to participate at the ritual of *Mujāhada Kubrā* in *Pesantren* Kedunglo (Madjid 1424:18-22). *Kyai* Abdul Latif describes *Wāḥidiyat* 's tolerance of other religions as follows:

> *Wāḥidiyat* followers need not become Muslims. *Wāḥidiyat* does not compel people, but we only ask people to approach Allah. It is not a problem if you are not Muslims, the most important thing is that you read the *Ṣalawāt Wāḥidiyat*...recently a non-Muslim from Metro practised for fifteen days. Everything has a cause. He had a problem which made him upset. Then he met with a *Wāḥidiyat* follower. The follower offered him *Ṣalawāt Wāḥidiyat* to read. After fifteen days his problem could be solved, but he did not want to convert to Islam.'

The inclusiveness and tolerance of *Wāḥidiyat* is not a unique phenomenon among Sufi groups elsewhere. For instance, there have been studies showing the inclusiveness and tolerance of Sufi groups and practices in South Asia. Saheb observes the inclusiveness and tolerance shown by a Sufi group in Nagore, India. Both Muslim and Hindus celebrate the anniversary of the death of the Sufi saint Sahul Hameed Nagore Andavar, known as *'urs* or *Kanduri,* and attend his tomb (Saheb 1998). Saheb's conclusion gains support from Werbner who concludes that most Sufi myths in South Asia contain a story of tolerance, inclusiveness and peace (Werbner 2003:26). Werbner further shows that the *shaikh* Zindapir, a Sufi master of the Naqshabandi order in Pakistan, for instance, is typical of Sufi saints in that he stresses the importance of inclusiveness and tolerance towards other religious faiths. As quoted by Werbner, the Sufi saint maintains that ' the 'true' Islam does not discriminate between people of different creeds and faiths.' The *shaikh* respects and treats other religious followers with generous hospitality because they are human beings and he does this for the love of God alone and no one else (Werbner, 2003:95). The successful history of Islamization in India, central Asia, Anatolia and Africa also shows that Sufi groups have played an important role in the process of the preaching of Islam since they have accommodated to the spiritual environment which has existed in those regions (Rahman 1979) and demonstrated flexibility in adaptation to incorporate 'local religious customs and belief into their eclectic fold' (Gilsenan, 1973).

4.7. Spiritual Experience and Spiritual Authority in *Wāḥidiyat*

Spiritual experience (I., *pengalaman rohani*) is inseparable from Sufi tradition. The term spiritual experience could also be translated as miracles (A. *karāmat*) experienced by a Sufi master or Sufi follower as a result of his closeness to God. Within the Sufi tradition, stories of miracles are well documented in Sufi hagiographical works that are responsible for the spreading of those miracles stories in Muslim societies. Most of these miracle stories tend to describe the extraordinary powers of saints that seem to surpass natural law (Schimmel 1975).

The main questions here are how the idea of spiritual experience (I., *pengalaman rohani*) is understood and what the role of this spritiual experience is among *Wāḥidiyat* followers. This section will discuss these questions by describing the role of the *Wāḥidiyat* spiritual leader and then analysing the stories of spiritual experience reported by the followers.

The fact that every *Wāḥidiyat* follower is able to be a leader (*imam*) in an *mujāhada* ritual does not necessarily mean that authority in *Wāḥidiyat* can be shared with others. Rather, the spiritual leader in *Wāḥidiyat* is *Kyai* Abdul Latif Madjid, who is the central leader of this Sufi group. All things to do with the group are centred on the leader. This includes not only organizational matters but also spiritual matters such as any *pengalaman rohani* experienced by his followers. In this sense, *pengalaman rohani* and unusual events that happen to the followers are perceived to be the result of the miraculous power (A. *maziyyat*) of *Ṣalawāt Waḥidiyat* and the miraculous intervention of their spiritual leader. These miracles thus prove his sacred quality. In other words, *pengalaman rohani* can be understood as what Ewing (1990:59) describes as a social phenomenon since it is believed that the spiritual experience has been directly brought about and its content shaped by the leader. In the case of *Waḥidiyat,* those spiritual experiences can be achieved by the followers while awake, though they mostly occur in dreams. This fact has inevitably made the leader central to the devotion of his followers in seeking his *barakah* (blessing) and attaining spiritual experience.

Therefore, it is not surprising that beside the quietness of heart which can be achieved by practising *Ṣalawāt Wāḥidiyat, pengalaman rohani* is also considered an important achievement. Furthermore, this is considered the highest achievement that most followers aspire to attain. For instance, commenting on a *Wāḥidiyat* follower who had published his experience of a vision of the Prophet in a magazine, an informant told me that he wanted to have the same spiritual experience. Although he had been practising *Ṣalawāt Wāḥidiyat* for a long time, he had not yet attained the same experience. This notion is also found elsewhere, such as in Egypt and Morocco, where miracle and *barakah* are not only a source of individual and group satisfaction but also based on dreams in which one finds refuge (Gilsenan 1992:95).

Within *Wāḥidiyat,* those who have themselves attained and those who have known other people who have achieved a spiritual experience should report this to the official board of *Wāḥidiyat.* This official instruction is mentioned in a leaflet as follows: 'write your experience or others' experiences as a result of *mujāhada* and tell it to the official board'(Anonymous 1989). A special team called The Spiritual Experience Team (*Tim Pengalaman Rohani*) has been set up to collect accounts of spiritual experiences from followers. In order to ensure the validity of these experiences, the team gives the followers a form which asks them to state that the *pengalaman rohani* they experienced really happened. After obtaining consent from them, the team then publishes the experience in a book or magazine. These accounts are similar to hagiographical Sufi stories. However, not all of the followers agree to share their spiritual experiences with the team. Some are reluctant to describe their experiences because they fear they are displaying *riyā'* (showing off), which is strongly opposed to Sufi teaching in general and the teaching of *Wāḥidiyat* in particular, since the latter emphasizes *ikhlāṣ* (absolute sincerity). Moreover, in the Sufi tradition, any kind of worship followed by *riyā'* is considered not only as commiting the greatest sin but also as meaningless and even dangerous. Some people also disagree with the publishing spiritual experiences because this may cause others who do not have such spiritual experiences to become jealous. On the other hand, others take the view that recounting spiritual experiences to the team only expresses a divine gift of grace (A., *taḥadduth bi al-ni'mat*).

In fact, the achievement of a spiritual experience or *karamah* is not the ultimate aim of *Wāḥidiyat* and other Sufi practices. Indeed, according to Sufi teaching, if disciples practise Sufi teachings just for the sake of gaining *karamah,* they will be hindered (A., *maḥjūb*) in their search to be near God. Some Sufi theorists have even warned that *karamah* constitutes a temptation given by God in order to test His servant (W.Ernst 2003:71). Nevertheless, stories of spiritual experiences are familiar among *Wāḥidiyat* followers. This is partly because such stories are introduced deliberately to the followers, not only through official rituals such as *mujāhada* but also through the publication of the book entitled *Shalawat Wahidiyah dan Pengalaman Rohani* as well as through a certain section of the *Aham* magazine which contains the stories of spiritual experience or *karamah* experienced by the followers. Like other hagiographical Sufi books, the book focuses on stories of the miraculous powers of the leader, as well as the peculiarities of *Ṣalawāt Wāḥidiyat,* and prophesy.

However, if we examine the stories of spiritual experience in the book, we find that the majority of stories feature the figure of the leader with his miraculous powers, most of which are experienced by the followers in a dream. Spiritual experiences after seeing the leader performing such miracles are seldom experienced while awake. The stories that followers tell can be divided into several themes. The first theme is to do with who is the *Ghauth* (the Help) of this age, and who is the real spiritual successor of the *Wāḥidiyat* leader after the death of *Kyai* Abdul Madjid Ma'ruf. Examples of stories with these themes are given below:

> A day before the ritual of *Mujāhada Kubrā Rajab* 1424 H. was held, I visited *Kyai* Abdul Latif Madjid asking him to pray for me to be able to join my soul with the holy soul of the servant of God. After doing *mujāhada,* I slept and had a vision of meeting with four people with white robes. The oldest man among these four people asked me, 'Who are you? He said to me, 'I am the prophet Abraham, this person is the prophet Moses, and this person is the prophet Solomon.' But, he did not introduce the fourth person. Then,

> I asked him,'Why are all of you here, and not in paradise?' He replied, ' I and all the prophets are here because we follow and support the struggle of the Prophet Muhammad which is now given to the His Majesty *Romo Kyai* Abdul Latif Madjid .' Abraham said,'He has a channel of *Nūr alA'ẓam* (great light) which is directly linked to the Prophet Muhammad. .... 'look at *Kyai* Abdul Latif Madjid whose light connects to the Prophet and spreads to the universe.' I witnessed that at that time the light was really coming out towards the Prophet Muhammad. Abraham continued to say, 'From now on, those who wish to *wuṣūl* toward God and His Prophet without *Kyai* Abdul Latif Madjid will not succeed in their journey, and my companions do not mind and I keep supporting *Kyai* Latif Madjid.'
>
> In the middle of 1998, I read a book on Sufism in the middle of the night. I fell a sleep and had a dream of visiting *Kyai* Abdul Latif Madjid. He asked me to wait for him in the living room, while he went into his room. Then he came and saw me with two plates of rice. He asked me to have dinner. After having dinner he showed me a letter of decision (*surat keputusan*) written by the Prophet Muhammad. The letter mentioned that *Kyai* Latif is the successor of *Kyai* Madjid, the author of *Ṣalawāt Wāḥidiyat*. He let me read the letter. I was impressed with the beauty of the paper and the writing of the letter. Suddenly the room where we met was filled with a pile of books, and he said to me, 'The letter from the Prophet has been given to me, yet why do people want to replace me, that is impossible…'
>
> …One night, I had a dream that I was in a large garden. The garden was the most beautiful garden I had ever seen. I walked into the garden to enjoy some flowers planted near the bank of a river. While I enjoyed the beauty of the flowers, I was surprised that I heard a voice from the river water saying, '*Kyai* Abdul Latif Madjid is *gauth hādha al-zamān* (the Help of this age). Then, another voice said the same thing, but the voice was spoken by flowers and subsequently the stones, fish, ground, and birds said the same thing as the water and flowers did. One day after experiencing such dreams I came and saw *Kyai* Latif Madjid. While I was sitting, he asked me, 'Have you had any spiritual experiences, Ocin?' 'Tell me'. 'I have known it.' It was strange that I could not tell him anything, I just cried loudly in front of him.

It is clear that these stories are told to give certainity to *Wāḥidiyat* followers, particularly, to define who is the successor to the *Wāḥidiyat* leadership after the demise of *Kyai* Abdul Madjid Ma'ruf. These stories also tell us that *Kyai* Abdul Latif Madjid is not only a valid leader but was also spiritually chosen by the Prophet Muhammad himself and the other prophets. Furthermore, during the period of internal conflict, these stories would have been effectively used by the proponents of Abdul Latif Madjid to convince other followers who were still in doubt about giving their allegiance to Abdul Latif Madjid rather than to another figure.

Other stories of spiritual experience relate the benefits and the miraculous power of reciting *Ṣalawāt Wāḥidiyat* and the curses which result from insulting *Ṣalawāt Wāḥidiyat* and the leader. Examples of these themes are as follows:

> At first, I was reluctant to recite *Ṣalawāt Wāḥidiyat* because I was still a teenager and I studied in a university which is opposed to the teaching of *Wāḥidiyat*. As my father urged me to practise *Ṣalawāt Wāḥidiyat,* I began to practise the forty day *mujāhada.* At day seventeen, I had a dream that I had died and lay in a grave alone. Suddenly two angels came to torture me. When these two angels were about to torture me, there was a voice saying, 'Do not torture my follower.' Suddenly, there was a gentleman standing in front of me. The two angels paid respect to the gentleman by bending their head to him asking: 'Oh the Prophet why do you forbid us to torture this body?' The Prophet replied,'[because] he is already practicing *Ṣalawāt Wāḥidiyat.*' Then I woke up.

> ...there is a leader of the people who is strongly opposed to *Ṣalawāt Wāḥidiyat* in my village. He does not believe in the existence of *Ghauth.* This person came to me and said to me: 'the *Ghauth* does not exist. The *Ghauth* is a fictional name created by Abdul Latif Madjid from Kedunglo, who wants to be respected by people since he does not have any positions in other established Muslim organizations...So it is better for you to leave *Waḥidiyat* and join other established organizations. *Wāḥidiyat* is guided by Satan.' After several days I met with his wife who behaved like her husband. After this occurrence, the leader and his wife suffered from disease for 100 days and he died after that. The wife died several weeks after her husband. They even experienced a tragic and critical moment before they died. It seems to me that the husband and wife died because of God's curse after they insulted *Ṣalawāt Wāḥidiyat* and *Kyai* Latif Madjid.

> *Kyai* Arif Iskandari is a *kyai* or *imam* in my village *mushalla* (place for prayer). He is well known for his *kesakten* (spiritual power). When we conducted a *mujāhada* ritual in the *mushalla,* he drove us out from the *mushalla...*We told this incident to the leader of the village, and because of this occurrence, the leader of village asked me and *Kyai* Arif to meet in the village office to discuss the incident. But, in the meeting, Pak Arif denied everything that he had done. As a result we were involved in a heated discussion with him. After this incident, Pak Arif suffered a serious illness which caused him to be sent to a hospital for a month at a high cost. From my point of view, this happened to him because of the miracle of *Ṣalawāt Wāḥidiyat.*

Like the previous stories, these stories are still related to the figure of the leader and the *Ṣalawāt Wāḥidiyat.* However, in these tales the leader of *Wāḥidiyat* and *Ṣalawāt Wāḥidiyat* are described by the followers as agents who not only bring about goodness for those who surrender (A., *taslīm*) themselves to the leader but also misfortune for those who oppose him.

Other stories are prophetic and involve the leader's insight into things to come as well as into present circumstances. The following story by a female follower can be categorised as one such prophetic story:

> At the beginning of *Muharram* month 1994, it was about 2.00 am, I woke up to perform night prayer (*tahajjud*) and ritual *mujāhada*. During *mujāhada Kyai* Abdul Latif Madjid came dressed in a suit. He asked me to sit down beside Mr. Karna Aji, and he sat in front of us as if he would marry us. He said to us: 'I will give both of you a task.' I and Mr. Karna were friends at university but we are in different departments. After experiencing the dream, I fell in love with him, but as woman I tried to hide the feeling. Finally, after some years Mr. Karna and I married. Then, *Kyai* Abdul Latif chose us as coordinators in the official board of *Ṣalawāt Wāḥidiyat.* At that time, I just shed tears because I remembered the dream that I had experienced several years ago.

Acccording to the dreamer, this experience proves that Abdul Latif Madjid is not only able to understand the destiny of every follower but is also able to communicate with his followers wherever they are (Rohani 2004:156-58).

Another theme of spiritual experience stories is the assistance and help given by the leader in both minor and major occurrences in his followers' daily life. The example illustrates Abdul Latif Madjid's intervention in a problem some followers were facing.

> Several weeks after practising *Ṣalawāt Wāḥidiyat,* I was working at a timber company. One day my company lost its motorcycle, which was kept in a warehouse. Because I worked at the warehouse, my boss was angry at me and at other workers who worked at the warehouse. He said to us: 'If you cannot find the motorcycle, I will accuse you of stealing the motorcycle.' In a state of confusion, I asked my friends to perform *mujāhada* after the midday prayers. We recited *yā sayyidī yā rasūlallah* for almost three hours. At the same time I focused my concentration (*tawajjuh*) towards *Kyai* Abdul Latif Madjid saying: '*Romo Yahi* please help us, if the motorcycle cannot be returned, we will be considered as a thieves.' I asked my friend to keep saying *nida'*, '*yā sayyidī yā rasūlullah'*, while I kept focusing my attention on *Kyai* Abdul Latif. At 19.00 pm the stolen motor was returned to the warehouse in which we worked.
>
> My wife was about to give birth. I brought her to Dr. Sahono Hospital in Kudus. According to the medical specialist, the blood pressure of my wife

> had reached 200. As a result, my wife was to be given special treatment by a medical specialist and she had to move to a specialist room…when she was moving to the specialist room, I asked her to perform *mujāhada*. When she entered the room, she saw *Kyai* Abdul Latif lying on a bed. When she was about to occupy the bed, *Kyai* Latif disappeared. After medical assistants put my wife on the bed, they began to prepare surgical instruments. Within a few minutes, before the surgical process could be conducted, my wife gave birth easily without surgery. All medical assistants were surprised to see this occurrence… I then thanked *Kyai* Latif for hearing his follower who was in trouble.

Another story which can be categorized according to this theme is the story of a student of Pesantren Kedunglo who met Abdul Latif Madjid in a dream. In his dream, he was visited by Abdul Latif Madjid who removed a dirty grass root from his heart (Rohani 2004:67). Another theme included in the spiritual experience book is a story about the miraculous power of Kyai Abdul Madjid Ma'ruf, the author of Ṣalawāt Waḥidiyat. Similar stories are often told about the current leader of *Wāḥidiyat*. A tale with this theme is as follows:

> After the fortieth day of *Kyai* Madjid's death, I dreamed of attending a *mujāhada* ritual. At the location of *mujāhada* I was suddenly embraced by *Kyai* Madjid. He asked me to go to the bank of the Brantas. At the bank of the river he said to me,' *Mujāhada Kubrā* will become divided into two groups. One group appears good outwardly, but actually it is inwardly dark. Another group appears not so good outwardly, but it should be good, because he [the leader of this group] just cleared a path for justice.' I asked him, 'Who is that ?' He replied,' He is Gus Latif [*Kyai* Abdul Latif Madjid]. Suddenly *Kyai* Abdul Latif appeared in front of *Kyai* Madjid, and I paid homage to him, then I woke up

These spiritual experiences can be seen either from the perspective of the *Wāḥidiyat* followers or from the perspective of *Ṣalawāt Wāḥidiyat* as an organization. From the followers' perspective, spiritual experiences achieved through dreams are significant in their social world not merely because of the content of the spiritual experience, but also because of the interactions between the followers and others in particular situations. In this sense, the spiritual experience can serve as one of strategies to resolve a conflict that the followers face. For example, through the spiritual experience, which is believed as a truth since it is sent by God via Abdul Latif Madjid, the followers are able to recognize who is the real *Ghauth* is and the successor of the author of *Ṣalawāt Waḥidiyat*. Moreover, as Ewing (1990:60) observed, dreams or spiritual experiences can validate the relationship between a follower and a leader, either before or after he or she has met the leader. For instance, before becoming a member of *Ṣalawāt Wāḥidiyat*, one might be just an ordinary person. After experiencing a dream of seeing a man with white robes who seems to be exactly the same as the man to whom he speaks, a person is much more confident that the leader of *Ṣalawāt Wāḥidiyat* is the spiritual leader for whom he has been searching in his spiritual life. Alternatively, an encounter with the leader in a dream after a person has become a member of *Wāḥidiyat,* can result in enhancing his belief that he has been allowed by his leader to experience an ultimate experience which not all followers are able to have. This, in turn, can cause the follower to feel that he has undergone a fundamental change in his spiritual life. Furthermore, those spiritual experiences also reflect the follower's wishes and goals. The followers may come to expect that the everyday world will be shaped by Abdul Latif Madjid as a *Ghauth hādha al zamān,* who can appear in person in a vision, and whose voice may be heard on every occasion.

From the perspective of a member of the official board of *Ṣalawāt Wāḥidiyat,* those spiritual experiences play a significant role in increasing and enhancing the spiritual authority and charisma of the leader and *Ṣalawāt Wāḥidiyat* among other Sufi groups. Strong charisma and spiritual authority are needed in order to increase the followers' love (A., *maḥabbat*) towards their leader (Anonymous 1424a:38). This can then be used as a glue to build cohesion within the group. The role played by those spiritual experiences in *Wāḥidiyat* is similar to Werbner's (2003:84) and Gilsenan's (1973:33) observations that the secondary legends surrounding a saint, such as the personal dreams of his disciples and their vision of the saint and his encounter with the Prophet, enhance his charisma and add further lustre to his reputation. In line with this, the spiritual experiences collected in a book as in *Wāḥidiyat* can also be used as a means to attract other followers to join with *Wāḥidiyat.* This strategy might have been accepted partly because other Sufi groups also offer a spiritual path which has the same aim as *Wāḥidiyat* , that is, to attain quietness of heart.

Chapter V: The Veneration of *Wali* and Holy Persons: The Case of *Istighāthat Iḥsāniyyat*

This chapter highlights another *Majlis Dhikr* group that has creatively developed its own practices and formulae to obtain spiritual experiences and religious knowledge absent in conventional Islamic proselytization (*dakwah*). In this chapter, I will show how this group defines itself as an alternative mystical path among other established Sufi orders while retaining legitimate Sufi practices and how it plays an important role in the *dakwah* project of Islam. In this chapter I will describe the foundation of *Iḥsāniyyat,* examine challenges and rivalries involving this group, describe the ritual of *Iḥsāniyyat,* discuss the structure of *Iḥsāniyyat,* and analyse the strategy of its *dakwah* project in the light of Islamic Sufi teachings. This chapter will argue that although the group cannot be categorised as a *tarekat mu'tabarah* (acknowledged Sufi orders) by Nahdlatul Ulama, this group does attract a lot of people and it is acceptable to both nominal Muslims (*abangan*)and Muslim *santri* (strict Muslim). Therefore, this group bridges the Geertzian cultural contrast between *abangan* and *santri.*

5.1. The Foundation of *Istighāthat Iḥsāniyyat*

Istighāthat is an Arabic word meaning 'calling for help' or 'appealing for help' in a critical moment. In this sense, the word *istighāthat* can be distinguished from the word *istanṣara,* which also means to ask someone for assistance but not in a critical moment (Wehr 1966:434). The word *istighāthat* in its verbal form (*yastaghīthu*) can be found in five different verses in the Qur'ān (Al-Kahfi: 29; Al-Qaṣaṣ 28; Al-Aḥqāf: 17; Al-Anfāl : 9), all of which imply asking or seeking help at a critical moment.

However, within the Indonesian Islamic context, a term *istighāthat* (I, *istighasah*), refers to a compilation of prayers or litanies recited on a particular occasion which consists of an invocation for divine help with the repetition of the sacred names of God and other prayers. In this sense, *istighāthat* might be considered similar to the *dhikr* ritual (remembrance), which is widely practised by other Muslims communities in the country. The word *istighāthat* is usually used by those affiliated with the Nahdlatul Ulama (NU) organization, rather than reformist organizations such as Muhammadiyah and PERSIS. The NU has a particular *istighāthat* prayer which is usually practised and recited by its members when the organization is facing a problem or is holding a major organizational event. *Istighāthat* is frequently practised in NU *pesantren* and *kelompok pengajian* (religious gatherings) once a week.

According to *Kyai* Masduki Mahfudz, a chairman of the Nahdlatul Ulama religious board of East Java, the *istighāthat* ritual, which is widely practised by Nahdlatul Ulama members, was originally taken from the Sufi tradition, particularly the Qadiriyah wa Naqsabandiyyah[1] group in Rejoso, Jombang, East Java. The late *Kyai* Ramli Tamim, the leader of the order, selecting from various sources such as the Qur'an, the Prophet tradition and Muslim scholars' books, compiled texts of *istighāthat* prayers.[2] The leader of this *tarekat* told me that compiling these texts took a long time because the author had to perform a special fasting ritual for about forty days for each text. The aim of this ritual fast was not only to ask God to give guidance as where a text should be place among other texts but also to ask Him to give a benefit for each text of prayer. This is partly because in Islam every prayer is believed to have its own particular function.[3]

The *istighāthat* ritual is often carried out during the opening ceremony of a religious gathering conducted by the Qadiriyah wa Naqabandiyyah order. The *istighāthat* prayers collected by *Kyai* Ramli were first used by the East Java regional board of Nahdlatul Ulama. In 1996, the *istighāthat* ritual was conducted by the organization following information that there would be a great disaster in Indonesia. It was expected that by conducting the ritual, Indonesia would be saved from the disaster. Then, the idea to hold the ritual was brought to the central board of the organization in Jakarta and widely spread in other branches throughout Indonesia. As a result, the ritual has become popular and is used by this organization not only for religious purposes but also for political purposes. For example, in 2001, a major prayer session known as *Istighāthat Kubrā* was held in Senayan, Jakarta to support the president Abdurrahman Wahid, former general chairman of the Nahdlatul Ulama, following his impeachment by the Indonesian parliament.

The word istighāthat is derived from the Qur'an and hence, the ritual istighāthat has a strong basis in the Islamic sources of law. The Qur'an states: 'When you

1 The combined *Qādiriyyat Naqṣabandiyyat* order was established by Ahmad Khāṭib Sambas (1802-1878). Dhofier as quoted by Mulyati (2004: 259) argues that during 1970's, there were four centres of this *tarekat* in Java including Rejoso, Jombang, East Java led by *Kyai* Tamim; Mranggen, Central Java, led by *Kyai* Muslih; Suralaya, Tasikmalaya, West Java led by *Kyai* Shohibulwafa Tajul 'Arifin (Abah Anom), and Pegantongan, Bogor, West Java led by *Kyai* Thohir Falak.

2 Interview with *Kyai* Masduki Mahfudz, Malang, January, 2005.

3 Interview with *Gus* Najib, Kediri, January, 2005.

sought aid from your Lord, so He answered you: I will assist you with a thousand of the angels following one another' (Al-Anfāl 8:9). Based on this verse, Kyai Mughni, a teacher in Pesantren Jampes, pointed out that the istighāthat ritual as practised by many Indonesian Muslims can be historically traced back to the Prophet himself. As described by Ibn Kathīr in his book, Tafsīr al-Qur'ān al-Karīm,[4] according to the prophetic tradition, in the Badr war, the Prophet felt pessimistic about waging a war against the enemy because the Muslim troops only numbered three hundred, while the enemy's troops numbered more than a thousand. It was reported that in this critical situation, the Prophet's companions asked the prophet to ask help from God (istighāthat) to defeat the enemy. In his prayer, the Prophet said: 'Oh! Lord, fulfill your promise to me, if these groups of Muslim perish, they will never worship you on this earth.'[5] It was believed that because of this *istighāthat,* the Muslims troops could defeat their enemy during the war.

Although the Nahdlatul Ulama (NU) has a specific *istighāthat* prayer, it does not officially and specifically give instruction to its members to recite and practise only that *istighāthat* prayer. As a result, each different community within NU might have different ways and formats of *istighāthat* prayer. Nevertheless, it is certain that most of these groups have similar objectives, namely, to ask for help and forgiveness from God through the combination of prayer and the repetition of the sacred names of God and *dhikr.* The *Istighāthat Iḥsāniyyat* group is one group among many others which has different ways and formats of *istighāthat* ritual compared to Nahdlatul Ulama.

The *Istighāthat Iḥsāniyyat* group was first set up by *Gus* Abdul Latif Muhammad (b.1968-), a Muslim cleric from *Pesantren* Jampes in Kediri. The leader of this group is a grandson of *Shaikh* Ihsan Muhammad ibn Daḥlān, the author of the two volumes of *Sirāj al-Ṭālibīn,*[6]a commentary on Al-Ghazālī's *Minhāj al-'Ābidīn Ilā Jannati Rabbi al-'Ālamīn* and two volumes of *Manāhij al-Imdād,*[7] a commentary on Zainuddin al-Malibari's *Irshād al-'Ibād* (Mughni 1982:31). *Gus* Abdul Latif was born in the *pesantren* milieu where he spent most of his

4 Ibn Kathīr 2006, Tafsīr al-Qur'ān al-Karīm. Jordan: Aal al-Bayt Institute for Islamic Thought, viewed 6 January 2007, 10:00 am, http://www.altafsir.com/Tafasir.asp?tMadhNo=0&tTafsirNo=7&tSoraNo=10&tAyahNo=62&tDisplay=yes&UserProfile=0.

5 "اللهم أنجز لي ما وعدتني، اللهم إن تهلك هذه العصابة من أهل الإسلام فلا تعبد في الأرض أبدا"

6 *Sirāj al-Ṭālibīn* is a Sufi book which is well known among *Pesantren* students in Java. It was written in 1932. This book was published, for the first time, in 1936 by Al-Nabhaniyah publishing house in Surabaya, printed by a big publisher in Egypt, Mustafa al-Babi al-Halabi. The book that I have contains 1098 pages, published by al-Madinah, Surabaya. In the *Pesantren* Jampes, this book is taught only during the month of *Ramaḍān*

7 This book written in 1940 has two volumes (1000 pages). When I was in the field, the book was first published by the family of the author. During *Ramaḍān* this book is taught to the student in *Jampes.* During *Ramadhan* in 2006, *Kyai* Said Agil Siraj, taught the officials of Nahdlatul Ulama using this book in the prayer room of the Jakarta headquarters.

time studying religious subjects from primary and secondary to tertiary school levels. He never studied at a secular school. His father, *Kyai* Muhammad Ibn Ihsan was a Muslim cleric (I., *kyai*) in the *pesantren* as well as a Muslim healer (I., *tabib*), a person who could heal various illnesses by spiritual methods. After finishing his study at his father's *pesantren, Gus* Abdul Latif held a teaching position at the *pesantren*. He taught spiritual healing subjects which were only followed by senior *santri* (students). Like father like son, he was also a *tabib* who received many guests who asked for healing or made other requests. He obtained expertise in spiritual healing through wandering from one teacher to another in Java. For example, he learned spiritual healing (I., *ketabiban*) from his uncle, *Kyai* Amin in Cirebon, West Java, *Kyai* Abdullah in Mantenan, Blitar, and *Kyai* Taraqqi in Malang, and studied *tabarrukan* (the obtaining of grace) with *Kyai* Abdul Hamid in Pasuruan, East Java.[8]

The *Istighāthat Iḥsāniyyat* group, which now has its central office in Kediri, was first set up in Banyuwangi. The selection of this regency in the eastern region of East Java for the first site for this group was not an accident. From July to November 1998, following the downfall of Suharto, several violent murders occurred in Banyuwangi in particular and many other regions in East Java in general. *Ninja* were believed to be involved in these violent murders. Local people believed that the killers of sorcerer (I., *dukun santet*) were *ninja,* trained killers who wore black masks and dark clothes when they killed their victims. The term *ninja* was first introduced by the press to identify those who had killed victims in other regions. At the beginning, the targets were *dukun santet,* but after several months, the range of victims became wider and included not only suspected *dukun santet* but also local Muslim clerics (*kyai*) and *guru ngaji* (Qur'an teachers). Data compiled by a Nahdlatul Ulama (NU) investigation team indicated that more than 147 suspected *dukun santet* were killed during September and October 1998 in Banyuwangi (Manan et al. 2001) along with another 105 victims in neighboring regions of East Java such as Jember, Sumenep and Pasuruan (Brown 2000). Forty percent of these other victims were identified as local Muslims clerics, Nadhlatul Ulama activists and *guru ngaji* (Wijayanta et al. 1998:12-13).

The situation certainly created panic among villagers in Banyuwangi. Although villagers intensified their vigilance, they found it difficult to identify the real killers. Consequently, suspicions increased as to the perpetrators of the killings in Banyuwangi. Moreover, this situation led most people, particularly Muslim clerics, to feel threatened because they felt that they might be future victims. This was not unreasonable because many Muslim clerics and *guru ngaji* were

8 Interview with *Gus* Latif, Kediri, September 2004.

reported to have been killed at that time. It is common among traditional Muslims, when individuals feel insecure because of a threat, that they ask for specific help from *kyai.*

Plate 5.1: Gus Abdul Latif (Gus Latif), the founder and the leader of the Istighāthat Iḥsāniyyat group.

As described by Mansurnoor, local people will ask *kyai* for protection especially during a time of unrest and upheaval (Mansurnoor 1990). It was in this situation that *Gus* Abdul Latif, referred as a *Gus*[9] and *Agus* because of his genealogy and *kesakten* was asked by local people to improve peace, security and trust among them. The first thing he did was to provide the local people with *gemblengan,* a form of invulnerability (I, *kekebalan*) by which he transferred a spiritual power so that they became invulnerable to sharp objects, fire and bullets. According to *Gus* Abdul Latif, cultivating invulnerability can provide a feeling of security because it can protect lives from murder. Due to the threat of murder, these practices were also conducted in other regions in East Java other than Banyuwangi.

The participants in the practice of invulnerability in Banyuwangi included not only those who were known as good people but also those considered bad individuals (I., *orang nakal*) by local people. The involvement of these individuals in *gemblengan* led to criticism from local *'ulamā'*. They worried that if those people were allowed to follow *gemblengan*, they would misuse their spiritual power. However, *Gus* Abdul Latif denied this, arguing that since the sense of insecurity was felt by everyone, *gemblengan* should be held both for good and bad people. For *dakwah* purposes, bad people should be involved in the *gemblengan* in order to bring them to the right path. In this sense, *Gus* Abdul Latif believed that people, including *orang nakal,* have their own sense of right (I., *hati nurani*). He argued that this sense would be touched if they faced a serious problem in their life and this would lead them to return to the path of God. In addition to this, the local *'ulamā'* also asked him to obtain permission from the local government before holding *gemblengan,* otherwise the local police and security officials would arrest *Gus* Abdul Latif as had happened in 1965 when a lot of people who held *gemblengan* were arrested by local security forces. However, *Gus* Abdul Latif continued to hold *gemblengan* without permission from the police. The success of these *gemblengan* contributed to his popularity and influence.[10] Services such as *gemblengan* and spiritual healing, rather than educational services, attracted many followers (Mansurnoor 1990).

One of his followers claimed that the success of *gemblengan* in Banyuwangi contributed to the improvement of peace within these regions. However, these improvements cannot be attributed solely to the *gemblengan* or *Gus* Abdul Latif's role. Muslim clerics from NU asked the Ministry of Security and Defense, General Wiranto and the Indonesian Army Forces (ABRI) to discover the killers of the *dukun santet* and transparently investigate this situation so

---

9 Term *Gus* is derived from *Agus* which means the son of *Kyai*. However, currently, the word *Gus* is also used to refer to those who have spiritual power.

10 Interview with *Gus* Abdul Latif, Kediri, January, 2005.

that it would not lead to social unrest (Rahim n.d.:16-20). The improvement of security in Banyuwangi was due to help from many people, including the local population of Banyuwangi.

From 1998 to 1999 was a period of turmoil in the Indonesian political landscape. The period was a political transition after the fall of Suharto's regime in May 1998, followed by religious, ethnic violence and social unrest in many Indonesian areas. On 7 June 1999, the first general election after the downfall of the New Order regime was held to elect the House of Representative members from forty eight parties with different political ideologies.

Heated competition during the general election campaign in 1999 among political parties was felt not only in Jakarta but also in many other provinces and regions in Indonesia. Banyuwangi became an arena for political parties, including Islamic parties, to gain as many voters as possible. In order to attract voters, some political parties recruited charismatic Muslims scholars as vote getters whom they believed had a lot of followers but also had the ability to attract voters in the region. During the campaign, every Muslim scholar supported his own political party and, without doubt, this contributed to the tension among them. In addition, as maintained by *Kyai* Muhammad Syaiful Hisham, they also strongly condemned local government for having failed to maintain security in Banyuwangi. As a result, relations between them and government or among themselves worsened.

Kyai Muhammad Syaiful Hisham one Muslim cleric (A.,'*ulamā*'; I., *ulama*) in Banyuwangi, believed that if the situation continued, more serious conflicts would break out, which would eventually threaten the unity of the social fabric in Banyuwangi. He came up with the idea of calling for unity among those '*ulamā*' involved in the political contestation and the government under the banner of *Pancasila*, the Indonesian ideology. The government (*umarā*'), according to him, should become a partner of the '*ulamā*', and the latter should serve as advisors to the local government. Therefore, he argued that instead of criticizing and condemning the government, '*ulamā*' should help the government if it faced a problem in dealing with security in Banyuwangi. He put it this way:

> The condemnation of the government conducted by '*ulamā*' in Banyuwangi is not only useless but it is also destructive. Therefore, it is pointless to condemn the government... Be careful, we live in Indonesia whose national basis is *Pancasila* and under the symbol of *Bhineka Tunggal Ika* (The Unity in Diversity). We are all brothers. Many Muslims and Non-Muslims are involved not only in the GOLKAR Party, PKB (The National Awakening Party) but also in PAN (The National Mandate Party) and PDIP (The Indonesian Democratic Party of Struggle). If we struggle to do something

> [on behalf of Islam], why should we depend too much on a particular political party. Therefore, do not besmirch other parties because there are a lot of Muslims in those parties…do not tarnish GOLKAR, PKB and PAN because if we tarnish one in GOLKAR, it will be similar to tarnishing Islam itself, and thus, it will damage the prestige of Islam.

Based on this view, *Kyai* Hisham, tried to find the best way to prevent '*ulamā*' from condemning the government by changing the political tension through religious activity which could involve government, '*ulamā*'and local people. From the beginning, he intended to help the government establish a peaceful situation in Banyuwangi. He was asked by local '*ulamā*'to seek a particular prayer which could be used to maintain peace in Banyuwangi after the *Ninja* and *Dukun Santet* tragedy. *Kyai* Hisham singled out *Gus* Abdul Latif because he was previously considered successful in holding *gemblengan* in Banyuwangi. In addition, he felt an affinity with him because both were classmates when they studied in *Pesantren* Jampes, Kediri. Therefore, *Kyai* Hisham chose *Gus* Abdul Latif. In this case, as observed by Mansurnoor, collegiate friendship developed at *pesantren* became an invaluable element in building a further network (Mansurnoor 1990).

Before composing the prayer, *Gus* Abdul Latif is said to have performed a particular ritual to seek guidance at his grandfather's grave. His grandfather, *Kyai* Ihsan Dahlan is believed among his followers to be a Muslim saint (I., *wali*) and his tomb has become an object of visitation and veneration. Some of his followers believe that *Gus* Abdul Latif can communicate with the late *Kyai* Ihsan Dahlan. This is based on the fact that traditionalist '*ulamā*' believe that communication between the pious dead and the pious living is possible (Pranowo 1991:47). After receiving guidance, *Gus* Abdul Latif offered a particular prayer to *Kyai* Hisham and asked him and other people in Banyuwangi to recite it in groups (I., *berjamaah*) or individually twice a month, once a week or everyday if needed. Before practising the prayer, *Kyai* Hisham submitted the prayer to *Kyai* Malik Ihsan Dahlan,[11] and asked his consent because he was the senior *kyai* in *Pesantren Jampes* and one of *Kyai* Ihsan Dahlan's sons who was still alive. *Kyai* Malik agreed with the composition of the prayer and added particular prayers to it.

Kyai Hisham brought the prayer to Banyuwangi and recited it together with seventeen people, who later became the first members of this new group. He, then, was elected by *Gus* Abdul Latif as a coordinator of the group in Banyuwangi. Establishing a new religious fraternity required a name to identify it from others. It was not easy to name and establish a new group, particularly

11 He has passed away when I returned to Australia.

among many other well-known Sufi orders and *istighāthat* groups which have existed for many years in Banyuwangi. Thus, the new group was challenged, not only to find a name which could attract the attention of a broad mass of people but also to offer a new type of fraternity which was not similar to others.

Gus Abdul Latif chose *Iḥsāniyyat* as the name of the group. The name *Iḥsāniyyat* was originally taken from the first name, Ihsan, of his grandfather, *Kyai* Ihsan Dahlan. The use of one's grandfather's name as the name of a Sufi order is unusual among Sufi orders. In Sufi tradition, the name of a Sufi order is traditionally taken from the name of their founder. For example, the Naqshabandiyah Order attributed its name to its founder, Bahā' al-Dīn al-Naqshābandī, the Qadiriyah Order is attributed to Syeikh Abdul Qādir al-Jaylānī, the Shadiliyat Order is attributed to Abu al-Ḥasan al-Shādhilī. *Gus* Abdul Latif argued that the use of his grandfather's name for the *istighāthat* was because he was not only as well-known Muslim *'ulamā'* but also considered to be the saint of God (A., *waliyullah*) who could be used as an object of mediation (A., *tawassul* or *wasīlat*) by those who sought for closeness with God. *Gus* Abdul Latif mentioned that a means (A., *wasīlat*) is necessary for lay people to achieve the love of God. However, for him, to achieve the love of God is difficult because God is an unseen object. By contrast, lay people can only love something concrete. Therefore, loving those loved by God (I., *waliullah*) is the way for them to achieve the love of God.

Furthermore, there might have been another reason for *Gus* Abdul Latif to choose his grandfather's name rather than his own name for the new group. He might have thought that other people would be unfamiliar with his name. So he chose *Kyai* Ihsan Dahlan's since his grandfather had the reputation of being a prolific writer on Sufism and was an internationally well known *'ulamā'* who was acknowledged among other Sufi groups and the *pesantren* community. Therefore, naming the new group *Iḥsāniyyat*, would give the impression to the public that this group was closely linked to the legacy of *Kyai* Ihsan Dahlan and, as a consequence, this group would become better known.

The name *Iḥsāniyyat* was initially used for this new *istīghāthat* group after *Gus* Abdul Latif experienced a visionary dream of meeting with *Gus* Mik, a well-known *wali* in Kediri. In his dream, *Gus* Abdul Latif received the late *Gus* Mik's consent to the name of *Iḥsāniyyat*. It is clear that *Gus* Abdul Latif relied on this other well-known *'ulamā'*, *Kyai* Hamim Jazuli, usually called *Gus* Mik, who was the founder of *Dhikr al-Ghāfilīn* which has many followers spread throughout Indonesia, to justify the foundation of his group. A dream, particularly a good dream, can be used as the basis of action for Muslims since it is believed to be revealed by God. Therefore, although received in a dream, the consent from *Gus* Mik was important for this newly born group.

The consent from *Gus* Mik had various meanings for the followers of *Iḥsāniyyat*. Firstly, it showed that there was a close relationship and spiritual chain between their leader and *Gus* Mik. Secondly, only those who had a similar spiritual level to that of *Gus* Mik could gain consent from him. In this sense, the followers would think that *Gus* Abdul Latif was entitled to receive this consent because he had reached the same level of spiritual capacity as *Gus* Mik. Thirdly, by giving his consent, *Gus* Mik allowed *Gus* Abdul Latif to continue his efforts to improve people's consciousness of God and the hereafter through the establishment of the *istighāthat* group. This would prevent *Iḥsāniyyat* from being considered as a competitor of *Dhikr al-Ghāfilīn* in Kediri because *Gus* Mik, as the founder of *Dhikr al-Ghāfilīn*, had given his consent to *Gus* Abdul Latif. All of these things contributed to enhance the authority of *Gus* Abdul Latif as well as his group among other groups.

Another challenge the group needed to address was to find a new model of *istighāthat* to distinguish it from other *istighāthat* groups. In dealing with this issue, *Gus* Abdul Latif, not only attempted to compose prayers of *istighāthat*which were not as lengthy as other *istighāthat* prayers, but also introduced vernacular rather than Arabic in the *istighāthat* ritual. Furthermore, he combined ritual *istighāthat* with interactive dialog on religious issues involving all participants in the ritual and he held cultural arts festivals such as *jaranan* (hobby-horse dance), *reog ponorogo* (tiger-mask dance), *barongsai* (a Chinese traditional dance), and *ruwatan*[12] and *dangdutan*.

Gus Abdul Latif established *Iḥsāniyyat* in Kediri on 9 September 1999, one year after the establishment of *Iḥsāniyyat* in Banyuwangi. This date coincided with the rumor among people that the day of judgment (I., *kiamat*) would occur on that date at 9:00 a.m. The inauguration of this group in Kediri was held in the graveyard of *Kyai* Ihsan Dahlan. The rationale behind this establishment was not just to follow upon the success of *Iḥsāniyyat* in Banyuwangi but also to respond to a request from some villagers who were addicted to drugs, alcohol and gambling. These people asked *Gus* Abdul Latif to help them escape from addiction. *Gus* Abdul Latif explained this as follows:

> The first members of *Iḥsāniyyat* in Putih village consisted of eleven people. Those people asked me to cure them from inner illness and help them cease from wrongdoing (I., *maksiat*) they had done. They could not cure those

12 *Ruwatan*is a sacred ceremony in the Javanese tradition to ward off misfortune.

> illnesses nor help themselves to cease from wrongdoing without help from God. As a result of their sincere wish, I established an *Iḥsāniyyat* group in Kediri as a means of improving morality among the people in Kediri.

At the beginning, the activity of this group was simple. The ritual of *istighāthat*was led by *Gus* Abdul Latif once in a week at the *Kyai* Ihsan Dahlan's tomb, followed by a small group gathering to talk about various topics. As the number of participants in the ritual grew, *Gus* Abdul Latif held interactive dialogues on religious topics based on questions from the audience before reciting *istighāthat* prayer.

At the same time, *Gus* Abdul Latif established a group called *Paguyuban Tombo Ati* (The Heart Healing Community). This group aimed to provide a venue to hold prayers and to discuss Islamic teachings and personal problems for those who were ignored, held in contempt by other religious leaders or regarded by others as local hodlum (I., *preman*), the dregs of society (I., *sampah masyarakat*) and bad individuals (I, *orang nakal*). An informant told me that the members of this group consisted of drug users, local hoodlum (I., *preman*), drug traffickers, gamblers, drunks, and prostitutes. *Gus* Abdul Latif believed that instead of changing their behavior, tagging them with such labels as *sampah masyarakat* and *orang nakal* not only prevented them from returning to the right path but also from integrating with other members of society. Therefore, the main target of his appeal was to those described by Gilsenan as people 'without a shepherd and those who were not touched and accommodated by the existing religious institutions'(Gilsenan 1973:37). Moreover, *Gus* Abdul Latif insisted that those who were considered *orang nakal* actually had a strong desire in their hearts to be good and to follow the right path, but they did not know the way they should take in order to be a good or to resolve their problems. In dealing with these people, as *Gus* Abdul Latif argued, a gradual approach and a long-term strategy were needed.

Actually, the ritual held both at the *Istighāthat Iḥsāniyyat* and the *Paguyuban Tombo Ati* was the same. *Istighāthat* prayers were recited in both groups. However, the name *Paguyuban Tombo Ati* was deliberately used to give the impression that the activity of the group could be attended by everybody, including those people who are still unfamiliar with *istighāthat* prayer. According to *Gus* Abdul Latif, this strategy was successful in attracting those who were fearful of attending *istighāthat* prayer. They realized that both the *Iḥsāniyyat* group and the *Paguyuban Tombo Ati* had a similar objective. As a result, they were no longer fearful of joining the group. One of the participants of the *Paguyuban Tombo Ati* said:

> As I realized that *Tombo Ati* was part of *Istighāthat Iḥsāniyyat* and both were led by *Gus* Abdul Latif, I joined joined the *Istighāthat Iḥsāniyya* without doubt. During the *Tombo Ati ritual,* I felt that *Gus* Abdul Latif paid his attention to me and helped me to solve my problems especially those to do with drug addiction.

5.2. Local Rivalry and Challenges

Although there are many other *Majlis Dhikr* groups and Sufi orders in Kediri, which provide similar ritual to that of *Istighāthat Iḥsāniyyat,* this group has hardly ever faced a serious challenge from those groups. In contrast, in Banyuwangi, this group faced serious challenges especially from local *kyai.* From its inception, the ritual of *Istighāthat Iḥsāniyyat,* held once every five weeks (J., *selapanan*) in Banyuwangi was attended not only by local people but also by many local *kyai* officially invited by the coordinator of the *Istighāthat Iḥsāniyyat* group. In fact, besides *Gus* Abdul Latif, local *kyai* contributed to attracting their followers to participate in the ritual.

As this new group in Banyuwangi made rapid progress and attracted many followers, this excited the jealousy and fear of other local *'ulamā'*in Banyuwangi. Because they were no longer involved by *Istighāthat Iḥsāniyyat* leader as official members of the group, these local *kyai* who had previously supported the establishment of the group in Banyuwangi withdrew their support. There can be little doubt that the real objections to this group was that it threatened the standing privileges of local *kyai.* This contributed to a rivalry that developed between the *Istighāthat Iḥsāniyyat* group and other groups.

As an informant observed, these *kyai* did not object to the *Istighāthat Iḥsāniyyat,* but they wanted the group to be run and led by local *kyai* without outside involvement. They argued that there were many *kyai* in Banyuwangi who were more capable of leading the *Istighāthat Iḥsāniyyat* ritual than those from Kediri. Moreover, they argued that because the ritual took place in Banyuwangi, it was more appropriate for this group to be run by involving *kyai* or leaders of *pesantren* who lived in Banyuwangi.

In dealing with these points, *Kyai* Hisham, the coordinator of the group, argued that he could not prevent *Gus* Abdul Latif, the author of *Istighāthat Iḥsāniyyat* prayer, from attending the *Istighāthat Iḥsāniyyat* ritual in Banyuwangi because he was the person who had given the *ijāza* (authorization, license) for the *Istighāthat Iḥsāniyyat* prayers. It was a courtesy that, as the recipient of the *ijāza, Kyai* Hisham should include *Gus* Abdul Latif in the *Istighāthat Iḥsāniyyat.*

Because *Kyai* Hisham regarded himself as a student of *Gus* Abdul Latif, even though both were colleagues, *Kyai* Hisham would not dare to destroy this teacher-student relationship. According to *pesantren* tradition, this relationship endures even after the teacher has passed away. If a student cuts this relationship, he will never obtain the sanctity of God through his teacher. It is for this reason that *Kyai* Hisham did not ask *Gus* Abdul Latif to stop attending the *Istighāthat Iḥsāniyyat* ritual in Banyuwangi, despite objections from many local *kyai*.

When consulted by *Kyai* Hisham about these objections, *Gus* Abdul Latif insisted that he and *Kyai* Hisham could not be separated in running the *Istighāthat Iḥsāniyyat* in Banyuwangi, and if others asked him to leave the group, he would witdraw the *ijāza* and dissolve the group. In the *pesantren* tradition the giver of *ijāza* (authorization) has the authority to withdraw *ijāza* from the recipient or to ask the recipient not to transmit the *ijāza* to others. For example, when the initiator of *ijāza*asks the recipient not to give it to others, the recipient should obey. If he or she ignores this rule, the *ijāza* will be no longer valid.

Kyai Hisham and *Gus* Abdul Latif needed to cooperate in order to obtain their objectives. On the one hand, *Gus* Abdul Latif needed *Kyai* Hisham as a liaison to spread the *Istighāthat Iḥsāniyyat* in Banyuwangi. His job as a religious books distributor allowed *Kyai* Hisham to make close contact with many leaders of *pesantren*. By approaching these *pesantren* leaders, *Kyai* Hisham succeeded in attracting a number local people to join with the *Istighāthat Iḥsāniyyat* ritual. It is for this reason that *Gus* Abdul Latif preferred him to be a coordinator of the group in Banyuwangi. Because *Gus* Abdul Latif solely determined the appointment of the coordinator, none of the members of the group could succeed *Kyai* Hisham. Therefore, *Kyai* Hisham needed *Gus* Abdul Latif to pave his way to control the *Istighāthat Iḥsāniyyat* group in Banyuwangi.

Another objection from the Banyuwangi *kyai* toward the *Istighāthat Iḥsāniyyat* group had to do with the involvement of this group in local politics. According to these *kyai*, some officials of the group used it for political and worldly interests by putting The Chief of Executive of the district's name (I., *bupati*) on the advisory board. Those *kyai* worried that the *bupati* would use the group to increase his popularity. This anxiety was reasonable because the popularity of the *bupati* had decreased following strong criticism of his moral behavior. As a result, those *kyai* strongly rejected an invitation from *bupati* to hold the *Istighāthat Iḥsāniyyat* ritual in his office. *Kyai* Hisham took the view that those who lived in Banyuwangi should obey the leader of regency, so they should accept the invitation despite various objections. Without consent from those *kyai*, *Kyai* Hisham and *Gus* Abdul Latif held *istighāthat* ritual in the *bupati's* office (I., *Pendopo Kabupaten*). This, of course, added to the *kyai* objections to *Kyai* Hisham and *Gus* Abdul Latif since the two ignored the opinion of the *kyai* in Banyuwangi.

As a result, some *kyai* who had previously supported the group established a new *istighāthat* group which did not include any *kyai* except those from Banyuwangi. In order to enhance its local nature, this new group was called *Dhikr al-Shafā'at,* a name which appeared to have been taken from the name of a local charismatic *kyai* in Banyuwangi, *Kyai* Muhammad Shafa'at. He was the founder of *Pesantren* Blok Agung, which is the oldest *pesantren* in Banyuwangi. Perhaps, the name of *Shafā'at* was used in the attempt to match the popularity of *Iḥsāniyyat.* This group might have deliberately used the name of *Kyai* Shafa'at in order to attract local people to join this new group. But according to *Kyai* Fahrur Rozi, a secretary of the group, this name was originally taken from the Arabic word *shafā'at* which means blessing and healing (*kesembuan*). Those who recited *Dhikr al-Shafā'at* prayers were expected to be able to obtain *kesembuhan* (healing) and *shafā'at* from the Prophet.[13] In order to attract followers, this group offered rituals and prayers which are very similar to those of *Istighāthat Iḥsāniyyat.* It also included some individuals who had become officials members of the *Istighāthat Iḥsāniyyat.* One of the members of the *Istighāthat Iḥsāniyyat* group claimed that this was done to lessen the popularity of *Istighāthat Iḥsāniyyat.* In response to the new group, *Kyai* Hisham let his followers freely choose to join any group they wanted to. He argued that if the content of the prayers were good, he would let them join the *Dhikr al-Shafā'at* group.

The *Istighāthat Iḥsāniyyat* group also faced another challenge from some *kyai* involved with the local branch of Nahdlatul Ulama (NU) in Banyuwangi. These *kyai* argued that since the activity of the group was closely related to *istighāthat* and most supporters of this group came from NU *pesantren,* this group should be integrated and reviewed regularly by NU. However, *Kyai* Hisham opposed that suggestion arguing that this group was not part of any organization, including NU, and did not use the symbol of NU, though it followed the spirit of *Ahlussunnah wa al-jama'ah* upon which NU was established. Thus, this group was not opposed to either NU or its teachings. He further stated that if this group were integrated under NU, this would reduce its popularity among people from other social and political backgrounds. Furthermore, according to *Kyai* Hisham it would also affect the development of the group since each official member of NU had their own opinion about how to administer the group. In

13 Interview with *Kyai* Fahrur Rozi, Banyuwangi, April, 2005.

this sense, *Kyai* Hisham was fully aware that if he allowed other local *kyai* or NU officials to review the *Iḥsāniyyat* group, he would gradually lose his role to control the group. Therefore, he was strongly opposed to that plan.

In its hometown, the *Istighāthat Iḥsāniyyat* had another competitor not from outside, but from one of the relatives of the leader of the *Istighāthat Iḥsāniyyat* group himself. *Gus* Abdul Latif lived within *Pesantren* Jampes, which many other descendants of the founder of the *pesantren* also occupied. These descendents were not only entitled to live in the *pesantren* but also to use the legacy of the *pesantren* founder, including the founder's name, for their own religious purposes. One of these descendants established another *istighāthat* group called *Yamisda al-Ihsan*. *Yamisda* stood for *Shaikh* Yahūda, *Shaikh* Mesir, *Shaikh* Isti'ānat, and *Shaikh* Dahlan, all of which are names of ancestral *kyai* of *Pesantren* Jampes and are regarded as saints (I., *wali*). The leader of this group claimed the names of *wali* would lead to obtaining blessing (I., *barakah*). It is for this reason that the group was called by the names of these *wali*. In addition, the name *Yamisda* also gave the impression to the public that this group had much greater legitimacy than *Iḥsāniyyat* since it had many transmitters, including *Kyai* Ihsan, and his father and grandfather.

Like *Iḥsāniyyat*, the *Yamisda* group also had *istighathat* prayers as the core of its ritual. However, unlike *Iḥsāniyyat,* this group used alumnae of the *pesantren* network to spread the *istighāthat*. This was possible because *Kyai* Malik, the oldest *kyai* in the *pesantren,* recommended that his students and *Pesantren* Jampes alumnae recite the *istighāthat* and develop it when they returned to their hometowns. As a result, this group developed branches in many regions in which these alumnae of the *pesantren* lived.

By contrast, *Iḥsāniyyat* does not have a formal network which can be used to spread the *istighāthat*. Students are not normally allowed to go out of the *pesantren* at night, so they rarely participate in the ritual of *Iḥsāniyyat*, which is mostly held on Thursday nights at the *pesantren* family's cemetery, situated outside the *pesantren.* Students are, however, allowed by the leader of *Pesantren* Jampes to take part in the ritual of *Yamisda,* held on Saturday nights at the cemetery or at the *pesantren*. Without doubt, *Yamisda* has benefited from this policy. Although it was not intended to prevent the progress of *Iḥsāniyyat,* it did limit the spread of the *Istighāthat Iḥsāniyyat* only to those who are categorized as lay people, while those who are categorized *santri* have not been involved. Although in fact there has been latent competition between the two groups, a student of the *pesantren* denied the competition and did not see the emergence of *Yamisda* as a competitor of *Iḥsāniyyat* or vice versa. The student argued as follows:

> Perhaps, outsiders see the emergence of two *istighāthah* groups within one *pesantren* as a rivalry between them. But, in fact there is a *hikma* or a blessing with the emergence of the two groups. The emergence of *Yamisda* will serve not only as a means for *Kyai* Malik to be active outside *pesantren* but also as a venue for alumnae to gather. Furthermore, the emergence of both groups has helped both to reach a wide area of preaching (*dakwah*). If there was only one group in the *pesantren,* it would be difficult to cope with the wide area of *dakwah.*[14]

This response, put forward by a student on the emergence of the two groups in his *pesantren,* is a typical view of the *santri.* This view is based on positive thinking (*husn al-ẓann*) rather than negative thinking (*sūu al-ẓann*) toward teachers. This view is also part of the courtesy (*adab*) of students toward their teachers, which is a quality strongly stressed in the relationship between students and teachers in *pesantren.*

The rivalry among *istighāthat* groups occurred when each attempted to promote their group based on the genealogy of their leaders and founders. Had the leaders of these groups been integrated in one group, this group might have had greater potential for spreading *istighāthat* prayer among people.

5.3. The Ritual of *Iḥsāniyyat*

The central ritual of this group is the recitation of *istighāthat.* One of the leaders of this group stated that this ritual includes pronouncing the name of the *shaikh* or teacher as mediator in the ritual (A., *tawassul*), remembrance (A., *dhikr*), the recitation of *Ṣalawāt,* prayer(A.,*du'ā'*), and a request for forgiveness (A., *istighfār*). All of these features are endorsed by Islam and regarded as *ibādat* (Muttahid 2004). *Ibādat* is understood by this group to refer to additional activities such as reciting the Qur'an, *tahlīl, tahmīd*and visiting tombs in addition to the five actions linked to the five pillars of Islam: the witness of faith (A., *shahāda*), prayer, charity, fasting, and pilgrimage (Muhaimin 1995). In other words, *ibādat* in this sense is understood in its broader sense, which includes doing things that can be used as a means to seek God's pleasure and to attain closeness to Him.

According to *Gus* Abdul Latif, all of these activities have a strong basis either in the Qur'ān or the hadith. *Dhikr,* for instance, is a practice drawn from many references in the Qur'an explaining the excellence of the remembrance of God

14 *Interview with a student of Pesantren Jampes, Kediri, November, 2004.*

(Al-Ahzāb: 41, al-Imrān: 191). In addition, the Prophet not only encouraged Muslims to practice *dhikr* but also explained that a reward could be earned by those who practice *dhikr*. For example, the Prophet said that when any group of people remembers God, angels surround them and mercy covers them, tranquility descends upon them, and God mentions them to those who are with Him (narrated by Muslim, Tirmīdhī, Ahmad, Ibn Mājah, and Bayhāqī).

Another component of *istighāthat* is *tawassul*. This practice is understood by the group as pronouncing the names of '*ulamā*' or Sufi masters as mediators in supplicating God, irrespective of whether they are alive or dead. This practice is not intended to ask something from those people but merely to identify them as righteous persons in the view of God. *Gus* Abdul Latif has argued that, since these people are believed to be the most beloved of God, pronouncing their names in prayer, will increase the likelihood that God will grant the prayer. He made the analogy to a person who wished to meet a manager. If they are accompanied by a person who is closely known to the manager, the person is much more likely to attract the manager's attention than if the person comes to the manager's office alone. This analogy is widely used among *kyai* in Java. Other *kyai* object to this since in this situation people recognize the authority of the intermediary as much as that of the manager. In contrast, other *kyai* compare the *tawassul* to people who use spectacles to read the Qur'an. In this way, people can be said to view only the Qur'an, not the glass in their spectacles (Dhofier 1999).

The recitation of *Ṣalawāt* (invoking the blessing on the Prophet) is also part of the *istighāthat* ritual and it is sanctioned by God. *Gus* Abdul Latif argued that since every Muslim receives guidance from God by virtue of the Prophet, they should invoke blessing on him. Furthermore, quoting the verse of Qur'an, *Gus* Abdul Latif mentioned that indeed, as God and His Angels invoke blessing on the Prophet, so should people. In addition, the Prophet is the right person to whom blessing is given because he was believed to be able to provide his intercession (*shafaat*) both in this world and in the hereafter.

Another important element of the *istighāthat* is *istighfār*.*Gus* Abdul Latif mentioned that the *istighfār* was included as a formula to invoke God's forgiveness. The importance of *istighfār* is well supported both by the Qur'an and the hadīth because it is closely related to the concept of repentance (A., *taubah*). According to Sufi tradition, repentance (A., *taubat*), which is considered to be the first station (*maqām*) in Sufi practice, is required of all Muslims, since no Muslim is able to perform God's order perfectly. Moreover, no one can be free from the intrigues of the devil nor from the lower soul's (*nafs*) desire, which contributes to disobedience (Muhaya 1993:43).

To perform *taubat,* it is not enough just say *istighfār,* without following three requirements. Qushairī notes three essential conditions in order for repentance to be acceptable. The first is contrition for acts of disobedience. The second is the immediate abandonment of sin through fulfilling the obligation to refrain from disobedience. The third is the determination not to sin again (al-Qushayri 2002:111). This is similar to *Gus* Abdul Latif's view that no son or daughter of Adam is immune from committing sins, and the best of those who have committed sin are those who repent from it. Moreover, it is believed that performing *istighfār* is able to purify hearts and get rid of sins.

The last component of this *istighāthat* is the prayer of supplication (A., *du'ā'*). This ritual is normally placed at the end of the *istighāthat.* It is at this time that people are urged to pray to God with the guidance of their leader, asking not only for their happiness in the hereafter but also for happiness in this life. As in other Sufi orders, *du'ā'* is stressed in this group because it is considered to be the most important practice of the *istighāthat.*

The ritual of *istighāthat* is normally led by the leader of the group or his representatives at the tombs of holy people or other places such as in mosques, a village public hall (I., *balai desa*) and member's houses. This ritual usually begins with a session called *arwahan.* As implied by this term, which is derived from the word meaning the soul of deceased person (I., *arwah*), this ritual involves the leader sending prayers or the *al-Fātiḥat* chapter[15] to deceased persons at the request of the participants. However, in this session many people request the leader to recite *al-Fātiḥat* not for deceased persons, but for their own worldly purposes. For example, during this session participants have asked for success in the local regency elections, Indonesian football competition, earning money, the military tests, selling houses, or for the recovery from a chronic disease. Normally, these requests are written on a piece of paper and given to the coordinator a few minutes before the session begins. Asking for a share in the blessing (I., *barakah*) and intercession from the personage in the tombs, the leader reads the request and makes a prayer. In return, those who make these requests should give some money voluntarily to the coordinator. The amount of money is not determined. In the great ritual of *istighāthat,* the *arwahan* session can take a long time since many people make requests.

When the *arwahan* has been concluded, the next session will be a religious lecture (A., *mau'iẓat al-hasanat*) followed by interactive dialogue involving the participants and the leader. The topic of the lecture is not determined beforehand

15 This first chapter of the Qur'an is considered by Muslim scholars as the core of the rest of the Qur'an in term of the content of its message. Therefore, it is believed that reciting this chapter is like reciting all the chapters of the Qur'an.

and is usually based on the preference of the leader. On some occasions, the lecture is given and developed from questions asked by the participants. Therefore, the lecture could include various topics on Islamic subjects and individual consultations. Usually during a major ceremony or ritual held by Sufi orders, this kind of lecture does not allow the audience time to ask questions.

Plate 5.2: People using trucks to get to the Istighāthat Iḥsāniyyat ritual Banyuwangi

Plate 5.3: Female participants at a Istighāthat Iḥsāniyyat group ritual in Kediri.

After the religious lecture, the main ritual of *istighāthat,* that is *tawassulan,* occurs. This consists in reciting the *al-Fātiḥat*chapter conveyed to the Prophet Muhammad, and from him in succession to his families, his companions, the generations after companions (A., *tābi'īn*), the generations after the *tābi'īn* (A., *tābi' al-tābi'īn*), the saints (A., *auliyā'*), Muslim scholars (I., *ulama*), and all virtuous Muslims (A.,*ṣāliḥin*). Other prophets such as Adam and Eve, Khiḍr, Elias, Christ, are also specifically mentioned. Other names recited can include 'Alī ibnAbīṬālib, the only one of the Prophet's companions specifically mentioned in the list; Abū Ḥāmid al-Ghazāly; 'Abd al-Qādir al-Jaylānī, the founder of Qadiriyah orders; 'Abd al-Salām Ibn Mashīsh (d.1228), the teacher of the founder of Shadhiliyyah orders; Abu al-Ḥasan 'Alī Ibn 'Abd Allah Ibn 'Abd al-Jabbār al-Shādhilī (d.1258), the founder of Shadhiliyyah orders; Abū al-'Abbās Aḥmad bin 'Aliy al-Būnī (d.1225), the author of *Shams al-Ma'ārif*(The Illumination of Knowledge) which is the most widely read medieval Islamic treatise on talismans, and the magical square (A.,*wifq*) in pesantren; 'Abd al-Wahhāb al-Sha'rānī (d.1565), the founder of Sha'rāniyyat orders, and Abū Madyān al-Maghrābī (d.1197), the teacher of Ibn Mashīsh.

It is clear that some of the names cited during *tawassulan* are renowned names, which have important positions in the chain of transmission in various famous Sufi orders. Pronouncing these names during the *tawassulan* session does not mean that these names are considered as transmitters (A., *isnād*or I., *silsilah*) of the *Iḥsāniyyat* group. These names are cited to help to obtain blessing from those who are considered to be 'the axis of saints' (A., *Qutb al-Aqtāb*). It is believed that these saints, despite their death, 'reside simultaneously in their tombs and in heaven' (Woodward 1989). Moreover, they are also believed to be capable of becoming involved in the lives of those who pray (Ewing 1997:117).

Other names cited during the *tawassulan* session are the leader's family ancestors including *Shaikh*Yahūda, *Shaikh* Mesir, *Shaikh* Ujang Ṣāliḥ, Nyai Isti'ānah, *Sheikh* Daḥlān, *Shaikh* Iḥsān, *Shaikh* Muḥammad, and *Nyai* Ḥasanah. Apart from the last two, these names are also cited during the *tawassulan* session held by the *Yamisda* group. The last two names are not mentioned by *Yamisda* because they are not regarded as family ancestors of the leader. Sheikh Muhammad was the elder brother and and *Nyai* Hasanah the sister-in-law of Yamisda's leader, *Kyai* Malik, so their status in the group is considered less significant.

Among those family ancestor names, *Shaikh* Ihsan is cited twice during the *tawassulan* session after reciting *al-Fātiḥat* for all deceased teachers of *Pesantren* Jampes, all deceased Muslim fathers, mothers, grandfathers, grandmothers, and all dead or live Muslims. For the *Iḥsāniyyat* leader, this name needs to be emphasized in the ritual and should be given special attention because he is regarded as a transmitter (A., *sanad*) of this group (Muttahid 2004). According to the rule of hadith (A., *'ulūm al-ḥadīth*), a *sanad* is understood to be the person who narrated the text of a hadith. The succession of these *sanad* starts with the last narrator and ends with the Prophet who spoke the hadith. It is not clear in this group whether or not *Shaikh* Ihsan is regarded as a *sanad* in the strict sense of this term. If he is, he should receive the *Istighāthat* formula through a chain of narrators which leads back to the Prophet. However, there seems to be no evidence that he has received this formula from the Prophet through a chain of transmitters.

After reciting *al-Fātiḥat* for *Shaikh* Ihsan, by asking for a share in his sacredness (A, *karāmat,* I., *karamah*[16]), blessing and secrets (A., *asrār*), the *tawassul* session is closed with a prayer. Unlike rituals held by others Sufi groups, this prayer is recited in both Arabic and Javanese. It can also be recited in other vernaculars depending on the language of the majority of supplicants. The reason for using the Javanese language is to steady the supplicants' hearts because all of them are Javanese and few of them understand Arabic. It is widely held in Sufi teachings that to invoke God, people should understand the meaning of the invocation because it will guarantee the success of the prayer. As al-Ghazālī said, praying without understanding the meaning is like a parrot that can say anything but understand nothing. Even, in the five times prayers, understanding the meaning will contribute to improve the focus (A., *khusū'*) of prayer. This prayer is as follows:

> O! Allah I ask of your *taufiq* and guidance, your mercy and blessing, as well as your contentment and forgiveness for me and for my family. And Oh! Allah I ask you to ease all of my problems, to meet all my needs, to make all business successful for my family and myself. And I ask you to make me and my family happy both in this world and the world to come, to increase my livelihood and wealth which are blessed and useful, and I ask you to save me and my family from trials, misfortune, dangers and from all unpleasant things. And I ask you to answer all of my requests by virtue of the blessing, the miracle and the secrets of *al-Fātiḥat* chapter [17](Muhammad n.d.:7).

16 The term *karāmat*(plural *karāmāt*) is an Arabic word meaning the wonders wrought by Muslim saints for the good of the people as well as in proof of their own saintship. In Javanese the term *karāmat*changes to *keramat* which refers to sacred place such as a holy grave or the shrine of a holy person.

17 'Ya Allah kulo nyuwun , kulo sekeluargo mugi tansah panjenengan paringi Taufiq lan Hidayah panjenengan, Rahmat lan Nikmat Panjenengan , Soho ridha lan pengampunan panjenengan , lan kulu nyuwun Ya Allah kulo sekeluarga mugio panjenengan gampilaken sedoyo urusanipun, hasil sedoyo hajatipun, sukses sedoyo usahanipun, lan kulo nyuwun Ya Allah kulo sekeluargo mugio panjenengan dadosaken tiang ingkang bahagia donyo lan akhiratipun, kathah rizkinipun,kathah bondonipun ingkang barakahi lan manfaati, lan kulo nyuwun Ya Allah kulo sekeluarga mugio panjenengan selametaken saking fitnah, bala' afat lan sedoyo perkawis ingkang mboten ngeremenaken. Lan kulo nyuwun Ya Allah mugio sedoyo panyuwun kulo kolowau panjenengan ijabahi sedoyo lantaran barokah, karomah, soho asroripun Surat a-Fatihah.'

This prayer is not the end of the ritual. Rather, this prayer is the beginning of the *dhikr* session that consists of the reciting of the first chapter of the Qur'an (*al-Fātiḥat*) forty times; the reciting of *al-Ikhlāṣ* chapter eleven times; the reciting of *istighfār* phrase, استغفر الله العظيم سبحان الله وبحمده (I beseech Allah's forgiveness, the Magnificent, glory be to Allah and praise be to him); the reciting of the *ṣalāwa* phrase a hundred times, السلام عليك ايهاالنبي ورحمة الله وبركاته (May the peace, the Mercy and the Blessing of Allah be upon you, O! Prophet); the reciting of *Kalīmat al-Ṭayyibat* a hundred times, لااله الا الله الملك الحقّ المبين (There is none worthy of worship except Allah, the sovereign Lord, the Truth, the Clear evident), the reciting of some of God's names a hundred times, بسم الله يافتّاح يارزّاق ياكفى ياغنيّ (In the name of Allah, O! the Opener, the Provider, the Most Sufficient, the Rich) and the reciting of *ḥauqala* phrase a hundred times, بسم الله الرحمن الرحيم لاحول ولاقوةالا بالله العلي العظيم (In the names of Allah the All Merciful and the All Compassionate, there is no change and power except through Allah). All of these formulae are recited vocally either by the leader or the participants. Eventually, the ritual is closed by a long prayer led by the leader.

It is important to note that the dominant feature of the *dhikr* ritual performed by this group is the recitation of God's names taken from the best names of God (A., *asmāul ḥusnā*). Although Muslim scholars have different opinions on the number of these names, it is widely held that there are ninety nine names. In addition to the use of His names focusing on his transcendence and power, this group also employs His names or attributes which imply His response to requests. For example, if one says *Ya Fattāḥ* (the Opener), *Ya Razzāq* (the Provider), it would mean 'be opening and be providing'. In other words, it is expected that by reciting these God's names, divine aid in opening and providing a livelihood for humans is sought. This practice is sanctioned by God in the Qur'an, which asks people to invoke God using His names (al-A'rāf : 180; al-Isrā' : 110). It is expected that mentioning God's attributes and his names in praying will cause the prayer to be granted by God, as well as creating optimism in the heart of supplicants (Shihab 1998:xxxvii). However, particular Sufi orders such as the Hamidiyyah Shadhiliyah order, recite God's names but not in connection with questions and requests. According to Hamidiyyah Shadhiliyyah group, the proper purpose of *dhikr* is to focus on the Absoluteness of God, on His transcendent, Eternal Being, with no thought of material purposes (Gilsenan 1973:167-68). In contrast, In the *Iḥsāniyyat* group, the participants are allowed to invoke God with respect to their own intentions.

The ritual of *istighāthāt* is conducted in a group (*berjamaah*) on a weekly and five-week (J., *selapanan*) basis. It may also be practised daily by individuals at any time. The weekly ritual is usually held in places such as the tombs of holy men or in some villages located in Kediri. These rituals are usually attended by a small number of people. On the other hand, the *selapanan* ritual is generally held outside Kediri and can be attended by a great number of people. In addition, the ritual is also specifically held in connection with the birthday of this group and the anniversary of the death of Muslim saints in the vicinity of Kediri such as *Shaikh* Ihsan Dahlan, *Shaikh* Muhammad and Nyai Hasanah, *Shaikh* Murshad, *Shaikh* Ali Laleyan (Pangeran Demang), and *Shaikh* Ageng Karanglo. Like the *selapanan* rituals, these rituals are held on the anniversary of the saints' deaths and involve many members of the group from different regions.

Only the *selapanan* ritual of *istighāthāt* is followed by other cultural performances such as hobby-horse dances (J., *jaranan*), the tiger-masked dances (I.,*Reog Ponorogo*), a Chinese traditional dances (I., *barongsai*), and *dangdutan*. On these occasions, a meal and special water are provided for the participants in the ritual. When the ritual has concluded, the committee that organized the ritual usually serves a meal from a general kitchen (I., *dapur umum*) set up in the location. The special meal provided during this ritual is rice served with eggplant vegetable curry. For the leader of this group this menu has a particular significance. According to him, the soft texture of eggplant symbolizes the softness of the heart after performing the *istighāthāt* ritual. Therefore, it is expected that reciting *istighāthāt*, can make the hearts of the participants soft and ready to receive guidance (I., *hidayah*) from God.

In addition to the meal, special water called blessed water (I., *air karamah*) is provided for the ritual participants at every entrance. To obtain this water people should voluntarily give a small amount of money. Before being offered to people, this water is specially prayed over by a group of selected *kyai* in turn so that this water is believed to have particular power (I., *karamah*) that can be used for many purposes. *Gus* Abdul Latif believes that this water can be used to heal or for other purposes because it has absorbed spiritually the sound waves of recited *dhikr*. In order to enhance the power of this water, a special prayer can be directed to it. *Gus* Abdul Latif argued that this practice was well supported by the fact that the Prophet himself carried out the same practice. It was said in a hadith that when one of the Prophet's companions was sick, the Prophet gave him water while reciting a prayer. It is for this reason that in order to obtain blessing (*barakah*) during a *manāqiban* ritual (reciting a particular Sufi saint's biography) or during a *istighāthāt* recitation held by some Sufi orders in Java, many participants bring a bottle of water from home, and place it in front of the ritual gathering with its lid open.

5.4. The Structure of the Group

Gilsenan, in his classical study on Saints and Sufi in Modern Egypt, used the terms, 'organization' and 'association' to describe the structure of Sufi orders. An organization emphasizes 'a high degree of stratification on the basis of differential expertise and/or efficiency'. An organization is also characterized by 'greater structural recognition of functional inequality' and formal control based on 'a hierarchy of authority statuses'. Another mark of organizations is that their holders are full time and fully paid. In contrast, an association is characterized by 'looseness of structure with minimal development of a status hierarchy.' Individual commitment in an association is also voluntary and egalitarian. Moreover, the appointment of officials is based on administrative convenience. He concluded that the majority of Sufi orders in Egypt could be placed on a continuum between association and organization (Gilsenan 1973:65-66). Sufi orders in Indonesia can also be shown to follow this typology.

However, Gilsenan's typology cannot be easily applied to the structure of *Majlis Dhikr* groups like *Istighāthat Iḥsaniyyat*. Unlike many Sufi orders in Indonesia which have hierarchical positions such as master (*murshid*), vice-master (*khalifah*), and disciple (*murid*), in the *Iḥsaniyyat* group these positions are not recognized. Instead, *Iḥsaniyyat* only recognises a single position of leader who is regarded as a central figure (I., *tokoh sentral*) in this group. Although there are chairpersons (I., *ketua*) in some branches, they function only as coordinators for major *istighāthat* rituals (*rutinan selapanan*) and other rituals held in these branches. If the *tokoh sentral* cannot come to the ritual, these chairpersons will substitute for him to lead the major *istighāthat* (*rutinan selapanan*) ritual. These branch representative chairpersons are appointed directly by the central leader without any further qualification and without any limit on the time. As a result, they are immediately responsible to him. In this sense, the position of these representatives is not like the *khalīfat* or *naib* in other Sufi orders who can function as intermediaries linking *murid* with *murshid* but also supervising the initiation of new *murid* on behalf of their *murshid.*

Because there is no intermediary person to link the members with the *tokoh sentral,* people find it easy to meet with him either privately or on public occasions. For example, prior to the weekly *istighāthat* ritual and at the end of the ritual, people can freely meet *Gus* Abdul Latif, in the relaxed context, sitting together and chatting (J., *jagongan)* with him. It is on this occasion that people can ask, consult, and discuss everything with their leader. Moreover, such occasions are sometimes used by the leader to give religious messages to his members informally. It is also evident on such occasions how the *tokoh sentral*

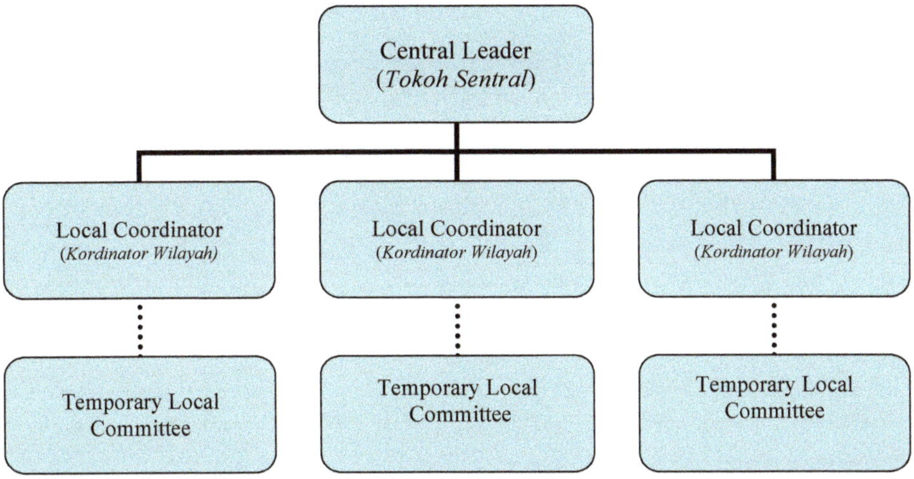

Figure 5.1 Orgnizational Structure of Iḥsāniyyat Group.

Source: Interview with Gus Abdul Latif, Kediri, November 2004.

demonstrates his sympathy and care toward his members by staying until midnight, if called upon to do so. In addition, if people want to consult privately, they can meet him directly in his house at any time or they can make a call through his assistants (J., *khadam*) to check on his availability.

As happens in many other Sufi groups, the exact number of members and their social background are unknown because the *Iḥsāniyyat* group keeps no official records, and the recruitment of new followers is not officially registered. The majority of its members come from the lower classes of society. Most of them come from rural areas rather than urban areas. The members of this group comprise not only elderly men and women but also younger people.

To become a member of *Iḥsāniyyat*, people do not need to take an oath or initiation (A., *bay'at,* I., *baiat*) to the leader or his representative or pass a test. In other words, the mode of entry is voluntary, so people can recite and practice the *wird* (*dhikr* formula) without asking direct permission from the *tokoh sentral.* Moreover, the *Iḥsāniyyat* group does not demand an exclusive commitment on the part of its members. Therefore, people can voluntary join this group while also being members of other *dhikr* groups. They are also able to practise the ritual of *istighāthat*intermittently without any sanction, even though the leader of this group recommends the members (*jamaah*) practise the *istighāthat* ritual continuously. In contrast, other Sufi orders require their members to take a vow of allegiance (*bay'at*) to their *shaikh* or *murshid,* before they can recite a special *dhikr* and more *aḥzāb* (Trimingham 1971:186). Even Sufi groups such as Hamidiyah Shadiliyah (Gilsenan 1973:94), and Tijaniyah demanded an exclusive commitment and allegiance from their members. For example, on joining the Tijaniyah order, people are expected to abandon their commitment to other orders. They will not suffer any harm if they abandon those orders. However, if they abandon their allegiance to the Tijaniyyah, they will experience harm and death (Sirriyeh 1999:17-18).

The relationship between the *tokoh sentral* and his members is not like the strong master-pupil (*murshid-murid*) relationship in many Sufi orders. The relationship is based on a general normative comportment (I., *adab*) as commonly practised in teacher-student relations in the Islamic learning tradition, while the relationship between *murshid* and *murid* in Sufi orders is strongly based on a complex set of *adab* as well as sanctions. *Kyai* Usman Ishaqi, a *murshid* of Qadiriyah wa Naqshabandiyah order from Surabaya, mentioned in his book, *al-Khulāṣat al-Wafiyyat fī al-Ādāb wa Kaifiyyat al-Dhikr 'Inda al-Sāda al-Qādiriyyat wa al-Naqshabandiyyat,* the *adab* by which the *murid* should completely respect their *murshid.* He put it this way:

> You should respect your *shaikh* and believe outwardly (*dhahir*) and inwardly (*batin*) that without the help of the *shaikh*, your objective will never be obtained. You should not complain about what the *shaikh* has done, even though the *shaikh* may have done something which is unlawful in appearance. Instead, avoiding negative prejudice against the *shaikh,* people should be convinced that what the *shaikh* has done is clearly based on God's orders. If you still do not understand this, you should think that this is because of your lack of knowledge in understanding the essence of matters. Sometimes what the *shaikh* has done seems to be blameworthy (*madhmūmat*) in appearance; however in its essence what he has done is praiseworthy. You should surrender yourselves to him because challenging him is like a disease , which is difficult to cure… the *murid* who ask their *shaikh* about his behaviour will never prosper. In all your life matters either in their totality or in their details, in devotional aspects or cultural aspects, you should abandon your own choice because your *shaikh* has chosen for you. In short, you should surrender yourself to him. The annihilation in *master* (A.,*fanā' fī al-shaikh*) is an introduction to the annihilation in God (A., *fanā' fī Allah*)…You should not talk in front of your *shaikh.* When he asks you, instead of answering too long, you should answer the question precisely. This is partly because speaking too much in front of the *shaikh* will eliminate his veneration. Therefore, the excellent *adab* of a *murid* toward his *shaikh* is that he should be silent, quiet and pay attention to what the *shaikh* says and do that which contributes to welfare (al-Ishaqi n.d.:5-6).

This *adab* is relevant to the famous expression in the Sufi tradition, 'Be with your *shaikh* like the corpse in the hands of the washer; he turns it over as he wishes and it is obedient' (Trimingham 1971:187). This long practical *adab* instruction in a Sufi order is always stressed, either by the *murshid* or his *khalīfat,* especially on the occasion of initiation (A., *bay'at*) and some other occasions. In contrast, although the members of *Iḥsāniyyat* do not engage in such *adab,* they still pay respect to their *tokoh sentral* as a teacher. For example, it is very common for *Iḥsāniyyat* members to chat with their *tokoh sentral* after an *istighāthāt* ritual session until midnight. Sometimes they laugh if the *tokoh sentral* makes a joke about one of his members. According to the *adab* prescribed in the Sufi orders, none of these practices is allowed.

Since the highest authority in the *Iḥsāniyyat* is in the hands of the *tokoh sentral* as founder as well as guider of the group, every decision related to the group is determined only with his approval. For example, every activity is conducted by establishing a temporary committee, the members of which are recruited from capable group members on his approval. When those activities have been completed, the committee is responsible for reporting about these activities to the *tokoh sentral.* When *tokoh sentral* has approved and accepted the report, he officially dismisses the committee. If he cannot attend and lead the weekly ritual, he delegates his representative to lead the ritual. Without a mandate from him, no one dares to lead the ritual.

In order to support and run the activities of *Iḥsāniyyat,* this group does not have particular ways to gain financial funding. For example, it has never asked its members to give money regularly to the leader of the group. The only financial funding that can be obtained by this group comes from events such as *ruwatan* (a special ritual to cleanse people's misfortune) and the regular *istighāthāt* ritual (I., *rutinan istighathat selapanan*). In an event like *ruwatan,* for instance, the event committee usually asks those who participate to give some money. Moreover, at another event such as a major *istighāthāt* ritual, this group can collect funds from the *arwahan* session, donation boxes, and *air karamah* provided to the participants. In order to be included in the *arwahan* session, people should give some money voluntarily to the coordinator of the session. Likewise, if they want to receive *air karomah,* they should give some money in return.

To encourage members of *Iḥsāniyyat* to give more alms, *Kyai* Hisham argued that prayers would be more easily granted by God if they are followed by alms and charity (I., *sadaqah*). The more people give the greater the chance their prayer will be granted by God. He described this notion to the members of *Iḥsāniyyat* by pointing out that 'if someone wants to catch a big fish, they should have big fish bait.' However, it is not clear what percentage of the money collected should be allocated to the group or given to the leader. It is therefore difficult to trace the stream of funding in this group because all financial matters are discussed internally among a few individuals. As a result, the members and public have no idea how much money has been collected by this organization so far.

It is interesting to note that although this group has not included *pesantren* in its structure, *pesantren* have still played an important role in the spreading of this local group. In the case of *Iḥsāniyyat,* the network of alumnae who graduated from *Pesantren* Jampes has played an important role in disseminating knowledge of this group. The position of *Gus* Abdul Latif as the leader of *Iḥsāniyyat,* as a son of a *kyai* of the *pesantren,* and as an Islamic preacher (I., *muballigh*) has attracted many alumnae to invite him to give religious lectures in their home towns. On such occasions *Gus* Abdul Latif often introduces *Iḥsāniyyat* to the participants. On many occasions, this group is deliberately introduced to the public as a group from *Pesantren* Jampes rather than from Kediri. In this way, *Pesantren* Jampes has become a part of the group's structure. *Pesantren* Jampes has contributed to popularizing this group.

5.5. From Tombs to Mosques: Implementing Sufi *Dakwah* and Religious Tolerance

Dakwah is a Qur'anic concept that has been widely used and practised by Muslims. However, since this term has different connotations and understandings, Muslims in diverse parts of the world conceive the practice of *dakwah* in various ways. Even in Indonesian Islam, *dakwah* is applied and interpreted in different ways. Some people use the concept in 'its restricted form (to apply only within Islam), while others use *dakwah* in its open form (for all of humanity).' As Gade has explained, *dakwah* basically means 'call to deepen one's own or encourage others' Islamic piety' (Gade 2004:16).

For the leader of *Iḥsāniyat, dakwah* is understood not only as encouraging others' Islamic piety but also seeking the guidance of God (I., *hidayah*), which is necessary for the success of *dakwah.* It is in line with this definition that the ritual of *Istighāthat Iḥsāniyyat* is combined with a religious lecture (A., *mauiẓat al-ḥasanat*). The first aim is to ask God's guidance and then to deepen and encourage others' Islamic piety. *Gus* Abdul Latif believes that without God guidance (I., *hidayah*), the objective of *dakwah* will not be perfectly achieved. Likewise, *istighāthat* without *mauiẓat al-ḥasanat* is like *ibāda* without knowledge (I., *ilmu*), which is considered worthless. To achieve *hidayah* entails the purification of one's heart from negative worldly desire. This purification can be done through *istighāthat* which contains continuous worship and repentance.

When *hidayah* has been achieved, people can deepen their understanding of Islamic knowledge from any source. This form of *dakwah* has been practised by the group since *Gus* Abdul Latif realized that the *dakwah* of Islamic preachers in Indonesia has not contributed to the improvement of Muslims' religious attitudes. This is partly because the practice of *dakwah* has placed too much stress on public lectures (I., *ceramah*), while ignoring the obtainment of *hidayah*. *Gus* Abdul Latif explained the importance of *istighāthat* in the *dakwah* project as follows:

> Human beings consist of two aspects: a physical aspect (I., *jasmani*) and a spiritual aspect (I., *rohani*). Both of them constitute life in unity which needs different food supplement. The former will become healthy and functional if it is supplied with enough nutrition and vitamins. Likewise, the latter will be healthy and functional if it is supplied with enough nutrition and vitamins. This nutrition and vitamins can be gained from sincere worship and religious activities which can bring one nearer to God through *istighāthat*. However, most people have forgotten this spiritual need. In fact, if this spiritual need can be fulfilled, all social problems such as drug and alcohol addiction, as well as social crimes can be resolved.[18]

Since its inception, this group has catered for those who are categorized as difficult people (I., *orang ruwet*) and marginalised people (I., *orang pinggiran*) though it is also open to other groups of people. *Iḥsāniyyat* even attracted those who were previously addicted to narcotics (I., *narkoba*), alcohol, ecstasy tablets, and opium (*sabu-sabu*). According to *Gus* Abdul Latif, the reason for recruiting those people into the *Iḥsāniyyat* group was that they had been ignored by other religious leaders in their *dakwah* projects. Instead of ignoring them, he stressed that these people should become the main target of Islamic *dakwah*. These people in his view were similar to government officials (I., *pejabat*), nobles (I., *orang pangkat*), and Muslims scholars (I., *ulama*) and these people should be treated patiently without labeling them as *orang nakal* or *orang ruwet*. However, some of *Gus* Abdul Latif's colleagues have objected to such *dakwah*. They feared that if such people were involved, they could ruin their status as *Gus* or *kyai*. In response to this objection, he argued as follows:

> The status of someone's *kyaiship* will not disappear because of associating with bad people, thieves, and drug addicts. The status of a person's *kyaiship* will be sustained so long as they maintain their consistency to conduct and hold their belief [religious belief]. Even if they associate with pious people but do not maintain their consistency, their status as *kyai* will decline.

18 Interview with *Gus* Latif, Kediri, January, 2005.

Gus Abdul Latif further argued that the recruitment of *orang ruwet* in the *dakwah* project was based on the fact that the Prophet himself was very concerned about these people. The Prophet give his advocacy (A., *shafā'at*) for those who committed capital offences (I., *dosa besar*). *Gus* Abdul Latif insisted that if *'ulamā'* are considered the Prophet's inheritors, they have to emulate him by welcoming, and embracing such people, and strengthening their Islamic piety rather than ignoring them. Therefore, in the context of *dakwah* he maintained that 'people should guide those who cannot walk rather than guiding those who are capable of walking.'

Involving those people in the *dakwah* project can also mean that they should be regarded as respected people (I., *orang terhormat*) rather than as the dregs of society (I., *sampah masyarakat*). For *Gus* Abdul Latif, respecting them and involving them in the *dakwah* project will enhance their confidence, which ultimately contributes to their consciousness to return to the right path. One of his ways to increase their confidence is by asking them not to be upset by their past deeds. He maintained that if those people are willing to repent seriously, God will forgive all their past sins; God only loves those sinners who are willing to repent. Furthermore, he motivates them by saying that the repentance of those sinners could be likened to fertilizer made from animal feces, which is useful for plantations. Without this fertilizer, plants will not grow perfectly. Thus, he believes that because of those people, the status of other people before God can improve. Therefore, instead of condemning them, people should thank them. According to *Gus* Abdul Latif, this notion is based on the hadith which he described as follows:

> 'Later, the flame of fire licks many Muslims on the Day of Judgment; no one including Muslim scholars (*ulama*) can prevent the fire. Suddenly, the Angel of Gabriel comes and brings water to extinguish the fire and it is out. The Prophet says to the Angel, 'What sort of water did you bring to extinguish the fire?' Gabriel answers, 'I collected this water from the tears of those who regret their sins.'

Furthermore, to those who have committed sins and would like to repent, *Gus* Abdul Latif says, 'Your rank (*derajat*) before God is higher than mine, because God loves much those who want to repent from their sins and only those who have sinned are able to repent.'

Here, *Gus* Abdul Latif's positive opinion toward those who have committed sins relies heavily on the teaching of Sufism (I., *tasawuf*). Based on this teaching, people's fate at the end of their lives is difficult to know: whether they will have a good death (A., *ḥusn al-khātimat*) or a bad death (A., *sū' al-khātimat*).

In this respect, some people may do good deeds during their life, but commit sins at the end of their life without having a chance to repent, so these people obviously die with *sū' al-khātimat.* Furthermore, he argued that people should not underestimate those who have committed sins during their life, because they might have the chance to repent at the end of their life so that they may die with *ḥusn al- khātimat.* Therefore, since people do not know their own fate, they should not underestimate others who are still sinning. In this sense, *Gus* Abdul Latif's opinion is similar to Ibn Aṭāillah who pointed out that, 'Bad deeds (I., *maksiat*) which bring someone to obedience to Allah (A., *ṭā'at*) are much better than good deeds (A., *ṭā'at*) which are coupled with, and lead, to pride (A., *takabbur*) (Pranowo 1991:50).'

Another approach taken by *Gus* Abdul Latif to attract those *orang ruwet* into his group is based on the teachings of the Qur'an. For example, when approaching drunken people who ultimately succeed in stopping drinking, he never overtly prohibits them from drinking. He believes that if they have not received *hidayah,* they will not stop drinking. Therefore, since quitting drinking is a matter of *hidayah,* he allows them to drink but at the same time, he asks them to keep in their mind that God prohibits drinking alcohol. This strategy was inspired by the way the Qur'an gradually prohibited drinking *khamr.* As described in the Qur'an, the prohibition took place four steps: the first step is that the Qur'an just informed people that:

> And of the fruits of the date-palm, and grapes, whence ye derive strong drink (*sakar*) and (also) good nourishment. Lo! therein is indeed a portent for people who have sense [An-Nahl 16:67].

At the second step, when one of the Prophet's companions reported that *khamr* can lead people to unconsciousness and bankruptcy, the Qur'an responded that:

> They will ask thee about intoxicants and games of chance. Say: 'In both there is great evil as well as some benefit for man; but the evil which they cause is greater than the benefit which they bring.' And they will ask thee as to what they should spend [in God's cause]. Say: 'Whatever you can spare'. In this way God makes clear unto you His messages, so that you might reflect [al-Baqarah 2:219]

In this verse, instead of explicitly prohibiting people from drinking strong liquor (A., *khamr*), the Qur'an only noted that the sin, which resulted from drinking khamr, was greater than its usefulness. At the third step, the Qur'an only prohibits people from drinking *khamr* while they are about to pray. The Qur'an explained that:

> O! ye who believe! Draw not near unto prayer when ye are drunken, until ye know that which ye utter [al-Nisa' 4:43].

At the fourth step, the Qur'an explicitly forbade people from drinking *khamr* because it is part of Satan's handiwork. The Qur'an said that:

O! ye who believe! Strong drink and games of chance and idols and divining arrows are only an infamy of Satan's handiwork. Leave it aside in order that ye may succeed. [al-Maidah 5:90]

All of these verses suggest that in order to prohibit *khamr,* God prescribed a gradual method rather than a direct method, and this method can be applied in *dakwah* projects. The application of this method is also stressed by the Prophetic tradition which encourages Muslims to behave according to God's ethics (A., *akhlāq Allāh*).

In line with this method, *Gus* Abdul Latif allowed Javanese popular arts such as the hobby-horse dance (J., *jaranan*), tiger-masked dance (I., *reog*), *dangdutan,* Chinese dragon dance (*leang-leong*), and *ruwatan* to be performed on the annual anniversary of *Iḥsāniyyat.* Such Javanese popular arts within the framework of *pesantren* and Sufi group are unusual. These popular arts are closely associated with the *abangan* group (nominal Muslims), a group that is seen by some scholars as being always contrary to the *santri* group (devout Muslims). However, *Gus* Abdul Latif believes that these performances can be used as a means to propagate Islam among those nominal Muslims. He put it this way:

> Holding *jaranan* on the anniversary day of *Iḥsāniyyat*could be seen as part of *lisān al-ḥāl*in the *dakwah* project. In other words, although without saying anything, I have shown to them that I can accept and accommodate those performances…As a result, we can bring the *jaranan* society or *abangan* group back to the Islamic path by respecting and appreciating them. If we have been accepted [by them], we can remove slowly the content of the performance arts that is prohibited by Islamic Law. If this succeeds, they can propagate Islam through the performance arts.[19]

In response to this statement, the leader of the Lukojoyo *Jaranan* Group commented as follows:

> As an *'ulāma, Gus* Abdul Latif was willing to watch our performance, without denouncing it. He, even, suggested we improve the quality of *jaranan* performance, whereas other *'ulāma'* have regarded us as people who are outside of social norms (*I., di luar norma sosial*) (Hisbi:2004).

19 Interview with *Gus* Abdul Latif, Kediri, January, 2005.

This response makes clear that these people felt happy to be embraced by *Gus* Abdul Latif in his *dakwah*. *Gus* Abdul Latif often involved this group in organizing *istighāthat* rituals in their own area. As a result, they were not reluctant to join other rituals held in other places.

According to *Gus* Abdul Latif, there were objections among other '*ulamā*' towards those Javanese performance arts. Some '*ulamā*' objected to those performances, saying that those arts were un-Islamic. However, *Gus* Abdul Latif criticized those who regarded Javanese arts such as *reog* and *jaranan* or *jatilan* as sinful arts (*kesenian yang berdosa*), while others such as *qasidah* and *gambus* were considered to be Islamic arts (*kesenian Islami*) . He questioned: 'What makes those Javanese arts un-Islamic, whereas the latter are considered Islamic arts (I., *Islami*)?' He argued that it is not fair to say that *jaranan* is an un-Islamic art, while *qasidah modern* is Islamic because it has an Arabic flavor. He argued that *qasidah*, in fact, must be considered as less Islamic than *jaranan*, since *qasidah* or *gambus*, even though they contain Arabic songs, always involve women who dance and sing. According to Islamic jurisprudence (*fiqh*), watching dancing women and hearing women singers can lead to immoral acts (I., *maksiat*) rather than spiritual benefits (*manfaat*).[20]

In fact, *Gus* Abdul Latif's predecessor also allowed various Javanese popular arts performances. My informant mentioned that *Shaikh* Ihsan Dahlan, Abdul *Gus* Latif's grandfather, included various popular Javanese arts when he conducted graduation (J., *khataman*) celebrations after he had finished reciting the whole chapters of *Ihyā' 'Ulūmuddīn* and his works, *Sirāj al-Ṭālibīn* in his *pesantren*[21]. At that time, *Kyai* Hasyim Ash'ari, the founder of the Nahdlatul Ulama organization, asked *Kyai* Ihsan about the involvement of these Javanese popular arts in the *khataman* celebration. Instead of answering, *Kyai* Ihsan Dahlan just opened his mouth. According to my informant, *Kyai* Hashim looked inside and saw the blue water of an ocean in *Kyai* Ihsan's mouth. My informant argued that this blue water of the deep ocean remains pure and clean even though dirty streams of water from rivers flow into it. This blue water of tthe deep ocean thus also symbolized the depth of *Kyai* Ihsan's Sufi practice that could purify all vices brought about by those Javanese popular arts. *Gus* Abdul Latif's acceptance of Javanese popular arts showed that *santri* culture is not always opposed to Javanese indigenous culture. Furthermore, *Gus* Abdul Latif's acceptance of Javanese popular arts reflects the nature of Sufi teachings which emphasizes continuity rather than change in local tradition and practices.

20 Interview with *Gus* Abdul Latif, Kediri, October, 2004.
21 Interview with *Gus* Abdul Latif, Kediri, October, 2004.

The involvement of Javanese performances in the *Iḥsāniyyat* group's *dakwah* reminds us of Sunan Kalijaga, one of the nine saints (I., *Wali Sanga*) of Java, who introduced Javanese gamelan of *sekaten* (I.,*gamelan sekaten*) in his *dakwah* in commemoration of Prophet Muhammad's birthday (I., *maulid nabi*). The word *sekaten* is a Javanese word which is adapted from the Arabic *shahādatain* (the two sentences of the declaration of faith), the first pillar of the five pillars of Islam. Sunan Kalijaga used the story and actors in shadow puppet (I.,*wayang kulit*) performances and creatively modified them to propagate Islam (Saksono 1995:91). In fact, as van Dijk (1998:225) has described, most *Wali Sanga* propagated Islam in Java with 'tact and moderation and accepted existing culture wherever possible.' They never touched, criticized or banned any sensitive issues and local customs in the society by rigidly imposing religious teachings, even though they lived in an *abangan-santri* society.

In addition to his tolerance toward Javanese culture and arts, *Gus* Abdul Latif also demonstrated his tolerance toward other religious followers. For example, he allowed a Christian to join regularly in the *istighāthat* ritual held by the *Iḥsāniyyat* group in Kediri without asking him to convert to Islam. *Gus* Abdul Latif further demonstrated his tolerance toward followers of other religious by praying sincerely for a Christian, at his request, for success in finding a new house. The reason for accepting this person as a member of the group is related to his *dakwah* strategy to show the tolerance and inclusiveness of Islam toward other religious believers. *Gus* Latif stressed that Islam and other religions have many more similarities than differences.[22]

Another reason to accept followers of other religions as *Iḥsāniyyat* members is to provide a bridge for interfaith dialogue and mutual understanding, which is essential in building religious life in Indonesia. The significance of this religious relationship can be concluded, for example, from a dialogue between a Christian and *Gus* Abdul Latif concerning a comment put forward by Abu Bakar Ba'asyir that, 'We have to destroy America, and enemies of Islam in Indonesia'. The Christian felt threatened by Ba'asyir's comment. In response, to this concern, *Gus* Abdul Latif said that every Muslim knows who Abu Bakar Ba'asyir is, and so one should not be worried by his threats. If this problem is not communicated in the frame of religious friendship, *Gus* Abdul Latif believed, followers of religions other than Islam will think that the majority of Muslims are like Abu Bakar Ba'asyir. Therefore, interfaith friendship and dialogue are important to reduce potential conflicts between religious beliefs because of misunderstandings. This mission is relevant to the motto of this group, that is, as a builder of a conscious and adhesive *ummat* (I., *pembina mental dan perekat umat*).

22 Interview with *Gus* Abdul Latif, Kediri, October 2004.

When asked about why he, as a Christian, was able to join with *Gus* Abdul Latif and become a member of the *Iḥsāniyyat*group, the Christian replied that he joined because he saw wisdom in the figure of *Gus* Abdul Latif. He said: 'As a Christian, I need wisdom as well as happiness in this life, and I can find these from everyone, regardless of their religion.' When he first joined the *istighāthat* group and actively listened to religious lectures given by *Gus* Abdul Latif, his parents worried that he would convert to Islam because of his closeness to the leader of *Iḥsāniyyat.* To convince his parents, he answered, 'If I was born a Christian, I will die a Christian.' In other words, he felt secure as a Christian because what he heard from *Gus* Abdul Latif's lecture (I., *pengajian*) and advice was relevant to the universal ethic, which is also prevalent in other religious teachings. He described *Gus* Abdul Latif as follows:

> As a drug addict, I want to quit my addiction. However, no one including my close friends could help me to quit. Instead of helping me, they all left me alone with my problem. Actually, I need those who can hear and help me to ease my problem. Finally, I found a person who could help and listen my problem. The person is *Gus* Latif. He is a wise man. I have spent many nights chatting with him until morning. He patiently heard my problem and gave advice to me. While he advised me, he never alluded to theological matters regarding Christianity'.[23]

Although *Gus* Abdul Latif pointed out that the recruitment of members was not the main objective of his group, nevertheless, as a *Majlis Dhikr* group which is missionary in nature, *Iḥsāniyyat* inevitably needs to recruit as many members as possible and to spread its influence to others. The need to recruit new members was evident when I attended a major *istighāthat* held in Banyuwangi, and *Gus* Abdul Latif proudly said to me that although this group was only established a few years ago, it had successfully attracted a large number of participants.[24] Moreover in every *istighāthat* ritual, he specifically invokes God's help so that *Iḥsāniyyat* can develop everywhere. Given the fact that various groups already exist in the region which offer programs such as *dhikr*, reciting the Qur'an and *Ṣalawāt*, the *Iḥsāniyyat* group needs to look for a distinct way to recruit members and spread its practice.

The first method used by the group to promote *Iḥsāniyyat* was to broadcast its events and programs on the radio. This method is not new among religious preachers. In fact, this method has been widely used by other Indonesian Islamic preachers and several *dhikr* groups in Indonesia. Following the boom in establishing new TV stations in Indonesia in the 1990's, famous national

23 Interview with Andik, Kediri, October, 2004.

24 Interview with *Gus* Abdul Latif, Kediri, November, 2004.

preachers such as *Kyai* Abdullah Gymnastiar (usually called 'Aa Gym), *Kyai* Ilham Arifin, Jeffri and Ustadz Haryono have all become widely known by Indonesian viewers through *dakwah* programs on particular TV stations. However, in the local context of Kediri, the use of radio stations by the *Iḥsāniyyat* group to teach and spread Islamic teachings and local *tarekat* is quite new.

Initially, one of the biggest radio stations in Kediri, *Wijangsongko* FM radio, which is well-known for its programs of Javanese music and songs and *keroncong* music, invited *Gus* Abdul Latif to host a weekly interactive program called *Sajadah* (*Sajian Amal dan Ibadah*). This program was intended to provide listeners with a discussion of Islamic subjects ranging from Islamic jurisprudence and theology to Muslim daily life based on questions from listeners. This radio program could be heard by those who lived in Kediri but also by those who lived in other cities such as Tulungagung, Nganjuk, and Jombang. Unlike other radio and television programs on Islamic subjects, this program was presented in Indonesian and Javanese so that it could be easily followed by its listeners. *Gus* Abdul Latif realized that this program could be used as a means to introduce *Iḥsāniyyat* and to announce its programs as well as to strengthen the unity of *Iḥsāniyyat* members. For example, at the beginning or at the end of the program, he always addresses his listeners and followers as well as invoking the help of God so that He will help to promote *Iḥsāniyyat* mission. In this way, as a leader of the group, he can communicate easily with his followers. For his followers who cannot visit him regularly, this program helps them to keep in touch with their leader.

A second avenue for making *dakwah* acceptable, especially to those categorized as *orang ruwet*, marginalized people (I., *orang pinggiran*) and nominal Muslims was through a *dakwah* project called 'from tombs to mosques' (I., *dari makam ke masjid*). This method involved conducting *istighāthat* rituals at several tombs of Muslim saints. Among 'modernist' Indonesian Muslims, this practice is regarded not only as an improper addition to religious ritual but also as a serious violation to the Islamic teachings verging on polytheism (*shirk*) because people may wrongly ask something directly from the deceased persons. The *istighāthat* in the Muslims tombs is usually held by this group at night. Fox maintains that Javanese people visit tombs at the appropriate times for various reasons, including 'to *nyekar*, offer flowers (and incense), to pray, to make a request or to fulfill a vow after having made request (*nyadran*) and, in the process, to gain a share in the blessing (*berkah*), possibly even the potency (*kesakten*) of the sleeping one (Fox 1991:20)'. However, *Gus* Abdul Latif explained that the aim of visiting the tombs of Muslim saints is by no means to ask for something from those buried within. By holding *istighāthat* rituals in those tombs, *Gus* Abdul Latif perhaps wanted to illustrate how to perform visits the tombs (I., *ziarah*) in a correct way so that people are not led to polytheism.

However, the main objective of holding *istighāthat* rituals in the tombs of Muslim saints rather than in mosques was to attract as many *orang ruwet* and nominal Muslims as possible to attend the ritual so that they could enhance their religious knowledge and practice. Since the tradition of visiting tombs is a well-established practice among Javanese, *Gus* Abdul Latif considered it easier to ask people to come to the tombs than directly to come to a mosque. When people understood the practices of Islamic teachings, they would be expected to come voluntarily to mosques.

As explained by *Kyai* Misbah, *Gus* Abdul Latif's brother, another reason why the *Iḥsāniyyat* group held its *istighāthat*ritual at tombs rather than in mosques was because this procedure is actually justified by Islam. It is sanctioned by the Prophetic tradition because it can encourage Muslims to remember death (A., *dhikr al-maut*). According to the Sufi tradition, *dhikr al-maut* is one way which can lead to an increase in asceticism (A., *zuhd*) from the world as well as the purification of heart. In regards to *dhikr al-maut,* the Prophet Muhammad in his hadith asked Muslims to remember death abundantly and regarded those who frequently remember death as people of genius.[25] As noted by al-Ghazālī in his *Ihyā' 'Ulūm al-Dīn,* the reason for the excellence of remembering death is because it can increase one's preparation to face the world-to-come (al-Ghazali 1973:434).

Furthermore, *Kyai* Misbah has argued that some *'ulamā'*consider the tombs of Muslim saints to be among the particular places in which people's prayers to God must be granted (A., *maqām mustajābat*). In other words, the tombs of saints are considered efficacious places from which to offer prayer (I, *doa*). This notion, he asserted, in fact was relevant to several hadith, which state that the tombs of Muslims are part of the gardens of paradise (A., *rauḍ min riyāḍ al-jannat*), whereas the tombs of unbelievers and hypocrites are part of the hollow of hell (*ḥufratun min ḥufar al-nīrān*).[26] Based on this hadith, the ritual practice of *istighāthat* at the tombs of Muslim saints is both lawful and strongly recommended as a means to remember death.

---

25 These *hadith* are as follows: (narrated Tirmidhi) تاذللا مذاه ركذ نماورثكا , 'Increase your remembrance to something which destroys the pleasant.'

26 Actually the original text of hadith he cited does not mention the tombs of Muslims and the tombs of unbelievers. The text of hadith, instead, states that the tombs [can become] paradise gardens or hell's abysses. So, this hadith can be interpreted as tombs becoming gardens of paradise if people follow properly the teachings of religion during their life in the world, or the tombs can become the abyss of hell if people transgress the teachings of religion.

Another reason for holding the *istighāthat* ritual at the tombs of venerated Muslim saints is to ask for the intercession and blessing of these deceased pious saints. According to *Gus* Abdul Latif, since it is difficult to guarantee that people's good deeds will be granted by God, these pious saints can be used as intercessors for the living so that God may grant people's prayer because of these pious people. Therefore, for *Gus* Abdul Latif, it is necessary to venerate and love those saints who are beloved of God so that God will give His love to the people.

There are several Muslim tombs where this group holds its rituals. Most of these tombs are located in Kediri but some are in Bali while other include several tombs of the Nine Saints (*Wali Sanga*) in Java. In Kediri, for example, the *Iḥsāniyyat* group has held its ritual at the tomb of *Shaikh* Ihsan Dahlan, the *Iḥsāniyyat* leader's ancestor, but also at the tombs of Raden Demang, *Shaikh* Mursyad, *Shaikh* Ali Lalean (Pangeran Demang), *Shaikh* Ageng Karanglo. These shrines are located in several regions of Kediri, enabling this group to attract people who live in the vicinity of these shrines. Interestingly, several tombs of Muslim saints in Kediri were also used by other local *tarekat* groups as ritual objects without raising any conflict and tension. When I attended a ritual in *Shaikh* Mursyad's tomb, I met some one who had actively participated in one ritual held there by another group. He attended the *istighāthat* ritual held by *Iḥsāniyyat* and had become a member of *Iḥsāniyyat* while also being a member of another group.[27]

Other shrines which have been subject to visitation and ritual, are located in Bali. Muslim tombs in Bali that have been said by local people and by this group to be Muslim saints' tombs are the tombs of Ḥabīb 'Alī Bafāqih in Negara, Pangeran Mas Sepuh (*Keramat Pantai Seseh*), Sayyidah Khadījat (Denpasar), *Shaikh* Abū Bakr al-Ḥamīd (*Keramat Kusumba*) in Klungkung, Ḥabīb 'Ali Zainal Idrus (*Keramat Kembar*) in Amlapura, *Shaikh* 'Abd al- Jalīl (*Keramat Saren Jawa*) in Bangli, *Shaikh* Ḥabīb 'Umar Yusūf (*Keramat Bedugul*) in Bedugul, and *Shaikh* 'Abd al-Qādir (*Keramat Temukus*) in Buleleng. During my visiting with *Iḥsāniyyat* pilgrims to these tombs, I found that one of these tombs, Pangeran Mas Sepuh's tombs (*Keramat Pantai Seseh*), was not like Muslim tomb. The ornamentation of the tomb was like most Hindu tombs. Situated near to the beach, the tomb was also venerated by Hindus. Visits to these tombs and the tombs of *Wali Sanga* (The Nine Javanese Saints) are usually made on an annual basis including the tombs of Sunan Ampel in Surabaya, Maulana Malik Ibrahim in Gresik, Sunan Giri in Gresik (East Java), Sunan Drajat in Drajat, Lamongan (East Java), Sunan Bonang in Tuban (East Java), Sunan Kudus in Kudus, Sunan Muria in Muria (Central Java), Sunan Kalijaga in Central Java, and Sunan Gunung Jati, in Cirebon.

---

27 Interview with Pak x, Kediri, August 2004.

Plate 5.4: Gus Abdul Latif (wearing a white hat) and the researcher (left) after conducting istighāthat ritual at the shrine of a Muslim saint.

Plate 5.5: The Yamisda group holding istighāthat at Kyai Ihsan Dahlan's tomb.

Plate 5.6: The participants of istighāthat at a Muslim saint's tomb.

Yet another method to attract people to join the *Iḥsāniyyat* is through publishing a small book consisting of *dhikr* formulae written by *Gus* Abdul Latif, along with the general and particular purpose (*khasiat)* of these *istighāthat* formulae. As stated in this book, the general purposes of this *istighāthat* are as follows:

> (1) To reach closeness with God (2) for salvation of life in this world and life in the hereafter (3) for happiness and welfare in life in this world (4)

> for removing sins (5) to obtain *shafa'at* from the Prophet Muhammad (6) as safeguard from jinn and satan (7) as safeguard from witchcraft (A., *sihr*) and sorcery (*santet*) (8) to facilitate all business (9) to facilitate all needs (10) to make successful all businesses (agriculture, commerce, farming, animal husbandry, and industry) (11) to facilitate the means of living (A., *rizq)* (12) to build a peaceful and harmonious family (I., *keluarga sakinah*) (Muhammad n.d.:17).

It is clear that the purpose of the *istighāthat* is not only for spiritual matters but also for 'worldly' matters. Explaining this cannot but help to attract people to join the group. This strategy is, in part, taken by *Gus* Abdul Latif to avoid attracting people to the *dakwah* project by emphasizing too much the *karamah* of the leader. In other words, every member of *Iḥsāniyyat* can practise and recite the formulae so that they can draw benefits for their life without depending on their leader. In this way, members of the group do not need to regard *Gus* Abdul Latif as a *wali* or *Ghauth*, constantly seeking blessings and *karamah* through physical contact. In fact, *Gus* Abdul Latif strongly criticizes the strategy of *dakwah* which stresses the *karamah* of the leader since it can undermine other preachers who do not posses the same qualities of *karamah*.

This book also notes that each formula has a particular and specific purpose if it is recited a specified number of times and in specific ways. For example, reciting the *al-Fātiḥat* chapter will help those who wish to succeed in their school exams as well as help them to strengthen their memory. This verse, according to this book, can also be used to help people who want to collect a debt so that they can get their money back. To do this, they should recite the chapter to the creditor 313 times. This practice should be performed for seven days consecutively at midnight or 10 pm. Another example is the specific purpose of *al-Iḥlāṣ* chapter in the the *Istighāthat Iḥsāniyyat* formulae. If this *al-Iḥlāṣ* chapter is recited a hundred times for seven days at midnight and is followed by a particular prayer each time, this chapter increase a person's charisma so that his or her boss or colleagues can respect and love them (Muhammad n.d.:17-30). To conclude, every single one of the *istighāthat* formulae has a purpose which is related to health, career, protection from evil spirit, husband and wife relationships, or seeking a soul mate (I., *jodoh*). In other words, the formulae of the *istighāthat* answer most people's needs.

The tradition of using the collection of *dhikr* formulae for specific purposes in the *Iḥsāniyyat* group might be strongly influenced by the spread of books about 'Islamic magic' as well as works on medicine (A., *tibb*) and occult sciences (A., *hikmat*) which are widely used in Javanese *pesantren*. As observed by Bruinesssen, the book on *hikmat* usually contains symbols which are derived from pre-Islamic tradition, whereas the book on *tibb* usually uses symbols taken from

Qur'anic texts as amulets. Among the books used by *santri* are al-Ghazāli's*al-Awfāq,* Ahmad ibn 'Ali al-Būnī's *Shams al-Ma'ārif al-Kubrā, Manbā' uṣūl al-Hikma* and Ibn al-Qayyim al-Jauzī's *Al-Ṭib al-Nabawīy* (Bruinessen 1990:261-262). In fact, during my research, the two works of al-Būni were taught by *Gus* Abdul Latif in *Pesantren* Jampes. When I asked about the particular meaning of the amulet, he explained by referring to al-Ghazāli's*al-Awfāq.*[28]

Plate 5.7: The Book of Istighāthat Iḥsāniyyat.

---

28 In addition to classical works on Islamic magic, medicine, and occult sciences, other works on similar subjects compiled and written by famous local *tabīb* are also used by some students in Javanese *pesantren.* Usually, in order to obtain access to these books, a student should individually seek *ijāza*for the book from its author. Local *tabib* have compiled materials for their books on the basis of *ijāza*obtained from other *tabib* or from their teachers. Some *tabib* ask that individual students to stay for some days to be taught the content of the books, while other *tabib* just give these books with their *ijāza.* These *santri* reciprocate with money to cover printing costs.

Chapter VI: The Awakening of the Negligent: The *Dhikr al- Ghāfilīn Group*

Chapter V highlighted the important role of the *Iḥsāniyyat* group in developing and spreading Islam among nominal Muslims (*abangan*) by means of cultural approaches. In doing so, the group has adopted the ideas of Sufi *dakwah* and Sufi tolerance, which have been practised since the introduction of Islam to the Indonesian Archipelago. This chapter will look at the role played by another group in developing and spreading Islamic values among Muslims, the *Dhikr al- Ghāfilīn*. In contrast to the previous chapter, this chapter will focus on the leader of the *Majlis Dhikr al-Ghāfilīn, Gus* Mik, whose reputation and charisma as a *wali* raised controversy among Muslims in Indonesia. Despite this, *Gus* Mik played an important role in introducing Islamic values to particular groups of people who have been characterized as *orang-orang malam,* a term used to indicate people such as prostitutes, nightclub singers and nightclub visitors.

6.1. The Foundation of the group

The composition of the religious litanies (*dhikr*, remembrance of God) used by the *Majlis Dhikr al- Ghāfilīn* was closely associated with three well known *kyai* in East Java, namely, the late *Kyai* Hamim Jazuli known as *Gus* Mik from *Pesantren* Ploso Kediri , East Java; the late *Kyai* Ahmad Siddiq (from Jember), who was a former chairman of the Nahdlatul Ulama (NU) religious board (*Ketua Syuriah*); and the late *Kyai* 'Abd al-Hamid (from Pasuruan). Indonesian Muslims, particularly from NU, believe that these three *kyai* possessed extraordinary miracle power (*karamah*) and divine blessings (*barakah*).

According to Kyai Ahmad Siddiq, all of these *kyai* contributed to the composition of the *Dhikr al- Ghāfilīn.* He said:

> In fact this formula [the *Dhikr al- Ghāfilīn*] belonged to *Kyai* 'Abd al- Hamid and *Gus* Mik. I only wrote and compiled it. However, I wanted to disclose the secret so that all my children understood that this formula was the work of three persons namely myself, *Gus* Mik and *Kyai* 'Abd al- Hamid. First of all I went to *Kyai* 'Abd al- Hamid. He gave me *ijazah* (authority) to recite the *al-Fātiḥat* chapter a hundred times together with the *Asma'ul Husna* (The beautiful names of God). Then, I went to *Gus* Mik when he was in the Pak Marliyan's house where we discussed the formula until 03.00 a.m. On that occasion, *Gus* Mik added to the formula by reciting *istighfār*a hundred times and *Ṣalawāt* three hundred times.

After asking permission from *Gus* Mik, *Kyai* Ahmad Siddiq recited the formula to *Kyai* 'Abd al-Hamid. During this meeting, *Kyai* 'Abd al-Ḥamid cried. According to *Kyai*Aḥmad Siddīq the compilation process of this formula took place in the month of *Sha'ban* and was first practiced in the month of *Ramaḍān*1972.

The founders of a Sufi group have often received *ilhām,* a spiritual order, or experience a visionary dream of the Prophet Muhammad before they established or introduced publicly their formulae (*aurad*). Thus, *Kyai* Ahmad Siddiq not only received consent from two respected *kyai* or *wali,* he also received consent from respected deceased *kyai* through his visionary dream to improve and expand the practice of the *Dhikr al-Ghāfilīn* litanies. He described his experience as follows:

> I had a clear dream that after reciting the *Dhikr al- Ghāfilīn,* my late brother *Kyai* Ahmad Qushairi Siddiq was waiting for me at a harbour when I disembarked from a ship. But I did not watch my ship. Then, he asked me to walk along with his friends, *habaib* (Prophet's descendants). We walked together. It seemed that we walked in the city of Mecca. But he left me behind and I lost him. So, I asked his friend in Arabic: 'Do you know *Kyai* Qushairi's house?' then he replied: 'How can I not know him, when he always prays for you.' Then I found *Kyai* Qushairi in the al-Ḥaram Mosque in Mecca and he said to me, 'Certainly, when you lead the recitation of the *Dhikr al- Ghāfilīn,* I always pray for you at this Ka'bah (Siddiq n.d.:40).'

Based on the consent he received in this dream, *Kyai* Ahmad Siddiq was much more confident to practice this *dhikr* formulae. Moreover, he claimed that although he did not promote and advertise this formula to the public, it attracted a large number of followers to practice the ritual of the group.

*Kyai*Ahmad Siddiq did not publicly launch the formula but only disclosed it to a limited number of people in Jember. Similarly, *Kyai* Saiful maintained that *Gus* Mik did not launch the formula to the general public because at that time many Muslims practiced *dhikr* formula given by Sufi orders. In 1983, *Gus* Mik only practised the formula personally in Tulungagung (East Java) and established a group called the *Dhikr al-Layliyyat.* However, this group did not attract many followers. Three years later, when friction occurred in some *tarekat* (Sufi orders) in relation to the succession of their leaders, *Gus* Mik began to introduce the formula of *Dhikr al- Ghāfilīn* to the public after receiving consent from *Kyai* Arwani, one of the prominent *tarekat* leaders from Kudus, Central Java. It seems that *Gus* Mik sought an appropriate time to launch his new group.

In addition to the introduction of the *Dhikr al- Ghāfilīn, Gus* Mik also began to introduce *Khatm al-Qur'an*[1](J., *khataman Qur'an*) to the public. Previously, *Gus* Mik held the *Khatm al-Qur'an,* a particular event involving the recitation of all the chapters of the Qur'an, on the anniversary of his father's death (A., *ḥaul*) and at graduations (A., *imtiḥān*) in *Pesantren* Ploso. During this *ḥaul*, the *Khatm al-Qur'an* not only included reciting the Qur'an (A., *bi al-naẓar*), but also memorizing all the chapters of the Qur'an. The former was intended for general participants, whereas the latter was particularly intended for memorizers (A., *ḥāfiẓ*) who were invited to the *haul. Gus* Mik called this event *semaan* (Javenese word), a word which is derived from the Arabic word *sami'a* which means to listen or pay attention. Persons who listen are called *sāmiin* (listeners). People who came to the event were supposed to listen to the memorizers or reciters and correct them if they make any mistakes (Thoha 2003:266-67). The first *semaan* was held outside the *pesantren* in the house of Drs. Muhtadi, an Indonesian Bank Rakyat employee in Kediri, followed by the recitation of the *Dhikr al-Ghāfilīn.* Since then, the *semaan* ritual has been conducted together with the reciting of the *Dhikr al- Ghāfilīn.* This first *semaan* held outside the *pesantren* was attended by hundreds of people. Since then, other *semaan* have been held in various houses, not only in Kediri but also in many other cities in East Java and in other provinces. According to Abdul Qadir, one of senior leaders in the group, in 1990, a *semaan* was even held in the Yogyakarta palace to commemorate the fortieth day of the death of Hamengku Buwono IX.

Gus Mik named the *semaan* group *Jantiko* which stands for *Majlis Anti Koler* (anti loss group, I., *anti hancur, anti mogok*). *Kyai* Saiful, *Gus* Mik's close friend explained to me that it was expected that by giving such a name, those who joined the group would limit their suffering a loss of spirituality in this world and the world-to-come. This name was inspired by *Gus* Mik's conversation with a car mechanic, his close friend. One day, *Gus* Mik asked the mechanic whether an old car fuelled by kerosene that he had designed would break down. The mechanic replied: 'Obviously not *Gus,* because this car is *anti koler* (I., *anti hancur, anti mogok*).' *Gus* Mik then gave his group the name, *Majlis Anti Koler.* However, because of *Kyai* Dahnan's suggestion, in 1989 the name was changed to *Mantab,* which means 'strong' and able to withstand a test (J., *tahan uji*) (El-Ahmad 1993). Abdul Qadir argued that the word *Mantab* stands for *Majlis Tapa Brata,* which means the place for remembering God, while *Kyai* Saiful argued that the word *Mantab* was taken from two Arabic words *man* and *tāba,* meaning a person who repents.[2]

---

1 This means the recitation of all chapters of the Qur'an by memorizers while the audiences listens to their recitation and makes correction if the memorizers make a mistake.

2 Interview with Abdul Qadir, Kediri, September, 2004.

The objective for establishing this *dhikr* group was based on *Gus* Mik's prediction that a great disaster would occur in the year 2000. This disaster was not related to natural disasters such as earthquakes, flooding or landslides, but to a decline in the quality of Muslims' spiritual life in connection with their *ibadah* to God. According to *Gus* Mik, because of the intensity of detrimental influences, Muslims would find it difficult to worship God sincerely (I., *ikhlas*). This disaster would affect all Muslims regardless of their social status, be they ordinary Muslims or *'ulāma'*. *Gus* Mik argued that no one would be safe from this disaster except those who had a strong spiritual basis as a result of their consistent (A., *istiqāmat*) religious practices. Furthermore, the people who would be saved from this disaster were those who always remembered God's saints by praying for them, because praying for them would open the door of God's blessing. Quoting a prominent Sufi, 'Abd al-Qādir al-Jaylānī, *Gus* Mik was convinced that people who remembered God's saints would obtain blessing from God. Therefore, by reciting the *Dhikr al- Ghāfilīn,* which includes praying for Muslim saints, people would have a strong basis to face the disaster.

Another objective of establishing the *semaan* group and using the *Dhikr al-Ghāfilīn* was to popularise (*membudayakan*) the recitation of the Qur'an and to start a movement of Qur'an recitation (I., *tadarus al-Qur'an*) in Indonesia. *Kyai* Saiful claimed that before this group was established, the memorization of the Qur'an was conducted only at particular events such as at the Qur'an recitation contests (I., *Musabaqah Tilawatil Qur'an,* MTQ) and other events in *pesantren,* which never attracted many participants. As argued by *Kyai* Saiful since the emergence of this group, it is not difficult to find such events in many cities in East Java and some other provinces on Java. The ritual is even held in many government offices (*pendopo kota*) in those cities, and is attended by many participants. For example, in the *semaan* held by this group on the anniversary of *Gus* Mik's death (*haul*), which I attended, over a thousand people, men and women, from several regions in Java flocked to the *semaan.* The venue of the *semaan* occupied almost one kilometre of the main road located in front of *Pesantren* Al-Falah, Ploso, Kediri. When *Gus* Mik was still alive, the ritual of reciting the Qur'an attracted many government officials and political party leaders and was supported by the introduction of the *Iqra'* recitation method nationally in 1992 and by the growing number of Qur'anic Kindergartens (I., *Taman Pendidikan al-Qur'an*) in Indonesia. This new use of recitation was regarded as a faster learning method than the traditional method (the *Baghdadi* method), enabling children less than five years old to read the chapters of the Qur'an with ease (Gade 2004:117).

Another goal in establishing the *Dhikr al- Ghāfilīn,* was to get people used to performing prayers collectively (I., *berjamaah*) and reciting prayers (I., *doa*) or *dhikr* after performing communal prayers (I., *shalat berjamaah*), as well as to enliven the time particularly between *Maghrib* prayer and *Isha* prayer. All of these activities are included in the ritual of *semaan* and in the recitation of the *Dhikr al- Ghāfilīn*. Those who join the *semaan* definitely practise such activities. As mentioned by Abdul Qadir, one of the *imam* in this group, it was expected that the *sāmi'īn* (the participants in a *semaan*) should practise these activities when they return to their communities. According to *Gus* Mik, the goal of holding *semaan* was to obtain the blessing (I., *barakah*) contained in the Qur'an as well as to communicate with God. He believed that the words of the Qur'an contain blessings that can be obtained by those who recite and listen to them.

Gus Mik also mentioned that another objective in reciting the *Dhikr al- Ghāfilīn* was to help people not only to face their problems in this world but also to face the Day of Judgment (A., *yaum al-ḥisāb*), the day in the hereafter when all people's conduct will be judged. It is expected that God will give His love to those who recite the *Dhikr al- Ghāfilīn*. *Gus* Mik explained the objectives as follows:

> Hopefully, the *Dhikr al- Ghāfilīn*, which might become [our] spiritual force, could be our support in facing occurrences on the Day of Judgment. This is an important thing to remember. When we find it difficult to manage our wives and families, to create beautiful lives and when the signs of calamity come, this means that we are strongly urged to strengthen our spirit so that so that God will give His love to us. That's it.[3]

The success of *Gus* Mik in spreading and developing his group has been supported by the network of alumnae of *Pesantren* Al-Falah, Ploso, Kediri who are spread throughout Java. Wherever *Gus* Mik conducted his *dhikr* ritual, these alumnae strongly supported him and his group. This fact is not surprising, because in *pesantren* tradition, *santri* of *pesantren* are still regarded as 'students' of their *pesantren*, even though they have graduated and returned to their community. Alumnae of *pesantren* have strong emotional attachment with their *pesantren*. With this status they have to respect their *kyai* and his family even though they have returned to their home and become *kyai* in their respective community. *Gus* Mik's position as the son of the founder of *Pesantren* Ploso deserved to receive support and respect from his father's students who have returned to their community.

---

3 Mugi-mugi termasuk Dhikr al- Ghāfilīn sing sampun dados ketahanan batiniyah, mangke dados penyangga kulo panjenengan wonten ing sidang-sidang yaumul hisab. Niku sing penting. Di tengah-tengah kulo panjenengan angel noto bojo, noto rumah tangga, sulitnya menciptakan sesuatu yang indah, tanda-tanda musibah badhe dugi katah, berarti kulo panjenengan dituntut nyusun ketahanan batiniyah, nyentuh duspundi supados Allah iku sayang, gati teng kulo panjenengan. Niku mawon.

6.2. The Ritual Practice of the Group

The ritual of this group focuses on the reciting of *dhikr*. In common with many other Sufi groups, *dhikr* for this group constitutes 'a way or a rule of life', which should be practised by its members to purify their soul (A., *nafs*) in order to approach God and be pious servants (I., *kehambaan yang tulus*). *Gus* Mik specifically said that the recitation of the *Dhikr al- Ghāfilīn* formulae can lead to tranquillity and the strengthening of the heart as well as being a safeguard against the horror of the world and the horror of the day of resurrection.

According to the guide book for the *Dhikr al- Ghāfilīn*(Anonymous n.d:2-30), this *dhikr* starts by seeking a means (A., *wasīlat*) through the recitation of *al-Fātiḥat,* hundred times. The merit of this recitation is conveyed to the spirit of the Prophet Muhammad, Abdul Qādir al-Jaylānī, Imam al-Ghazālī, Habib Abdillah ibn 'Alwi al-Ḥaddād (the author of *Rātib al-Ḥaddād*) and closes with the prayer of *al-Fātiḥat*. Those figures are mentioned in the formulae because they were believed by *Gus* Mik to be figures who continuously recited *al-Fātiḥat* hundred times every day. The section then continues with the recitation of *Ayat Kursi* and *Asmāul Ḥusnā*(ninety names of God), followed by a short prayer repeated ten times in unison.

In the second section, then, the *al-Fātiḥat tawassul* is recited again three times, specifically, to be conveyed to the spirits of God's previous prophets, particularly those who have received the title of '*Ulul Azmi* (those with firm resolution) such as Abraham, Moses, Jesus, Muhammad and Noah (46:34), and all the Angels of God. An exaltation known as *Ṣalawāt Muqarrabīn* is recited for those Angels who are regarded as the closest Angels to God, including Gabriel, Michael, Isrofil, Azrael, the *'Arsh* Guardian Angels, and for all God's Prophets. This *Ṣalawāt Muqarrabīn* continues with the recitation of *al-Fātiḥat* three times whose merit is conveyed to the Prophet Muhammad and his wives, children, descendants, companions, *ahl al-Badr* (those who died in the battle of *Badr*) from either the *Muhājirīn* (the Prophet's companions from Mecca) or the *Anṣār* (the Prophet's Companions from Medina), all the Prophet's followers, martyrs (I., *shuhadā'*), *'ulamā',* all Muslim saints, all the pious, all Muslim authors, participants' grandfathers, grandmothers, fathers, and mothers. The next procedure is to recite *al-Fātiḥat* specifically directed to the Prophet Muhammad as the source of intercession (*shafā'at*). This is continued by the reciting *istighfār* one hundred times.

Then follows the recitation of *al-Fātiḥat tawassul* for the Prophet Khidr, the Prophet's grandsons, Ḥasan and Ḥusain, 'Alī ibn Abī Ṭālib, and Faṭīmat, the Prophet's daughter. The other people for whom *al-Fātiḥat* is recited include well known Muslim Sufi, Prophetic tradition scholars, the founders of Sufi orders, of the four schools of Muslim Jurists, Muslim saints both male and female, and all Muslim authors, the Nine Saints of Java, Muslims saints of Madura and all the participants of the group. The reciting of *al-Fātiḥat* to these people is followed by reciting the exaltation to the Prophet of Muhammad three hundred times and *tahlīl* (the recitation of *lāilāha illallah* phrase) hundred times. The *Dhikr al-Ghāfilīn* closes with the recitation of the part of the *kasidah burdah* (odes) and poetic Arabic (A., *sha'ir*) prayers written by *Gus* Mik and Aḥmad ibn 'Umār ibn Samt. The names of all the persons mentioned in this formulae are as follows:

- The prophet Muhammad
- 'Abd al-Qādir al-Jailānī
- 'Abd Allah b. 'Alwī al-Ḥaddād
- Khiḍr
- Ḥasan b. Abi Ṭālib
- Ḥusain b. Abi Ṭālib
- Abū Ṭālib
- Fāṭimat
- Abd al-Qādir al-Jailānī
- Muḥammad Bahā al-Dīn al-Naqshabandī
- Abū Ḥāmid al-Ghazālī
- His brother Aḥmad al-Ghazālī
- Abu Bakr al-Shiblī
- 'Abd Allah b. 'Alwī al-Ḥaddād
- Abu Yazīd Ṭaifūr b. 'Īsā al-Busṭāmī
- Muḥammad al-Ḥanafī
- Yūsuf b. Ismā'īl al-Nabhānī
- Jalāl al-dīn al-Suyūṭī
- Abu Zakariyyā Yahyā b. Sharaf al-Nawāwī
- 'Abd al-Wahhāb al-Sha''rānī
- 'Alī Nūr al-Dīn al-Shaunī
- Abu al-'Abbas Aḥmad b. 'Alī al-Būnī
- Ibrāhim b. Adham
- Ibrāhim al-Dasūqī
- Shihab al-Dīn Ahmad b. 'Umar al-Anṣārī al-Mursī
- Abī Sa'īd 'Abd al-Karīm al-Būṣīrī
- Abu al-Ḥasan al-Bakrī

- Abū ʻAbd Allah Muḥammad b. Ismāʼīl al-Bukhārī
- Zain al-Dīn b. ʻAbd al-ʻAzīz al-Malībārī al-Fannānī
- Tāj al-Dīn b. ʻAṭāʼ Allah al-Sakandarī
- Muḥammad b. Idrīs al-Shāfiʼī
- Abu Ḥafṣ ʻUmar al-Suhrawardī
- Abu Madyan
- Ibn al-Mālik al-Andalusī
- Abu ʻAbd Allah Muḥammad b. Sulaiman al-Jāzūlī
- Muḥyi al-Dīn b. al-ʻArabī
- ʻImrān b. Ḥuṣain
- ʻAbd al-Salām b. Mashīsh
- Abu al-Ḥasan ʻʼAlī b. ʻAbd Allah b. ʻAbd al-Jabbār al-Shādhilī
- Abū Maḥfūẓ Maʼrūf al-Karkhī
- Abu al-Ḥasan al-Sariy al-Saqṭī
- Abu al-Qāsim al-Imām al-Junaid al-Baghdādī
- Abu al-Abbā.s Aḥmad al-Badāwī
- Ahmad b. Abi Ḥusain al-Rifāʼī
- Al-Imām al-Ḥasan b. Abī al-Hasan Abī Saʼīd al-Baṣrī
- Rābiʼat al-ʻAdawiyyat
- ʻUbaida binti Abī Kilāb
- Abū Sulaimān al-Dārainī
- ʻAbd al-Hārith b. Asad al-Muhāsibī
- Dhu al-Nūn al- Miṣrī
- Abu Zakariyyā Yahyā Muʼādh al-Rāzī
- Abu Ṣāliḥ Ḥamdūn al-Qaṣṣār al-Naisābūrī
- Ḥusain b. Manṣūr al-Ḥallāj
- Jalāl al-Dīn al-Rūmī

Abū Ḥafṣ Sharaf al-Dīn ʻUmar b. al-Fāriḍ al-Ḥamawī al-Miṣrī

It can be seen clearly from the ritual of the *Dhikr al- Ghāfilīn* that it is dominated by the recitation of *al-Fātiḥat* during the *tawassul* sessions. This practice is closely linked to *Gus* Mik's conviction that even though these people have died, they are still capable of hearing *al-Fātiḥat* conveyed to them by the living. As a result, God will give the merit of the recitation to them and, just like living persons, these deceased people will respond by praying for those who recite *al-Fātiḥat*.

It is interesting to note here that the individuals named include the founders of other respected Sufi orders such as 'Abd al-Qādir al-Jaylānī (d. (Qādiriyyah order), Abū al-Ḥasan 'Ālī b. Abdillah b. Abd al-Jabbār al-Syādhilī (d.1258) (Shādhiliyyah order), 'AlīMuḥammad Bahā' al-Dīn al-Naqshābandī (The Naqshabandiyah order), Ahmad b. Abī Ḥusain al-Rifā'iy (d.1178) (The Rifa'iyah order), Jalāl al-dīn al-Rūmī (The Maulawiyah order), Abu Madyān al-Tilmisānī (d.1197) (The Madyaniyya order) and Abu al-'Abbās Ahmad al-Badāwiy (d.1276) (The Badawiyah order). Other names in the *tawassul* sessions are considered controversial Sufis, such as Ibn 'Arabī and Ḥusain b. Manṣūr al-Ḥallāj, as well as the woman Sufi, Rabī'at al-'Adāwiyyat. Moreover, the *Dhikr al-Ghāfilīn* group also puts in the formulae the names of those who have been important in the Shiite tradition including 'Ālī b. Abi Ṭālib, Fāṭimat al-Zahrā', and their sons, Ḥasan and the Martyr, Ḥusain. Indeed, the group characterizes these individuals as the youngest dwellers in Paradise.

It is interesting to examine why these names are included in the *tawassul* sessions. One informant told me that the *Dhikr al- Ghāfilīn* group names these figures merely because these people are believed to be *auliyā'*(The Saints of God) who can spiritually help people to approach God. In this respect, *Gus* Mik put it this way:

> In the world to come (I., *akhirat*) we will follow those respected *ulama* as well as those whose names were written in *Dhikr al-Ghāfilīn* formula to whom we recited al-Fātiḥat(Ibad 2005:10).

This reason is similar to *Kyai*Ahamad Siddiq's statement that those *wali* whose names are mentioned in the formulae have reached the highest station (A., *maqām*). Although the members of the *Dhikr al- Ghāfilīn* group cannot reach their *maqām,* at least these *wali* can help them in the world to come. *Kyai*Aḥmad Siddiq's son told me that his father argued that those named are like those who travel by a first class train, while the group members were like passengers in economy class. The first class passengers occupy the front car which is served with special meals, while the economy class passengers occupy the rear car. Although these economy class passengers are not being served with special meals, they will arrive at the same destination as the first class passengers.[4]

Another logical foundation underpinning the practice of praying to God for those people mentioned in the formulae relates to the following Sufi teaching: 'You should be with Allah. If you cannot be with Him, you should be with

4 Interview with *Gus* Fahri, Kediri, January, 2005.

those who have been with Allah because these persons can bring you to be with Allah.' According to *Gus* Mik, those who can bring someone to Allah might be alive or dead. In other words, *Gus* Mik believed those persons named in the formula could become a means to bring people nearer to God. This notion is relevant to the motto printed on the cover of *Dhikr al-Ghāfilīn* litany book which reads 'this litany is intended for those who are keen to be gathered with Muslim saints and pious people.'[5]

It is strongly recommended that new members first recite the *dhikr* once a day for forty days consecutively. The formula should be recited for forty days because this is the minimal time necessary to show whether or not a Muslim's good acts are able to be considered *istiqāmat* (steadfastness). In fact, for this group, the notion of forty days is taken from the Qur'anic teaching that after fasting for forty days consecutively, Moses received the Book from God. This practice is also based on the notion that good virtues can only be accepted by God if practised for forty days consecutively. In addition, forty days is also used by this group as a requirement for those who want to benefit from the formulae. For example, the leader of this group told me that one *kyai* practised the formulae for thirty eight days consecutively, but then missed the thirty ninth day. As a result, this *kyai* failed to gain any benefit; he therefore needed to restart the ritual from the first day.

To practise the ritual of the *Dhikr al-Ghāfilīn*, people can practise individually or together in a group led by a leader (A., *imām*) elected by the *Dhikr al-Ghāfilīn* leader. At an important event such as the anniversary of the founder of this group which I attended, this ritual was combined with a *semaan* event. At the event I attended, the *dhikr* formula was recited after the *Maghrib* prayer when the participants who were reciting from memory reached the final *juz* (section) of the the Qur'an. The reciting of the *dhikr* formula took almost one hour. There was no particular position or separation between the leader and the members during the ritual. However, when the ritual is held at the tombs of local saints in Kediri, all the members face these tombs, while the leader of the ritual faces the members. Unlike rituals held by Sufi orders, no specific ritual dress is worn by participants and the leader. At the ritual I attended no one displayed the hysterical behaviour as is commonly found in the rituals held by other Sufi orders as result of the heightened tension in the different sections of their formulae. When the reciting of the *dhikr* formulae was complete, it was followed by the recitation the rest of the Qur'an by memory, and the ritual closed with the *Isha'* prayer.

---

5 ان يحشرمع الاولياءوالصلحا لحينمن احب

As for the *semaan* event that I attended, this event began after completing the dawn prayer and ended at the *Isha'* prayer. During this event, all chapters of the Qur'an were recited from memory by male memorizers (A., *ḥāfidhīn*) using a loud speaker. As usual they sat on a stage which was higher than the participants' seats so that the participants could observe them easily. All the female and male participants in the *semaan* directly faced the stage. The position for female and male participants was separated during this ritual. Those who attended the *semaan* had to follow and listen carefully to what the memorizers recited by looking at their own Qur'an provided by the host of the event. In this way, the participants were not only able to correct the recitation of the memorizers, but they were also able to gain the merit of the recitation even though they just followed and listened because, according to the Prophet, both those who recite the Qur'an from memory and those who listen to the reciting are able to obtain merit. The reciting of the Qur'an in the *semaan* was conducted continuously, and was only stopped for the performance of obligatory prayers. After noon prayer (I., *Shalat Dhuhur*), the memorizers and all the participants had lunch together, which was provided by the host of the event. For an important event such as the commemoration of the death of the founder, the host provides lunch for all participants. Previously, my informant told me, when *Gus* Mik (the founder) was alive, it was recommended that the memorizers and all participants fasted during this event.

At the rituals that I attended, the leader of this group often gave a very short religious message to the participants at the end of the ritual and the *semaan*. The topic of the message was usually based on the preference of the leader. The leader often talked about the spiritual experience or *karamah* of *Gus* Mik, the founder of the group. It is likely that this was to keep him in the collective memory of the participants. This is partly because after *Gus* Mik died, no one, including his children could replace his popularity as a *wali*. Nevertheless, many members of the group still believed that the charisma of *Gus* Mik should be inherited by one of his sons. This is shown by the fact that after the ritual, most of the participants wished to meet and seek *barakah* from *Gus* Mik's sons by kissing their hands. In order to do that, these participants sometimes stood for a long time waiting their turn to kiss the leader's hand. Before *Gus* Mik's sons led the ritual, some of his followers visited their home to ask for their *barakah* or to consult them about their problems.

In addition to holding the ritual on specific occasions like the anniversary of the death of particular Muslim saints and the founder, this group also conducted the ritual on a weekly basis and every *selapanan* (every five weeks) in a group. At the weekly event, the ritual was usually held at the household of the leader or at one of the tombs of Muslim Saints located in Kediri. The tombs which provided a venue for the ritual included the tomb of *Setono Gedong,* the tomb of Muhammad Abdullah Umar (Sumber Dlingu, Kediri), the tomb of Ki Demang (Mbadal, Kediri), and the tomb of *Shaikh* Ihsan Dahlan (Jampes, Kediri). On the other hand, the major ritual held every five weeks (*selapanan*) was conducted at the Tomb of Saints (*Makam Auliya'*) at which *Gus* Mik was buried. The ritual held at his tomb could be attended by thousands of people, who travelled from all over Java to attend.

Gus Farih Fauzi , one of leaders of this group, told me that the first reason for holding the ritual at Muslim saints' tombs was to remember death. Secondly, it was to pray for all Muslims. Thirdly, it was to gain blessing (*barakah*) since it is recommended to visit the tombs of pious Muslims to gain their blessing and to emulate their virtues in fulfilling religious duties. The fourth reason was to fulfil the obligation to parents and fellow Muslims who need to be prayed for if they have died. Fifthly, the ritual could express one's respect to someone whom one has known and loved. Another was that the tombs of saints are efficacious places from which to offer prayer.[6]

In common with Sufi orders elsewhere, as in Pakistan and Egypt, the *Dhikr al-Ghāfilīn* group focuses its activities at the tomb of its founder. *Gus* Mik's tomb, called *Makam Auliya'* is located on three hectares of land in Tambak hamlet, Ngadi village, Ploso subdistrict, Kediri. This site was chosen by *Gus* Mik in 1990. Like other tombs of Muslim saints in Java, the *Makam Auliya'* consists of several mausoleums, a small mosque and is surrounded by kiosks which sell pamphlets and food (Fox 2002:161). *Gus* Mik expected that forty Muslim saints would be buried at that place, and he himself determined personages who would be given the privilege to rest in that place. It is said that previously there were only three tombs of Muslim saints on the site, including Shaikh 'Abd al-Qādir Khairi (allegedly from Iskandariah, Egypt), Muhammad Ḥirmān, and Shaikh 'Abd Allah Ṣaliḥ (allegedly from Istanbul, Turkey). According to Abdul Wahid, the custodian of the tomb (*juru kunci*), these graves were first founded in the 1830's by Seno Atmojo, one of Pangeran Diponegoro's soldiers. People who lived around the site believed these old tombs had *keramat*. The three personages buried in that place were believed to be the first preachers of Islam in the region. It is reported that *Gus* Mik often spent much of his time visiting and meditating at that site (Jawapos 1993). Currently, there are fifteen personages buried there, including *Gus* Mik and *Kyai* Aḥmad Ṣiddīq. In addition to the tombs of *Wali Sanga,* this site is well known as an object of veneration and visitation in Java.

It was not clear why *Gus* Mik had the idea to establish the *Makam Auliya'*. Only he knew the objective. Even one of his close companions never understood

6 Interview with *Gus* Fahri, Kediri, September, 2007.

why the *Makam Auliya* was established. One possible reason relates to the notion pointed out by Ibn Abī Hajala that 'it is essential to bury the dead close to persons whose righteous and grace is assured and as far from the graves of the sinful as possible.' This notion is based on several hadith in which the Prophet asked Muslims to bury their dead near to deceased righteous Muslims rather than sinful people because the dead can be hurt by bad neighbours. In other words, just as in life, being close to bad neighbours could be injurious for the dead, being close to good neighbours can benefit them. This explains why when many Muslim saints were near to death, they asked to be buried near to the graves of other saints in order to obtain some of the saints' *barakah* (Taylor 1998:47-49). Therefore, *Gus* Mik might have thought that those righteous Muslims should be buried together with other righteous Muslims in one tomb in order to receive the other saints' *barakah*.

After *Gus* Mik died, the question arose as to who would have the right to decide the next personages or Muslim saints (*wali*) to be buried at the site. *Gus* Ali, one of *Gus* Mik's close companions, argued that only *Gus* Mik knew about this and should decide who would be buried at the site. The fact that *Gus* Mik had died did not hinder him from spiritually determining the personages to be buried at the site. *Gus* Ali believed that before *Gus* Mik died, he had already informed some other *wali* that they could be buried at the site. However, it is difficult to know whether or not anyone received this information from *Gus* Mik. In addition, *Gus* Ali mentioned that those who have been prioritised to be buried at the site are all memorisers (A., *ḥāfiẓ*) who have been actively involved in the *semaan*. This criterion might have partly been due to the fact his group did not have a *wali* like *Gus* Mik to determine who could be buried at the site. However, the decision to give the memorisers the privilege of being buried at the site also raised difficulties. The criteria to determine which memorisers should be buried there is not clear. In addition to asking for spiritual guidance (I., *petunjuk spiritual*) from *Gus* Mik to solve this problem, *Gus* Ali finally used another mechanism, that is, through discussion (*musyawarah*) involving many respected Muslim scholars, to decide who should be buried at the site.

6.3. *Gus* Mik: a Living Saint and Controversial *Kyai*

Gus Mik was born in Kediri in 1941 and died in 1993. He was born in the *Pesantren* community because his father, *Kyai* Jazuli Usman (1900-1976) was the founder of *Pesantren* Ploso which became one of the centres of Islamic studies in East Java. *Gus* Mik is an important figure for the *Dhikr al-Ghāfilīn* and the *Semaan al-Qur'an*. Indeed, it is almost impossible to study the group without recognising the figure of *Gus* Mik. This section will look at the position of *Gus* Mik, both within his group and within an Indonesian Islamic context.

Gus Mik was frequently seen by people and the media as a controversial Islamic scholar (I., *kyai nyeleneh* and *nyentrik*). This controversy was triggered by the fact that *Gus* Mik was frequently seen in night clubs, brothels, pubs and casinos in Surabaya. It was reported that *Gus* Mik regularly spent his nights at the Elmi Hotel, Surabaya. At such places, he was also frequently seen drinking black beer (I., *bir hitam*) with pub singers and visitors (Muryadi 1992:63). Some people and *'ulamā'* maintained that this was not suitable behaviour for an *'ulamā'* like *Gus* Mik and not acceptable in Islamic law. As an *'ulamā'*, he should not visit such places and drink alcohol, which is prohibited by Islamic law. If the *'ulamā'* visited such places, it could cause misbehaviour among people because they might follow his conduct.[7]

Kyai Zainudiin, one of *Gus* Mik's brothers could not explain *Gus* Mik's controversial behaviour. Since *Kyai* Zainuddin did not witness *Gus* Mik's actions outside the *pesantren,* he and his family still regarded *Gus* Mik as a model of the *pesantren* family member. *Kyai* Zainuddin argued that because he did not witness *Gus* Mik drinking alcohol, he could not make any comments on the matter. All he could say about *Gus* Mik was that everything that he did was difficult for others to emulate. According to *Kyai* Zainuddin, the objective of *Gus* Mik's actions was to glorify Islam. If the methods he used were different from other *'ulamā'*, this was part of his ability that could not be copied by others (Rahmat 1993).

To deal with this controversy, one of the charismatic *'ulamā'*, *Kyai* al-Hamid, argued that *Gus* Mik's actions were part of his Islamic preaching (I., *dakwah*). However, the way *Gus* Mik chose to preach Islam was not like other *'ulamā'*, who usually preached Islam through sermons (I., *ceramah*) in mosques, *pesantren,* and *pengajian* groups (I., *majlis taklim*). In contrast, *Gus* Mik conducted his mission by preaching Islam in places such as night clubs, brothels, casinos and hotel pubs which are commonly considered immoral places (I., *dunia hitam* and *tempat maksiat*) (Hidayat 1993). In this regard, *Gus* Mik admitted that he did not have a particular *pesantren* but considered those places to be his real '*pesantren*'. He described his mission as follows:

> These places are my real *pesantren.* Most of my *jamaah* (followers) meet in those places. 90% of them have not said *asyhadu* yet (*belum asyahdu*), namely, those who always hang around at night with their psychological

7 Interview with *Kyai* Saiful, Kediri, November, 2004.

> problems. They are not good people (I., *bukan orang baik-baik*). I have never involved other *kyai* in these places because they wear *surban* [*kyai*'s scarf] (Muryadi 1992:63).

Kyai al-Hamid considered that, the mission of preaching Islam in such places was more difficult than preaching in other places because it often resulted in exclusion by other *'ulamā'* and insults from people. *Kyai* Zainuddin, *Gus* Mik's brother, agreed that 'the night world of *Gus* Mik could not be reached by other *kyai*. I myself could not afford to carry out the mission as *Gus* Mik did.' Not all *'ulamā'* have been given a power by God to conduct Islamic preaching mission in such places. *Gus* Mik, according to *Kyai* al-Hamid, was one of the *'ulamā'* whom God chose to give his spiritual power to perform that mission. As a *Jawa Pos* journalist, Sholihin Hidayat wrote, at such places *Gus* Mik met with many people including artists, singers, military officials, government officials, gamblers and alcoholics. Because of *Gus* Mik, many of them refrained from drinking and gambling and started to pray five times a day (Hidayat 1993a). One of those people was Erna Jaelani, a singer from Surabaya. Before meeting with *Gus* Mik, she was a pub singer in Surabaya. She admitted that after meeting him she not only stopped singing in pubs but also avoided entering them. She then became a wedding stylist and opened a fashion shop in her carport (Jawa Pos 1993). Another famous rock singer from Bali who converted to Islam after meeting *Gus* Mik was Ayu Wedhayanti. She is now an active participant in every ritual of the *Dhikr al-Ghāfilīn* and *semaan*.

One of *Gus* Mik's students explained to me that the reason why *Gus* Mik mostly spent his nights in pubs, bars, and karaoke places with other visitors, prostitutes, and singers was to pray that they could return to the straight path since no other *'ulamā'* wanted to pray for those people. For example, one day *Gus* Mik asked *Gus* Rofiq Siraj to accompany him to brothels in Surabaya. *Gus* Mik and *Gus* Rofiq Siraj spent all night reciting *al-Fātiḥat* many times until morning. As usual, after reciting the *al-Fātiḥat*, *Gus* Mik was approached by a prostitute who wanted to repent. This story was also told in an interview held by a journalist from Matra magazine. When asked about his controversial activities in pubs, *Gus* Mik replied that he just enjoyed those places. In addition, he was excited to emulate what has been practised by another Muslim *'ulamā'*, Aḥmad Ibn Hanbal, when he entered places entertainment which were forbidden by Islamic law. According to *Gus* Mik, it was reported that when Ibnu Hambal entered such places, he always prayed for the people there. One of Ibnu Hambal's prayers was as follows:

> O! Allah just as you have made these people have a party in this place, may these people also have a party in the world -to- come. Just as these people are happy in this place, I ask God to make these people happy in the world –to- come (*akhirat*).

Another reason why *Gus* Mik visited such places was to check whether or not his followers went there. When *Gus* Mik met any of his followers there, he claimed that although they were sitting in these places, they remained conscious of improving the recitation of *al-Fātiḥat* and remembering God. The sound of music did not prevent them from reciting *al-Fātiḥat*. *Gus* Mik was very proud of his students who were able to remember God and to draw close to Him not only in mosques but also in such places (Siregar 1992)

Gus Mik's willingness to hear and receive prostitutes, sinners and gamblers might have been inspired by the story of a prostitute and a virtuous person mentioned in the Sufi book, *al-Hikam*. Because of his intensive worship of God, the virtuous person was endowed with the power of miracles (I., *karamah*). It is said that one of his miracles was that wherever he walked in the desert, a cloud shaded him so that he was protected from the hot sun. One day, a prostitute came to him so that she could receive God's blessing. But the virtuous person refused the prostitute and asked her to go away. At that time, God said to the current prophet that He had forgiven any sins committed by the prostitute. God then withdrew the power of miracles he had given to the person and gave it to the prostitute.

Another interesting comment regarding *Gus* Mik's behaviour was made by *Gus* Ali Mashuri, a senior *kyai* in East Java, who fully understood everything to do with *Gus* Mik. However, he never regarded *Gus* Mik as a saint (*wali*) because the title of *wali* can be known only by *Gus* Mik and God, and no one can give the title of *wali* to another. Based on this notion, *Gus* Ali argued that although *Gus* Mik committed acts considered by others as evils, he committed such acts without asking others to do so. Furthermore, *Gus* Ali pointed out that if God has given someone the highest spiritual position (*maqam*), this person would never be happy if other people praised him nor be sad if anyone insulted him. Praise and insults would not prevent such a person from obtaining God's blessing. *Gus* Mik, according to *Gus* Ali, was one of those people on whom God had bestowed with the highest *maqam*.[8] This can be seen by the fact that although other *'ulamā'*regarded him as a 'beer *kyai*' and 'bar *kyai*' (I., *kyai bir* and *kyai bar*) who destroyed the image of Islam,*Gus* Mik never felt sad about this title and continued his mission of preaching Islam.

---

8 Interview with *Kyai* Ali Mashuri, Sidoarjo, Januari, 2005.

Plate 6.1: Gus Mik meeting with Ir. Akbar Tanjung, the former minister in Suharto era.

Source : Matra Magazine, October, 1992.

His son, Thābut, told me that *Gus* Mik preferred humiliation to praise, and always prayed for those who humiliated him.[9] According to *Gus* Ali Mashuri, *Gus* Mik made himself an object of blame, while nevertheless believing that in the eyes of God he was considered good. In this sense, *Gus* Mik could be regarded as a Sufi who sought the glory of God through the gate of humbleness. This notion is relevant to something frequently taught by *Gus* Mik, that in order to obtain God's blessing, instead of showing off their good deeds to others, people should hide their virtues and keep them a secret between themselves and God. According to *Gus* Ali, this is the highest teaching of Sufism, which not all ordinary people are able to practise. For him, this teaching, was in fact, deeply rooted in the story of Moses and Khidr[10] in the Qur'an. This story tells us that Khidr was allowed by God to do things which seemed to be evil and malicious in the eyes of lay people but had benefits later. Not every one can emulate Khidr and even the prophet of God, Moses, failed to understand what Khidr was doing.

9 Interview with Thabut, Kediri, November, 2004.

10 This prominent figure plays a part in many legend and stories. His name is Balya ibn Malkan. Al-Khidr is his epithet which means 'the green man.' According to Sufi tradition, he is regarded as saint. Every age has its Khidr. His immortality is emphasized in Islamic tradition (Gibb and Kramers 1953:232-35).

Moreover, *Gus* Ali argued that what *Gus* Mik did could be compared with the teaching of the Malamatiyah Sufi group which required struggle to hide one's virtuous and pious actions. As result, this group only showed bad qualities and became an object of blame by others (Gibb 1996:223). In line with this, al-Ghazālī wrote that in order to get rid of the love of pride (A., *jāh*), which, according to him, is dangerous for Sufi in their efforts to approach God, they may commit deeds which result in their status falling in the eyes of others. However, al-Ghazālī argued that they are allowed only to commit deeds which are categorised as permissible (*mubāḥ*), not those categorised as forbidden. In doing so they can feel secure in their camouflage and they be satisfied with the reception of God (al-Ghazali 1973:281).

Gus Mik fully realized that other people would question his activities in bars and pubs and regard his activities as violating Islamic laws. Asked why as a Muslim he drank beer in bars, he replied that he knew nothing about alcohol and only knew about *mushkir*, a kind of beverage that can make people drunk. He claimed that no one had told him whether beer can be categorised as *mushkir*. Therefore, *Gus* Mik argued that he could not prohibit (*mengharamkan*) the drinking of beer, even though this kind of beverage was commonly considered an intoxicant (I., *memabukkan*). However, he asked people not to drink beer because it caused health problems and also because it was expensive and useless (A., *mubādhir*). *Gus* Mik was concerned about the social effect of drinking beer. He argued that instead of spending money buying something so useless, people should use the money for other purposes such as helping the poor. *Gus* Mik asked his followers not to drink, even though he himself did not stop drinking because he drunk the beer as a means to maintain friendships with other people.

Gus Mik's view of drinking alcohol can be clearly explained in the perspective of Islamic jurisprudence (A., *fiqh al-Islām*). All Muslim jurists mention that any drink which may cause drunkenness is prohibited. This notion is based on the Prophetic hadith, 'if it intoxicates in a large amount, it is forbidden even in a small amount' (*kullu mushkirin ḥarām qolīluhu wa kathīruhu*). However, according to Abū Ḥanīfat, although both *khamr* and *nabīdh*can cause drunkenness, there is a distinction between them. *Khamr* is a kind of drink made from wine, while *nabīdh*is a kind of drink made from anything other than grapes. Abū Ḥanīfat argued that *khamr* (wine) was prohibited because of its essence, while *nabīdh* was not. Therefore, people are allowed to drink *nabīdh*as long as they do not get drunk on it (Qudamah n.d). Perhaps, based on Abū Ḥanīfat's view, *Gus* Mik categorised beer as *nabīdh*because it is not made from grapes.

Plate 6.2: Gus Mik with his followers in a pub in Surabaya.

Source: Matra Magazine, October, 1992.

Plate 6.3: Gus Mik chatting with Sultan Hameng Kubuwono X (The Ruler of Yogyakarta).

Source: Matra Magazine, October, 1992.

One of *Gus* Mik's students maintained that because of his *karamah,* any beer that *Gus* Mik drank turned into spring water. Therefore, *Gus* Mik was never drunk although he consumed large amounts of beer. As regards gambling, an informant told me that while *Gus* Mik was often seen gambling with other gamblers, his purpose was to appeal to people to stop gambling. My informant was convinced that as result of his *karamah,* if *Gus* Mik gambled in particular places, these places would close and no gambling activities would be done there. This story was often told by his followers and it relates to the way *Gus* Mik appealed to other people to stop them from drinking and gambling.

Some of *Gus* Mik followers who accompanied him for many years found it difficult to judge what *Gus* Mik did. They believed that only God could understand *Gus* Mik's conduct. Furthermore, *Gus* Mik never asked his followers to emulate his deeds. Therefore, one *kyai* whom I asked about *Gus* Mik preferred to think positively (A., *ḥusn al-ẓann*) rather than to think negatively (A., *sū'u al-ẓann*) about what he did. In this respect, *ḥusn al-ẓann* is encouraged even if *Gus* Mik did conduct negative acts. On the other hand, if people think negatively about *Gus* Mik, when in fact his acts are positive, these people commit a sin because of this negative thinking.[11]

It is clear that the responses given by people about *Gus* Mik were based on the idea of *khāriq al 'āda,* which is prevalent in the Sufi tradition. This term is given to those who can perform deeds that break the custom of God (I., *sunnatullah*). *Gus* Mik, for example, was believed by his followers to performing deeds which could be categorised as *khāriq al 'āda,* so no one should emulate him. In this sense, *Gus* Mik was considered by his followers to be a *wali* who possessed *karamah* which in the Sufi tradition is closely related the idea of *khāriq al 'āda.* In addition, the positive responses given to *Gus* Mik relied on *ḥusn al-ẓann,* according to which, every single act conducted by *Gus* Mik had the good purpose of spreading Islam (I., *syiar Islam*). His followers therefore believe that the success of *Gus* Mik in promoting the reciting of the Qur'an, *dhikr,* resolving people's problems and stopping people from gambling and drinking alcohol far outweigh *Gus* Mik habit of drinking and visiting bars.

6.4. *Gus* Mik: His *Karamah*

Among his followers, *Gus* Mik was believed to be a *wali* sent by God to bring people to the right path. To fulfil this mission his followers also believed *Gus* Mik had been endowed by God with an extraordinary power (J., *kekuatan*

11 Interview with *Kyai* Idris, November, Kediri, 2004.

linuwih) called *karamah.* As a *wali*, what he did during his lifetime had religious significance. He was always guided by God, either through visions or dreams. With this guidance, he may have committed minor trespasses but he immediately repented. Although *Gus* Mik never regarded himself as an '*Ārif bi Allah* ('one who has Gnosis of God'), his followers believed that he reached the state of *ma'rifat* so that he could be regarded as an '*Ārif bi Allah.* With this title he deserved to be a spiritual teacher (A., *murshid*) of the *Dhikr al-Ghāfilīn* group and no one could succeed him after his death. One of his followers even considered he had the same *karamah,* as was possessed by 'Abd al-Qādir al-Jailānī, the founder of the Qadiriyah Sufi group.

Stories about *Gus* Mik's *karamah* are told and circulate by word of mouth. In order to keep the collective memory of *Gus* Mik alive among his followers, these stories are often retold during the ritual of the *Dhikr al-Ghāfilīn* especially on the annual anniversary of his death (*haul*). Most of these stories about *Gus* Mik's *karamah* deal specifically with his miraculous powers. They serve as an important model of exemplary piety for his followers. Moreover, these stories about *Gus* Mik's *karamah* increase his followers' spiritual beliefs about him. As result, this improves their spiritual focus (A., *tawajjuh*). Some examples of his *karamah* were told to me by his close friends as follows:

First karamah: *Gus* Mik showed his *karamah* when he was a teenager. Unlike his two brothers who spent their time studying hard in the *pesantren* and had a normal life typical of the sons of a *kyai*, *Gus* Mik spent his time outside the *pesantren* travelling (J., *keluyuran*) everywhere. He left his hair uncut. He was often found fishing alone on the bank of the River Brantas. One day he walked along the river up to the city of Surabaya. During his wanderings, many people witnessed him walking on the surface of the water. He himself never realized that he had such *karamah.*

Second karamah: His parents worried about *Gus* Mik's behaviour which was so different to his two brothers. As a result, his parents asked many *kyai* to give advice and pray for *Gus* Mik so that he would stop being eccentric (I., *kenyelenehannya*) and live a normal life. However, many *kyai* were reluctant to give advice and pray for *Gus* Mik. One day his parents asked *Gus* Mik to come and visit the mourning family of *Kyai* Romli, the late leader of Pesantren Darul Ulum and the Qadiriyah wa Naqshabandiyah Sufi group in Jombang. His parents hoped that during this visit, they could ask *kyai* who attended the burial ritual to pray for their son. *Gus* Mik refused to come with his family to the funeral of *Kyai* Ramli. However, when his parents arrived at *Kyai* Romli's, they found that *Gus* Mik had already arrived and was sitting at the side of *Kyai* Romli's corpse.

Third karamah: My informant told me that *Gus* Mik could understand things to come (J., *weruh sandurungi winarak*) – these things would happen a week, month or year later. For example, *Gus* Mik told my informant that he would perform the pilgrimage (*hajj*) some years later. My informant thought it would not be possible to perform the *hajj,* as he did not have the financial ability to undertake the journey. However, few years later, his friends gave him enough money to pay the cost of the *hajj.* After his first *hajj, Gus* Mik told him that he would perform a second *hajj* four years later. One year before this second *hajj,* my informant dreamed that he met *Gus* Mik and another person. This person wished to perform *hajj* with *Gus* Mik and offered to pay all the costs of the journey (I., *Ongkos Naik Haji*, ONH). However, *Gus* Mik declined this offer and instead, gave this offer to my informant. *Gus* Mik asked my informant to pray and not to thiŋk about the cost of the *hajj.* One year after experiencing this dream, my informant undertook his second *hajj* because two people gave him the money to cover the cost. This kind of *karamah,* according to my informant, was similar to that of 'Abd al-Qadir al-Jaylāni when he said in his *manaqib* that he knew everything that would happen in the upcoming weeks, months and years.

Fourth karamah: One day *Gus* Mik told my informant that he understood everything that would happen to my informant's family for the next ten years. For example, *Gus* Mik forecast that my informant's wife would give birth six years later. This forecast proved true when six years later my informant's wife gave birth to her third child. *Gus* Mik also forecast that *Kyai*Ahmad Siddiq would experience a trial for six years. After six years *Kyai*Ahmad Siddiq succeeded in passing this trial and was nominated chairman of the National Board of Nahdlatul Ulama.

Fifth karamah: My informant believed that God endowed *Gus* Mik with one of His *kun* characteristics. *Kun* is an Arabic word which refers to an act of manifesting, existing or being. In the Qur'an, God commands the universe *to be* ('*kun!*') and it is (*fayakūn*). Someone who possesses this characteristic can predict that something will happen and it should happen. According to my informant, *Gus* Mik told him that he could make *Kyai*Ṣaliḥ, who was poor, a rich man. Before getting married, *Kyai*Ṣalih was poor and pious person but after his married, he became a rich.

Sixth karamah: Abu Bakr Kalabadzi mentioned that it is widely believed among Sufi that a *wali* may possesses various kinds of *karamah,* such as being able to walk on the surface of water, talk with animals and appear in two places at the same time (Kalabadzi 1985:79). *Gus* Mik is said by his followers to have had the ability to appear in three places at the same time. *Gus* Ali Muhammad, *Gus*

Farid, and *Gus* Muqarrabin said that when this group held *semaan* in Jember, Surabaya and Yogyakarta, *Gus* Mik appeared in all these three places at the same time. Because of this *karamah,* one of my informants rejected the claim that *Gus* Mik never performed a prayer during his life based on the fact that no one found him praying at prayer times. Since he could appear in three places at the same time, my informant pointed out that *Gus* Mik might not be praying at one place, but he might possibly be praying at another place.

Seventh karamah: One day *Gus* Mik wanted to visit *Kyai* Ahmad Shiddiq in Jember. At that time, *Kyai* Ahmad Siddiq was looking for citations from books, and *Gus* Mik brought a piece of paper with the citation texts that *Kyai* Ahmad Siddiq was looking for (Memorandum, 11/06/1993).

Eighth karamah: *Gus* Mik was believed to be capable of giving his followers solutions to problem. Adi Siswanto, a businessman from Sidoarjo, claimed that what *Gus* Mik ordered to him do when he had a difficult problem, contained a hidden meaning. *Gus* Mik gave him a solution which made him happy. This also happened to many other artists, businessmen, and government officials who sought advice and solutions from *Gus* Mik about their problems. An informant told of how his advice was always correct, even though it might at first have seemed puzzling. As an example, Oscar regretted not complying with *Gus* Mik's advice. If he had done so, his business would not have failed totally. He at first thought it was not possible to follow *Gus* Mik's advice.

Niinth karamah: One day my informant went out with *Gus* Mik to eat at a famous restaurant in Kediri. When waiters served *Gus* Mik with his favourite satay, *Gus* Mik told my informant that the waitress was not a virgin. On this occasion my informant believed that *Gus* Mik not only understood hidden things in the hearts of people but also recognised every sin that had been committed by others. In a similar story, *Gus* Mik and my informant attended a *Dhikr al Ghāfilīn* ritual in a *pesantren,* and sat in the front seats with other *kyai*. Among these *kyai,* there was one *kyai* who sat wordlessly in the corner. *Gus* Mik commented to my informant that this *kyai* was an extraordinary person because his heart always remembered death and God.

Tenth karamah: *Kyai* Farih Fauzi said that *Gus* Mik was absent from Friday prayer one day. A few hours later, *Gus* Mik arrived bringing a branch of fresh dates which had been taken from a date tree. This must have been taken from the holy land.

The moral message of these different *Gus* Mik's *karamah* is the same: *Gus* Mik's knowledge transcended place and time and penetrated the inners hearts of his followers. However, his knowledge did not just signal his ability to foresee the future or to know what is in men's hearts wherever they are, it was also part of God's power and love, indicated by *Gus* Mik's power to become involved in a bad environments without committing any sin in such places.

The most significant evidence of his *karamah*, which could be seen after he died, was his ability to attract many people to the ritual of *Dhikr al-Ghāfilīn* and *semaan*. Although *Gus* Mik had died, the *semaan* and the *Dhikr al-Ghāfilīn* still continued to attract many participants. This ability was seen by his companions and followers as part of God's plan to send one of his servants to preserve the Qur'an from being forgotten. This initiative of *Gus* Mik to hold *semaan al-Qur'an* (memorizing the Qur'an) was often related to what God said in the Qur'an, 'Verily, We, it is We Who have sent down the *Dhikr* (i.e. the Qur'an) and surely We will guard it (from corruption)' (15:9). According to his companions, *Gus* Mik with his *karamah* was the preserver of the Qur'an itself. This notion is not difficult to understand. It was argued on the basis of the interpretation of the text of the Qur'anic verse in which God says *we* rather than *I*. According to common exegesis, when God uses *we* rather than *I*, it means that the process of His works involving humans. Therefore, when God says that *we* will preserve the Qur'an, this preservation involves humans. In this sense, *Gus* Mik was one whom God used to preserve the Qur'an.

6.5. *Gus* Mik: His Teachings

To describe and understand *Gus* Mik's teachings comprehensively is a difficult task. This is partly because he was neither a writer who expressed his thoughts systematically in a book nor a preacher who explained in detail the teachings of *tasawuf* in front of his followers. *Gus* Mik chose to practise these teachings rather than explain them in detail to his followers. This can be seen through his advice given to his followers after the ritual of the *Dhikr al-Ghāfilīn* was completed. *Kyai* Saiful, one of his close companions, told me that on such occasions, *Gus* Mik usually gave a short speech which took only five to ten minutes. Nevertheless, in this short time he could convey as the depths of *tasawuf*. For *Gus* Mik, the current concept of *dakwah* should stress giving an example in practice (A., *lisān al-hal*) rather than placing too much stress on sermons and lectures (Mantab n.d:8). Through his brief sermons, his followers could understand the moral and ethical ideas needed in their lives. For his followers, *Gus* Mik's advice was easy to remember, even though its content was not easy to practise. In addition to *tasawuf* teachings, the topics of his advice were very broad, touching on many aspects of life. Therefore, this section will examine his teachings and analyse them in the light of *tasawuf* teachings.

One of *Gus* Mik's teachings emphasizes the importance of Muslims keeping their pious acts (I., *amal saleh*) secret from other people. He asked his followers to conceal their pious acts, even though these virtues were little things such as praying for their hosts before visiting them. This teaching is simple, but in the context of *tasawuf* teachings it is important since it is closely related to the essence of people's worship of their God. According to Islamic teachings, Muslims are required to worship God and perform good deeds sincerely (I., *ikhlas*). In other words, Muslims should worship and do good deeds to seek reward from God, and not for the sake of people's praise (A., *riyā'*). Based on this notion, all *ibadah* necessitates the purity of intention. As a result, if people perform good deeds, but have an intention other than seeking God's blessing, these good deeds will be meaningless in the eyes of God. In fact, what *Gus* Mik taught on this matter was strongly based on Sufi teachings. For example, Ibn 'Aṭāillah suggested to those who want to seek closeness to God:

> 'Bury your existence in the earth of obscurity, for whatever sprouts forth, without having first been buried, flowers imperfectly'[12]

After stressing the importance of pure intention and the hiding of virtuous deeds, *Gus* Mik asked his followers not to regard themselves as the purer and holier (I., *orang yang paling suci*) than others. *Gus* Mik pointed out that there are two kinds of people: First, people who feel that they are the most holy, clean, successful, and purest persons in the world, and secondly, people who feel that they are nothing. Instead of regarding themselves as very pure, *Gus* Mik asked people to inculcate a sense of worthlessness (I., *rasa penghambaan*) such as feeling guilty, humble, sinful, and full of weakness. With regard to this teaching *Gus* Mik said as follows:

> We do not need to seek others' faults and despise people around us who have gone astray (I.,*maksiat*) because we cannot be sure that we are better than they are (Mantab n.d:1).[13]

These feelings would increase people's humility and willingness to ask for God's forgiveness. However, *Gus* Mik admitted that imparting these feelings was difficult and needed continuous practice. He argued that this teaching was easy to explain but he himself found it difficult to practise. In this respect, *Gus* Mik always taught the following special prayer to his followers: 'Oh Lord! We have wronged ourselves, if you forgive us not and have not mercy on us; surely we are of the lost.'

---

12 نتاجه يتم لا يدفن لم مما نبت فما الخمول الارض فى وجودك ادفن

13 *Kita tidak perlu mencari kesalahan orang lain dan membenci orang-orang di sekitar kita yang melakukan maksiat.*

As regards this teaching, my informant explained to me that if God wants to make people pious, He will endow them with knowledge of their weaknesses. My informant further mentioned that according to a hadith, the luckiest person is he who is always busy looking at his own weaknesses so that he has no time to look at other people's weaknesses. According to my informant, people always look at others' weaknesses because they feel that they have none. *Gus* Mik pointed out as follows:

> In my village, I lived with different people, the most important thing to do is to remember God, do not regard yourself as holier than others, do not pay attention and seek out others' fault, and have a good heart toward other people, these are the characteristics of the followers of the *Dhikr al-Ghāfilīn.*[14]

This teaching is supported by the Qur'anic text which asks people not to regard themselves as pure. Moreover, this teaching was elaborated further by Ibn 'Aṭāillah who said in his book that sinful acts (*maksiat*) that make a person feel humble and ashamed are better than proper actions that give rise to pride (I., *takabbur*) and feelings of superiority.

In addition to hiding good acts, *Gus* Mik also stressed the importance of focusing people's minds on always remembering God in all conditions, places and times. As reported by my informant, *Gus* Mik said that 'When you engage with something, do not let this prevent you from remembering God and when you engage with someone, do not let them prevent you from remembering God.' This notion, according to my informant, was practised by *Gus* Mik himself so he could undergo *khalwa,* a silent situation enabling him to communicate with God and to draw near to Him, even if he was in a noisy place such as a bar.[15]

Another piece of *Gus* Mik's advice told to me by his son, *Gus* Sabut, was that 'we should not make our neighbours jealous (A., *hasad*) of us.' According to his son, this advice contained deep Sufi moral teaching, although it was difficult to practice, particularly today.[16] In *tasawuf* teachings, envy is regarded as the worst of spiritual diseases. Al-Ghazālī defines *ḥasad*as the feeling of hate towards the goodness of others and desire for the elimination of others' bounty (al-Ghazali 1973:185). Many Qur'anic texts and Prophetic traditions regarded *ḥasad* as a destructive force (A., *muhlikat*) which leads to the destruction of the good acts of envious people. Therefore, according to Qur'anic teachings, people

14 *'Kulo teng kampong niku sareng tiyang katah, Sing penting imut teng Allah, mboten rumaos langkung suci ketimbang liyane, ora sempat melirik maksiati wong liyo, kaleh sinten-sinten nggadah manah ingkang sahe, ngih niku cirikhase pengamal Dzikr al-Ghafilin.'*

15 Interview with *Kyai* Saiful, Kediri, December, 2004.

16 Interview with *Kyai* Saiful, Kediri, December, 2004.

should seek refuge in God from envious people (*A.,ḥāsid*) and from jealousy itself (al-Falaq:5). However, asking for refuge is not enough; people should act to stop others from being jealous of them. According to *Gus* Mik's son, in order to avoid others' jealousy, people should share some of their bounty (I., *rizki*) with others. For him, this is important way to overcome the social problems in Indonesia, where many people tend to become selfish and ignore their less fortunate neighbours.

In relation to his previous advice, *Gus* Mik tried to console his followers who happened to be experiencing calamity, misfortune, or poverty. *Gus* Mik pointed out that these people should thank God rather than complaining about their difficulties. This is because living in such conditions can increase one's awareness and remembrance of God. In contrast, if God determines that some should live in this world with happiness and wealth, this can make people easily forgetful of their God. *Gus* Mik not only advised his followers but he also practised what he advised. For example, when he suffered cancer he never complained about his illness to his companions. Instead of complaining to God, he always thanked God for his illness.

In supporting his followers who lived in poverty, *Gus* Mik said that every single person in this world is keen to be wealthy. In fact, however, those wealthy will become needy persons in the world-to-come. In contrast, those who are poor in this world and are patient with their poverty will become wealthy persons in the world-to-come. This notion was based on *Gus* Mik's belief in the Prophet's sayings that poor patient people will enter paradise five hundreds years earlier than good rich people. *Gus* Mik said:

> The poor who can stand suffering, smile, be joyful, and always grateful are much more respected than anyone else. The pious poor are more excellent than philanthropists who have spent ninety nine percent of their wealth for the sake of God.[17]

The point of his advice was that people should be patient in all conditions, both in comfort and in hardship, and should always praise God by saying *alhamdulillah* (all praise due to God) (Mantab n.d:6). The poor should not demonstrate their poverty to other people, but should try to be like the Prophet Muhammad who never complained about his poverty. *Gus* Mik suggested that instead of submitting to their own fate, the poor should earn a living and obtain

17 Manusia fakir yang tahan uji, yang mampu tertawa, mampu menjadi periang, batinnya mensyukuri, ini lebih terhormat dari siapa saja. Termasuk orang dermawan yang sembilan puluh sembilan persen hak miliknya dibuang karena Allah, masih unggul fakir yang sholeh.

everything by lawful means (I., *halal*) (Mantab n.d:4). On the other hand, *Gus* Mik also recommended that other people should respect the poor (Mantab n.d:39).

Gus Mik also taught his followers how to love God correctly. *Gus* Mik pointed out that loving God was similar to the concept of *taqwa,* that is, avoiding what God dislikes and practising what God has instructed. However, in the context of loving God, avoiding what God has forbidden should not be followed by the fear of His torment, and practising what God has asked should not be followed by expectation of His paradise. All of these acts, according to my informant, should be conducted only to obtain His consent (A., *riḍā*). On another occasion, *Gus* Mik stressed the importance of doing something which can cause God to give His love to his servants. This idea reminds us of the teaching of the Saint, Rabī'at al-'Adawiyyat, who first introduced the idea of love in Sufi practice.

It is clear that the teachings that *Gus* Mik gave to his followers were deeply inspired by the teachings of prominent Sufi. Sometimes, he taught his followers about good conduct, positive attitudes, and morality taken from local tradition without making any religious reference, and presented this advice using their vernacular language. As a result, his followers who were mainly villagers easily understood this type of teaching.

6.6. The Group after *Gus* Mik

Kyai Saiful, senior *'ulamā'*in the *Dhikr al-Ghāfilīn* group, told me that before *Gus* Mik passed away, he did not give any message of advice (I., *wasiat*) to his children about who should be his successor as the leader of the *Dhikr al-Ghāfilīn* group[18]. Instead of choosing his successor from one of his sons, *Gus* Mik said that all the members of this group (A., *sami'īn*) and memorizers (A., *khuffāẓ*) involved in the group could be the next leaders. Several days before he died, one of his students asked him when he was critically sick in the hospital (*Rumah Sakit Budi Mulya*) in Surabaya, 'Who will you choose as your successor to lead the group while you are being treated in this hospital?' he replied, 'Do you mean my successor after I die?' Then the student did not dare to ask further (Hidayat 1993b). This situation without doubt confused *Gus* Mik's followers. *Kyai* Saiful told me that although *Gus* Mik did not choose a successor, this does not necessarily mean that no one could succeed him as leader. *Kyai* Saiful believed that one of *Gus* Mik's sons or his close friends had to become his successor. However, selecting the next leader of the group either from one of his

18 Interview with *Kyai* Saiful, Kediri, July 2005.

sons or his close friends was not an easy task for *Gus* Mik's family. It was even more difficult to seek a leader who possessed the same charisma as *Gus* Mik. There were also questions regarding the mechanism of election; for example who might be chosen as the committee to conduct the election, which parties would be included within the election, and what would be the requirements needed to determine who would be candidates for *Gus* Mik's position. Because of these difficulties, *Gus* Mik's family and close friends have not yet decided who will succeed *Gus* Mik.

The absence of a sign from *Gus* Mik about his successor has given an opportunity to both his sons and the sons of *Kyai* Ahmad Siddiq to become involved in running and establishing their own *dhikr* groups. *Kyai* Ahmad Siddiq's sons feel that since the group was established not only by *Gus* Mik, but also by their father and *Kyai* al-Hamid, they are also entitled develop the group after *Gus* Mik. *Kyai* Aḥmad Siddiq was important figure in the establishment of the group. *Gus* Mik appointed him as a coordinator of the group for several years. *Gus* Mik took his position following *Kyai* Ahmad Siddiq's death. Thus, *Kyai* Ahmad Siddiq's role in developing the organisation of the group cannot be overlooked. His position as a leader of Nahdlatul Ulama, the largest Muslim organisation in Indonesia, attracted people from the Nahdlatul Ulama community to join the group.

During my fieldwork, eleven years after *Gus* Mik had died, all of his sons and several sons of *Kyai* Ahmad Siddiq were running their own groups (I., *jamaah*) which had similar names to the *Dhikr al-Ghāfilīn*. At that time, there were seven large groups of *Majlis Dhikr* and several small groups with the same name in the hands of different leaders including Tajuddin Heru Cokro, Sabut Suwijan Pranoto Projo, Tijani Robert Saifunnawas, Orbar Sadewo Ahmad (see the genealogy of of *Gus* Mik's family: Figure 6.1), *Gus* Farih Fauzi , Farid Wajdi (see the genealogy of *Kyai* Ahmad Siddiq's family: Figure 6.2) and *Gus* Ali (*Gus* Mik's close colleague). All of these groups had their own members and held similar *dhikr* rituals and *semaan al-Qur'an* regularly in cities in Indonesia. In some cases, three or four of these groups have been established in one city by different leaders.

These groups not only held most of their rituals at Muslim saints' graves or holy graves situated in those cities, but also shared the same ritual venues at these graves. For example, when I visited *Kyai* Murshad's grave, one of famous pilgrimage sites in Kediri, I saw a schedule board next to the Mosque mentioning two groups, one under the leadership of *Gus* Sabut (*Gus* Mik's son) and the other under *Gus* Farih Fauzi (*Kyai* Ahmad Siddiq's son) who were using the same venue for their ritual practice on different days. Specific venues for rituals usually become exclusive to particular groups and not to others. For example, the complex of Muslim saints' graves known as *Makam Auliya' Tambak* in Kediri, where *Gus* Mik and many others personages including *Kyai* Ahmad Siddiq are buried has become the special venue for all *Gus* Mik' sons but not for *Kyai* Ahmad Siddiq's sons. In addition, each group holds their own activities to celebrate the anniversary of the group and the death of the founders. For example, in order to commemorate the anniversary of the death (I., *haul*) of *Gus* Mik, they celebrated on different days rather than on the same days. One group might hold their celebration one week after the date of *Gus* Mik's death; others might celebrate his death one week later.

Commenting on the different leaders and groups, Abdul Qadir one of important figures in these groups, told me that having various group leaders with the same name is God's blessing to the *Dhikr al-Ghāfilīn* and to members. The situation gives people more options to join a particular group with a particular leader. In addition, previously, he added, the ritual of *dhikr* and *semaan* was held once a week. Because of these different leaders, the reciting of the formula and *semaan al-Qur'an* can now be held as many times as possible within a week. Abdul Qadir himself joined the group of one of *Gus* Mik's sons because of his respect for *Gus* Mik as a *murshid* (leader) of the group.[19]

Even though all of the founders of the *Dhikr al-Ghāfilīn* have died, the current leaders of these groups claim that the *Dzikr al-Ghāfilīn* groups have continued to develop rapidly. They claim that these groups have established branches in most cities in Indonesia. However, the absence of charismatic figures such as *Gus* Mik and *Kyai* Ahmad Siddiq has led the current leaders to find ways to encourage their followers to remember those figures. This happens in many Sufi orders (*tarekat*) in Java, particularly when the founders or senior leaders of these groups have died and no one, including their own children, possesses the charismatic qualities that their fathers had. This is one reason why stories about the founder's *karamah* and religious advice are frequently told to the followers of the *Dhikr al- Ghāfilīn* on numerous occasions. In addition, some groups not only collect and publish the religious advice presented by *Gus* Mik but also print his picture so that he can be remembered by his followers. The formation of these groups under the same name following the death of the founders of the *Dhikr al-Ghāfilīn*has led to competing claims about which groups are more worthy of representing the founders to their followers. Some leaders have tried to identify their groups as distinctive and 'authentic' compared to others. For example, *Gus* Sabut, one of leaders of these groups, claimed that his father, *Gus* Mik, was not only the founder, a central leader (I., *Tokoh Sentral*), and spiritual master (A., *murshid*) of the group, but also the only one who created the formula of the *Dhikr al-Ghāfilīn* (I., *Pencipta Tunggal Dhikr al- Ghāfilīn*).

19 Interview with Abdul Qadir, Kediri, September, 2004.

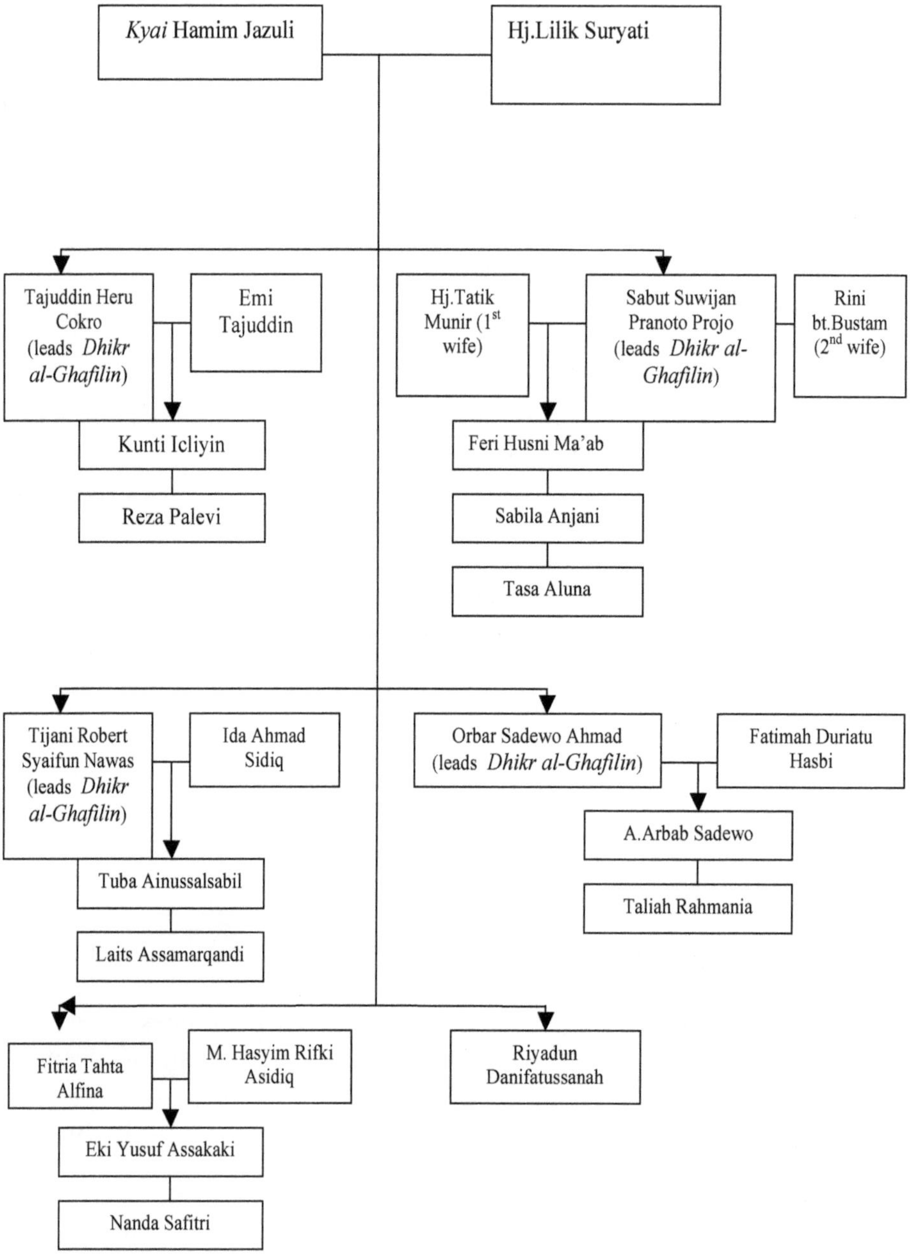

Figure 6.1. Kyai Hamim Jazuli's (Gus Mik's) Family.

Source : Biographi Kyai Djazuli Usman, n.d.

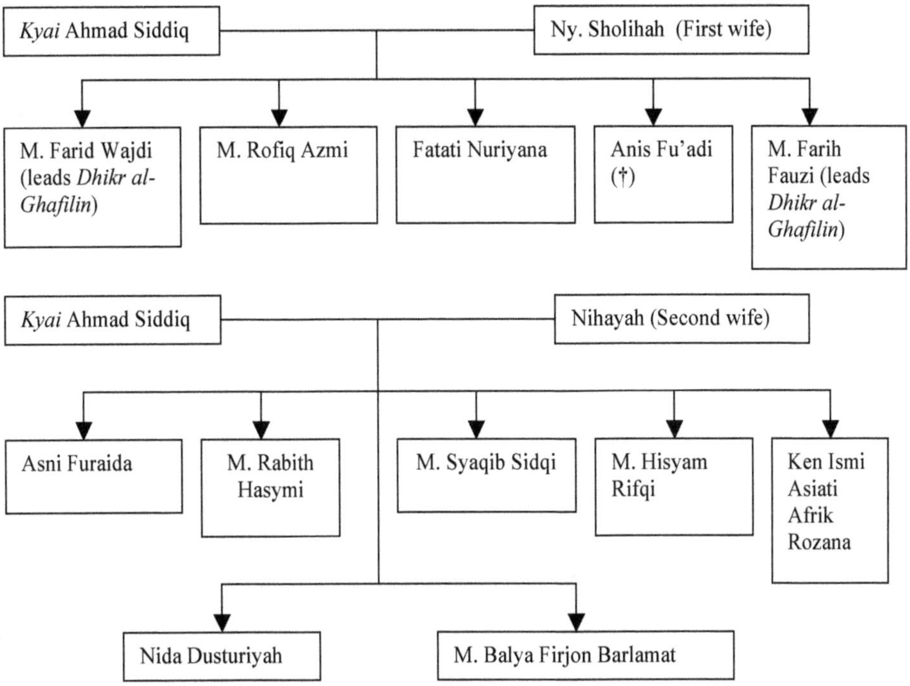

Figure 6.2. Kyai Ahmad Siddīq's Family.

Source: Interview with Gus Farih Fauzi

According to Sabut, other figures like *Kyai* Aḥmad Ṣiddīq were asked by *Gus* Mik to write the formula of *Dhikr al-Ghāfilīn* but were not founders of the group. By doing this, *Gus* Sabut probably wishes to convince his followers and others that his group and his brothers' groups are more authentic than other groups. He is also responding to *Gus* Farih's claim that the *Dhikr al-Ghāfilīn* was established not only by *Gus* Mik but also by *Kyai* Ahmad Siddiq and *Kyai* 'Abd al-Ḥamid who both contributed to its formula. *Gus* Farih told me that the formula was not created by *Gus* Mik alone but it was collected from one of prayers created by several prominent Muslim scholars and Sufi, and that *Kyai* Ahmad Siddiq was a compiler of those prayers. An example of claims made by these leaders can be seen clearly from a comparison of the covers of the manual published by their groups below:

Plate 6.4: The front cover of the Dhikr al-Ghafīlīn book published by Gus Sabut Panoto Projo.

Plate 6.5: The back cover of the Dhikr al-Ghafīlīn book published by Gus Sabut Panoto Projo.

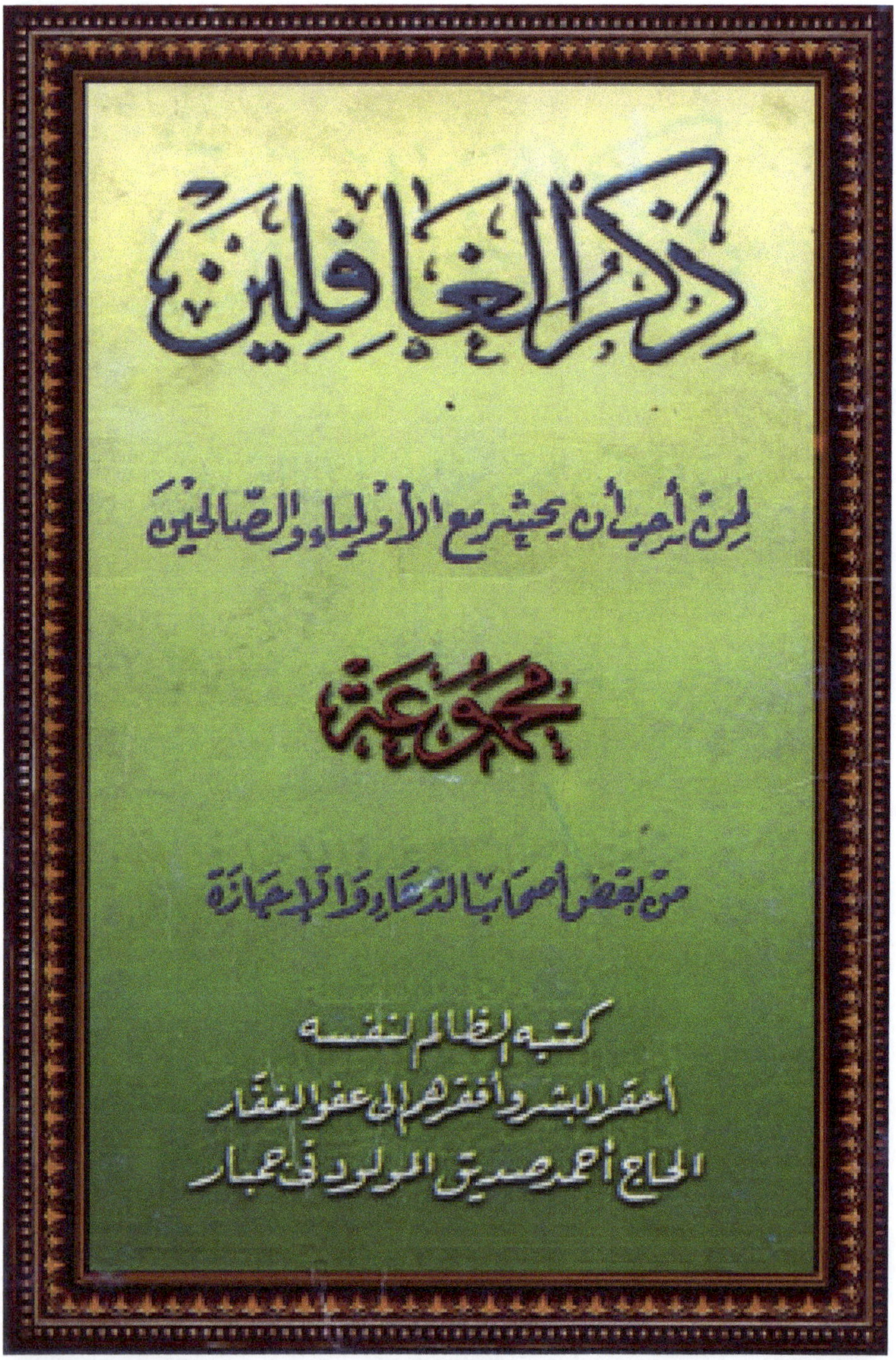

Plate 6.6: The front cover of the Dhikr al-Ghafīlīn book published by Gus Farih Fauzi.

Plate 6.7: The back cover of the Dhikr al-Ghafī līn book published by Gus Farih Fauzi.

The front cover of the manual of *Dhikr al-Ghāfilīn* (Plate 6.4) shows *Gus* Mik as the founder, *Tokoh Sentral* and *murshid* (the sole composer of the formula). In contrast, instead of putting the picture of his father, *Kyai*Ahmad Siddiq, on the front page or his own picture, *Gus* Farih puts the following long sentence indicating that his father was a compiler of the formula collected from one of the owners of these prayers with proper *ijāzat* (authorisation) (Plate 6.6):

> The book was written by a person who is unjust to himself, the lowest human and who is the most in need of forgiveness from the Most-Forgiving, Haji Ahmad Shiddiq, born in Jember.[20]

Both books cite the motto of the group, which is that group is intended for those who want to gather with the saints and pious people. Plate 6.6 notes that Sabut Panoto Projo (the son of *Gus* Mik) is the coordinator of the *Dhikr al-Ghāfilīn* on Friday night Kliwon at *Gus* Mik's grave. In contrast, Plate 6.8 has a picture of three founders. This is intended to show the public that *Dhikr al-Ghāfilīn* was the creation of these three persons: *Kyai* Ahamad Siddiq, *Gus* Mik, and *Kyai* al-Hamid.

Like their predecessors, these various *dhikr* groups do not have the structure of other modern organizations, equipped with a deputy leader, secretary, treasurer

20 *Majmū'atun min ba'ḍi aṣḥābi al-du'āī wa al-ijāza* (it is collected from one of the owners of prayers and *ijāzat*). *Katabahū al-ẓālimu linafsihī Aḥqaru al-bashari wa Afqarahum ilā 'afwi al-Ghaffāri al-hāj Aḥmad Ṣiddīq al-maulūdi fī Jimbāra.*

and registered membership. As a result, all the activities of these groups are controlled by the leaders of these groups. Some of these leaders even handle administrative matters personally. For example, during my fieldwork, a leader of one group sent a short message to invite me and my friends to one of the group's rituals. These groups do not even have an office to handle activities and administrative matters. In order to hold a major ritual event such as the commemoration of a founder's death, these groups usually form temporary committees. When these activities have completed their work, the leaders of the group then dismiss the committee.

The leaders of these groups do not have any particular method to obtain financial funding to support and run the activities of their groups. They rarely ask their members to give money and charity to them. However, they distribute donation boxes among their members during regular weekly or *selapanan* rituals. Money collected from these events will be used not only to operate these groups but also for the operating expenses at the particular places where these rituals are held, such as the electricity bill at a grave, for the custodian (I., *juru kunci*), and for cleaning fees. The leaders strongly encourage donations when the groups need funding for particular purposes. For example, when I was in the field, *Gus* Farih, a leader one of the groups, who held a regular ritual at the famous pilgrimage site of Mbah Wasil's tomb in the city centre of Kediri, needed to buy another sound system because the participants in the ritual was so numerous that the old sound system in the inner area of the tomb was not powerful enough to be heard by participants sitting outside the area. Therefore *Gus* Farih urged his *jamaah* to donate money to the group to buy a new sound system.

6.7. Conclusion

This chapter has examined that the role played by the late *Gus* Mik in developing and maintaining the continuity of the *Dhikr al-Ghāfilīn* group. Through his charisma and *karamah, Gus* Mik was able to practice *dakwah* in an unusual way, i.e. among those categorised as *orang malam,* nightclub visitors and gamblers. However, after his death, his *karamah* and charisma could not be passed on to his sons. None of his sons or other leaders of these groups are able to engage in this unusual practice of *dakwah.* As a result, the leaders of the current *Dhikr al-Ghāfilīn* groups confine their *dakwah* activities to people who engage in the ritual practices of these groups.

Chapter VII

Conclusion

The main object of this study has been to examine the emergence of forms of Islamic spirituality in Indonesia identified as *Majlis Dhikr.* Various *Majlis Dhikr* offer similar Islamic ritual practices to those of the increasing popular *tarekat* in Indonesia. I have argued in this study that despite criticism from other Indonesian Muslims, the ritual practices of *Majlis Dhikr* can be legitimately accepted as proper Islamic ritual since the aim of these practices is to attain closeness to God and His Prophet. Throughout this work, I have presented a wide-ranging discussion of *Majlis Dhikr* groups. Most of their rituals are observable because they are widespread in many areas of Java. This discussion includes consideration as to how *Majlis Dhikr* groups regard their practices within Islam despite the criticism from Indonesian Salafi groups and members of Indonesian *tarekat.* I also consider the extent to which the teachings and ritual of *Majlis Dhikr* groups are related to the teachings of the Qur'an, hadith and Islamic teaching and orthodox Sufism. I then examine how *Majlis Dhikr* groups disseminate their teachings and the role of *pesantren* in spreading these groups. In this concluding chapter I summarise the findings of this study and offer answers to the research questions posed in Chapter I, emphasizing the contribution this work has endeavoured to make to the scholarly literature.

The prediction of some Indonesianists that Sufi groups, along with their rural Muslim scholar proponents, would disappear from the Indonesian landscape as Indonesian society modernised has proved to be flawed. This study has provided evidence that *Majlis Dhikr* have proliferated among rural and urban people and continue to attract new membership, following on the increasing popularity of Sufi *tarekat.* Not only have peasants increased their interest in Majlis Dhikr, the urban middle class and many educated Muslims have been attracted to join *Majlis Dhikr* groups. The central figures in these *Majlis Dhikr* groups are *kyai* (Muslim scholars) or *ustādh* (Muslim teachers) who have mostly graduated from *pesantren.* In contrast to the predicted decline in Sufism, *pesantren* have continued to produce Muslim scholars (*kyai*) both in rural and urban Javanese areas who play an important role not only in inculcating Islamic values and norms in the lives of Muslims but also in developing *Majlis Dhikr* as venues for practising Islamic ritual.

However, despite this, there have been criticism of the emergence of *Majlis Dhikr* groups as a new phenomenon of Islamic spiritual practice in Indonesia. The most notable criticism comes from two different groups, either from supporters of *tarekat* or from members of Indonesian Salafi groups such as *Dewan Dakwah Islamiah Indonesia* (The Indonesian Council for Islamic Preaching, DDII). The followers of *tarekat* have particularly addressed the issue of the validity of *isnād* (transmission) in *Majlis Dhikr,* since such groups do not have an unbroken line of links between their founders and the Prophet. In contrast, the Salafi have criticised the way *Majlis Dhikr* groups recite *dhikr* vocally and in unison, and have charged them with *bid'ah* and heresy because such practices, it is claimed, were never practised by the Prophet and his Companions. Despite these criticisms, these *Majlis Dhikr* groups regard their ritual as legitimate practice that offers an alternative to *tarekat* for Muslims to practise Islamic spirituality. In responding to the issue of the *isnād,* members of *Majlis Dhikr* group have argued that their ritual does not necessarily need a chain of transmission (*isnād*) back to the Prophet since what they practise in their ritual, such as reciting *Ṣalāwa,*was strongly recommended by the Prophet himself. Furthermore, they argue that even though their groups are not regarded as *mu'tabarah* by the *Jam'iyyah Ahl al-Thariqah al-Mu'tabarah,* the Forum for *tarekat mu'tabarah* in Indonesia within Nahdlatul Ulama, this does not necessarily mean that their *dhikr* ritual should be prohibited since the aim of this ritual is similar to that of *dhikr* rituals conducted by *tarekat*, namely to attain closeness to God.

In order to prove that their ritual practices are legitimate, *Majlis Dhikr* groups have based their argument not only on the prescriptions of the Qur'an and hadith, but also on the views of authoritative Muslim scholars. Based on their understanding and interpretation of these sources, members of *Majlis Dhikr* groups believe that their ritual of vocal recitation of *dhikr* in unison is both lawful and sanctioned by God and His Prophet. Closer examination of the debates involving the proponents and opponents of *Majlis Dhikr* in Indonesia reveals that both parties base their arguments on the interpretation of Qur'anic verses, hadith and the views of Muslim scholars. In addition, both groups have similar views on the practice of *dhikr,* but they differ on the particular issue of whether the recitation of *dhikr* has to be conducted in unison and recited vocally or has to be conducted individually and quietly. Their differences are due to different interpretations of the textual evidence, not to presence or absence of textual evidence. As argued by Quraish Shihab, a renowned Indonesian exegete, in the matter of interpretation, no one can regard their interpretation as absolutely true, while regarding other interpretations as false. This is partly because when one group of Muslims gives its interpretation of a particular religious text, this is commonly challenged by another group of Muslims. The interpretation of one group of Muslims is therefore only absolute for them, but not for another group (Shihab 1992:219-220).

Different interpretations of some aspects of Islamic teaching will happen in part when Muslims discuss multi-interpretable texts of the Qur'an and hadith. In the case of debates about the *dhikr* ritual in Indonesia, therefore I argue in this study that both the proponents and opponents of *Majlis Dhikr* base their views on interpretable Islamic teachings; as a result one should not regard one group as being truly Islamic, while accusing the other Muslim group of practising *bid'ah* and superstition in this matter. Furthermore, I argue that interpretations can be regarded as belonging to the field of *ijtihad* which allows the use of all the capabilities of reason in deducing a conclusion based on the Qur'an and hadith. If this is the case, one can expect different results of *ijtihad* among Muslims scholars. Muslims should not therefore claim that their own results of *ijtihad* are deemed to be true, while others' *ijtihad* are false, because all of such efforts will be justified later in the hereafter. If the result is true according to the meaning and purpose of God and the Prophet's purpose, then it will have two rewards. In contrast, if the result is wrong because it does not agree with God's and the Prophet's purpose, it will have only one reward.

This study also offers important findings about the extent to which *Majlis Dhikr* groups comply with the teachings of the Qur'an, hadith and orthodox Sufism. In relation to this question, I have examined several aspects of *Majlis Dhikr* ritual, including their usage of *Ṣalāwa* as a means to approach God, their concept of sainthood (*wali*), seeking intermediaries (*tawassul*), sending the merit of pious deeds to deceased persons, and seeking blessing (*tabarruk*). In these ritual aspects, rather than innovating within Islam (I., *melaksanakan bid'ah*), *Majlis Dhikr* groups rely heavily on the prescriptions of the Qur'an, hadith, and the views of authoritative Muslim theologians. Interestingly, their theological responses in these aspects are similar to those prevalent in the practices of major Sufi groups in Java. Therefore, in this sense, despite their *ghairu mu'tabarah* status according to the *Jam'iyyah, Majlis Dhikr* groups can be considered to be in accordance with orthodox Sufi teachings, which still stress the importance of the observance of *sharī'a*. In this sense, these groups can serve as an alternative venue for Indonesian Muslims to practice the inner aspects of Islam.

Majlis Dhikr groups in Java function as a venue for Muslims to practise *dhikr* ritual and to seek spiritual closeness to God; they also serve as institutions for deepening and preaching Islamic values (I., *dakwah Islam*). This study examines how specific *Majlis Dhikr* groups employ different strategies to do this. For instance, in order to spread its teachings in particular and to preach Islamic values in general, the *Wāḥidiyat* group has been opened by its proponents to all people regardless of their age, cultural or religious background. With this strategy, this group accepts people from different religions to join and practise the group's ritual without asking them to convert to Islam. Further, in order to attract new followers, this group has stressed the efficacy of its *dhikr* formula not only to solve the problems commonly faced by people but also to effectively obtain *ma'rifatullah* (Gnosis of God), the highest achievement in Sufi practice.

In contrast, the *Istighāthat Iḥsāniyyat,* another *Majlis Dhikr,* uses a different strategy to promote Islamic values and teachings among Muslims. Since the *Istighāthat Iḥsāniyyat* group was established initially to attract those who have been categorised sociologically as marginalised people and theologically as nominal Muslims, it has tried to accommodate cultural aspects which are prevalent among these people into its *dakwah.* In line with this approach, this group allows Javanese popular arts such as the hobby-horse dance (J., *jaranan*), tiger-masked dance (I., *reog*), *dangdutan,* Chinese dragon dance (J., *leang-leong*), and *ruwatan* to be performed on the annual anniversary of *Iḥsāniyyat.* Including such Javanese popular arts within the framework of *pesantren* and Sufi group is unusual. Moreover, this group also applies the strategy 'from tombs to mosques' (I., *dari kubur ke masjid*) in order to attract people to join the group. They have found that it is easier to ask such people to come to the tombs than directly to a mosque. It is expected that once these people have enough Islamic knowledge and have practised Islam, they will voluntarily come to the mosque. Through such methods, the presence of these *Majlis Dhikr* groups in the landscape of Indonesian Islam has contributed to narrowing the gap between *santri* Muslims and nominal Muslims, who have long been ideologically opposed to one another. Moreover, in implementing Sufi *dakwah* and religious tolerance, the *Istighāthat Iḥsāniyyat* group also allows people from different religions to join the group without asking them to convert to Islam. This strategy helps to create a peaceful religious life in Indonesia.

Similar to the *Iḥsāniyyat,* the *Dhikr al-Ghāfilīn* group uses tombs as a venue for attracting members. Like the *Iḥsāniyyat,* in addition to holding a *dhikr* ritual at Muslim saints' tombs, this group also gives religious lectures (*ceramah agama*) during the ritual in the expectation that people will not only gain spiritual enlightenment by reciting *dhikr* but also obtain knowledge of Islamic teachings and values. Furthermore, in order to spread its influence, this group accentuates the figure of the founder of the group as an icon to attract new members. This strategy is not unique among *Majlis Dhikr* groups whose current leaders are not as charismatic as their founders. The *Dhikr al-Ghāfilīn* group in particular seems to rely on this strategy because none of its leaders has the same capability as the late *Gus* Mik, the original founder of *Dhikr al-Ghāfilīn* who was known among people as a *wali.*

My study also clearly shows that *pesantren* have played an important role in the maintenance and the development of these *Majlis Dhikr* groups. Most of the leaders of these groups have graduated from *pesantren,* and they are mostly the sons of *kyai* from famous *pesantren* in East Java. As a result, they have used their *pesantren* networks to spread their groups. The networks of alumni of particular *pesantren* have been important in the dissemination of *Majlis Dhikr* groups to wherever these alumni live. In this way, some *pesantren* not only function as places for educating students about Islamic knowledge but have also become centres for the teaching and the propagation of *Majlis Dhikr.* Students of these *pesantren* are obliged to practise and join the recitation of *dhikr* held by these groups. One *pesantren, Pesantren* Kedunglo, where *Majlis Dhikr Ṣalāwa Wāḥidiyat* is based, even obliges its students to propagate the teachings of the group when they have graduated and returned home.

The role played by *pesantren* in the maintenance and development of *Majlis Dhikr* indicates that they are effective places to maintain both the outer and inner aspects of Islam on Java. A similar role has been revealed by previous studies on the role of *pesantren* in the maintenance of Sufism in Java. Such studies have noted that *pesantren* in Java can be divided into two categories. The first maintains Sufism without being necessarily being affiliated with a particular *tarekat, a*lthough they nevertheless practise *dhikr* and *wirid* as in *tarekat,* and apply Sufi teachings in daily life. The second category is that of *pesantren* that specialise in the teaching and the development of *tarekat.* This study has added another category of *pesantren* in Java, that is, *pesantren* that not only practise *dhikr* and *wird* regularly but also organise and establish *Majlis Dhikr* groups and propagate these among people outside the *pesantren.*

One point which needs to be emphasised is that *pesantren* and *tarekat* in Java have been conceived by previous researchers as inseparable institutions for the maintenance of traditional Islam within the Javanese Muslim community. Most *pesantren* in Java function as places to mould students with Islamic knowledge, while some of them also function as instruments for the recruitment of members of *tarekat,* which are organized around the figure of a particular scholar and teacher. This study highlights the rise of new Islamic spiritual groups in Java, the *Majlis Dhikr,* which suggests that another institution should be taken into account when considering the maintenance of traditional Islam among Javanese.

It has been argued that Indonesia has undergone an Islamic revival since 1970's (Howell 2001). This resurgence is measured by scholars in considering phenomena as diverse as the boom in the publication of books on Islam, the reinvigoration of Islamic political parties, the prevalence of Muslim fashion among middle class urban population, the growing number of mosques, the appearance of new forms of student activity on university campuses, and the establishment of Islamic banking. This kind of representation of Indonesia's Islamic revival puts too much emphasis on the outer aspects of Islam, while tending to ignore the increasing popularity of Islamic spiritual expression as articulated by the proliferation of both Sufi groups and *Majlis Dhikr* groups in urban and rural areas. This study has attempted to redress this imbalance by enriching perspectives on the development of Islam in Indonesia, while presenting another piece of evidence for Islamic revival in Indonesia.

Appendix

Names of Tarekat Considered As Mu'tabarah by Jam'iyyat Ahl al-Tarīqat al-Mu'tabarat al-Nahdliyyat in Its 9th Congress held in Pekalongan, Central Java. (26-28 February 2000)

1. Rumiyyah	25. Ghazaliyyah
2. Rifaiyyah	26. Hamzawiyyah
3. Sai'diyyah	27. Haddadiyyah
4. Bakriyyah	28. Madbuliyyah
5. Justiyyah	29. Sumbuliyyah
6. Umariyyah	30. Idrusiyyah
7. Alawiyyah	31. Uthmaniyyah
8. Abasiyyah	32. Shadhiliyyah
9. Zainiyyah	33. Sha'baniyyah
10. Dasuqiyyah	34. Kalshaniyyah
11. Akbariyyah	35. Khadliriyyah
12. Bayumiyyah	36. Shattariyyah
13. Malamiyyah	37. Khalwatiyyah
14. Ghaiyyah	38. Bakdashiyyah
15. Tijaniyyah	39. Shuhruwiyyah
16. Uwasiyyah	40. Thariqah Almadiyyah
17. Idrisiyyah	41. 'Isawiyyah
18. Samaniyyah	42. Thuruqil Akabiril Auliya'
19. Buhuriyyah	43. Qadiriyah wa Naqshabandiyyah
20. Usyaqiyyah	44. Khalidiyyah wa Naqshabandiyyah
21. Kubrawiyyah	45. Junaid al-Baghdadi
22. Maulawiyyah	46. Ahli Mulazamatil Qur'an wa Sunnah wa Dala'ilil
23. Jalwatiyyah	47. Khairati Wa Ta'limi Fathil Qaribi au Kifayatil Awami
24. Bairumiyyah	

Bibliography

Abdurrahman, Moeslim

1978 Sufism in Kediri. *In* Dialog. Pp. 23-40. Jakarta.

Abu Bakr, bin Muhammad bin As-Sayyid Al-Hanbali

2004 Karamah Wali Menurut Pandangan Ahlussunnah Wal Jama'ah. D.S. MS, transl. Jakarta: Darus Sunnah Press.

Al-Albāni, Muḥammad Nāsir al-Dīn

1975 Al-Tawassul: An wā'uhū wa Aḥkāmuhū. Beirut: Rasail al-Da'wah al-Salafiyyah.

Al-Ghazālī, Abu Ḥāmid Muḥammad ibn Muḥammad

1973 Ihyā' 'Ulūm al-Dīn. Volume III. Egypt: Mustafa al-Babi al-Halabi wa Auladihi.

Al-Hilali, Muḥammad Taqiyy al-Dīn, Muḥammad Muḥsin Khan

1996 The Noble Qur'an: Transliteration in Roman Script with Original Arabic Text (Mushaf Al-Madinah). Saudi Arabia: Darussalam.

Al-Hujwirī, Syed Ali bin Uthmān

1997 Kashful Maḥjūb. M.W.B. Rabbani, transl. Kuala Lumpur: A.S. Noordeen.

Al-Jauziyah, Ibnu Qayyim

1999 Roh. K. Suhardi, transl. Jakarta: Pustaka Al-Kautsar.

Al-Mālikī, Muḥammad ibn 'Alwi

1993 Mafāhim Yajib An Tusaḥḥaḥ. Cairo: Dar Jawāmi' al-Kalam.

Al-Mālikī, Muḥammad ibn 'Alwi

N.d. Tahqīq al-Amal Fī Mā Yanfa' al-Mayyiti min al-A'māl. Cairo: Dar Jawāmi' al-Kalam.

Al-Mukaffi, Abdurraḥman

2003 Rapot Merah AA Gym: MQ di Penjara Tasawuf. Jakarta: Darul Falah.

Al-Nabhānī, Yusuf b. Ismail
N.d. Sa'adat al-Daraini Fi Salat 'ala Sayyidi al-Kaunaini Sallawahu 'Alaihi Wasallam. Beirut: Dar al-Kutub al-'Ilmiyya.

Al-Qurṭūbī
2006, al-Jāmi' li Aḥkām al-Qur'ān. Jordan: Aal al-Bayt Institute for Islamic Thought, viewed 14 July 2006, 11:00 am,http://www.altafsir.com/Tafasir.asp?tMadhNo=0&tTafsirNo=5&tSoraNo=10&tAyahNo=62&tDisplay=yes&UserProfile=0.

Al-Tabari
2002 Jāmi' al-Bayān fī Tafsīr al-Qur'ān. Jordan: Aal al-Bayt Institute for Islamic Thought, viewed 13 July 2006, 10:00 am, http://www.altafsir.com/Tafasir.asp?tMadhNo=0&tTafsirNo=1&tSoraNo=10&tAyahNo=62&tDisplay=yes&Page=2&Size=1.

Al-Zamakhshārī
2006 Tafsīr al-Kashshāf,Aal al-Bayt. Jordan: Institute for Islamic Thought, viewed 14 July 2006,10:30 am, http://www.altafsir.com/Tafasir.asp?tMadhNo=0&tTafsirNo=2&tSoraNo=10&tAyahNo=62&tDisplay=yes&UserProfile=0.

Amien, Shiddiq
2005 Persis dan Tantangan Dakwah. *In* Pikiran Rakyat. Bandung, viewed 13 January 2007, 10:00am,
http://www.pikiran-rakyat.com/cetak/2005/0905/03/0801.htm

Amsaka, Abu
2003 Koreksi Dzikir Jamaa'ah Mohammad Arifin Ilham. Jakarta: Darul Falah.

Anonymous
1423a Berdana Sebagai Penyempurna Iman dan Makrifat. *In* Aham. Pp. 31-32, Vol. 44.

Anonymous
1423b DKW Adalah Mustahiq. *In* Aham. Pp. 9, Vol. VI.

Anonymous
1424a Romo Yahi ra. Menunggui Kanak-kanak Yang Sedang Menghafal Shalawat Wahidiyah. *In* Aham. Pp. 38, Vol. VI.

Anonymous
1424b Sumbangan Pendapatan dan Zakat. *In* Aham. Pp. 30-31, Vol. VI.

Anonymous
1425a Adab Membaca Shalawat Wahidiyah. *In* Aham. Pp. 23, Vol. VII.

Anonymous
1425b Menentukan Pilihan Dengan Taqdiimul Aham fal Aham tsummal Anfa' fal Anfa'. *In* Aham. Pp. 30, Vol. VII.

Anonymous
1425c Wahidiyah Menatap Masa Depan. *In* Aham. Pp. 10-14, Vol. VII.

Anonymous
1985 5 Undang-undang Baru di Bidang Politik Serta Peraturan-peraturan Pelaksanaannya. Jakarta: Ghalia Indonesia.

Anonymous
1989 Bahan Up Grading Da'i Wahidiyah Bagian B. Kediri: Penyiar Shalawat Wahidiyah Pusat.

Anonymous
1996 Tuntunan Mujahadah dan Acara-acara Wahidiyah. Jombang: Dewan Pimpinan Pusat Penyiar Sholawat Wahidiyah.

Anonymous
1999a Bahan Up Grading Da'i Wahidiyah Bagian A. Kediri: Yayasan Perjuangan Wahidiyah dan Pondok Pesantren Kedunglo.

Anonymous
1999b Kumpulan Teks Kuliah Wahidiyah. Kediri: Departemen Pembina Wanita Wahidiyah Pusat.

Anonymous
2000 Hasil-hasil Muktamar IX Jam'iyyah Ahlith Thoriqoh al-Mu'tabaraoh al-Nahdliyyah. Pekalongan: Sekretariat Muktamar IX.

Anonymous
N.d.-a Dhikr al-Ghāfilīn Li man Aḥabba An Yuhshara Ma'a al-Auliyā' wa al-Ṣalihīn. Kediri: Jama'ah Dzikrul Ghāfilīn Rutin Malam Jum'at Kliwon di Makam Gus Mik.

Anonymous
N.d.-a Kuliah Wahidiyah Untuk Menjernihkan Hati dan Ma'rifat Billah Wa Birosulihi. Kediri: Yayasan Perjuangan Wahidiyah dan Pondok Pesantren Kedunglo Kota Kediri Jawa Timur.

Anonymous
N.d.-b Pedoman Pokok-Pokok Ajaran Wahidiyah. kediri: Yayasan Perjuangan Wahidiyah dan Pondok Pesantren Kedunglo.

Anwar, C. Ramli Bihar
2002 Bertasawuf Tanpa Tarekat. Jakarta: Penerbit IIMAN dan Hikmah

Aqib, Kharisudin
1999 Al-Hikmah: Memahami Teosofi Tarekat Qadiriyah Wa Naqsyabandiyah. Surabaya: Dunia Ilmu.

Ash-Shiddieqy, Hasbi
1964 Pedoman Dzikir dan Do'a. Jakarta: Bulan Bintang.

Asy'ari, Hasyim
2005 Sang Kyai Fatwa, KH.M.Hasyim Asy'ari. Yogyakarta: Qirtas.

Badruzzaman, Ahmad Dimyati
2003 Zikir Berjamaah: Sunnah Atau Bid'ah. Jakatra: Penerbit Republika.

Bakri
N.d I'ānat al-Ṭālibīn. Volume IV. Bandung, Indonesia: Syirkah al-Ma'arif.

Bawani, Imam
1981 Profil K.H. Abdul Madjid Ma'ruf Kedunglo - Kediri. Pp. 1-31. Jakarta: Proyek Penelitian Keagamaan Badan Penelitian dan Pengembangan Agama Departemen Agama R.I.

Brown, Jason
2000 The Banyuwangi Murders, Why Did Over a Hundred Black Magic Practitioners Die in East Java Late in 1998?, viewed 13 October 2006, 11:00 am, http://www.insideindonesia.org/edit62/jason.htm.

Bruinessen, Martin Van
1990 Books in Arabic Script used in the *Pesantren* Milieu. Bijdragen tot de taal-, land- en volkenkunde 146:226-269.

Bruinessen, Martin Van
1992 Tarekat Naqsyabandiyah di Indonesia. Bandung: Mizan.

Bruinessen, Martin Van
1995 Tarekat and Tarekat Teachers in Madurese Society. *In* Across Madura Strait: The Dynamics of an Insular Society. H.d.J.a.E. Touwen-Bouwsma, ed. Pp. 108-115. Leiden: KITLV Press.

Buinessen, Martin Van
1999 Controversies and Polemics Involving the Sufi Orders in Twentieth-Century Indonesia. *In* Islamic Mysticism Contested B.R. Frederick De Jong ed. Pp. 705-728. Leiden Brill.

Colin, G S
1978 Baraka. *In* The Encyclopaedia of Islam. B. Lewis, J.H. Kramers, and J. Schacht, eds. Leiden: E.J. Brill.

Dahlan, Iḥsān
N.d Sirāj al-Ṭālibīn Sharḥ Minhāj al-ʻĀbidīn. 2 vols. Volume 1. Surabaya: Al-Hidayah.

Damarhuda, and Imawan Mashuri
2005 Zikir Penyembuhan Ala Ustadz Haryono. Surabaya: Pustaka Zikir.

Dhofier, Z.
1982 Tradisi Pesantren: Studi Tentang Pandangan Hidup Kyai. Jakarta: LP3ES.

Dhofier, Z.
1999 The Pesantren Tradition The Role of the Kyai in the Maintenance of Traditional Islam in Java. Arizona: Program for Southeast Asian Studies Arizona State University.

Djaelani, Abdul Qadir
1996 Koreksi Terhadap Ajaran Tasawuf. Jakarta: Gema Insani Press.

El-Ahmad, Bajuri
1993 Tiga Hari Wafatnya Gus Mik, Seluruh Jama'ah Semaan 'Mantab' Masi Berduka. *In* Karya Darma, Surabaya, June 8: 1.

Ewing, Katherine P.
1990 The Dream of Spiritual Initiation and the Organization of Self Representations among Pakistani Sufis. American Ethnologist 17(1):56-74.

Ewing, Katherine Pratt
1997 Arguing Sainthood. Durham: Duke University Press.

Fealy, Greg, Virginia Hooker, and Sally White
2006 Indonesia. *In* Voices of Islam in Southeast Asia: A Contemporary Sourcebook. G. Fealy and V. Hooker, eds. Pp. 43-44. Singapore: Institute of Southeast Asian Studies.

Fierro, Maribel
1992 The Treatises Against Innovations *(Kutub al-Bida'i).* Der Islam 69(2):205-246.

Fox, James J.
2004 Currents in Contemporary Islam in Indonesia. Harvard Asia Vision 21, Massachusetts, 2004, pp. 1-24. Unpublished.

Fox, James J.
1991 Ziarah Visits to the Tombs of Wali, the Founder of Islam on Java. In Islam in Indonesian Social Context. M.C. Ricklefs, ed. Melbourne: CSEAS Monash University.

Fox, James J.
2002 Interpreting the Historical Significance of Tombs and Chronicles in Contemporary Java. *In* The Potent Dead: Ancestors, Saints and Heroes in Contemporary Indonesia. Henri Chambert-Loir and Anthony Reid, eds. Honolulu: Allen and Unwin and University of Hawaii Press.

Gade, Anna M.
2004 Perfection Makes Practice: Learning, Emotion, and the Recited Qur'an in Indonesia. Honolulu: University of Hawaii Press.

Gibb, H.A.R.
1996 Encyclopaedia of Islam. Leiden: E.J. Brill.

Gilsenan, Michael
1973 Saint and Sufi in Modern Egypt: An Essay in the Sociology of Religion. Oxford: The Clarendon Press.

Gilsenan, Michael
1992 Recognizing Islam: Religion and Society in the Modern Middle East. London: I.B. Tauris.

Hallaq, Wael B
Innovation. *In* The Encyclopaedia of Qur'an. Pp. 536-537. Leiden: EJ Brill.

Hamka
1990 Tasawuf Modern. Jakarta: Pustaka Panjimas.

Haryono, Ustadz
2006 Amalan Doa-doa Penyembuh, Enteng Jodoh Pembuka Aura dan Pemenuh Segala Kebutuhan. Depok: Penerbit Berkah.

Hasan, Muhammad Tholhah
2006 Ahlussunnah Wal-Jama'ah Dalam Persepsi dan Tradisi NU. Jakarta: Lantabora Press.

Hidayat, Sholihin
1993a Derita itu Dianggap Nikmat. *In* Jawa Pos. Surabaya, June 6:1.

Hidayat, Sholihin
1993b Setelah Gus Mik, Siapa ke Makam Auliya'? *In* Jawa Pos. Surabaya, June 9:1

Hooker, Virginia
2006 Personal Expressions of Faith. *In* Voices of Islam in Southeast Asia: A Contemporary Sourcebook. G. Fealy and V. Hooker, eds. Singapore: Institute of Southeast Asian Studies.

Howell, Julia Day
2001 Sufism and the Indonesian Islamic Revival. The Journal of Asian Studies 60(3):701-729.

Howell, Julia D, M.A. Subandi, and Peter L. Nelson
2001 New Faces of Indonesian Sufism: A Demographic Profile of Tarekat Qodiriyyah-Naqsyabandiyyah, Pesantren Suralaya, in the 1990s. Review of Indonesian and Malaysian Affairs 35(2):33-60.

Ibad, Mn.
Bulan dan Matahari: Kumpulan Dawuh KH. Hamim Jazuly (GusMik). Surabaya: Unesa University Press.

Ibn Kathīr
2006, Tafsīr al-Qur'ān al-Karīm. Jordan: Aal al-Bayt Institute for Islamic Thought, viewed 14 July 2006, 10:45 am, http://www.altafsir.com/Tafasir.asp?tMadhNo=0&tTafsirNo=7&tSoraNo=10&tAyahNo=62&tDisplay=yes&UserProfile=0.

Imran, AM
1990 Kitab Manakib Syekh ABdulQadir Jaelani Merusak Aqidah Islam. Bangil: Amprint.

Jahar, Asep Saipudin
1999 Abu Ishaq Al-Shatibi's Reformulation of the Concept of Bid'ah: A Study of His *Al-I'tiṣām*, McGill University.

Jaiz, Hartono Ahmad
2004 Aliran dan Paham Sesat di Indonesia. Jakarta: Pustaka Al-Kautsar.

Jaiz, Hartono Ahmad
1999 Gus Dur Wali?: Mendudukkan Tasawuf. Jakarta Darul Falah.

Jawapos
1993 Masih banyak yang Bertakziah ke Makam Gus Mik. *In* Jawa Pos. Surabaya, June 8:1

Jawas, Yazid Abdul Qadir
1423 Doa dan Wirid: Mengobati Guna-guna dan Sihir Menurut Al-Qur'an dan As-Sunnah. Bogor: Pustaka Imam Asy-Syafi'i.

Julian, Patrick Millie
2006 Splashed by The Saint: Ritual Reading and Islamic Sanctity in West Java, Leiden University.

Kalabadzi, Abu Bakar M.
1985 Ajaran-ajaran Sufi. Bandung: Penerbit Pustaka.

Madjid, Abdul Latif
1423a Krisis Iman Sumber Berbagai Krisis. *In* Aham. Pp. 20-25, Vol. V.

Madjid, Abdul Latif
1423b Menyelami Kedalaman Makrifat Wahidiyah. *In* Aham. Pp. 29-33, Vol. VI.

Madjid, Abdul Latif
1424 Kaum Ibu Pemegang Kunci Surga. *In* Aham. Pp. 18-22, Vol. IV.

Madjid, Abdul Latif
1425 Jangan Sekali-kali Meragukan Janji Allah. *In* Aham. Pp. 34-37, Vol. VII.

Madjid, Abdul Latif
1999 Tengah-tengahe Napung Datang Fadhal Allah SWT. *In* Aham. Pp. 10, Vol. III.

Madjid, Abdul Latif
2000a Back to Basic dengan Riadhah dan Mujahadah. *In* Aham. Pp. 30, Vol. IV.

Madjid, Abdul Latif
2000b Persoalan Wushul kepada Allah, Jangan Anggap Enteng. *In* Aham. Pp. 25-31, Vol. IV.

Madjid, Abdul Latif
2001 Wahidiyah Mengemban Misi Nubuwah. *In* Aham. Pp. 21-27, Vol. IV.

Manan, Abdul, Imam Sumaatmadja, and Veven Sp Wardhana
2001 Geger Santet Banyuwangi. Jakarta: Institute Studi Arus Informasi (ISAI).

Mansurnoor, Iik Arifin
1990 Islam in Indonesian World: Ulama of Madura. Yogyakarta: Gadjah Mada University Press.

Mantab, Sesepuh
N.d. Kumpulan Pidato Kyai Hamim Djazuli (*Gus* Mik). Nganjuk: Majelis Semaan Al-Qur'an "Mantab" dan Dzikrul Ghofilin Kabupaten Nganjuk.

Mufid, Ahmad Syafi'i
2006 Tangklukan, Abangan, dan Tarekat. Jakarta: Yayasan Obor Indonesia.

Mughni, Ahmad Busyra
1982 Syekh Muhammad Ihsan Dahlan. Kediri: Pesantren Jampes

Muhaimin, A.G
1995 The Islamic Traditions of Cirebeon: *Ibadat* and *Adat* Among Javanese Muslims, The Australian National University.

Muhaimin, A.G

2006 The Islamic Traditions of Cirebeon: *Ibadat* and *Adat* Among Javanese Muslims. Canberra: ANU E Press.

Muhammad, Husein

2004 Kitab Mu'tabar dan Ghayr Mu'tabar Versus Arus Liberatif Generasi Baru NU. Tashwirul Afkar 17:75-83.

Muhammad, K.H. Abdul Latif

N.d. Al-Ihsaniyyah. Kediri: Jama'ah Istighotsah Ihsaniyyah.

Muhaya, Abdul

1993 *Maqāmāt* (stations) and *Aḥwāl* (states) According to Al-Qusyairi and Al- Hujwiri : A Comparative Study, Mc Gill University.

Muryadi, Wahyu

1992 Kiai-kiai dengan Kekuatan Plus. *In* Tempo. Pp. 43-66, Vol. XXII.

Muttahid, Moh. Hisbi

2004 Efektifitas Istighasah Ihsaniyyah Dalam Mengembangkan Dakwah Islamiyah, Institut Agama Islam Tribakti (IAIT) Kediri.

Ni'am, Muhammad

2007 Bid'ah Secara Etimologis dan Terminologis. Indonesia: Pesantrenvirtual.com, viewed 20 March 2007, 12:00 am, http://www.pesantrenvirtual.com/index.php?option=com_contact&task=view&contact_id=1&Itemid=18.

Noorhaidi

2005 Laskar Jihad: Islam, Militancy, and the Quest for Identity in Post-New Order Indonesia, Utrecht University.

Penyiar Shalawat Wahidiyah, Dewan Pimpinan Pusat

N.d. Anggaran Dasar dan Anggaran Rumah Tangga Penyiar Shalawat Wahidiyah. Rejoagung Ngoro Jombang: Pesantren At-Tahdzib (PA).

Pijper, G.F.

1987 Fragmenta Islamica. Tudjimah, transl. Jakarta Penerbit Universitas Indonesia (UI-Press).

Pranowo, Bambang

1991 Traditional Islam in Rural Contemporary Java. *In* Islam in Indonesian Social Context. M.C. Ricklefs, ed. Pp. 39-55. Melbourne: CSEAS Monash University.

Qardhawi, Yusuf
1995 Fatwa-fatwa Kontemporer. Volume I. Jakarta: Gema Insani Press.

Qawa'id
1992 Tarekat Shiddiqiyah: Antara Kekhusukan dan Gerakan. Pesantren IX(1):89-96.

Qomar, Muzammil
2002 NU Liberal dari Tradisionalisme Ahlussunnah ke Universalisme Islam. Bandung: Mizan.

Qomari, Mukhtar
2003 Sejarah Dari Awal Perjuangan Wahidiyah. Kediri.

Qudamah, Ibn
N.d. Al-Mughnī: Saudi Arabia: Wizara al-Syuūn al-Islāmiyyat wa al-Auqāfwaal-Da'wa wa al-Irshād. viewed 12 April 2006, 10:00 pm. http://feqh.alislam.com/Display.asp?DocID=21&MaksamID=6317&ParagraphID=6435&Sharh=0.

Radtke, Bernd, and John O'kane
1996 The Concept of Sainthood in Early islamic Mysticism. Richmond Surrey: CurzonPress.

Rahim, Saiful
N.d. Merah Darah Santet di Banyuwangi. PT Metro Pos.

Rahman, Fazlur
1979 Islam. Chicago: The University of Chicago Press.

Rahmat
1993 Di balik Menghilangnya Gus Mik, Lahir Sebagai Insan Istimewa. *In* Memorandum. Surabaya.

Rakhmat, Jalaluddin
1998 Reformasi Sufistik Halaman Akhir Fikri Yathir. Bandung: Pustaka Hidayah.

Rispler, Vardit
1991 Toward a New Understanding of The Term *bid'a*. Der Islam 68(12):320-328.

Robson, James
1936 Blessing on the prophet. The Muslim World 26:365-371.

Rohani, Team Pengalaman
2004 Shalawat Wahidiyah dan Pengalaman Rohani. Kediri: Qalamuna Pondok Pesantren Kedunglo.

Sa'id, M. Ridlwan Qayyum
2004 Fiqh Klenik. Kediri: Mitra Gayatri.

Saheb, S.A.A.
1998 A"Festival of Flags": Hindu-Muslim Devotion and the Sacralising of Localism at the Shrine of Nagore-e-Sharif in Tamil Nadu. *In* Embodying Charisma: Modernity, Locality, and the Performancec of Emotion in Sufi Cults. P.W.a.H. Basu, ed. London: Routledge.

Saksono, Widji
1995 Mengislamkan Tanah Jawa: Telaah Atas Metode Dakwah Walisongo. Bandung: Mizan.

Salih bin Abdul-Aziz bin Muhammad Aal ash-Shaikh
1995, The Understanding of Tabarruk with Ahl al-Sunnah: Salafi Publications.com, viewed 2 January 2007, 11:04 am, http://www.spubs.com/sps/sp.cfm?subsecID=TAW04&articleID=TAW040001&articlePages=1.

Satori, Saefulloh M
2003 Koreksi Zikir Keblinger: Kearifan Menilai Zikir Berjamaah dan Bisnis M. Arifin Ilham. Jakarta: Pustaka Medina.

Sawi, Ahmad
N.d. Hasyiyatul 'Alamatis Showi 'Ala Tafsiril Jalalain. Volume 3. Semarang: Toha Putra.

Schimmel, Annemarie
1978 Mystical Dimensions of Islam. Chapel Hill: The University of North Carolina Press.

Schimmel, Annemarie
1985 And Muhammad is His Messenger: The Veneration of the Prophet in Islamic Piety. Chapel Hill and London: The University of North Carolina Press.

Shiddieqy, Hasbi Ash
1983 Kriteria antara Sunnah dan Bid'ah. Jakarta: Bulan Bintang.

Shihab, M. Quraish
1998 Menyingkap Tabir Ilahi. Jakarta: Lentera Hati.

Shihab, M. Quraish
1996 Wawasan Al-Qur'an: Tafsir Maudhu'i atas Pelbagai Persoalan Umat. Bandung: Mizan.

Shihab, M. Quraish
2006 Wawasan Al-Qur'an Tentang Zikir dan Do'a. Jakarta: Lentera Hati.

Siddiq, Ahmad
N.d. Buku Dhikr al-Ghāfilīn. Kediri.

Siregar, Arif Bargot
1992 Saya Sudah Terbawa Globalisasi, Gus Mik, Semaan, Night-Club, Bir dan Golkar. *In* Matra.

Sirriyeh, Elizabeth
1999 Sufis and Anti-Sufis: The Defence Rethinking and Rejection of Sufism in The Modern World. Great Britain: Curzon Press.

Sodli, Ahmad
1990 Tarekat Wahidiyah di Jawa Timur dan Jawa Tengah. Pp. 1-48. Semarang: Departemen Agama R.I. Balai Penelitian Aliran Kerohanian / Keagamaan.

Subhani, Ja'far
1989 Tawassul, Tabarruk, Ziarah Kubur, Karamah Wali, Termasuk Ajaran Islam: Kritik Atas Faham Wahabi. Jakarta: Pustaka Al-Hidayah.

Sujuti, Mahmud
2001 Politik Tarekat Qadiriyah wa Naqshabandiyah Jombang: Hubungan Agama, Negara dan Masyarakat. Yogyakarta: Galang Press.

Syadzily, Tb. Ace Hasan
2005 Arifin Ilham: Dai Kota Penabur Kedamaian Jiwa. Bandung: Hikmah (PT Mizan Publika).

Tanthowi, Pramono U
2003 Dakwah Kultural: Revisi Paham Keagamaan Muhammadiyah? *In* Muhammadiyah Sebagai Tenda Kultural. M. Abdurrahman, ed. Jakarta: Ideo Press and Ma'arif Institute.

Taylor, Christopher S.
1998 In the Vicinity of the Righteous : Ziyara and the Veneration of Muslim Saints in late Medieval Egypt. Leiden: Brill.

Taymiyyah, Ibn
1987 Tawassul dan Wasilah. S.a. Sa'ad, transl. Jakarta: Pustaka Panjimas.

Taymiyyah, Ibn
1999 Al-Mukjizatu wa Karamatu al-Auliya'. A. Yahya, transl. Jakarta: PT Lentera Basritama.

Taymiyyah, Ibn
N.d-a Majmū' al-Fatāwā. Volume 11. Saudi Arabiah: Al-Maktab al-Ta'limiy Al-Sa'udiy bi al-Maghrib.

Taymiyyah, Ibn
N.d-b Majmū' al-Fatāwā Shaikh al-Islam Ahmad Ibn Taymiyyah. Volume 1. Saudi Arabiah: Al-Maktab al-Ta'limiy Al-Sa'udiy bi al-Maghrib.

Thoha, Zainal Arifin
2003 Runtuhnya Singgasana Kiai. Yogyakarta: Kutub.

Trimingham, J. Spencer
1971 The Sufi Orders in Islam. Oxford: At The Clarendon Press.

Turmudi, Endang
2003 Perselingkuhan Kyai dan Kekuasaan. Yogyakarta: LKiS.

Turmudi, Endang
2006 Struggling For The Umma: Changing Leadership Roles of *Kiai* in Jombang, East Java. Canberra: ANU E Press.

Van Dijk, Kees
1998 *Dakwah* and Indigenous Culture: The Dissemination of Islam. Bijdragen tot de taal-, land- en volkenkunde 154(2):218-235.

Vety, Arovah
2001 Mbah KH. Muhammad Ma'roef RA. *In* Aham. Pp. 54-61.

W.Ernst, Carl
2003 Ajaran dan Amaliah Tasawuf: Sebuah Pengantar. A. Anwar, transl. Jogjakarta: Pustaka Sufi.

Watson, C W
2005 A Popular Indonesian Preacher: The Significance of AA Gymnastiar. Royal Anthropological Institute 11(4):773-792.

Wehr, Hans
1966 A Dictionary of Modern Written Arabic. Itacha: Cornell University Press.

Werbner, Pnina
2003 Pilgrims of Love: The Anthropology of a Global Sufi Cult. Indiana: Indiana University Press.

Wijayanta, Hanibal W.Y., Ivan Haris, and Muhammad Toha
1998 Darah Mengalir di Tapal Kuda. *In* Forum Keadilan. Pp. 12-15, Vol. VII.

Woodward, Mark R.
1989 Islam in Java: Normative Piety and Mysticism in the Sultanate of Yogyakarta. Tucson: Tthe University of Arizona Press.

Yusuf, Muhammad Djazuli
1994 Tanya Jawab. *In* Bulletin Kembali. Pp. 14-15, Vol. III.

Yusuf, Muhammad Djazuli
2003 Aku Pengganti Mualif Shalawat Wahidiyah. Surabaya: Tarbiyah.

Zulkifli
2001 The Role of the Pesantren in the Maintenance of Sufism in Java. Leiden: INIS.

www.ingramcontent.com/pod-product-compliance
Lightning Source LLC
Chambersburg PA
CBHW060928170426
43192CB00031B/2865
* 9 7 8 1 9 2 1 6 6 6 2 4 7 *